"*Biometrics* is a timely, rich, and comprehensive addition to the biometric literature, and it belongs in every library as a valuable source of information, both interesting for casual technical reading and essential for technical reference. The important issues are fairly presented and discussed. This is a rare book that is at once a textbook and required reading for all of us in today's biometric society, where the human body has become the password for access. Organized efficiently, this book builds from definitions and history to technologies, issues, privacy, and policy, ending with a thorough discussion of the idea for a national ID. The writing style is excellent, using case study and scenarios appropriately, yet dealing directly with issues such as privacy and law, and test and evaluation. I did not put the book aside until I had reached its final page."

—Edwin P. Rood, Ph.D.
Director
The Biometric Knowledge Center at West Virginia University

"John Woodward and his colleagues have written a timely book on a hot topic. They explain biometrics in easy-to-understand terms and helpfully review the technology's many applications in the 21st century. The authors also include a welcome discussion of the many law, policy, and privacy concerns raised by this emerging technology. The three in-depth case studies on Super Bowl surveillance, the FBI's use of fingerprints, and the feasibility of a national identification system are sure to stimulate thought and ignite controversy."

—James L. Swanson
Constitutional Law Scholar and
Editor of the *First Amendment Law Handbook*

place index finger in window

Biometrics

place index finger in window

Biometrics

John D. Woodward, Jr.
Nicholas M. Orlans
Peter T. Higgins

McGraw-Hill/Osborne

New York   Chicago   San Francisco
Lisbon   London   Madrid   Mexico City
Milan   New Delhi   San Juan
Seoul   Singapore   Sydney   Toronto

The McGraw-Hill Companies

McGraw-Hill/Osborne
2600 Tenth Street
Berkeley, California 94710
U.S.A.

To arrange bulk purchase discounts for sales promotions, premiums, or fund-raisers, please contact **McGraw-Hill**/Osborne at the above address. For information on translations or book distributors outside the U.S.A., please see the International Contact Information page immediately following the index of this book.

Biometrics

1234567890 FGR FGR 0198765432

ISBN 0-07-222227-1

Publisher Brandon A. Nordin	**Proofreader** Marian Selig
Vice President & Associate Publisher Scott Rogers	**Indexer** Jack Lewis
Editorial Director Tracy Dunkelberger	**Computer Designer** Tara A. Davis
Executive Editor Jane K. Brownlow	**Illustrators** Lyssa Wald, Melinda Lytle, Michael Mueller
Project Editor Jenn Tust	**Series Design** Peter F. Hancik
Acquisitions Coordinator Martin Przybyla	**Cover Design & Illustration** Reed Loar and Greg Scott
Technical Editor Sarah Granger	**Face & Hand Photos (Back Cover/ Internal Part and Chapter Openers)**
Copy Editors Lisa Theobald, Marcia Baker, Emily Rader	Courtesy of Biometrics Research Lab, Michigan State University, http://biometrics.cse.msu.edu.

The following used with permission from RAND: "Searching the FBI's Civil Files: Public Safety v. Civil Liberty," *U.S. Law Week*, September 17, 2002; also published in *Privacy & Security Law*, September 2, 2002. Copyright RAND 2002. John D. Woodward, Jr., et al., *Army Biometric Applications: Identifying and Addressing Sociocultural Concerns*, RAND/MR-1237-A, Santa Monica, CA: RAND, 2001. Copyright RAND 2001. John D. Woodward, Jr., *Super Bowl Surveillance: Facing Up to Biometrics*, RAND/IP-209, Santa Monica, CA: RAND, 2001. Copyright RAND 2001.

The following used with permission from Kluwer: An earlier version of Chapter 12 appeared as Chapter 19: entitled "Biometrics: Identifying Law and Policy Concerns," in *Biometrics: Personal Identification in Networked Society*, edited by Anil Jain, Ruud Bolle, Sharath Pankanti, published by Kluwer Academic Publishers. Copyright Klumer 1999.

This book was composed with Corel VENTURA™ Publisher.

About the Author

John D. Woodward, Jr., is a senior policy analyst at RAND, a public policy research organization. He works on national security, intelligence, and technology policy issues. He has testified on biometrics before Congress and his articles on the subject have appeared in publications such as the *Legal Times*, *Pittsburgh Post-Gazette*, *Proceedings of the Institute of Electrical and Electronics Engineers*, *United States Law Week*, *University of Pittsburgh Law Review*, *Washington Post*, among others. He previously served as an operations officer for the Central Intelligence Agency in several overseas assignments. Mr. Woodward received his Juris Doctor degree magna cum laude from Georgetown University Law Center in Washington, D.C. He was a Thouron Scholar at the London School of Economics, University of London, where he received his M.S. in economics. He received his B.S. in economics from the Wharton School of the University of Pennsylvania.

Nicholas M. Orlans is a principal investigator for MITRE experimentation in biometrics and is interested in performance prediction techniques for large systems. After earning a B.S. in mathematics, a Masters in architecture, and a full graduate minor in computer science, Mr. Orlans worked in the computer graphics industry where he developed and supported 3D and image processing applications. He then went on to support engineering, analysis, and testing projects on the IRIDIUM Satellite program. Since 1996, he has worked at the MITRE Corporation in McLean, Virginia, where he supports a number of Department of Defense projects, primarily in the areas of counterdrug and information assurance. As a lead engineer he worked on the design, development, and testing of multi-source identity correlation and query systems for counterdrug and criminal justice. He has also been a part of research efforts into link analysis and data fusion systems.

Peter T. Higgins started a consulting practice soon after his retirement from the FBI where he served as the deputy assistant director in charge of the world's largest fingerprint automation project, IAFIS. In addition to providing support to several North American federal and state agencies in the procurement of biometric systems as a consultant, he lecturers in biometrics at the UCLA Extension School and is a volunteer instructor in the Presidential Classroom for Young Americans. He serves on the board of directors of several companies including Printrak International, before it was sold to Motorola.

After receiving his M.S. in theoretical math and computer science from Stevens Institute of Technology, he joined the CIA where he worked in various technical and management positions. He was appointed to the Senior Intelligence Service in his 30s, and after a year in a Congressional Fellowship awarded by the American Political Science Association, he served as a group chief in the CIA's Office of Research and Development where he was first involved in biometrics— in the late 1980s. He went on to establish the function that is now the chief information officer position while serving in the Office of the Director. In 1992, he was loaned to the FBI and eventually transferred there.

About the Contributing Authors

Dr. Martin Libicki, a senior policy analyst at RAND since 1998, is the principal contributor of Chapter 19, "Biometrics and the Feasibility of a National ID Card." He works on the relationship between information technology and public policy, notably national security. This work is documented in numerous monographs, the most recent of which is *Scaffolding the New Web: Standards and Standards Policy for the Digital Economy*. It follows the commercially published *Information Technology Standards: Quest for the Common Byte*. Prior employment includes twelve years at the National Defense University, three years on the Navy Staff as program sponsor for industrial preparedness and three years as a policy analyst for the General Accounting Office's Energy and Minerals Division. Dr. Libicki received his Ph.D. from U.C. Berkeley (1978) writing on industrial economics. He has also received a Master's in city planning from U.C. Berkeley (1974), and a Bachelor's degree in mathematics from MIT (1972).

Kapil Raina, CISSP, is a security expert with years of experience in security consulting and product marketing of products and services. He is the principal contributor of Chapter 2, "How Biometrics Work." Mr. Raina has worked for leading companies such as VeriSign and Lucent (INS Netcare Consulting) with clients ranging from KPN Telecom to DHL Systems. At VeriSign, Mr. Raina managed the product marketing, product development, and business development of enterprise partner related security products and services. Mr. Raina is well recognized in the industry through his contribution to numerous books including *mCommerce Security: A Beginner's Guide* (McGraw-Hill/Osborne, January 2002) and *PKI Trust Solutions* (Wiley and Sons, March 2003). In addition, Mr. Raina is a sought-after speaker, having given talks to leading universities such as the U.C. Berkeley Haas Business School and industry forums such as InfoSec 2003. Mr. Raina also guides eVincible, a secure forms signing company, on product marketing strategy, as a respected member of its advisory board. Currently, Mr. Raina serves as a technical marketing consultant to Probix as a director of marketing establishing their product marketing and European channel strategy.

Richard E. Smith, Ph.D., CISSP, is a writer, educator, and consultant. He contributed Chapter 1, "How Authentication Technologies Work." He is the author of two books on information security: *Authentication: From Passwords to Public Keys* (Addison-Wesley, 2001) and *Internet Cryptography* (Addison-Wesley, 1997), as well as numerous papers and articles. Dr. Smith's activities in information security and assurance have included work on DARPA cyber defense research, cryptographic systems, the Sidewinder Internet firewall, and the NSA Standard Mail Guard. He also developed protocol software for the ARPA Network, the forerunner to today's Internet. Dr. Smith holds a B.S. in engineering from Boston University and a M.S. and Ph.D. in information science from the University of Minnesota.

Jeff Stapleton contributed Chapter 10, "Biometric Standards." He is a manager with KPMG LLP in the Risk Advisory Services (RAS) practice focusing on business risks, payment systems, cryptography, PKI, and biometrics. He has over 20 years experience at KPMG, RSA Security, MasterCard International, and Citicorp, and he has provided consulting services to the financial, healthcare, and entertainment industries. Mr. Stapleton holds Bachelor's and Master's of Science degrees in computer science from the University of Missouri. He is the chair of the X9F4 working group, which developed the ANSI standard X9.84-2001 *Biometric Information Management and Security*, and he is currently working on X9.95 *Trusted Timestamps*. He has also participated in developing numerous national and international cryptography and security standards for the financial industry with ISO TC68 and ASC X9, instructed at Washington University (St. Louis), and is a frequent speaker at security conferences.

Dr. Valorie Valencia, a cofounder and CEO of Authenti-Corp, contributed Chapter 8, "Biometric Liveness Testing." She began working in the biometrics arena in 1995 at Sandia National Laboratories. She received her B.S. in mechanical engineering with honors and high distinction, M.S. in optical sciences, and Ph.D. in optical sciences, all from the University of Arizona. Started in August of 2000, Authenti-Corp is an authentication technology consulting firm that serves both public and private clients.

About the Research Assistants

Julius Gatune has a B. S. in civil engineering and an M.B.A. from the University of Nairobi, as well as a Diploma in computer science from the University of Cambridge. He has worked as an engineer and a lecturer in information systems, and as an information systems manager. He is currently a doctoral fellow at the RAND Graduate School, Santa Monica, California.

Christopher Horn is a research assistant at RAND. He graduated from Brown University with a B.A. in economics. He plans to pursue a doctoral degree in economics.

Aryn Thomas is an administrative assistant at RAND. Ms. Thomas was a Dean's Honors Scholar at Tulane University, where she received her B.A. cum laude in political economy.

About the Technical Editor

Sarah Granger, an experienced network security consultant, writes and edits articles on topics such as hacking, encryption, and biometrics for Security Focus, Mindjack, and the Electronic Frontier Foundation, to name a few. This is the third book for which she has been a technical editor.

Contents at a Glance

Contents

Acknowledgments

Having three friends serve as principal authors to write a book on a dynamic subject like biometrics (and remain friends) is no small feat. It requires lots of work, the occasional inspiration, and heavy doses of humor. The three of us became fast friends through our work in biometrics; we decided to join forces to write this book because we wanted to produce a comprehensive one-volume resource on an emerging technology that we believe will become commonplace as a means of providing identity assurance in the information age.

While our names are on the cover, we had abundant assistance along the way. Our contributing authors, Rick Smith, Kapil Raina, Valorie Valencia, Jeff Stapleton, and Martin Libicki, are all subject matter experts who shared their knowledge. We are honored to have their contributions. Julius Gatune, Christopher Horn, Aryn Thomas, and Rick Chavez helped with research and analysis. McGraw Hill/Osborne provided us with a first-rate editorial team who helped turn dreary drafts into readable reality. We have all greatly benefited from the Biometric Consortium, the U.S. Government's focal point for research, development, testing, evaluation, and application of biometrics (www.biometrics.org). Since 1995, the "BC" has served as a tremendous national resource, even when its list serve sometimes floods us with more noise than signal. Its leadership over the years, Joe Campbell, Lisa Alyea, Jeff Dunn, and Fernando Podio, deserve our thanks. We all thank Jim Wayman, a distinguished biometrics expert and our friend.

While this book reflects and hopefully benefits from our research and work done for various organizations over the years, the views expressed are not endorsed by RAND, MITRE, or any of our sponsors. We are responsible for the book's contents and we share the blame for any mistakes contained herein.

Peter Higgins writes: I would also like to acknowledge and thank my friends in the International Association for Identification, in particular Frederic Biarnes and David Hall for sharing their knowledge of history and philosophy; special thanks to Don Harrison of the Royal Canadian Mounted Police for his willingness to share information and his friendship, and to my wife, Kathy, for her tireless research and support.

Nicholas Orlans writes: I would also like to acknowledge and thank my colleagues at MITRE and in the government for their support and interest, particularly Al Piszcz, Chuck Howell, Paul Lehner, Dan Venese, and Eileen Boettcher. Dr. John Daugman kindly answered my questions on iris recognition. And kayaking sensei Jim Stuart, thanks for helping me realize whatever nominal abilities I have on the river.

John Woodward writes: I appreciate the support I received from RAND to undertake this endeavor and the interest of my RAND colleagues, particularly Kathi Webb, John Baker, Elaine Newton, Ken Horn, Dave Brannan, Martin Libicki, Ed Balkovich, Kevin O'Connell, Diane Snyder, Willis Ware, Michael Tseng, and Bob

Preston. I have learned much from colleagues at the Department of Defense, the Department of Justice, and other government agencies that I support in my work. I thank Mike Absher, Astrid Albrecht, Duane Blackburn, Paul Collier, Arthur S. Di Dio, Ed German, Austin Hicklin, A.M. Jacocks, Jr., Professor Anil Jain, George Kiebuzinski, Jim Loudermilk, David Mintie, Raj and Samir Nanavati, Rick Norton, Jonathan Phillips, Gary Pluck, Clive Reedman, Edwin Rood, Marc Rotenberg, and Tim Schellberg for patiently listening to my ideas and generously sharing their insights. Ben Miller and Liz Wenchel of CardTech/ SecurTech, Bill Rogers of Biometric Digest, Mark Lockie of Biometric Technology Today, C. Wayne Crews, Jr. of CATO, and Marcia Sullivan and William Coats of the American Bar Association invited me to speak at conferences hosted by their organizations and I have greatly benefited from these experiences.

Paul Burkett and Gordon A. McNeil provided helpful logistical support for my research in the United Kingdom. The Hon. Michael N. Castle and the Hon. Constance Morella invited me to testify on biometrics and related topics before Congress; I thank them for providing me with this honor.

The Hon. H. Morgan Griffith and the Hon. Kenneth W. Stolle invited me to serve on the Virginia State Crime Commission's Subcommittee on Facial Recognition Technology, which greatly contributed to my understanding of law and policy concerns of biometrics. Ivan Fong and Professor Julie O'Sullivan provided helpful comments on earlier drafts of the text. Professor Steve Goldberg helped give me my start in biometrics when he agreed to sponsor my independent study project at Georgetown University Law Center. He continues to dispense wisdom. My wife, Shirley Cassin Woodward, has read endless drafts of text and provided countless comments on them. She has supported my efforts without fail and with complete encouragement.

Introduction

Several years ago, several biometric industry analysts, an author of this book included, regularly appeared at annual conferences to speak on the future of biometrics and proclaimed:

"1997 is the Year of Biometrics."

The following year, the pronouncement became:

"1998 is the Year of Biometrics."

Each year, a pattern developed:

"1999 is the Year of Biometrics."

"2000 is the Year of Biometrics."

"2001 is the Year of Biometrics."

Eventually, a variable got inserted into the pronouncement, firm in the realization that eventually one year we would be correct:

" [Insert Year] is the Year of Biometrics."

Although biometrics have not become a required part of all authentication systems, this emerging industry has come a long way from its "modern founding" in 1972 with the installation of a commercial finger measurement device on Wall Street. For example, in 2001, the highly respected *MIT Technology Review* named biometrics one of the "top ten emerging technologies that will change the world."

The numbers also show industry growth. Rick Norton, the executive director of the International Biometric Industry Association (IBIA), the industry's trade association, has pointed out that biometric revenues over recent years have increased by an order of magnitude. In 1996, biometric revenues were $20 million. In 2001, they reached $200 million. Norton believes that in another five years, (2006), they will reach $2 billion.

Forecasts by the International Biometric Group (IBG), a biometric consulting and integration firm in New York City, estimate that biometric revenues totaled

$399 million in 2000 and will increase to $1.9 billion by 2005. Both the IBIA and IBG believe that much of this growth will be in the private sector.[1]

Following the September 11, 2001 terrorist attacks, the U.S. government and other governments and organizations throughout the world became greatly interested in this emerging human recognition technology. For example, on January 7, 2002, the Office of Homeland Security announced its "Specifics of Secure and Smart Border Action Plan," which lists "biometric identifiers" as its first priority.[2] Similarly, President Bush, in his State of the Union Address on January 29, 2002, said, "We will…use technology to track the arrivals and departures of visitors to the United States." He followed up on this subtle reference to biometrics by finally saying the word on May 14, 2002 when he signed the Enhanced Border Security and Visa Entry Reform Act.

The well-known "Uniting and Strengthening America by Providing Appropriate Tools Required to Intercept and Obstruct Terrorism (USA PATRIOT Act) Act of 2001" and other legislation, such as the Enhanced Border Security and Visa Entry Reform Act and the Aviation and Transportation Security Act, also make reference to biometric technologies in the context of using biometrics in conjunction with official government-issued travel documents, official government-issued identification credentials for transportation workers and others. Through its appropriations process, Congress has also made monies available to government agencies for biometric technologies.

While biometric revenues have not increased markedly in 2002, industry experts like the IBIA's Norton consider 2002 a great year for the discovery of biometrics. Because of the press attention paid to the subject, more and more people realize that biometrics is not science fiction but for real. More and more organizations have become aware of and interested in biometrics, and they no longer regard it as a fringe technology but rather perceive it as mainstream. Reacting to this interest, systems integrators and other major players are looking at biometrics as a business opportunity. At the same time, the betting is that the U.S. government will continue its enthusiasm for the technology.

The three basic factors influencing the adoption of biometrics are:

- Security
- Convenience
- Cost

---

[1]   Rick Norton, "The Biometrics Industry 2002: Are Government Initiatives Driving Development and Growth?" Biometrics 2002 Conference, London, United Kingdom, November 8, 2002. International Biometric Group, "Biometric Market Report 2000-2005," 2001, available at http://www.biometricgroup/ e/biometric_market_report.htm.

[2]   Office of Homeland Security, "Specifics of Secure and Smart Border Action Plan," January 7, 2002, available at http://www.whitehouse.gov/news/releases/2002/01/print/20020107.html.

To make the best business case for adoption, biometric authentication should provide greater security, greater convenience, and less cost than the status quo methods. Private sector end-users, in particular, want to see a return on investment.

End-users with high security requirements can afford to be more flexible on the business case. Government agencies, faced with the need to freeze or fix a person's identity to ensure integrity in a government program, or to identify threats to national security and public safety, have turned to biometrics as a way to provide these desired capabilities.

Over the past several years, the biometrics industry, due in part to the industry's competitive nature and numerous IT advances, improved its products in the following important ways: products have attained better operational performance (in terms of accuracy and throughput); at the same time, they are at much lower cost; and enhanced user friendliness is apparent as products are smaller, slicker and sexier, and ergonomically improved.

Biometrics are an integral and distinctive part of human beings. As such, they offer a natural convenience and technical efficiency that other authentication mechanisms, which must be mentally remembered or physically produced, do not. For this reason, biometrics can provide identity assurance for countless everyday activities currently protected by traditional means of access control—cards, personal identification numbers (PINs), and passwords. Biometrics can also be used in conjunction with cards and PINs to enhance security. A high security application could require all three factors for authentication. In many applications, a biometric could replace the card or PIN entirely, thus adding to convenience because there are no cards to lose or numbers to remember.

How This Book Is Organized

This book is organized into five parts.

Part I starts by providing an overview of authentication, explaining the concept of identity assurance, or the need to verify our own identities or someone else's, or otherwise determine who someone is. We explain how authentication mechanisms work, their common traits, and discuss different types of authentication mechanisms such as what you know (PINs and passwords), what you have (cards and keys), and what you are (biometrics). Next, we introduce biometrics by providing a definition, brief history, and an explanation of how biometrics work by focusing on their key elements.

Part II discusses in detail the different types of biometrics. These include fingerprint and hand geometry, facial and voice recognition, eye biometrics such as iris and retina scanning, signature recognition and keystroke dynamics, as well as esoteric biometrics, such as vein patterns, facial thermography, DNA, and sweat pores, among others.

Part III discusses current issues involving biometrics from the technical perspective. These hot topics include biometric liveness testing, or the steps taken to make certain that a biometric system is not spoofed or otherwise fooled. Next, we offer practical advice for anyone interested in using biometrics in large-scale systems, by helping a potential end-user answer the question: "Which biometric do I need for my application?" We then discuss biometric standards, which are essential if biometric systems are to achieve interoperability, and the various international and national standards groups that are involved in standards work. Part III concludes with a discussion of biometric testing and evaluation, a particularly important topic so that potential end-users will know how to judge their systems.

Part IV provides a detailed treatment of the privacy, policy, and legal concerns raised by biometrics. Biometrics as a technology has arrived and this necessarily means privacy, policy, and legal concerns have arrived with it. We begin by discussing privacy in the specific context of biometrics. Next, we explain legal considerations of government use of biometrics—what happens, for example, when the government requires a person to provide a biometric? We then offer a case study on a controversial facial recognition application—Super Bowl surveillance when Tampa police used facial recognition to scan spectators at America's preeminent sporting event. Part IV concludes by discussing the many legal considerations related to private-sector use of biometrics—what factors does a private-sector end-user need to consider when using biometrics?

Part V is our review of selected biometric programs. These include many government and military programs, which are discussed from the perspective of lessons learned. We also offer an in-depth case study of the Federal Bureau of Investigation's use of fingerprints in the context of its civil files, containing fingerprints of about 40 million law-abiding Americans. We then proceed to an analysis of private-sector programs, detailing real-world biometric applications used by many different organizations. Part V concludes with a feasibility study of a national identification card in the U.S.—a topic about which many Americans have strongly held opinions.

Who Should Read This Book

We have created what we hope is a comprehensive one-volume resource on biometrics that should appeal to all sorts of professionals and students with diverse interests. Background knowledge of biometrics is not a prerequisite for this book; we have organized the content in such a way that we start with the fundamentals and logically build. This book is not overly technical; we have kept equations to a minimum. If you know nothing or very little about biometrics and want to learn, you have selected the correct book: start with Part I, Chapter 1 and read on.

We have worked hard to make certain that each chapter stands alone. That is, you should be able to randomly turn to a chapter, read it, and become better informed about the topic. Those readers who count themselves among the biometric cognoscenti may feel free to skim certain chapters and dig into the ones that appeal to their particular interest. Those readers who are interested in law and policy aspects of this emerging technology will most appreciate Part IV, where we discuss these issues in detail. We have also not shied away from controversy, deliberately including case studies that will provoke lively debate.

We also designed this book to be a useful reference for anyone considering using biometrics. Potential end-users in the public or private sector will benefit from the many examples we offer about how various organizations currently use biometrics.

The Future

Since ancient times, man has used distances based on parts of his *body* to create measuring instruments. The Pharoah's Royal Cubit (the distance of the arm from the bent elbow to the tip of the extended middle finger), Henry I's yard (the distance from the tip of the King's nose to the end of his outstretched thumb), and their modern descendants have enabled man to better describe the world around him. Biometrics uses automated techniques to measure man in order to better describe himself.

We believe that biometrics will be commonly used for identity assurance. In the very near future, we will purchase an increasing number of IT products that will have biometric devices smartly imbedded in their design, thus readily offering biometrics for such everyday activities as entering a home or office, starting a vehicle, talking on a cellular telephone, logging onto a computer, paying for a purchase, and so on. In the near future, we predict a paradigm shift to where biometrics becomes the preferred method of identity assurance. Pitfalls and impediments remain in the technical and policy arenas. For example, the need for liveness testing, biometric standards, and testing and evaluation protocols remain a critical challenge and the industry, end-users, and government bodies must address privacy and related concerns. Challenges may be numerous but the opportunities are great.

Part I

place index finger in window

Authentication and Biometrics Overview

Chapter 1

How Authentication Technologies Work

By Richard E. Smith, Ph.D., CISSP

As we go about our daily lives, we often need to verify our identities or someone else's identity, or otherwise determine who someone is. Reliable identification makes life go more smoothly. For example, it improves public safety by helping to distinguish benign members of the general public from recognized criminals and other threats. Reliable identification also makes financial and business dealings safer and more efficient, if only by making the participants more accountable for their actions. When we automate the authentication process, we broaden the range of valuable tasks that computers and other devices can perform for us. These automated authentication processes can bring greater security, efficiency, and convenience to our lives.

Automated authentication makes it possible to tailor the way that a device responds to different people and to ensure that it confidently responds to people in a correct manner. In practice, this involves two separate actions: an *authentication* mechanism verifies the identity, and a separate *authorization* mechanism ties the appropriate actions to a person's identity. The distinction between these two actions is particularly important when changing how the system should react to a particular person. For example, if an employee named Bob resigns from his company, the company computers should cease granting him access to company resources. Strictly speaking, there's no problem if the computers continue to authenticate Bob reliably as long as they revoke his authorization to use the company's systems.

Three fundamental techniques, or factors, are used in authentication mechanisms:

- Something you *know*, which usually refers to passwords and PINs
- Something you *have*, which usually refers to cards or tokens
- Something you *are*, which refers to *biometrics*—the measurement of physical characteristics or personal traits

The earliest computer-based authentication mechanism was established as part of the Compatible Time Sharing System (CTSS) at the Massachusetts Institute of Technology in the early 1960s. The system's designer introduced the notion of a "private code" that students would memorize, much like they memorized the numbers for their combination locks on their student lockers. Today, of course, we use the term *password* to refer to such private codes (Smith, 2002).

Modern life today is littered with passwords: they stand in front of everything from children's personal computers to extensive business and financial resources. In theory, a password is memorized by a single person, it's hard to guess, it's never written down, and it's never shared. In practice, however, people constantly violate these expectations. Passwords are often written down, shared with other people, or chosen from among a small number of easy-to-guess words. There is an inevitable tug-of-war between choosing a password that's easy to remember and one that's hard to guess. Some systems try to force people to choose hard-to-guess passwords, and many people respond by keeping written lists of their hard-to-guess (and hard to remember) passwords. Of course, once this list is copied or stolen, the passwords provide no protection at all.

Although passwords are both widely used and easily compromised, they illustrate the fundamental mechanism of automated authentication: the user must provide some information or input that cannot be provided by someone else. Consider what happens if an authorized user named Cathy tries to log in to a server, such as an e-mail server. The server takes information Cathy provides and compares it with her previously stored information. If the comparison is satisfactory, the server acknowledges Cathy's identity. If a different person, Henry, for example, tries to impersonate Cathy, he should not be able to provide the same information, so the comparison should fail. We summarize these features as follows:

- **Cathy provides an *authenticator***   A data item that cannot be provided by anyone else
- **The server contains a *verifier***   A data item that can verify the correctness of the authenticator

- **The server uses a *verification procedure*** An algorithm that compares an authenticator with a verifier
- **There is generally a *base secret*** A data item in Cathy's possession that produces the authenticator

As we will see shortly, an authentication system's features take different forms according to the authentication factors involved. We examine this with examples in which Cathy tries to log in to her mail server while Henry tries to masquerade as Cathy. Different authentication factors provide subtly different types of information about a person's identity. In some cases, this simply affects the confidence we have in the results, while in other cases it enables other uses of the authentication.

What You Know: Passwords and PINs

The simplest implementations of passwords and personal identification numbers (PINs) yield the simplest of all authentication mechanisms. Cathy's memorized password serves as the authenticator, verifier, and base secret. The verification procedure simply performs a character string comparison of the authenticator (the password provided by Cathy) and verifier (a copy of the password stored in the mail server). In practice, password-based systems incorporate various cryptographic techniques to resist attacks, notably password hashing (Wilkes 1968).

Passwords work reliably only as long as they are not guessed or otherwise disclosed to potential adversaries through accident, subversion, or intentional sharing. If Cathy chooses her favorite color as a password, an acquaintance might guess it and try to log on as her. Since she chose a common word as a password, it's also possible that Henry or some other attacker might use a "dictionary attack" to discover her password in a file of hashed passwords. If Cathy logs in to her mail server across the Internet, Henry might be able to intercept her password while in transit, and then use it himself.

Although there are technical procedures to reduce the risks of guessing, accident, or subversion, there is no way to prevent Cathy or any other user from sharing passwords. Some enterprises enact strict security policies that prohibit such sharing, but such sharing often occurs anyway. Within the rank and file of an organization, coworkers will often share passwords if computer access is necessary for getting a job done but computer accounts aren't easy to establish. If Cathy is an administrative assistant, it's quite possible that she'll share her password with a temporary assistant who's called in to replace her if she's sick; the alternative is to create an account for the temp, and many people aren't likely to bother with that hassle. And if Cathy is like most people, she may have multiple accounts. To simplify life, she may decide to use the same password, even if the other accounts are intended for different purposes (for example, employee reviews or payroll information).

Password sharing also occurs at higher levels. If Cathy is a senior executive, there's a good chance that she'll share her password with her own administrative assistant, who might share it with the temp. Then the assistant can process Cathy's e-mail and even log in Cathy's computer for her every morning. Such flexibility might provide more benefits than shortcomings for some organizations, but it undermines the accountability that the authentication system is supposed to provide. There's no way to look at computer audit trails and distinguish Cathy's own activities from those of her assistant or the temp. Moreover, a secret, like a password, becomes easier to steal as it is shared among more and more people—thus reflecting the wisdom of the old saying: "Two people can keep a secret if one of them is dead."

What You Have: Cards and Tokens

Physical authentication devices, such as smart cards and password tokens, were developed to eliminate certain weaknesses associated with passwords. A major benefit of cards and tokens is that they can't be shared with the same freedom as sharing passwords. If Cathy shares her token with someone else, the other person can log in, but Cathy cannot.

In general, these devices store a large base secret (larger, in any case, than typical passwords). Since the token carries the secret, Cathy doesn't need to memorize it: she simply has to carry the token and have it available when she logs in. The devices usually contain a special procedure that uses the base secret to generate a hard-to-predict value for the authenticator. When Cathy needs to log in, her device generates the correct authenticator. Then she either types it in instead of a password, or she relies on a special authentication client to transmit the authenticator to the mail server.

To authenticate Cathy, the mail server uses a specialized verification procedure designed for the particular device Cathy uses. Usually, however, these procedures won't accept the same authenticator value twice. This increases security since Henry can't intercept and reuse an authenticator transmitted by Cathy's device. However, it may also inconvenience Cathy if she is able to access her mail only from access points that have the particular device. The appropriate verification procedures usually fall into two categories: those using secret-key cryptography and those using public-key cryptography.

The first password tokens were implemented using secret-key cryptography. To log in with one of the earliest tokens, Cathy needed to follow this procedure:

1. Cathy typed in her user name.
2. The server replied by displaying a numerical value, called the *challenge*.

3. Cathy typed the challenge into the keypad on her authentication token.

4. The authentication token used a cryptographic function (often the Data Encryption Standard, or DES) to combine the challenge with her base secret, stored inside the token.

5. The token displayed the result on a digital display; this was called the *response*.

6. Cathy transcribed the response into the server's password prompt, using it as the authenticator.

7. Internally, the server combined the challenge it sent with its own copy of Cathy's base secret. If the result matched Cathy's response, the server would log her in.

As these tokens became more sophisticated, they incorporated techniques to generate the challenge value internally. Some vendors produce tokens that use the value from a time-of-day clock as the challenge value, while others use an internal counter, and some combine both. These techniques greatly simplified matters: when Cathy needs to log in, the token simply displays the password she needs to use.

Other devices, notably smart cards and USB tokens, use public-key cryptography. If Cathy uses a public-key smart card, Cathy's private key serves as the base secret for authentication, and that key resides on the smart card. When Cathy logs in, most of the authentication process is handled automatically by client software, which performs a challenge-response exchange, similar to what was originally used in tokens. There is an important difference: the verifier is Cathy's public key, not her private key. She never has to divulge her private key to a server to log into it. This reduces the risks to Cathy's base secret, since it doesn't have to reside anywhere except on her smart card.

Like passwords, authentication devices can be stolen. Unlike passwords, the owner can tell if the device has been stolen. By itself, however, the authentication system won't be able to tell whether an authenticator comes from a stolen device or not.

What You Are: Biometrics

Biometric authentication, the subject of this book, relies on any automatically measurable physical characteristic or personal trait that is distinctive to an individual. Common biometric verification techniques try to match measurements from Cathy's fingerprint, hand, eye, face, or voice to measurements that were previously collected from her. There are two general applications for this: identification and verification. With identification, the biometric system asks and attempts to answer the question, "Who is X?" In an identification application, the biometric device reads a sample, processes it, and compares it against every record or template in the database. This type of comparison is called a "one-to-many" search (1:N). Depending on how the system is designed, it can make a "best" match, or it can score possible matches, ranking them in order of likelihood. Identification applications are common when the goal is to identify criminals, terrorists, or other "wolves in sheep's clothing."

Verification occurs when the biometric system asks and attempts to answer the question, "Is this X?" after the user claims to be X. In a verification application, the biometric system requires input from the user, at which time the user claims his or her identity via a password, token, or user name (or any combination of the three). This user input points the system to a template in the database. The system also requires a biometric sample from the user. It then processes and compares the sample to or against the user-defined template. This is called a "one-to-one" search (1:1). The system will either find or fail to find a match between the two.

For example, if Cathy's system relies on fingerprints, she must place her finger on a fingerprint reader when she logs in. The reader will examine the fingerprint reading she provides and try to match it to measurements that were previously collected from her. If the latest measurement matches closely enough, the system acknowledges that Cathy is present and logs her in or grants her access. Cathy has no device to lose or password to forget: she can authenticate herself as long as the appropriate physical characteristic or personal trait hasn't been badly injured or degraded.

The biometric authentication process begins with a biometric sensor of some kind. When Cathy tries to log in, the sensor collects a biometric reading from her and generates a biometric template from the reading, which becomes the authenticator. The verifier is based on one or more biometric readings previously collected from Cathy. The verification procedure essentially measures how closely the authenticator matches the verifier. If the system decides that the match is "close enough," the system authenticates Cathy; otherwise authentication is denied.

The measured properties of Cathy's biometric trait serve the role of the base secret in a biometric system. However, it's important to recognize that her biometric traits aren't really secrets. Cathy often leaves measurable traces of these "secrets" wherever she goes, such as fingerprints on surfaces, the recorded sound of her voice, or even video records of her face and body. This "latency" provides a way for attackers to generate a bogus authenticator and use it to trick the system into thinking that Cathy is actually present. Moreover, it may be possible to intercept a genuine authenticator collected from Cathy and replay it later. Thus, accurate authentication depends in part on whether the system can ensure that biometric authenticators are actually presented by live people, as discussed in Chapter 10.

Multi-Factor Authentication

As a general rule, if an authentication system is made by humans, it can be defeated by humans. Passwords can be intercepted and reused. Password tokens can be stolen. Biometric readings can be copied and replayed. All authentication factors suffer from fundamental weaknesses. Practical systems incorporate at least two factors to neutralize individual weaknesses. Plastic cards for ATMs provide a classic example: Cathy must possess the correct card and she must know the appropriate PIN; otherwise she can't use the teller machine. Most password tokens incorporate PINs in some fashion, and most biometric systems rely on token-like devices to collect readings and to protect them cryptographically.

Subverting the System

We use authentication systems because people occasionally try to misrepresent their identities. The previous section talked about Henry, who tried on occasion to assume Cathy's identity. Henry may be pursuing particular outcomes when he tries to subvert the authentication system; the next subsection characterizes those outcomes as *risks*. Henry might take a small number of general approaches to subvert the authentication system; the subsequent two subsections characterize those approaches as *attacks*. The final subsection reviews defenses used to resist these attacks.

Risks

The following risks represent different objectives an attacker like Henry might have when trying to subvert an authentication system. The attacker usually has a grander goal in mind, such as the embezzlement of a certain amount of money or the capture of certain goods or services. But for the authentication system itself, the attacker's goal is usually limited to one of the three described next: masquerade, multiple identities, or identity theft.

Masquerade

This is the classic risk to an authentication system. If Henry's goal is masquerade, he's simply trying to convince the system that he is in fact someone else, perhaps Cathy, since the system already knows how to recognize her. Henry proceeds by trying to trick the system into accepting him as being the other person.

Once the masquerade has succeeded, Henry can take advantage of the situation in various ways. For example, if Henry gets himself authenticated as Cathy, he might help himself to any particular abilities Cathy might have in the computing system, such as access to confidential files, sensitive applications, or equipment. In some cases, Henry might not expect his victim to have any unusual abilities, in which case he simply takes advantage of the fact that the system attributes his actions to Cathy. For example, Henry might use Cathy's identity while modifying some important files. If these activities were detected, they would be attributed to Cathy, casting suspicion on her instead of Henry.

Multiple Identities

Some systems, particularly those that dispense a government's social services program, are obligated to provide service to qualifying individuals within their jurisdiction. These individuals generally show up in person and request services. For many reasons, however, some people have found it profitable to register two or more times for the same benefits. For example, Henry might try to register himself twice or more so that he can collect multiple entitlement payments (a phenomenon known as "double-dipping"), or perhaps he can sell the registration to someone else, who, for whatever reason, may not qualify for the social services. Driver's license systems and other systems that in turn rely on driver's licenses, such as voter registration systems, are similarly undermined if fraudulent identities are allowed to enter the system.

Classic registration systems can't detect multiple registrations since Henry can provide different identifying information each time—such as a different name, birth date, place of birth, and so on—along with easily obtained fraudulent documentation to support the alias identity. A practical solution to this problem is to use biometric data as part of the registration process. If each registrant submits biometric data to the system, the system can perform an identification function by searching for matches between a new registrant and all the existing registrants. If Henry the registrant is truly new to the program, searching Henry's biometric against the records of the registrants should result in no matches. A match indicates Henry could be a double dipper. A number of jurisdictions have installed such systems and have reported dramatic reductions in double dipping and related fraud, as discussed in Chapter 13.

Identity Theft

This is the extreme case of authentication risks—when an attacker establishes new accounts that are attributed to a particular victim but authenticated by the attacker. In a simple masquerade, the attacker may assume the victim's identity temporarily in the context of systems the victim already uses. In an identity theft, the attacker collects personal identification information for a victim (name, social security number, date of birth, mother's maiden name, and so on) and uses it to assume the victim's identity in a broad range of transactions. In a typical fraud, Henry opens credit accounts in Cathy's name, although it's also common for the criminal to loot existing accounts.[1]

---

[1]   See, for example, U.S. General Accounting Office, "Identity Fraud: Information on Prevalence, Cost, and Internet Impact Is Limited," 1998, Rept. GAO/GGD-98-100BR.

Although law enforcement agencies have only started to collect data on identity theft cases, other sources of information show that it is a growing problem. In 1999, the U.S. Federal Trade Commission opened a hotline for identity theft reports. In its first month, the FTC hotline received an average of 445 calls per week. By December 2001, the hotline was receiving an average of 3,000 calls per week. According to the Social Security Administration, 81 percent of all reported incidents of social security number misuse involve identity theft. The Visa and MasterCard payment card associations estimate that card-related identity theft losses rose from $79.9 million in 1996 to $114.3 million in 2000.[2]

The crux of the problem for most cases of identity theft is that typical consumer financial transactions use relatively limited amounts of personal data for authentication. If the consumer is physically present during the transaction, the merchant will probably rely on a single identity card, such as a driver's license, to help verify the person's identity.

Trial-and-Error Attacks

When Henry goes after an authentication system, the first thing he considers is whether trial-and-error attempts are likely to succeed. Every authentication system is subject to some type of trial-and-error attack. The classic attack on passwords is an *interactive* attack, in which the attacker simply types one possible password after another, until either the list of possible passwords, or the attacker, is exhausted. Most systems resist such attacks by keeping track of the number of unsuccessful authentication attempts and then sounding an alarm when such things occur.

Password Guessing

With the introduction of password hashing and other techniques for obscuring a password cryptographically, a different technique emerged: the *offline* attack. These attacks take a copy of a cryptographically protected password and use a computer to try to "crack" it. An offline attack may succeed in two cases: when cracking small passwords and when using a *dictionary attack*. If people use small passwords or easily memorized common English terms (such as favorite sports teams), the offline attack can exhaustively check every possible password by comparing its hashed equivalent against the hashed or otherwise encrypted password being cracked. In a dictionary attack, the exhaustive search is against words in a list (the "dictionary") that are presumed to be likely choices for passwords. In fact, dictionary attacks are fast enough that the dictionary can contain lots of unlikely words as well. In studies performed on hashed password files, dictionaries of English words have been successfully used in dictionary attacks to crack between 24.2 percent and 35 percent of the files' passwords (Smith 2002).

---

[2]   U.S. General Accounting Office, "Identity Fraud: Prevalence and Cost Appear To Be Growing," 2002, Rept. GAO-02-363.

Tokens and Smart Cards

Authentication devices are also subject to interactive and offline attacks, although they are far less likely to succeed. An interactive attack would attempt to generate a legitimate authenticator value. The attack's likelihood of success depends on the size of the authenticator. Since authenticators tend to have at least six digits, the chances of success could be less than one in a million. Moreover, the interactive attempts can be detected by the system receiving them, and the system can then sound the alarm.

Offline attacks against tokens are more likely to succeed since they cannot be detected. The goal of the attack is to derive the base secret stored in the token or smart card. The offline attack begins by collecting a number of authenticators (and challenges, too, if they're available, as they are for systems using classic Microsoft Windows domain login protocols). The attack tries all plausible values for the base secret and tests them against the intercepted authenticators to determine whether a particular base secret value would generate that authenticator. These attacks may be practical against tokens that use DES or other algorithms with similarly short key lengths.

Biometrics

Biometric systems are much less susceptible to the same type of trial-and-error guessing than passwords or tokens. There's no obvious way for Henry to present his face differently several times in succession to try to look like Cathy, unless perhaps Henry and Cathy were identical twins. On the other hand, Henry might be able to produce a *team* attack against certain biometric sensors. In this attack, Henry collects a number of people and has them take turns pretending to be Cathy to a biometric sensor. If the sensor is a fingerprint reader, each person tries with each of his or her fingers. If the sensor is for voice recognition, each team member takes a turn trying to sound like Cathy. In theory, a large enough team could eventually succeed. However, the system should be able to detect the numerous failed attempts and sound the alarm before attacks succeed.

Measuring Vulnerability to Trial-and-Error

Since trial-and-error attacks represent a fairly obvious type of attack, most authentication systems are designed with them in mind. This is why some servers enforce a minimum length on passwords: a longer password should increase the number of guesses an attacker must make. This is also why password tokens display six or more digits instead of four or five.

A more accurate way of representing the practicality of trial-and-error attacks is the *average attack space*: a large number that is usually represented as a power of two. The average attack space indicates the number of attempts an attacker must make to achieve a 50 percent chance of discovering an authenticator that matches the expected value. If we are attacking hashed passwords, practical attacks can involve incredibly large numbers, since a computer can automatically test tens of millions of passwords in a relatively short time. If we use a comfortably large dictionary of likely passwords and take into account the fact that 24 to 35 percent of passwords we might encounter will be in a dictionary, we find an average attack space of about 8 million trials (2^{23}). If a practical offline attack can easily perform tens of millions of trials, 8 million pose no real challenge. For secret-key tokens, the space is tied to the size of the authenticator it emits or to the size of the base secret, depending on whether the attack is interactive or offline (Smith 2002).

Another way of representing the success rate of a trial-and-error attack is the *false acceptance rate* (FAR), also known as the *false match rate* (FMR). If we perform a large number of trials in which people attempt to be authenticated as someone else, the FAR may be thought of as the percentage of time they succeed. This is most often used to compare biometric systems. The FAR is one of several metrics often used to assess the effectiveness of the biometric's system. The average attack space for a biometric is tied to its FAR.

Other Attacks

Beyond trial-and-error attacks, Henry's toolbox has three additional tools for attacking authentication systems: replication, theft, and digital spoofing. These have different impacts on different systems, depending on the authentication factors being used.

Replication

In this attack, Henry produces a copy of whatever Cathy is using to authenticate herself. If Cathy has written down her password somewhere, Henry can perform a replication attack by finding the written password and copying it for his own use. This is similar to the delegation problem noted earlier except that it takes place without Cathy's knowledge or intentional cooperation.

As the number of password users, and the number of passwords themselves, have proliferated over the past decade, so has the number of passwords that are written down. Consider what happens if we search the immediate vicinity of workstations in an office environment, peeking under mouse pads and among nearby papers, to look for written passwords. In practice, such "mouse pad" searches uncover a password between 4 and 39 percent of the time, depending on the environment. If we characterize a mouse pad search as a single attempted attack, we have an average attack space of as little as 2^1. When attacking devices such as tokens or cards, the replication attack must duplicate the functionality of the device by either extracting its base secret or by deriving it through a trial-and-error attack (Smith 2002).

Replication attacks on biometrics try to mimic the personal traits or behaviors that the biometric sensor tries to read. This attack is a common fixture in motion pictures, though it often goes to science fiction extremes (see, for example, *Never Say Never Again*, 1983, or *Charlie's Angels*, 2000). In practice, however, it may be relatively easy to fool a biometric sensor, depending on the sensor, the verification procedure it uses, and whether it incorporates liveness testing (Thalheim, Krissler, and Ziegler 2002, 114).

Replication attacks against biometrics can be further broken down into mimics (disguises) and artifacts (facsimiles). *Mimics* are when a user is able to impersonate another identity. *Artifacts* are when an attacker is able to present a manufactured biometric (such as a fake finger) to the system.

Theft

In this attack, Henry physically steals whatever Cathy uses to log in. While this might refer to the slip of paper on which Cathy has written her password, this often means that Henry has stolen her password token or smart card. Cathy's one consolation is that she can readily detect that the theft has occurred; in most other cases she can't detect Henry's attack. Biometrics are relatively difficult to physically steal. Theft of latent biometrics and using them in subsequent replication attacks have been demonstrated.

Digital Spoofing

Also known as a *playback attack*, this attack takes advantage of the fact that all authentication data is ultimately reduced to bits on a wire. If the system expects a particular value for the authenticator, the attacker intercepts this value and replays it to masquerade as someone else. The classic example is for Henry to intercept Cathy's password as it travels in bits from her workstation to the server. This posed a serious problem for Internet traffic until cryptographic protection became a standard feature in web browsers.[3]

In biometrics, the attack manifests itself in roughly the same way as with passwords: Henry starts by intercepting a copy of Cathy's latest biometric reading. Later, Henry masquerades as Cathy by substituting the data message containing his own biometric reading with the earlier reading of Cathy's. Digital spoof attacks are generally sophisticated attacks. To be successful, they require the attacker to have good knowledge of the system as well as some basic level of network access and user privileges.

Defenses

Although authentication system design has often focused on trial-and-error attacks, basic defensive strategies can be used for all of these attacks. In many cases, the defense consists of combining one authentication factor with another.

Trial-and-Error

The essential strategy for reducing the threat of trial-and-error attacks is to increase the size of the base secret and the sensitivity of the verification procedure.

---

[3]   See, for example, Computer Emergency Response Team, "Advisory CA-1994-01: Ongoing Network Monitoring Attacks," February 3, 1994, http://www.cert.org/advisories/CA-1994-01.html.

In password-based systems, this consists of requiring longer and more difficult-to-remember passwords, while steadfastly refusing to recognize partial matches. With authentication devices, this consists of using longer base secrets and ensuring that authenticators are long and varied enough to resist offline attacks.

Another fundamental strategy is to limit the number of guesses: If someone provides a series of authenticators, none of which are correct, the authentication system should sound the alarm that an attack may be in progress. In many cases, systems restrict the number of successive failed matches on the assumption that the legitimate user would eventually match, while an attacker would continue trying unsuccessfully.

In biometric systems, we reduce the risk of trial-and-error attacks by pursuing a lower FAR (or FMR). Two strategies are used for doing this. First, the system can be designed to use additional information from the biometric sensor, which involves constructing a more complicated authenticator and a more sophisticated verification procedure. A second approach is adjusting how closely an authenticator must match a verifier. We can increase the FAR by tightening the match. Unfortunately, this second approach may impact the usability of the system by causing it to reject too many legitimate matches.

The FAR captures errors in which the system accepts illegitimate matches; for example, the wolf in sheep's clothing just got into the sheep pasture. A corresponding measure called the *false rejection rate* (FRR) or *false non-match rate* (FNMR) captures the rate at which the system incorrectly rejects legitimate matches; for example, the sheep just got denied entry to the sheep pasture. An effective biometric system should have a low FRR as well as a low FAR. If the FRR is too high, legitimate users won't be able to log in to the system reliably or get access to what they should be able to access. The sheep will soon become highly frustrated with its inability to access the pasture.

Replication

While there is no way to prevent the replication of passwords, a number of techniques can reduce the risk of replicating authentication devices and biometric traits. If an authentication device already uses base secrets and authenticators that are strong enough to resist trial-and-error attack, the remaining problem is to prevent attackers from extracting a device's secrets. Commercial tokens and smart cards incorporate a number of techniques to prevent replication, though these techniques do not always deter an attacker who has access to a good laboratory.[4]

Countermeasures for biometric replication depend on the type of biometric data being collected. A common strategy is to incorporate *liveness* information: the measurement of traits or behaviors that aren't present if an attacker presents a static copy of a biometric trait. For example, some fingerprint readers

---

[4]   Anderson and Kuhn, "Tamper Resistance—A Cautionary Note," Proceedings of the Second
      USENIX Workshop on Electronic Commerce (Berkeley: USENIX Association, 1996).

are designed to be sensitive to the finger's temperature or pulse, and face or eye recognition systems may require the user to move while it takes its readings. A voice recognition system could require Cathy to recite a different phrase each time she logs in; this would prevent Henry from simply recording her voice and editing her own words to match a preset authentication phrase. While these techniques increase the cost and complexity of the biometric systems, they help make them more reliable.

Theft

Theft is primarily a problem faced by authentication devices such as password tokens and smart cards. Biometrics aren't often subject to physical theft, since that would involve the removal of body parts. The most common defense against device theft is, of course, to associate a PIN with the device. If Henry steals Cathy's smart card, he shouldn't be able to use it because he shouldn't know her PIN and he shouldn't be able to guess it. Some devices incorporate biometrics, usually a fingerprint reader, which either substitutes for the PIN or operates in conjunction with it.

Although theft isn't usually a problem with biometrics, an inevitable question heard at every "Introduction to Biometrics" seminar is this: "What happens if they cut off my finger to try to access my ATM account?" The problem is similar to that of replication and it is addressed using similar techniques, as described in the previous section.

Digital Spoofing

The challenge-response procedure described earlier serves as the model for how most systems resist digital spoofing attacks. Instead of simply transmitting a base secret between a workstation and a server, the workstation uses the base secret to construct a nonrepeating authenticator value. Password-based systems such as Microsoft's Windows domain login mechanism use such an approach, and it is also the basis of all password tokens, smart cards, and other authentication devices.

Biometrics must take a different approach, however. Since biometric systems perform approximate matches, the authenticator must incorporate the actual biometric measurements collected by the sensor. To prevent digital spoofing, a biometric reader typically uses cryptographic techniques so that the verification procedure can confirm that the data came from the biometric reader. If the biometric reading is simply being used to authenticate the person (verification), and not being used to detect duplicate enrollments (identification), an alternative is to use the biometric as a substitute for a device PIN as described in the previous section.

Deploying Authentication Systems

While potential attacks traditionally motivate designs for many features of authentication systems, deployment and administration also play a fundamental role. Unless organizations can deploy and administer the systems economically, the systems won't be used. In authentication systems, the important features are enrollment, maintenance, revocation, and the handling of operational problems. To a large extent, these features take on particular properties depending on the authentication factors being used.

Enrollment

The enrollment process essentially introduces a person to the authentication system. From a technical standpoint, we enroll Cathy in the system simply by providing a verifier associated with her. The exact procedure depends on the authentication factors being used as well as the organization's security concerns. Organizations with high security concerns will likely require a trusted administrator to participate in Cathy's enrollment, even though this increases administrative costs. Many organizations are willing to automate the enrollment process as much as possible, and this leads to *self-enrollment* systems.

In a typical self-enrollment system, the user will enroll on a web page on the organization's internal network. If Cathy self-enrolls, for example, she visits the specified page and enters some identifying information, such as her employee number, so the system enrolls the correct person. Usually, she must also provide some additional personal information that the organization already has on file; this information is used to further authenticate her identity.

Once Cathy has been identified and authenticated, the system establishes the correct verifier. If the system uses passwords, it may either generate one and tell it to Cathy, or it may prompt her to enter a password of her own choosing. If the system uses password tokens, smart cards, or other physical devices, Cathy must have the device in her possession to proceed. To self-enroll a secret-key device, such as a password token, Cathy typically must type in the device's serial number. When the device vendor delivers a number of tokens to a customer, it generally provides a confidential list of serial numbers along with the corresponding base secrets. An administrator installs this list in the authentication server so that the server can retrieve the correct base secret when enrolling a new device.

If Cathy is self-enrolling with a public-key device, such as a smart card or a USB token, she must generally self-enroll at a workstation that has a reader for the card or token. When she plugs in the device and enrolls, the workstation retrieves her public key from the device. Since the data is a public key, there is no serious risk in retrieving it and transmitting it.

Similarly, Cathy could self-enroll with a biometric system as long as she enrolls at a workstation that has the appropriate biometric reader. She would still have to provide one or more biometric readings to create her verifier, but the self-enrollment system would associate that verifier with Cathy's user record. A problem with unsupervised self-enrollment is that Henry might try to enroll himself as Cathy in a form of ultimate masquerade, using her identity and his biometrics. For this reason, self-enrollment is not as secure as supervised enrollment.

Maintenance

Authentication system maintenance incorporates periodic procedures that keep the system operating reliably. Some of these procedures might be at the system level, like database backup and server replication; these procedures aren't distinctive to authentication systems except that databases of secret keys must remain confidential during the operations. Other maintenance procedures involve components of the authentication operation itself. Most authentication devices require little or no maintenance, but most password systems and some biometrics systems must deal with periodic maintenance.

Many organizations implement "password aging" and require users to change their passwords periodically. This reflects a tradition inherited from cryptographic systems: the notion that a key "wears out" after a long period of use and that we strengthen security by replacing it. Many systems provide for automatic password expiration, and almost all password systems provide an interactive service for replacing the existing password with a new one. However, some research suggests that the security of password systems is actually impaired by periodic password changes. A major problem is that users seem more likely to save written copies of passwords if they are induced to change them often (Adams and Sasse 1999). An alternative, more user-friendly policy is to enable keystroke dynamics in conjunction with conventional passwords. This technique is discussed in Chapter 6.

If a biometric system needs to recognize a person over a long period of time, the system must contend with aging and other physiological changes that could affect the characteristic or trait being measured. For example, a building entry system in a large housing project uses hand measurements for biometric authentication. Children reportedly start using the system at about age eight, and the system automatically adjusts a child's verifier as the child grows (Junkel 1999). This automatic adjustment over time is sometimes referred to as *template averaging*. The most efficient way of dealing with periodic maintenance tasks is, of course, to automate them.

Revocation

It is usually necessary to remove people from the authentication system over time. Typically, people are removed when they are no longer authorized to use the system. For example, if Cathy stops paying for her e-mail service, the service provider will remove her information from the system and have another paying customer reuse the space.

Revocation is a relatively direct and simple process with authentication systems that use secret keys or biometric verifiers. The administrator can make it impossible for the system to authenticate Cathy simply by removing her records from the authentication database.

In theory, the provider could leave a user's identity information and verifier in its databases. For example, Cathy's e-mail service provider could retain her name and password as long as a separate access control system can revoke Cathy's access until she pays her bills. For many administrators, however, it is most practical and efficient to delete all of a user's records at one time to avoid collecting a lot of "dangling" records belonging to users who no longer exist on a system.

This distinction between authentication data and access control becomes important when using public-key systems for authentication. Public keys are "public" data, just as any other published material. Like other published material, errors are extremely difficult to correct: you can publish a retraction but there's no guarantee that the retraction will reach everyone who read the original report. If Cathy is using a public-key pair for authentication and discovers that the private key has been stolen somehow, there's no way she can be certain that she's informed everyone who might use her public key to authenticate her. The best she can do is contact every system operator who might use her public key for authentication and tell them to revoke access when that key is used. This doesn't prevent all possible masquerades, since Cathy might fail to contact one or more sites, and some systems may have collected her public key without her knowing it.

Operational Problems

Authentication systems encounter operational problems as entropy takes its toll. Users forget passwords, injure biometric traits, or lose devices, and devices that aren't lost will occasionally float out of synchronization, necessitating adjustments in the authentication server. All of these are natural and even inevitable problems, but they all pose security risks to the authentication system. In practice, many such problems are reported over the telephone and there's rarely a reliable procedure in place to authenticate the person making the call.

Passwords are notorious for generating help desk calls: one study estimates that as many as 25 percent of help desk calls are for resetting passwords.[5] Administrators who answer these calls must either decide that it's too risky to restore a user's access via a telephone call, or they must give the user a password that will work. Secure systems tend to use password hashing, but the hashing makes it impractical to retrieve a user's password if the user has forgotten it. Instead, the help desk would need to assign a new password and provide it to the user over the telephone.

Vendors of password tokens advertise them as a worry-free alternative, although the devices can float out of synchronization. This causes the device to produce passwords that the server doesn't expect and thus won't accept. This can happen with either clock-based or counter-based devices. In the counter-based device, the device becomes out of synch if the button is pressed too many

[5]   Brittain and Paquet, "The Cost of a Nonautomated Help Desk," Research Note DF-14-7228, Gartner, Inc., January 14, 2002.

times, exceeding the range of values the device will accept. The clock-based devices drift out of synch as the clock on the device drifts out of synch with standard time. In both cases, the servers try to keep track of device "drift" in order to adapt to it. Some vendors, notably of counter-based products, have developed automatic resynchronization procedures that don't require a help desk call, while some products will require a help desk call whenever they float out of synch. To date, no study has been published that compares the cost of password maintenance against that of password token maintenance or biometrics maintenance (including enrollment costs).

Biometric users seem much less likely to lose the associated biometric trait, although they can encounter difficulties if a trait changes because of injury or if it changes significantly with age. Moreover, some biometric techniques provide a form of redundancy. For example, Cathy might always use her right index finger when authenticating with a fingerprint reader, but most systems will allow her to provide patterns of other fingers as well. If a bandage covers her right index finger, she can use her left index finger. Iris-based recognition can, of course, enroll both eyes in the system; the user can then use either one, which is helpful if a bandage covers one. Typically Cathy can simply provide the alternate eye and the system will recognize it automatically.

If the problem requires help desk intervention, the help desk must be careful to authenticate the caller. Obviously, anyone can telephone the help desk and claim to be a vice president who needs his password reset; a well-run help desk anticipates such requests and has procedures in place to handle them. High security environments will simply have to apologize and refuse to help, though other environments can provide the help desk with dossiers on employees for authentication purposes.

Economics of Authentication

Authentication systems aren't free, even when they are implemented almost entirely in software. It is always important to consider the total cost of ownership when comparing the cost of different authentication systems. Over its lifetime, an authentication system incurs costs for the original equipment and software, for the administrative costs of enrolling users, and for updating information for purposes of maintenance, problem recovery, or access revocation. In addition, some systems incorporate special hardware. While additional hardware may increase initial costs, those costs can reduce the total cost of ownership or, in high security environments, reduce risks and fraud losses.

Following is a summary of incremental costs associated with authentication systems. Depending on the authentication system being deployed, each of these may or may not represent additional costs over the cost of the base computing system. The total cost of ownership of an authentication system should take all of these into account.

Software—Per Enterprise, Per Site, Per Workstation

Password systems do not generally incur additional software costs, since most products incorporate passwords already. However, password-based, single sign-on products usually incur additional software costs. Systems that incorporate authentication devices or biometrics will usually incur further expenses for additional software.

Hardware—Per Site, Per User, Per Workstation

Authentication devices need to be purchased for every user to whom they are assigned. Biometric readers need to be purchased for every workstation from which a biometric-authenticated user is going to log in. An exception is Apple's Macintosh OS 9, which incorporates voice recognition for authentication, using the built-in microphone provided with most Macintosh computers. Keystroke biometrics are a second exception, as they are designed to work in conjunction with existing keyboards.

Some authentication systems allow different users to be assigned different authentication mechanisms: one might use a password while another might use a password token, and another might use a biometric reader. This changes the cost picture and allows the site to customize authentication according to user needs and specific risks.

Device-based and biometric-based systems will often require an authentication server, which should be hosted on a dedicated computer; a back-up server should usually be included to provide authentication services if the primary server goes down.

Enrollment Costs—Administrators, Per User

Per-user enrollment costs generally involve labor time that is diverted from the user's normal work tasks. At a minimum, the cost involves a minute or two to open an envelope and handle an assigned password or authentication device for the first time. More often, the user must interact with the authentication system as part of the enrollment process. For example, the user might need to change a default or initial password or demonstrate that a newly received device works correctly.

Biometric systems incur per-user enrollment costs as the user trains the system to recognize the biometric trait. This time period will be shorter or longer depending on details of the biometric system's implementation: some systems are designed for rapid training while others may require an extended training period.

In addition to per-user labor costs, some systems will require an administrator to participate in the enrollment. Depending on the system, administrators may need to be present to ensure the quality of the enrollment biometric or to check credentials. Such systems are the most expensive and least convenient to operate, since enrollment is delayed until an administrator is available, and administrators are diverted from other tasks to enroll new users. Enrollment costs also increase if an identification capability is required to guard against the problem of a person enrolled with multiple identities. Systems that support self-enrollment can eliminate many or all of these costs.

Biometric systems will have a *failure to enroll rate* (FTER). That is, a certain small percentage of the enrollment population will not be able to provide the biometric sought. This is because, as biometric expert Dr. James Wayman has so aptly noted: "The human body is weird." Those with no hands lack fingerprints. Of those of us with fingerprints, not all of us (1–4 percent, depending on the source) have good enough quality fingerprints to use in automated biometric applications, due to occupational, environmental, and other factors.

Per-Use Costs—Per User

Authentication procedures are a necessary evil: they are not productive activities and they always require a certain amount of time to perform. The best techniques are so easy to perform that the user isn't distracted from whatever important task is about to be performed on the computer. However, it's hard to estimate the amount of time lost through a distracting authentication process, since it's hard to quantify the loss associated with losing one's train of thought.

It is possible, however, to measure the time lost to authentication failures. Some authentication techniques are difficult to perform reliably. Some may necessitate two or more attempts before succeeding. Unreliable techniques will cost individual users more time than reliable procedures. Even worse, some systems are excessively sensitive to authentication failures and introduce the additional delay of a help desk call if the user has too much trouble completing the process correctly.

Maintenance Costs—Administrators, Per User

Password systems often incur per-user periodic maintenance costs, because many sites require users to change their passwords periodically. While the computer security community has a long tradition of promoting password expiration, some experts are beginning to question its real benefit to system security. Moreover, each time a user changes passwords, there is a risk that the user will lose or forget the new password, leading to a help desk call.

Maintenance functions for most other authentication systems tend to be handled automatically.

Problem Recovery—Forgotten Passwords, Lost Devices

As noted, as many as 25 percent of all help desk calls involve lost passwords that must be reset. The occurrence of lost authentication devices and the corresponding recovery costs are not well known. Moreover, when devices are reported lost, they must be deactivated and a replacement device must be issued. Similar problems with biometric systems tend to be rare. Biometric systems can enroll multiple biometrics (for example, different fingers, different eyes) so a user can substitute (or re-enroll) another if an injury interferes with the usual trait.

However, it's possible for biometric systems to fail due to false rejections: for some reason, the legitimate user can't reliably produce an acceptable biometric reading. Such failures may be due to inadequate training while the user was being enrolled, or they may be due to changes to the sensor's environment. For example, Cathy's workstation might be moved into an area with different ambient noise levels, and the background sounds might interfere with previously reliable voice recognition.

System Availability Costs—Lost Services

Related to problem recovery, if an authentication system fails completely it can result in a population of valid users being unable to access a service or a resource. If the service is a business function, such as eBay or Amazon, the cost of the downtime can be significant. For services and resources that use a networked authentication server, its availability depends heavily on the reliability of the authentication server.

Revocation Costs—Per User

As time marches on, peoples' roles change; they change jobs, employers, and locations. Therefore, a system's total cost should incorporate the cost of removing each user that is added to the system. These costs are rarely associated with the authentication factors being used; instead, the costs often reflect the presence or absence of centralized authentication servers and the degree to which authorization decisions are distributed to other computers (Smith 2002).

Chapter 2

How Biometrics Work

By Kapil Raina, John D. Woodward, Jr., and Nicholas Orlans

As humans, we all use our natural abilities to recognize people through their voices, faces, and other characteristics. Machines, on the other hand, must be programmatically instructed how to use the same observable information to perform human recognition. Technology advances, particularly in biometrics, are helping to close the gap between human perception and machine recognition. A priority goal of the use of biometrics is to provide identity assurance—or the capability to accurately recognize individuals—with greater reliability, speed, and convenience, as well as lower cost. Biometric methods vary greatly and as the technology continues to improve, new options will also come to the fore. This chapter introduces the idea of biometrics and the needs it fulfills, and then covers the fundamental concepts that apply to all biometric systems. Chapters 3–6 cover the major biometric technologies, fingerprint, hand geometry, face, voice, iris, retina, signature and keystroke, and how they perform. Chapter 7 discusses esoteric biometrics.

Brief History of Biometrics

References to biometrics, as a concept, date back over a thousand years. In East Asia, potters placed their fingerprints on their wares as an early form of brand identity. In Egypt's Nile Valley, traders were formally identified based on physical characteristics such as height, eye color, and complexion. This information helped identify trusted traders whom merchants had successfully transacted business with in the past.

The Old Testament also provides early (if not perfect) examples of voice recognition and biometric spoofing. The Book of Judges (12:5-6) reports that the men of Gilead identified enemy Ephraimites in their midst by making suspected Ephraimites say "Shibboleth." When a suspect answered, " 'Sibboleth,' for he could not pronounce it right; then they seized him and slew him at the fords of the Jordan. And there fell at that time forty-two thousand of the Ephraimites." Apparently, the Gileadites had great faith in the accuracy of their biometric system.

An instance of biblically documented biometric spoofing occurred when Jacob fooled his blind, aged father, Isaac, into thinking smooth-skinned Jacob was Esau, his hirsute, older brother. Aided by his mother, Rebekah, Jacob carried off this subterfuge by putting goat skins on his hands and on the back of his neck so that his skin would feel hairy to his father's touch. The Book of Genesis (27:11-28) explains that Isaac, perhaps suspecting a ruse, said to Jacob, "Come near, that I may feel you, my son, to know whether you are really my son Esau or not." Jacob approached Isaac, who felt him and said, "The voice is Jacob's voice, but the hands are the hands of Esau." Isaac should have trusted his inherent voice recognition skills, but he was impressed by the hairy arms of Jacob, and fell for the biometric spoofing. Jacob thus became a case of a false accept (or false match), as discussed below.

In the nineteenth century, law enforcement professionals and researchers, spurred by the need to identify recidivist criminals, tried to find better ways to identify people. In France, Alphonse Bertillon developed anthropometrics, or a method of taking multiple physical measurements of the human body as well as noting peculiar characteristics of a person (scars, tattoos). In the United Kingdom, attention focused on fingerprints, thanks, in part, to work done by police officials in British India. As explained in future chapters, fingerprints came to be the recognized dependable identifiers for law enforcement purposes.

Interestingly enough, biometric technology, in the sense of automated methods of human recognition, first appeared as an application for physical access control. This evolution did not track the growth of e-commerce but created more efficient and reliable authentication for physical access. Biometrics as a commercial, modern technology has been around since the early 1970's, when the first commercially available device was brought to market. One of the first commercial applications was used in 1972 when a Wall Street company, Shearson Hamil, installed Identimat, a finger-measurement device that served as a time keeping and monitoring application. Since this 1972 deployment, biometrics has improved tremendously in ease of use and diversity of applications. The advancement of biometrics has been driven by the increased computing power at lower costs, better algorithms, and cheaper storage mechanisms available today.

NOTE:

What is in a name? Biometrics translates literally as "life measurement." The word refers to automated methods of authentication based on physical or behavioral characteristics of an individual. Biometric industry guru Ben Miller introduced the following definition in 1987: "Biometric technologies are automated methods of verifying or recognizing the identity of a living person based on a physical or behavioral characteristic." (For more information see E-mail from Ben Miller to the Biometric Consortium ListServ, dated August 2, 2002. The International Biometric Industry Association, the industry's trade association, defines biometrics as "automated methods for verifying or identifying the identity of a living individual based on physiological or behavioral characteristics." (For more information go to the Internal Biometric Industry Association's website at www.ibia.org.)

Why Use Biometrics?

There are several key reasons why biometrics are becoming increasingly popular:

- **Convenient authentication**   The convenience of quick-and-easy authentication makes for a smoother system of identity assurance than using keys, cards, tokens, or PINs. With biometric technology, there is nothing to lose or forget since the characteristics or traits of the person serve as the identifiers. Many of these "individual" identifiers remain relatively unchanged and are enduring over time. In addition, biometric technologies also provide greater convenience for the information technology (IT) and support organizations that manage user authentication. For example, biometrics helps to eliminate the need to replace badges or reset PINs.

- **Increased need for strong authentication**   Passwords and PINs can be stolen easily. Biometrics should reduce the risk of compromise—the likelihood that an adversary can present a suitable identifier and gain unauthorized access. With today's intense focus on greater security for logical (computer) and physical access, biometrics offer an attractive method for guarding against stolen or lost identifiers, such as cards or passwords.

- **Decreased costs**   Over the years improvement in hardware and software technologies has brought down the costs of biometric authentication to be affordable at the commercial market level. In addition, advancements in computing power, networking, and database systems have allowed biometric systems to become easier to use over wide geographical and networked areas. Management systems have been developed to administer a cluster of devices.

Increased government and industry adoption   Today, numerous public and private organizations are using biometrics. As an outgrowth of the September 11, 2001, terrorist attacks, an increased awareness of physical security and public safety has also helped make biometrics attractive. Manufacturers are increasingly looking to provide biometrics with computer equipment and products. Many companies offer biometric authentication options and include biometric sensors and matching capabilities as part of their products. For example, there are instances of fingerprint sensors built right into keyboards, mice, and laptops, and second generation sensors are becoming much more "plug and play." As discussed in case studies presented in Chapters 16 and 18, biometrics are becoming increasingly popular.

Key Elements of Biometric Systems

This section discusses biometrics systems' key components: characteristics and traits, standards, enrollment, enrollment policy, processing, matching, and template management and repository issue.

Biometric Characteristics and Traits

There are several key aspects that contribute to a biometric's development and, inherently, its robustness and distinctiveness. These two terms require explanation. *Robustness* refers to the ability of a particular biometric to be repeatedly presented over time to the biometric system for successful automated measurement. Robustness is a function of the particular biometric's permanence and stability. (An iris is more robust than a voice.) *Distinctiveness* refers to the ability of a person's particular biometric to be different from others in the user population, and the difference can be measured. (A fingerprint is more distinctive than hand or finger geometry.)

- **Genetics**   These inherited features (like hair color and eye color) are derived from the subject's parents. In theory, some genetic aspects, such as face structure, are very difficult to change, which makes them appealing for their distinctiveness.

- **Phenotypic**   These traits are developed in the early stages of embryonic development that lead to distinctive development. We can view these as a sort of randomizer on the genetic roadmap, allowing for greater distinctiveness in the general population for certain biometric characteristics, such as iris patterns and vascular networks.

■ **Behavioral** These learned, or trained, behaviors identify patterns of usage (as in handwriting or speaking). In theory, these can be changed and/or relearned. Generally after reaching adult age, however, it becomes difficult to vary these behaviors even with a specific, sustained effort.

To a certain extent, all biometrics consist of genetic, phenotypic, and behavioral aspects. For example, the way a person presents a finger onto a biometric device or a face to a camera can have a behavioral aspect. However, in basic terms, many commercially available, or mainstream, biometrics rely on genetics as the basis of the distinctiveness of the biometric measurements (like hand geometry). Of all the various biometrics, iris and retinal patterns are believed to be the most robust, or consistent, over time. As a result, authentication systems based on these methods will find more accurate authentications over a longer time period (without reenrollment). The traits that tend to change the most over time are voice and pattern matching like keyboard stroke analysis.

Figure 2-1 shows the general flow of a biometric system. The system consists of the following components:

■ **Data acquisition** This is where the biometric is presented to the system. It consists of the digital capture of the biometric and the transfer of the resulting data to the signal processing functions. If data acquisition occurs at a remote location from the signal processing, the data might also be compressed (and encrypted) prior to transmission.

■ **Transmission channel** This process refers to the communication paths between the primary functional components. Some systems are self-contained and the transmission channels are internal to the device. Other systems are more distributed and might have central data storage with many remote data acquisition points. The transmission channel for distributed systems might be a local area network (LAN), a private Intranet, or even the Internet.

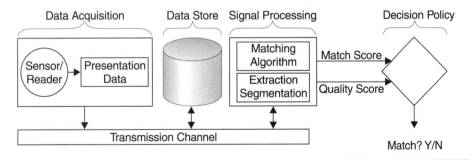

Figure 2-1   Biometric system components and flow diagram

> ## Standards
>
> One of the challenges the biometric industry faces is the range and diversity of technologies and platforms available to anyone trying to leverage biometric authentication applications. This diversity can lead to a situation where various systems lack interoperability because they are built to different standards or are working on incompatible platforms. Impressive work has been done in standards development, particularly with respect to fingerprints. Chapter 10 discusses biometric standards in detail.

- **Signal Processing** This is where the raw biometric data (or biometric sample) is processed for matching. Processing consists of segmentating the sample, then isolating and extracting relevant features from the data, and creating a biometric template—a mathematical representation of the original biometric. *Segmentation* is the process of separating (segmenting) relevant biometric data from background information (for example, cropping a voice sample to remove signals before and after an utterance). The result of feature extraction and segmentation is a *quality score*, reflecting the quality of the input by how successful the feature extraction was. Depending on the application, the newly created template is then compared to one or more reference templates by the matching algorithm. The result of the matching algorithm is a *match score*, indicating how similar the templates are.

- **Decision Policy** This is the final step where the application considers the signal processing outputs (consisting of the quality score and the match score) and makes a yes/no final determination whether there is a match. Normally, empirically determined thresholds are used for both the quality score and match score and a match is produced when both scores are above those thresholds (yes). Alternately, if the quality threshold is met but the match threshold is not, the application returns a negative match (no). If the quality threshold is not met, the application might refuse the match because of the poor quality data and instead request a new sample from the individual. The decision policy described is an example of a fairly common decision policy; however, other decision policies are possible, as they are determined and set by the end-user based on end-user requirements.

We will discuss the details of these components in the remainder of the chapter.

Enrollment

Enrollment is the procedure in which a data subject (or prospective enrollee) presents one or more biometric samples for processing into an acceptable template for future matching. The number of samples required for the creation of such a template varies depending on several factors. These include the type of biometric device selected, user and environmental considerations, and performance considerations (primarily, the level of the threshold—the minimum acceptable level— necessary for matching). If the biometric device selected is based on a fingerprint, for example, user and environmental considerations such as angle and placement of the finger on the scanner; injury (cut), residue, or obstruction (bandage) on the finger itself; and dirt or residue on the sensor can affect the processing necessary for template generation. Multiple samples are taken because the match performance of certain algorithms can benefit from considering multiple samples at the time of enrollment. The template, generated from the average of these samples, is then securely stored. Because multiple samples are taken, enrollment takes longer than a typical matching operation.

Many systems generate an enrollment score based on the samples to indicate the quality of enrollment. Based on the preset parameters for the system, the score is determined to be above a certain minimum acceptable standard. The threshold for the enrollment score has to be balanced with system considerations, such as user inconvenience and throughput rates, faced during the enrollment process. A high/low enrollment score means a likely chance of high/low matching later. In some special cases, a template might be based on only one sample. Such a case could be a surveillance application where people's faces in a public area would be scanned and a template (clandestinely) created based on that one sample. The template could then be used to do future matches to examine patterns of suspect behavior. In one-to-one matching scenarios, the enrollment can be purely voluntary. For example, customers of a credit union may enroll into the credit union's database to access tellerless kiosks. Customers are not required to enroll; it is optional. However, for certain applications, enrollment is mandatory. In a one-to-many scenario designed to identify double-dippers, the biometric system is checking against a pre-enrolled database where enrollment is usually done by a trusted third party (such as by state civil servants enrolling clients of government entitlement programs). All entitlement recipients must enroll, otherwise double-dippers will simply defeat the biometric system by choosing not to participate in it.

Some systems can provide dynamic thresholds. *Dynamic thresholds* are thresholds set per user (as opposed to all users having the same threshold for enrollment). Dynamic thresholds can be tied to the value or the importance of a particular transaction. For example, requesting access to an unrestricted area of a building may require a lower enrollment score, while requesting access to the data center of a building may require higher enrollment thresholds. In addition, traffic and frequency of use are factors required in determining threshold values in a dynamic threshold model. Generally, the more often the device must be used, the better enrollment score might be required. An enrollment policy may cover this scenario by determining how often users must access a certain resource (such as a data center, a wiring closet, or a factory floor).

Accuracy is also important as the master template is created from the enrollment process. The lack of success of enrollment is measured by the Failure to Enroll Rate (FTER). FTER, as shown by the fraction below, is determined over the number of total persons attempting to enroll and those that were unsuccessful within the enrollment policy. In other words, the higher the FTER, the more likely that the biometric system will become ineffective for large numbers of enrollments.

$$\frac{Numerator:\ Number\ of\ unsuccessful\ enrollments}{Denominator:\ Number\ of\ total\ persons\ attempting\ to\ enroll}$$

FTER can be influenced by many factors related to the environment as well as the data subject (for example, the occupation, ethnicity, age, and lifestyle of the enrollee). People who work aggressively with their hands (such as in the construction and bricklaying trades) tend to wear down their fingerprints over time. This degradation makes it very hard or even impossible for a fingerprint scanning device to capture enough features from the fingerprint to create a satisfactory template. Various ethnic groups also have different fingerprint characteristics.[1] All of these factors must be considered when establishing a biometric system because they will have an impact on the FTER. Figure 2-2 shows some relative rankings of how the various biometric methods compare for FTER, based on recent United Kingdom testing.

Enrollment Policy

An enrollment policy is necessary to establish the parameters for how to capture the data needed to produce the templates to be used for matching. Some of the points that need to be covered in an enrollment policy include:

- Determination of additional data required with enrollment to uniquely identify an individual (such as a name or password). Depending upon the function of the biometric system data required may include personal identification information of the individual associated with the biometric.

---

[1]   See, for example, John Berry, "Race Relationships," *Fingerprint Whorld*, vol. 2 (January 1977), 48-50. For extensive information on fingerprints, see Simon A. Cole, *Suspect Identities, A History of Fingerprinting and Criminal Identification* (Harvard 2001).

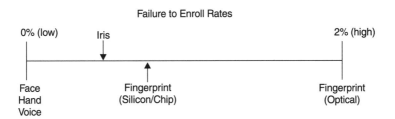

Based on test results from Tony Mansfield et al., "Biometric Product Testing: Final Report," March 21, 2001. Information on the U.K. government's biometric work, including testing, is available at http://www.cesg.gov.uk/technology/biometrics/.

Figure 2-2　Relative FTER among various biometric devices

- Number of enrollment attempts allowed. While an average enrollment may only require four or five samples to meet the enrollment threshold, it's possible that some users may require additional attempts as a result of user and environmental factors. In the case of a high-traffic scenario, it may be best to limit the number of attempts and force the user to consult the security officer or system administrator for assistance.

- The enrollment data storage location. Most likely, the location—at a central location or via portable storage (such as a smart card)—will be dictated by the choice of biometric system in use. In general, storage only on the smart card, while providing increased privacy (since the template used for matching remains on the card and thus within the owner's control) also means less efficiency (because it creates higher user support overhead) and less convenience (because it requires the owner to remember his card to access a biometric system).

- Requirement for an enrollment office and staff. Generally, best practices require an enrollment office and staff to not only ease the use of the system, but also to supervise the enrollment process (to eliminate fraud).

- Need for a multimodal enrollment. Multimodal enrollment allows the user to enroll via multiple biometric methods. For example, industrial workers who use gloves for their work may need to use iris recognition or other biometrics that allow authentication. Similarly, some military applications may require authentication in difficult environmental conditions, such as when soldiers have to wear chemical protective gear that includes gloves and masks. However, for most applications, a wide variety of biometrics will perform well.

Signal Processing

Signal processing, sometimes referred to as image processing, is a class of algorithms used to remove irrelevant noise from data or to help enhance important features. With biometrics, the objectives of signal processing are to remove noise from the data, locate the important parts of the data, and extract just the desired biometric features—a process also known simply as *template creation*. Once biometric data is reduced to a template, core comparison procedures can then either enroll the template or compare the template to one or more reference templates. The comparison process produces a matching score, and the process of template creation procedures produces a quality score. The quality score indicates either how good the original data was or how successful the signal processing procedures were in reducing the data down to its main, salient components.

TIP:

Generally, most algorithms used to perform extractions are proprietary and are considered the core intellectual property of the biometric vendors. Ask vendors questions about how they perform this processing as it plays a major role in system quality and performance. But beware: vendors are usually reluctant to discuss specifics—after all, it's proprietary.

Segmentation is the process that seeks to crop irrelevant background information from the biometric data, and it is a desirable and necessary step before the feature extraction can be performed. Segmentation improves the performance of subsequent algorithms, allowing them to more effectively locate and extract the relevant features (with less data to worry about). During the template creation process, there typically are also data normalization steps. *Normalization* is the process of adjusting or scaling data such that its range of values always falls within a friendly, known range. Normalization is useful for a variety of purposes and can be applied to raw data as well as the "finished" templates. Basically, normalization helps to eliminate surprises that might otherwise plague the matching procedures.

The output of a biometric system's signal processing is generally the quality score and matching score. This information is used by the decision-making application, per the threshold policy set by the end user (or system administrator), to determine if there is an acceptable match or enrollment.

Decision Policy

Matching accuracy is perhaps one of the most talked about aspects of biometrics. It is a critical part of the decision policy. Generally, it is easier to maintain higher levels and more predictable levels of accuracy using one-to-one authentication matching, also referred to as *verification* or *positive matching*, since each subject matches one and only one template. These systems are relatively simple to manage and administer compared to identification.

Identification, or a one-many match, is a more difficult function because all the records of the registered user population in the database are searched for a match. Identification becomes especially difficult as the size of the database to be searched grows. More and more records have to be searched, requiring more time and resources. Consequently, as more and more records are searched, the number of possible matches grows. (Chapter 17 explains this challenge in greater detail.) Given that identification is more difficult, identification programs are still relatively difficult and costly for population sizes that reach millions or more people. Identification matches return an ordered list of candidate matches (such as a list of possible criminals that might match a face in a shopping mall). This concept is also sometimes referred to as *negative matching* or *negative identification* (since generally the system discards those that do not match a predetermined list, like a criminal list). These systems tend to be more expensive as a result of the hardware and software needs.

Some of the key measurements in accuracy include the *False Acceptance Rate* (FAR) and the *False Rejection Rate* (FRR)—see Figure 2-3 for the formulas. The FAR, also known as a False Match Rate or Type II error, describes the number of times someone is inaccurately positively matched. The FRR, also known as a False Non-Match Rate or Type I error, derives the number of times someone who should be identified positively is instead rejected. The combination of the FAR and FRR can help determine which biometric device is more useful in a particular scenario. Generally, the crossover rate, or the equal error rate, is the intersection of the rate of these two events (see Figure 2-4). The lower the crossover rate, the better the rating of the biometric system.

Usually in the course of matching (between a presented sample and a stored template), a score is developed. Based on a set of parameters, the score is determined and if it reaches past a predetermined threshold, then the match is confirmed. Matches can be done as a binary option or in multiple sequences. In the binary option the score reaches the predetermined threshold or it does not. In the multiple sequence scenario, a match score below the threshold triggers another biometric query (perhaps from a different device or perhaps the same device, which averages the score over several tries).

Figure 2-3
FAR/FRR
formulas

FAR (False Acceptance Rate)

$$(\%)FAR = \frac{FA}{N} \times 100$$

FA = Number of incidents of false acceptance
N = Total number of samples

FRR (False Rejection Rate)

$$(\%)FRR = \frac{FR}{N} \times 100$$

FR = Number of incidents of false rejections
N = Total number of samples

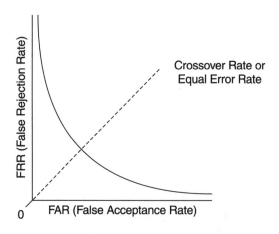

Figure 2-4
FAR/FRR
crossover rate
intersection

TIP:

Since matching results only in a score, there is no such thing as an absolute or exact match. Rather we can say matching is a degree of confidence that we have a match. If you wish to include exact match mechanisms, consider adding additional authentication, such as a PIN or badge access.

Matching can be done either in cooperative or noncooperative modes. In cooperative, the subject is presenting himself willingly to the system. In noncooperative modes, subjects are being scanned without their explicit consent. Most biometric systems, by their designs, require the data subject's de facto consent; you knowingly and willfully place your hand in the hand geometry reader. Some biometrics, however, notably facial recognition, permit clandestine use, so you don't necessarily know that the system is capturing your face.

Generally speaking, we refer to biometrics as matching "living" persons, otherwise we would venture into the world of forensics. As Chapter 8 discusses in detail, many biometric systems have checks to determine if an attack on the system is being attempted through artificial characteristics (such as a faux body part). Biometric liveness tests can range from thermal sensors for body heat to movements and other characteristics. Many authentication systems have duress fail safes to account for a scenario in which an individual is forcibly made to authenticate him or herself for the benefit of another to gain entry into a restricted resource. Biometric systems do not generally have these built in, but they can easily be implemented. For example, authenticating with a specific finger is considered normal access, but authentication with any other finger would be considered a duress situation. In this case, entry would be granted, but a silent alarm sent for additional security help. The national security community is particularly interested in how biometrics can be used as duress fail safe mechanisms in tactical situations.

Not all biometric applications necessarily check to see if the match is of a living person. The reason has to do with both cost and performance. Not many vendors sought to incur the extra costs of including additional sensors and software to test for liveness. Their initial motivation was to establish market share via good data acquisition matching of the primary biometric. The extra liveness testing also takes time and can slow down overall throughput. Thus, a word of caution is in order: never assume that a biometric device tests for liveness; do your homework.

Matching is susceptible to various user and environmental and biological factors (see Table 2-1) and their impact varies based on the particular device. For example, weather, light, or heat may affect certain biometric systems and increase the crossover rate. Other factors such as aging, facial hair, and eyeglasses can also affect the quality of matching for certain systems. In addition, user training and education are a clear factor in the success of the deployment and subsequent matching of users.

Template Management

The utility of all biometric systems is based on the quality and integrity of its template database. Since matching of a subject always requires comparison against a stored reference template, template management is critical to ensure low error rates, high system performance, high availability, and smooth operation. Templates are not raw data or the scanned images of a biometric sample, but rather they are an accumulation of the distinctive features extracted by the biometric system. For fingerprints, these features could be minutiae points. By using these points, the algorithm can allow for variances during the matching

Biometric	Factors Causing Errors	Possible Resolutions
ALL	Template aging as a result of age, gender, other factors	Periodic reenrollment
Fingerprint	Degradation of fingerprints caused by occupation, age, trauma	Enrollment of multiple fingers
Facial	Environmental factors such as lighting, background, contrast; pose, movement of subject, glasses	Use in controlled environmental scenarios; use multiple scans from different angles
Voice	Illness, age, quality of communication system	Allow for reenrollment as necessary
Hand	Injury, trauma to hand	Enrollment of both hands to reduce reliance on single hand
Iris	Positioning, eye angle, glasses	Increased user training and proper placement of scanner

Table 2-1   Factors Affecting Enrollment and Matching

process as a result of slight movement, some environmental factors such as dirt on the hand, or other common variances. In reality, no two presentations to a biometric device are ever exactly the same, but the distinctive features, however, do remain constant.

One challenge with a template is that it acts as a snapshot of certain biometric characteristics taken at a particular point in time. For biometrics such as voice, the characteristic or trait may change over time due to age or abnormal circumstances (like trauma). This change over time is referred to as template aging (or other natural template "drifting"). As a result, to ensure that a proper, up-to-date template is being used, reenrollment on a periodic basis may be desirable. There is no long-term test data available; however, common sense suggests that template aging becomes worse over a long period of time and over a large population that spans all age groups. Some biometric systems can continually average a person's template upon each presentation so that the stored template is always updated.

For certain applications, it may be necessary to store failed attempt templates as a method of ensuring against imposter attempts. A failed attempt template would simply be a recording, perhaps after a few failed tries, of a biometric characteristic that appeared to be repeatedly trying to enter the system. Storing failed attempt templates helps to prevent future attempts and also stores the information for subsequent investigation.

One key aspect of template management is the storage size required for the template. Depending on the biometric used, the size of the template will vary. See Table 2-2 for approximate template sizes in bytes.

A number of efforts have been undertaken in the area of compression technology, which allows a standard biometric template (as well as images) to be compressed into a very small space, thus making storage less expensive. Generally, compression is most useful for large-scale deployments, such as the FBI's Integrated Automated Fingerprint Identification System (known as IAFIS, discussed in Chapter 3).

Keep in mind that several templates may need to be stored for each enrolled user. This approach allows for small variances in day-to-day differences of the templates. Plan on using three or four templates per user and estimate storage space needed for your application accordingly.

Table 2-2	Biometric	Approx. Template Size in Bytes (B)
Approximate Biometric Template Sizes	Voice	70–80B/second
	Face	84–2000B
	Signature	500B–1000B
	Fingerprint	256B–1200B
	Hand Geometry	9B
	Iris	256B–512B
	Retina	96B

There are three main methods that can be employed for template storage:

- Local
- Network
- Portable device

Local Storage

Local storage of a template requires that all templates be stored on the biometric device itself. Generally, local storage is suitable for applications such as physical access by a small number of personnel to a particular location. Limitation of storage (of templates and therefore users) is based on the particular device and design; however, local storage is a robust authentication method since network failure and network compromise are not issues. Also, a higher level of security can be maintained (assuming the device is relatively secure itself) since no data passes over a network. One major drawback for this system is that it derives none of the advantages of a network. Template management is more difficult since a separate user enrollment must occur for each local storage device. For example, if a factory has four entrances all with locally stored devices, then users have to register at all four devices to have complete access to the building. In addition, there is no easy way to back up the templates. Therefore, local storage can become an impractical option.

For certain types of biometric systems, the device itself can be moved and made portable. This provides maximum flexibility in deployment. Portable devices also eliminate the need for possible redundant wiring as might be required for networked devices.

Network Storage

Network storage means that templates will be stored in a database that is available over a data network. This approach is required for large numbers of templates and for one-to-many matching scenarios, which may require access to thousands or even millions of records. One advantage of network storage is that the database can then also store helpful audit logs, which can help in detecting imposter attempts (especially repeated ones). However, this logging may also slow down the system (as with facial recognition systems) and as a result not every vendor will provide logging for the biometric system. One key advantage of this method is that enrollment only needs to occur at a master station. All other devices throughout the network can then access that same enrollment template, making enrollment usage very easy and convenient. Another advantage is that templates used by an entire network of devices can be adequately backed up as part of a disaster recovery or continuity of operations plan.

Portable Device Storage

For fixed template storage systems (such as hardwired systems that have a dedicated database), storage size is usually not an issue. However, for mobile or card-based template storage systems, it may be necessary to choose devices based on the template size. A typical smart card can have from 8K of memory up to more expensive ones that can hold 64K or more. Generally, the smart card in most applications is used to hold other information, including username/passwords for various systems, digital certificates, and more. As a result, for the cheaper smart cards, referred to as memory cards, the maximum space available for template storage is about 2K–4K. Portable template storage generally is the best method of maintaining individual privacy since the template does not have to also reside in an online "master" database. One key difference between the cheaper smart cards and those more expensive is the ability for them to encrypt data. Generally, more expensive cards that can encrypt the template are necessary since the loss of the card itself could force a compromise of the biometric system. This option, while maintaining a high level of privacy, leaves open the greatest user support issues. Should the card be lost, damaged, or stolen a number of security issues are raised. Replacement programs and reenrollment procedures also need to be developed for the cards.

The other key aspect of template storage is that the template must be stored in a very secure manner. If the template could be altered or somehow manipulated, it would compromise the entire system. This security issue is perhaps the weakest aspect of a biometric system since usually all of the templates are stored in a single database. This honey pot must be well protected. Some systems will store templates locally (directly on the device), while others will interact over a network to a central server. Other factors also must be considered, such as whether the templates will be stored in a dedicated database or in a multi-use database. A multi-use database may contain additional information about the user, such as her employee number, social security number, and other personal identification information. Risk of stolen identity increases as more information is tied to the biometric template.

One challenge related to interoperability is that templates are usually stored in proprietary formats, unique to each biometric vendor. This absence of uniform standards poses a challenge when a company attempts to require multiple biometric devices or merges heterogeneous biometric systems. Chapter 10 discusses this issue.

Repository Issues

Repository management is a key issue that affects biometric system architecture and design. Earlier, we discussed the need for secure storage of templates and alternatives to network storage. For large-scale projects however, a comprehensive repository system must be built, taking into account the following considerations:

- Sufficient capacity for the maximum target user population (number of records)
- Auto population of templates (from other data sources)
- Data structure construction (used for creating queries and manual research into the database)

■ Distributed architecture for match processing (to maximize processing power)

For such large enterprise or national level projects, commercial databases, such as Oracle, are used. These databases have several features including the ability to rollback to a previous state in case of database corruption, auditing and record locking, and security.

CAUTION:
In the configuration of the database it is important to note that most databases require a username and password for allowing a software query (usually through SQL). This username and password should be changed from the default! Also consider using internal firewalls and a standard security infrastructure to limit possible attacks, including those from inside the organization.

A number of biometric systems that feature advance template management features provide for encrypted template storage. Generally, however, the weakest aspect of the biometric system is in the transmission of the template and match information between a device and the network database. Biometric system vulnerabilities are covered in more detail in Chapter 8.

User Training

Given that there is a range of biometrics and each biometric system uses a different variation, user training is important for improving enrollment and match rates. Training covers presentation of a sample to the device. For example, some fingerprint scanning devices use optical technology, which requires a clean scanning lens. Users may have to periodically clean the lens, their fingers, or both for an acceptable presentation. Other fingerprint scanning devices use silicon, which does not suffer from the same issue, but proper finger placement is important. In addition, it is important to understand fail-safe mechanisms in case the device fails to operate. For example, if a biometric reader fails at an entrance to a data center during a system emergency, what is the backup plan? What are the alternatives?

For certain environments, such as industrial settings, it may not always be possible to present to a biometric device (like when safety glasses or safety gloves must be worn). Also, a certain small percentage of the user population will not be able to provide the desired biometric because of failure to enroll issues. In these cases alternative biometric devices or other authentication mechanisms may be needed as backups. Training is necessary for users to understand under what circumstances which method of authentication is allowed.

The ultimate goal of training is to reduce the failure to enroll rate (FTER) and increase the true match rates. This keeps costs down and user satisfaction high.

Part II

Types of Biometrics

place index finger in window

Chapter 3

Fingerprint and Hand Geometry

By Peter T. Higgins

Fingerprints are the oldest and most widely recognized biometric markers. They are the impressions of the papillary or friction ridges on the surfaces of the hand. In police and civil applications, the primary interest is in the ridges on the front of the fingers above the end joint. In certain forensic applications, the area of interest is broader and includes all of the friction ridge surfaces on the hands. This includes the fingers, the palms, and the so-called writers' palms (that is, the area on the little finger side of each hand, the part that rests on the paper when one writes).

Latent impressions that remain on objects that are touched or handled are a deposited residue made up of a combination of perspiration, organic solids such as amino acids, and inorganic solids such as salts or blood or other susceptible material the finger might have touched recently.

History of Fingerprints

Fingerprints were used as personal marks or signatures in parts of Asia as early as the third century B.C. Since the late 1800s, people have collected fingerprints using ink and paper in Western societies. Starting in July 1858, William Herschel collected them in Bengal, India, as prints of the whole hand or the right index and middle fingers to verify the identity of people signing contracts with the British-owned East India Company and later to be able to link criminals to their past arrests (Cole 2001, 64). Herschel started as a clerk for the East India Company and then became the Administrator of the Hooghly District of Bengal, India. He was eventually knighted for his services to the Crown.

In the 1870s an Englishman named Dr. Henry Faulds, while serving in Japan as a missionary doctor, uncovered ancient fingerprint impressions imbedded on pottery shards found in shell pits. He determined that the impressions were the distinctive marks of the artists. Thus inspired, he started collecting fingerprint impressions and studying them. He had students working for him and he collected students' fingerprints and samples of those infants to determine whether fingerprints changed as they aged.

In the late 1870s, Faulds made a major breakthrough by using fingerprints to aid a "criminal investigation." An unknown party had taken alcohol for, one assumes, unauthorized consumption from a beaker at Faulds's laboratory. Faulds identified the culprit by matching a student's fingerprints to the latent fingerprints left on the beaker. Subsequently, Faulds identified the perpetrator of a break-in at his laboratory from latent fingerprints left on the outside of the building. Faulds thus demonstrated that it was possible to match a latent, or partial, fingerprint left at a crime scene with a person (Beavin 2001, 71). He published an article in *Nature* (Faulds 1880, vol. xxii: 605) on fingerprints, the first published article on the subject, and went so far as to propose that Scotland Yard establish a fingerprint office.

While most of the recorded early interest in fingerprints involved Europeans, serious work was going on in South America as well. Juan Vucetich, an Argentine police official, began the first fingerprint files based on Galton pattern types. In 1892, Vucetich made the first criminal fingerprint identification taken to court. He was able to identify a woman who had murdered her two sons and cut her own throat in an attempt to place blame on another (Faulds 1880, vol. xxii: 112).

Also in 1892, Francis Galton published his book *Finger Prints* that stated for the first time that fingerprints had individuality and permanence. Herschel, Galton, and others eclipsed Faulds and Vucetich in recognition partially through chicanery—for details of this interesting story read *Suspect Identities* by Simon Cole.

As more and more fingerprints were collected, the greatest challenge was to classify them in a fashion that would permit searches against the collection for both new sets of fingerprints and latent fingerprints. The first such robust system was developed in India by Azizul Haque for Sir Edward Henry, Inspector General of Police in Bengal, India, and is documented in Henry's book, *Classification and Uses of Finger Prints*. In 1926, Sir Henry acknowledged Haque's "contribution in a conspicuous degree" in a letter endorsing a grant of land to Haque for his work on fingerprint classification (Sodhi and Kaur 2002; vol.28, no. 110:200).

Use of this classification system quickly spread across India. Henry got the credit for developing the system and in 1901 became the first director of the Metropolitan Police of London's (the Met) fingerprint division. He was promoted to Commissioner of Police in Scotland Yard in 1905. The classification system became known as the Henry System, and it and its variants were used well into the age of fingerprint automation that started in about 1970. The Henry System is analogous to the Dewey Decimal System that classifies books and journals so that people can search a physical library by topic rather than by just title and author, information a researcher might not have.

The Henry System relied on classification of each individual fingerprint into one of three classes: loop, arch, and whorl. Francis Galton initially described these classes in his 1892 book, *Finger Prints*. The results were expressed as a primary classification of two numbers written as a fraction. The top (numerator) number represented the number and position of any whorls on the odd-numbered fingers and the lower number (denominator) represented the data for whorls on the even-numbered fingers. To further classify the fingerprints for an individual, Henry employed one or more secondary classifications.

Over the years, the FBI and others augmented Henry's system to deal with larger and larger repositories of fingerprint cards. More data was added in the secondary classification area to reflect such items as finger position for the first finger with a loop, if any. By 1992, the FBI had more than 32 million sets of fingerprint cards in its master repository. This augmented classification system permitted the grouping of these 32 million records into classes in which the largest class was no more than 8 percent of the entire repository. It is easy to see that reducing the search by 92 percent of 32 million records surely made the problem easier. (Tens of millions more fingerprint cards in other FBI repositories were not routinely searched.)

In 1905, latent fingerprints were used for the first time in a British criminal case, when the Farrows family were murdered in their combination home and paint shop. A fingerprint was found on a cashbox tray. The fingerprint lab photographed the latent impression and fingerprinted all of the police officers to eliminate any chance of their fingerprints being the one on the cash tray. Eventually, they fingerprinted two brothers who had been seen in the neighborhood and matched the latent impression to the right thumb of one of the brothers.

By the first half of the twentieth century, the use of fingerprints to link arrestees to their criminal records and to identify suspects based on latent fingerprints left at a crime scene was widespread. By 1903, New York state had established a Fingerprint Bureau in its State Bureau of Prisons. Use of the Henry System and thousands of skilled personnel permitted the FBI to move from a criminal arrest and latent case system to an applicant-clearance-check system during World War II. Millions of military personnel and defense factory workers had to be background checked quickly.

Many countries started using fingerprints to vet their wartime personnel. In the United States, the practice is still in place for all government employees, including military personnel and Postal Service employees. Chapter 17 discusses in greater detail how the FBI uses criminal and civil fingerprints.

Fingerprint Cards

Independent of the intended use (criminal or civil) of fingerprints, a clear need to standardize the fingerprint data collection forms was recognized. The cards had to fit into common filing cabinets and needed clear fingerprint impressions identified as to which finger they were from. A comprehensive set of standards was developed by the FBI to include card size, type of ink, text fields, location of fingerprints, and other factors.

The FBI fingerprint cards, and most other police fingerprint cards, have room for 14 fingerprint blocks that support the collection of all 10 fingers in a "rolled" format and the 4 fingers of each hand simultaneously in a "flat" or "slap" format as well as flat impressions of each of the thumbs. These forms have evolved over time as the interest in and use of biographic and demographic data has evolved.

The rolled impressions, the top two rows of fingerprint blocks, are taken by inking and rolling each finger "from nail to nail"—that is, a technician captures all of the papillary or friction ridges from one side of the finger across the face of the finger and back up the other side of the finger. This nail-to-nail approach ensures that two sets of prints taken at different times would have sufficient overlap to support matching and that the entire surface will be available for future latent comparisons.

The flat impressions, or bottom row of the fingerprint card, ensure that the rolled impressions are in the correct sequence. They also provide clearer impressions of the center of the fingerprints than the rolled impressions. The rolled impressions are subject to small but perceptible pressure and motion-induced distortions.

Manual Matching of Fingerprints

To deal with searches against large numbers of fingerprints, law enforcement had two requirements: a classification system that could be used to find similar prints (the Henry System) and a way to describe the features that were matched on two fingerprints. That ended up focusing on *minutia*. The NIST Standard for Forensic Identification definition of a minutia (singular) or minutiae (plural) is this: "Friction ridge characteristics that are used to individualize that print. Minutiae occur at points where a single friction ridge deviates from an uninterrupted flow. Deviation may take the form of ending, division, or immediate origination and termination" (ANSI Glossary 1988). In current usage, we refer to these "events" on a ridge as an *end*, a *bifurcation*, or a *dot*, respectively.

Over the years, the science of fingerprint examination has matured to a point at which examiners discuss three levels of detail in fingerprints.

- **Level 1, or the Galton Level**   Overall appearance of fingerprint—the pattern and general ridge flow, classification, ridge count, focal areas, and orientation.

- **Level 2**   Friction ridge detail and path: the location of the major changes in individual ridges—endings, bifurcations, islands, dots, combinations—and their relationships. These events or minutiae can be described as having X and Y locations in a Cartesian coordinate system overlaid on the fingerprint as well as having an angle, Theta or θ, of flow relative to the X axis.

- **Level 3**   Individual ridge details such as ridge dimensional attributes—edge shape and width (may be dependent on the inking process or pressure) as well as location of pores and their relationships.

The image in Figure 3-1 is from a fingerprint card. It is a right thumb or Finger 1, as the fingerprint examiners number them. Note the ridges, endings, and bifurcations.

Figure 3-1

Fingerprint impression marked to show bifurcation and ridge ending

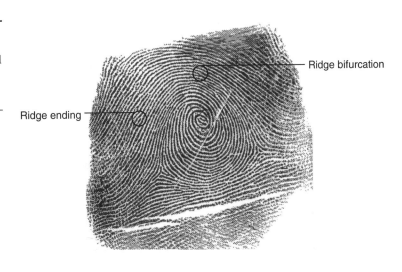

Ridge bifurcation

Ridge ending

If two fingerprint impressions have the same first level data and there is general agreement as to the Level 2 minutiae points and their relationships with no unexplainable dissimilarities, an examiner can number and mark the minutiae that match to show that the two impressions are from the same finger of the same individual. This is the type of data presented by latent examiners when they testify in court that two finger impressions are from the same individual.

It is important to note that each time a fingerprint image is captured, the results are slightly different. Many of the differences between rolled and flat impressions are obvious. The differences between two rolled or two flat impressions are subtler, however. Over or under inking of the finger can cause ridges to merge or not show up, which may result in ridge endings appearing as bifurcations or bifurcations appearing as ridge endings. Dirt or oils can interfere with the uniform transfer of the ridge detail. On an even subtler level, the differences in pressure applied when collecting the fingerprints can change the relative X and Y location of minutiae within an impression.

In the process of capturing fingerprint impressions, several sources of variations cause the separate representations to appear to be different. The most frequent sources of differences taken from a paper published in the Proceedings of the IEEE (Jain, Hong, and Bolle 1997; vol. 85, no. 9:1,365) include the following:

- Presentation could be in a different position on the capture device (for example, further up or down on the scanner).

- The presented finger could be in a different orientation.

- Pressure differences can cause spatial scaling of the location of all features.

- Genuine minutiae might be missing in any capture process.

- Local perturbations of minutiae can result from local pressure differences.

- Nonuniformity of contact between the ridges and the capture device can be caused by humidity, dirt, or damaged and diseased fingers.

The First Age of Automation

As early as 1961, papers were being published on the automated comparison of fingerprints. Interestingly, the first such paper was published in *Nature*, the same journal that Faulds and Hershel had published in earlier. Mitchell Trauring of Hughes Research Laboratories prepared an internal Hughes report, Research Report No. 190, entitled "On the Automatic Comparison of Finger Ridge Patterns for Personal-Identity Verification." A revised report was published in *Nature* in March 1963 (Trauring 1963; vol. 197, no 4,871:938). In his revised report, Trauring referred to a patent issued in September 1960 entitled "Methods and Apparatus for Automated Identification of Finger Prints" and dismissed the algorithm in it as not providing sufficient accuracy. Trauring proposed a system for verification of claimed identity and acknowledged that automating the searching of large repositories to identify people was not yet feasible.

A major push for applying automation to fingerprint comparison came from the FBI about eight years after the researchers first wrote about the possibility. By 1969, the FBI had more than 16 million sets of criminal fingerprints it was using for three primary services:

- Linking newly arrested people to their criminal histories as well as updating those records

- Solving crimes through matching latent fingerprints to records in the repository

- Linking various civil service, military, and citizenship applicants to any criminal history they might have

FBI Special Agent Carl Voelker saw both the repository and search load growing to a point where the current FBI staff would not be able to keep up with the workload. Voelker led the FBI in contracting with the National Bureau of Standards (NBS) (now the Commerce Department's National Institute of Standards and Technology, or NIST). The FBI turned to the NBS to study automation; the principal researchers were Ray Moore and Joe Wegstein. NBS identified two key automation challenges (Lee and Gaensslen 1991):

- Scanning fingerprint cards and identifying minutiae

- Comparing and matching lists of minutiae

Matching Studies

The contract to study automated matching of lists of minutiae was signed with the NBS with Wegstein as the principal investigator. This contract led to the development of the M40 algorithm, the first matching algorithm used operationally at the FBI.

By 1969, the FBI became convinced that fingerprint matching could be automated to the extent that human technicians could be provided a manageably small list of candidates (or possible matches) for each fingerprint card searched against the repository. Similar research was also occurring in France and the United Kingdom. The FBI visited these research teams to share and to learn.

French and British Research

The French and British researchers focused on automating the identification of latent fingerprints. In Paris, the FBI visited Inspector Thiebault, who was experimenting with special purpose matcher boards driven by a computer. Thiebault was also experimenting with Livescan technology rather than ink and paper for collecting fingerprints. These experiments took advantage of "frustrated total internal reflection" to capture ridge detail in the form of digital images. The finger is placed on a glass (or plastic) platen and light is scanned across the platen from below. Where a ridge is in contact with the platen, the light rays are frustrated from exiting the top of the platen and are scattered back into the platen and then onto the detector. Where a valley is present, the light is reflected in a focused ray and a strong signal is detected. Figure 3-2 from UltraScan Corporation demonstrates the process.

In the late 1970s, a public sector organization, SINORG,[1] a subsidiary of the French State Financial Institution, *Caisse des Depots et Consignation*, received a contract to use fingerprints to enroll the voters of Senegal. That effort was unsuccessful for two primary reasons: the immaturity of the technology and the lack of an infrastructure in Senegal.

Inspector Thiebault had a collaborator, Pierre Bodez, who continued his work and developed matching algorithms that he later sold to SINORG. Researchers from the *Ecole des Mines de Paris*, a technical school in Paris, joined the team and advanced the technology. Eventually, that group created a new company, *Morpho Systemes*, in 1982. Sagem Group purchased *Morpho Systemes* in March 1993 and it became *Sagem Morpho SA*. Currently, *Sagem Morpho* is the world leader in civil AFIS technology sales as well as one of the top three players in the criminal AFIS business, along with NEC and Printrak Motorola.

Sagem's first North American installation was in Tacoma, Washington, in 1985, where they then moved their North American operations from Southern California. When Sagem purchased *Morpho Systemes*, its fully owned subsidiary in the U.S., North American Morpho Systems (NAMSI), was renamed Sagem Morpho Inc.

Other Research

Behind the Iron Curtain, academic and industrial research in and development of AFIS technology was under way. Several research groups in the USSR had developed the technology simultaneously and several tried to sell it to western businesses after 1989. For example, Identicator's fingerprint processing algorithms originally come from Russian researchers. Identicator was one of the pioneers in the single finger and small-scale AFIS market. Oscar "Oz" Pieper founded Identicator in California in 1991. BioLinkUSA in Florida has also benefitted from Russian research and development of algorithms and special matcher boards.

A Russian company and product called Papillon, along with Sonda, another company originating from the same research group, claim to have many small-scale installations in Russia. Sonda Laboratory is located in the city of Miass in Chelyabinsk, Russia, and is supported by several Russian universities. (See their web site www.sonda.ru for more information.) Sonda has been in busi-

---

[1] Based on conversations (August 2002) and subsequent e-mail communications between Frederic Biarnes of Sagem Morpho and the author.

Figure 3-2

How Livescan technology works

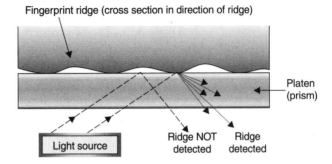

Cross-Section View (Optical Scan)

Fingerprint ridge (cross section in direction of ridge)

Platen (prism)

Light source

Ridge NOT detected   Ridge detected

ness since 1989; by 1991, Sonda installed a prototype system in the Chelyabinsk Department of Home Affairs. Sonda claims its systems are in operation in more than 120 cities around the world.

Fingerprint technology was developed during the end of the 1980s and the beginning of the 1990s in Hungary, Russia, and China. Several universities developed the technology in Hungary and Russia, and several dozen small-scale AFIS installations are running in China. Cogent technology originated, in part, from work done at a Chinese university. Today, Cogent is a well-established American AFIS vendor with systems in many countries.

South Korean companies have developed large-scale AFIS technology and are leaders in smart card use—a field where they see strong demand for fingerprint verification. Several South Korean companies are involved in the single-finger side of the automation of fingerprint identification. Likewise, several Indian companies are entering this market at the single-finger end of the spectrum.

FBI Makes Progress

FBI funded development of Scanners & Minutiae Extraction technology at Rockwell's Autonetics division in Los Angeles. This led to a prototype reader, known as the Finder, that was part of a pilot search system. Then the Bureau awarded a contract for five production card readers that were built in 1975 and 1976.

These card scanners were used to convert the FBI's paper-based card file from 1977 through 1980. The card scanning devices captured grayscale images at 500 pixels per inch (ppi) and extracted the minutiae on the fly for eight of the ten fingers—the little fingers were not imaged to save processing time and record size. The rolled finger blocks on fingerprint cards are 1.6 inches wide and 1.5 inches high. Thus, the eight images represented an area of 6. 4 inches by 3 inches on an 8-inch square fingerprint card.

At 500 ppi in the X and Y direction, the eight images were just less than 5MB in size. Given the price of disk technology, more than $500 per megabyte, the cost to store 14 million such records was unthinkable. Therefore, only the extracted minutiae from the eight fingers were stored.

The NBS work in minutiae matching had progressed to the point where it was able to implement comparison algorithms, and Rockwell built the first comparison software implementing the NBS M-40 algorithm.

FBI/Printrak Spin-offs   As a result of the progress at the FBI, several early adaptors purchased Rockwell (later the division, Printrak, was sold to Thomas de la Rue, they in turn sold it to a management team led by Richard Giles, and eventually he sold it to Motorola Automated Fingerprint Identification Systems (AFIS). Some of the initial Printrak sites were Minnesota/St. Paul, operational by February 1979; The California Department of Justice Latent System, operational in January 1980; and Miami Police Department operational in December 1980.

Canadian Progress

While the FBI was experimenting and pushing the understanding of automating fingerprint matching, the Royal Canadian Mounted Police (RCMP) installed an operational system before the FBI or anyone else. The Mounties imaged their entire fingerprint card file onto AMPEX videotapes, known as a Videofile, and indexed them by pattern type, name, and other parameters. The index data was on punched cards that could be machine sorted to reduce the search space, and then the tapes were loaded and the images of interest downloaded from the wideband analog tapes to video display stations. This semiautomated system was operational by 1973. By 1978, the RCMP had added a Rockwell minutiae extraction and matching system and operated the first digital AFIS—integrated with their AMPEX video, image repository. By 1989 the cost of disks had reached the point, about $10/MB, at which the RCMP was able to move to disk image storage.

British Progress

British Home Office researchers developed a proprietary algorithm and built a latent search system around it with help from Ferranti, and it was operational in the late 1970s. Later, the Home Office contracted with Logica (subsequently merged with Systems Development, Ltd.) to upgrade it. It was housed in an R&D office at Horseferry House, London. The repository consisted primarily of fingerprints collected from persons convicted of breaking and entering. The system was used by the Met, which then commissioned a larger system called *FOCUS*. FOCUS was installed at New Scotland Yard and, like the Canadian system, the images were stored on Ampex tapes as videofiles.

Although the Home Office decided not to compete on algorithm development with industry, it nonetheless maintained a strong in-house R&D staff. In the 1990s, while the Home Office was planning for the introduction of a national AFIS, the constables contracted with IBM to install a Sagem Morpho AFIS for their use. The system was eventually run remotely out of Tacoma, Washington. It has since been shut down, and the Home Office now uses the United Kingdom National AFIS (NAFIS) system.

The NAFIS system was built in the 1990s by TRW with help from Cogent. This successful system employs a semidistributed model with a central repository with tenprint search capability and a distributed latent search system. The centralized tenprint system supports more than 20 regional latent processing sites. The repository is filtered by region, and forensic personnel on the staff of the local constabularies perform the latent searches. The Met runs and operates this system in New Scotland Yard.

The Current FBI System

The FBI's major upgrade was the Integrated Automated Fingerprint Identification System (IAFIS) built in the 1990s. This program, also highly successful, was responsible for development of the ANSI-NIST standard for the Interchange of Fingerprint Images and the Image Quality Specification (IQS) for livescans, card scanners, monitors, and printers. The IQS is an appendix to the FBI's Electronic Fingerprint Transmission Specification (EFTS). That IQS Appendix is a de facto standard used in all livescan and AFIS procurements—worldwide. This program also was responsible for the selection and tuning of Wavelet Scalar Quantization (WSQ) as the compression standard for fingerprints captured at 500 ppi. This program involved scanning more than 32 million inked and laser printed fingerprint cards to comply with the ANSI-NIST Type 4 record format.

IAFIS was developed in response to state and local law enforcement pressure to improve response time for criminal searches and applicant processing. State and local law enforcement were investing in livescan systems and AFIS technology, but there was a need for a more automated federal infrastructure as it would be unreasonable to expect Delaware, for example, to search the fingerprints of all people arrested in California. In the late 1980s, criminal submittals were experiencing months of delays. Congress (led by Senator Robert Byrd of West Virginia) and FBI Director William S. Sessions accepted the challenge and started a program to develop an AFIS fully integrated with the computerized criminal history (CCH) files. The system employs the first Lockheed Martin/ Sagem Morpho based AFIS. The system went operational in 1999 and now provides responses in less than two hours for over 97 percent of the approximately 40,000 electronically submitted arrest fingerprints (seven days a week) and same-day turnaround for the approximately 40,000 daily applicant searches (five days a week). Chapter 17 also discusses the IAFIS operation.

Japanese Background

Japan's National Police Agency (NPA) approached NEC about automating storing and matching of fingerprints in the late 1960s. In response, NEC started a research project. The NPA worked out an agreement to have a guest worker at the U.S. government's NBS. In addition, NPA representatives visited the British Home Office researchers and French experts. The NPA started on a five-year production project in 1974 and demonstrated a pilot in Tokyo in 1981. This was quickly followed by conversion of the NPA fingerprint cards and the start of automated searching in 1982. NEC's first North American installation was in the San Francisco Police Department with the contract awarded in 1982 and the AFIS operational in 1984.

Palmprint Automation History

There has been a strong interest in capturing palmprints from criminals so that latent impressions left by the friction ridges on any part of the hand—not just the top third of the fingers—can be used to identify a print. This interest was based on an estimate that 30 percent of latent prints collected are of palms. It is not always obvious if a small latent impression is from a finger or a palm. Therefore, having an integrated repository of latent impressions independent of the type is important.

By February 1994, a palmprint system called Recoderm was installed by the Hungarian company Recoware in the Police headquarters of Szolnog, a suburb of Budapest, Hungary. This operational system is still in use. It was demonstrated for the first time outside Hungary in 1993 at the IPEC trade show in England. Frederic Biarnes of Sagem Morpho provided an extract of a positive report of a benchmark conducted by Ron Smith, dated June 25–27, 1995. Ron's first two paragraphs follow:

> In June of 1995 I had the opportunity to travel in Hungary to benchmark a system that was reported to not only conduct automated fingerprint searches but also palmprint searches as well. This concept has been talked about for many years but I had never before seen a system that could actually perform an automatic palmprint search. The system is called RECODERM and after three days of intense testing which involved several hours each day, I was fully convinced that the system can perform as advertised.[2]

However, Recoderm was never a commercial success, because of Recoware's inability to sell it. The company eventually sold the technology to Lockheed Martin in the late 1990s. By 1996, another integrated automated palm and finger matching system was available. This system was installed in Slovakia by Cogent Systems, Inc., of South Pasadena, California.

NOTE:
Chapter 16 includes a mini case study on the San Francisco Police Department's Automatic Palmprint Identification System.

---

[2]   Based on e-mails between Frederic Biarnes and the author (August 28 and September 5, 2002).

Evolution of Livescan Technology

As early as 1970, people were experimenting with ways to collect fingerprints without using ink. This was of great interest for several reasons:

- To reduce the time required in capturing multiple sets of prints (for example, one for local use, one for the state police, and one for the FBI)

- To eliminate the need to cleanup after collecting fingerprints or being fingerprinted

- To ensure consistency between sets

Thibedau in Paris did the first work in the early 1970s using digital scanning that employed total frustrated internal reflection.

The first production system was made by Fingermatrix to capture flats digitally in 1982. It was not until 1988 that the company was able to capture rolled impressions. As one can imagine, capturing rolled impressions is tricky because either the camera needs to roll around the finger or the finger needs to be rolled over the camera lens to capture the round finger surface. The way this is accomplished in a livescan fingerprint system is to roll the finger across the top of a platen in synchrony with the light source moving across the bottom of the platen. One of the scanners Thibedau was working on was a half cylinder in which you could place the finger with a moving sensor turning around it. That was similar to the design used by Identix in its first rolled finger scanner 10 years later.

Fingermatrix delivered the first system with rolled and flats to the San Francisco Police Department in 1988. A year later, Digital Biometrics Inc. (DBI), now part of Identix, delivered the first grayscale fingerprint printer, the 1135R-40, so that grayscale fingerprint cards could be produced from livescan systems.

By the early 1990s, there was a movement to connect the digital output of livescan equipment to AFIS systems. The FBI worked with the National Institute of Standards and Technology (NIST) to develop a standard for this interface. At that point, four AFIS companies and three livescan companies had different, proprietary data records and image densities.

NIST held a series of three workshops with participation from law enforcement, industry, academia, and so on. The result was an American National Standards Institute/National Institute of Standards and Technology (ANSI/NIST) standard for the exchange of fingerprint images. This standard was updated in 1997 to add mug shot exchange standards and again in 2000 to add variable density images and palm transactions. The official title of the current version is Data Format for the Interchange of Fingerprint, Facial, & Scar Mark & Tattoo (SMT) Information, ANSI/NIST-ITL 1-2000. It is known informally in the fingerprint community as the "ANSI/NIST Standard."

The standard was a compromise among the companies that wanted grayscale images and those who wanted binary images. It was also a compromise between those who wanted 300 ppi and those who wanted to scan at 600 ppi.

The compromise was that the standard supported all types of images—all scanned at a minimum of 500 ppi and transmitted at this rate or at 250 ppi. The ANSI/NIST Standard permitted communities of interest to select a set of record types that they would accept.

While IAFIS was being developed, latent examiners expressed a strong desire to capture fingerprints at higher scan rates to enable them to perform Level 2 and Level 3 comparisons using digital images. Capturing fingerprints at higher scan rates would permit them to make the same comparisons permitted with analog inked fingerprint cards. In 2000, the NIST sponsored a workshop to update the ANSI/NIST Standard for the Interchange of Fingerprint Images to include higher density images. The workshop participants expressed a desire to keep the current 500 ppi Type 4 records so legacy systems could continue to work but to add a higher density record type. Mike McCabe, the NIST workshop coordinator, drafted an update to the ANSI/NIST Standard that was accepted by ballot. It called for the addition of variable density images. Currently at least two AFIS procurements are specifying those new record Types at 1,000 ppi.

With the movement toward 1,000 ppi systems, there was a need to go back and look at the WSQ algorithm that had been tuned for 500 ppi image compression. The common approach that is emerging is that JPEG 2000 will be used for these higher density images. Unlike JPEG, which compressed sub-blocks of an image using discrete cosines, JPEG 2000 uses wavelets to compress whole images.

The ANSI/NIST standard, as approved in 1993, supported nine record types. By the second revision in 2000 it supported the sixteen record types listed in Table 3-1.

The FBI then published the Electronic Fingerprint Transmission Specification (EFTS) that specified which ANSI/NIST records the Bureau would accept, and within those records which data fields and formats. In effect the FBI eliminated many of the compromises by specifying that it would accept only Type 4 fingerprint images that are grayscale and high resolution. Based on that FBI decision, the Type 3, Type 5, and Type 6 images were never used.

Once the FBI promulgated the EFTS, other national and international agencies followed suit. The U.K. Home Office wrote its spec, and it became the foundation for the Interpol interpretation of the ANSI/NIST standard. The RCMP wrote its interpretation, known as the National Police Service-Interchange Control Document (NPS-ICD).

Initially police departments were using livescan technology to reduce labor time and to send the virtual fingerprint cards to their central fingerprint shops for laser printing. This approach permitted them to avoid the time and labor costs of driving the fingerprint cards to the central site.

It was not until the fall of 1995 that fingerprints were electronically submitted to the FBI. They were submitted as part of an initial pilot for the eventual nationwide interchange of fingerprint records electronically with the FBI's IAFIS system, at that point still under development. The pilot was the Electronic

Table 3-1	Logical Record Identifier	Logical Record Contents	Type of Data
The ANSI/NIST Standard's 16 Record Types	1	Transaction Information	ASCII
	2	Descriptive Text (User-defined)	ASCII
	3	Fingerprint Image Data (Low-resolution grayscale)	Binary
	4	Fingerprint Image Data (High-resolution grayscale)	Binary
	5	Fingerprint Image Data (Low-resolution binary)	Binary
	6	Fingerprint Image Data (High-resolution binary)	Binary
	7	Image Data (User-defined)	Binary
	8	Signature Image Data	Binary
	9	Minutiae Data	ASCII
	10	Facial & SMT Image Data	ASCII/Binary
	11	Reserved for Future Use	-
	12	Reserved for Future Use	-
	13	Latent Image Data (Variable-resolution)	ASCII/Binary
	14	Tenprint Fingerprint Impressions (Variable-resolution)	ASCII/Binary
	15	Palmprint Image Data (Variable-resolution)	ASCII/Binary
	16	User-defined Testing Image Data (Variable-resolution)	ASCII/Binary

Fingerprint Image Printing System (EFIPS). EFIPS permitted the Boston Police Department to capture fingerprints on its newly installed booking system that had Identix Livescan engines integrated by Comnetix Computer Systems of Ontario, Canada. The images and related text data were first transmitted to the Boston PD ID branch using ANSI/NIST transactions and from there to the FBI. At the FBI, the virtual fingerprint cards were printed and scanned into the AFIS system. A special priority was placed on these transactions and responses were available back in Boston within hours rather than the normal months. Deputy Superintendent Bill Casey of the Boston Police Department and the entire EFIPS team paved the way for what is today a routine process.

In 1996 and 1997, the International Association for Identification's (IAI) AFIS Committee ran a series of interoperability demonstrations to show the usefulness of the ANSI/NIST Standard. The first year the demonstrations involved the exchange of virtual fingerprint cards and search responses between Comnetix Systems livescans and Cogent, Printrak, and Sagem Morpho AFIS systems. The second year the demonstrations were run with operational AFIS sites from the same AFIS vendors with records sent from Comnetix and Aware software. These tests were very successful and helped push the idea of interoperability of AFIS technologies, independent of the vendor, as a real possibility for law enforcement.

Today more than 70 percent of all fingerprint cards submitted to the FBI arrive electronically from livescan stations and are directly fed into IAFIS as ANSI/NIST transactions as part of a paperless workflow.

The Second Age of Automation

With the ANSI/NIST Standard and the IAFIS and the UK's NAFIS systems taking the lead, end-to-end electronic fingerprint processing is becoming the norm. At about the same time IAFIS was being built, the number of background checks started to eclipse the number of criminal searches. During WW II, millions of applicant searches were conducted per year. With some high publicity, child abuse and abduction cases in the 1980s and 90s, the demand for background checks on people dealing with children and the elderly increased substantially. This demand was part of the incentive to build the IAFIS system. It was unreasonable, for example, to ask the smaller states such as Delaware and Rhode Island to search the fingerprints of each schoolteacher applicant in California just as it was unreasonable to ask them to run criminal searches for California arrests. This was one of the driving needs for a national repository searchable in near real-time and a standard way to exchange fingerprints and responses. About this time governments started automating civil searches for welfare— a new use for AFIS technology.

The first totally civil system in the U.S., the LA-AFIRM (Automated Fingerprint Image Reporting and Match) system built by EDS for the Los Angeles County Welfare Department, became operational on June 3, 1991. According to *Government Technology* magazine, "Los Angeles County actually began manually fingerprinting welfare applicants in 1986, when the county's Department of Public Social Services (DPSS), the second largest county-operated welfare department in the U.S., was required to provide housing benefits to homeless applicants without identification. Fearing abuse, the DPSS began manually fingerprinting and photographing applicants as a way to deter fraud in its General Relief program. Within three years, the county had a stack of 50,000 fingerprint cards and little in the way of results. Realizing that the existing system wasn't working, the county began to investigate automated fingerprint identification systems currently in use by law enforcement agencies." (For more information, see Tod Newcombe's "Finger Imaging Points to Welfare Savings" in *Government Technology* at http://www.govtech.net/magazine/gt/1996/apr/welfare/welfare.phtml.)

LA-AFIRM was part of an effort to control spiraling welfare costs through fingerprint matching of enrollees to keep people from enrolling under multiple names. Part of the incentive was a TV expose on so-called "welfare queens," one of whom had a mansion and drove a Rolls Royce to pick up her more than 30 welfare checks each month. The system was widely hailed as a success; it reduced the number of enrollees by more than 20 percent. No data is available to determine whether the fraud rate had been that high or how many people were frightened off by the prospect of having their fingerprints taken.

The system had a small Printrak AFIS back end and single finger, flat impression readers at each welfare office. Participants had to verify their identity with a fingerprint each month when they received their check. Based on the success of this system and a general concern about cost controls and the potential for fraudsters moving to adjacent counties, California has subsequently instituted such a system statewide. Other states and counties have also adopted this technology; Chapter 16 discusses some of these cases. Go to http://www.dss.state .ct.us/digital.htm for up-to-date information on use of AFIS systems in welfare management.

This trend led to a business in civil AFIS systems (that is, systems without an expensive latent capability) and single-finger readers. Simultaneously, a market was emerging for single-finger systems for access control and other information technology and physical security applications.

Interestingly, the ability to use one or two flat impressions in a near real-time AFIS application led full circle back to the law enforcement community. In the mid 1990s, the INS deployed the IDENT system using ANSI/NIST Standards for Type 4 records compressed at 15:1 but for flat impressions. Scanners were placed at border patrol enforcement centers such as Chula Vista, California. The application was a clever use of the LA-AFIRM model. Here people would claim not to be prior offenders, and the system was used to determine whether they had been detained previously or were wanted for some crime such as re-entering the U.S. after having been deported.

Two index finger impressions and a mug shot were collected primarily from persons detained while entering the U.S. at other than an official border crossing. They were sent back to INS headquarters electronically and within two minutes a response would be available at the border. The response would either be negative—a new illegal border crosser—or positive. In the positive case, the response would include data on previous encounters, a prior mug shot, and prior fingerprint images. Given the use of only two fingers, the hostile working environment (that is, dirty fingers and the uncooperative people), and the intense workload (up to 1,800 people per day at just one site), the IDENT system was far from as accurate as a tenprint system, but it was a significant milestone in the use of fingerprints in law enforcement. It also marked the first demonstration of the robustness of the ANSI/NIST Standard as the INS used a Cogent AFIS and, for a short while, also had a Printrak AFIS searching the same data stream.

The Defense Manpower Data Center (DMDC) deployed yet another civil application. It used a single finger from the fingerprints of military personnel to verify issuance of certain benefits and identification documents. The Defense Enrollment Eligibility Reporting System (DEERS) and the Real-Time Automated Personnel Identification System (RAPIDS) applications rely on a system developed by Identicator. Identicator later merged with Identix.

Today scores of companies are in the single-finger capture device business and almost all of them bundle a matching algorithm with their products. They are typically designed for a few hundred people using an information technology system or application. The majority work on minutiae-based technology, but a few employ image correlation techniques. Correlation techniques employ either spatial correlation of ridge flow or frequency domain correlation using two-dimensional Fast Fourier Transforms.

Single-finger flat scanners use a myriad of capture technologies:

- **Optical**   Typically using a light emitting diode or a flat luminescent panel for the light source and a Charged Coupled Device (CCD) array for the image capture device.

- **Thermal**   A solid-state device that measures thermal differences between ridge contact and the air in a valley between ridges.

- **Capacitive**   A solid-state device that measures the microvolt differences in potential energy between ridges and valleys.

- **Ultrasonic**   A transducer system that pulses the finger with ultrasonic waves at three wavelengths to locate and measure ridge detail. While the most expensive of the current readers, these devices can "see" through dirt, ink, and other noise that can impact lower cost devices.

These devices come in two models:

- **Two-dimensional arrays**   The more prevalent packaging that permits the finger to be placed once and captured in a static fashion

- **Single-row scanners**   The more compact packaging format that requires the finger to be moved, at a set rate, across a small scanning surface

Template Extraction and Size

To extract the minutiae and other feature data, the typical system goes through a multistep process. First the image is acquired and then the fingerprint is segmented from the background. This step involves edge detection and ridge flow algorithms such as two-dimensional Fourier Transforms for vertical and horizontal edge detection and Gabor filters to detect frequency and direction. These algorithms take advantage of ridge properties such as the maximum grayscale values on a ridge are along a direction normal to the ridge flow.

Then the fingerprint region is processed to thin the ridges to 1 pix
and binarize them. The reason for originally capturing them at 500 p
of grayscale was twofold: to capture as much information as possib
accurate ridge location and analysis, and to support human fingerprint imag
examination.

The thinned, binary image can then be processed to find the minutiae. This
involves the use of Gabor filters that are moved across the image. The calcula-
tions show ridge location and flow direction as well as ridge endings and
changes of direction. The differentiator of the various proprietary algorithms is
what data they add to the X, Y, and *Theta* values. Typically they include a subset
of the following fingerprint attributes: overall pattern, core or delta location and
overall image quality; and minutiae attributes: minutiae quality or confidence,
nearest neighbors, ridge crossings between neighbors, quadrant the minutiae
are in, and length and curvature of the ridge a minutia is located on.

After the features are extracted, usually in a record that averages about
1,000 bytes, they are matched with records in a repository to calculate a match
score. A threshold is applied to the sorted match scores to find a match or candidate. If the search is to authenticate a claimed identity, the match is against
one or possibly a few records associated with that claimed identity. If the claim
is that the person is not enrolled (for example, the case of a person applying for
a benefit such as a drivers license where possession of a current license precludes issuance of a new one), a so-called cold search is initiated. In this case,
the search can be limited by information external to the fingerprint such as
gender or age range. Likewise, the search can be limited by information derived
from the fingerprint such as pattern type. These types of information are sometimes called *exogenous* and *endogenous* information, respectively.

Robustness, Expected Accuracy

Traditionally the fingerprint community described the performance of AFIS
systems in terms of accuracy and reliability.

- **Accuracy** The probability of no false matches being made (that is,
  that the AFIS system will *not* match a fingerprint to the wrong record
  in the repository)

- **Reliability** The probability that the AFIS system will find the correct
  matching fingerprint if it is in the repository

- **Selectivity** The number of candidates that are returned from a search
  with scores above the threshold.

These terms, defined in the IAI NIST AFIS Definitions Standard, are being
replaced by the newer terms used in the broader biometric market place: Failure
to Enroll Rate, False Reject Rate, False Match Rate or False Accept Rate, and
Failure to Acquire Rate.

The performance of large-scale AFIS systems is different from that of single-finger systems used for access control. In the law enforcement applications with all ten fingers and both rolled and flat impressions, a failure to acquire an individual finger can be tolerated. In these tenprint systems, the failure to match rate is very close to zero as is the false match rate.

In the newer civil applications using only flat impressions, typically four or fewer fingers, the error rates can be quite a bit higher. The University of Bologna Tests in 2001 evaluated many of the best commercial algorithms and several experimental ones. The results are available at http://bias.csr.unibo.it/fvc2002/.

For single finger systems such as those used for access control to a computer system, the error rates can be higher still, which is not unexpected given the broad range of users, the infrequency of use, the low likelihood of proper platen cleaning, and other factors. It is important to note that while the false match rate can seem to be unacceptably high, say 5 percent, that does not warrant as much concern as it would first appear to justify. That number says that if 100 people make it through any other security your facility might have, such as locked doors and badge checks, and they know an account name or number, no more than five of them are likely to falsely match the stored fingerprint template. Before worrying about those five, it would be smart to strengthen physical and personnel security to keep out the 100 intruders.

Vulnerabilities

Over the past few years, several interesting papers have been written on the vulnerabilities of biometrics or liveness issues. Chapter 8 examines biometric liveness issues. Fingerprint capture devices are susceptible to two types of attack: masking the finger to avoid a match, and spoofing the capture device to force a false match. In Europe, for example, instances have been reported of refugees soaking their fingers in henna, a reddish-brown dye, to avoid ridge detection on low-cost optical scanners. Technical papers have been presented in journals describing the use of thin fingerprint pads adhered to the finger and successfully verified against a real finger of another person. The reality is that both are possible under worst-case scenarios. Fingerprint biometrics are like all other technologies—not magic and not foolproof.

Fingerprints are the most mature biometric, however, because they have been successfully used in both a manual and automated fashion for many years. The standards for interoperability of fingerprint systems are also the most mature biometric interchange standards in that they contain record format details that most minutiae-based systems can use and other formats for images that all systems can use. While 1 to 3 percent of the population has a hard time reliably using a fingerprint system, it remains the biometric with the largest population base in use—with more than 100 million persons enrolled worldwide.

Hand Geometry

The second most widely used biometric marker is the hand itself. This biometric technology measures much coarser information than even the Level 1 fingerprint data. In fact it uses a binary (that is pure black and white) image to extract measurement of features such as finger length.

History of Hand Geometry

The use of images of the hand to memorialize artists and to tell stories in petroglyphs, or images carved or pecked into a rock face using stone tools, is older than written history. Hands frequently appeared as symbols in prehistoric African petroglyphs (and sometimes foot tracings were included) and they were seen in North American petroglyphs, too. (You can read more about petroglyphs as http://www.crystalinks.com/petroglyphs.html.)

No recorded uses of hand tracings were used to differentiate people prior to the introduction of hand geometry readers in the late 1980s by Recognition Systems, Inc., (RSI) of California. RSI, founded in 1986, today is a division of Ingersoll-Rand, Inc. (http://www.recogsys.com). RSI sells approximately 90 percent of the hand geometry products sold in the marketplace. In far-off second place is Biomet Partners of Murten, Switzerland, established in the early 1990s.

The Technology

Every hand is unique. Hand geometry scanners, such as those made by RSI, take measurements of the length, width, thickness, and surface area of the hand and four fingers. These features are distinctive enough to permit verification of a claimed identity; however, they are not enough for an identification search. The technology uses a 32,000-pixel CCD digital camera to record the hand's three-dimensional shape from silhouetted images projected within the scanner. A picture of a typical RSI system is shown in Figure 3-3.

The RSI image acquisition system comprises a light source, a camera, a single mirror, and a flat surface (with five pegs arranged on it). The user places his hand—palm facing downward—on the flat surface of the device. The five pegs serve as control points for an appropriate placement of the user's right hand. The device is hooked to a PC with an application that can provide a live visual feedback of the top view and the side view of the hand. The user interface aids in capturing the hand image. The lone mirror projects the side view of the user's hand onto the camera. RSI's device captures two images of the hand.

The user places his or her hand on a highly reflective surface. After an image is captured, the location and size of the hand is determined by segmenting the reflected light from the dark mask created by the hand-obscuring portions of the reflective surface. The second image is acquired using the same camera and a mirror—to measure the thickness profile of the hand. Using only the binary image of the hand and the reflective background, the system is incapable of

Figure 3-3
A typical hand geometry reader with keypad

recording scars, ridges, or even tattoos. However, large rings, bandages, and gloves can change the image and resultant measurements sufficiently to cause a false rejection (or false non-match).

RSI uses the silhouetted images to calculate the length, width, thickness, and surface area of the four fingers of interest; the thumb is not used. More than 90 measurements are taken, and the hand and fingers' characteristics are represented as a 9-byte template. Pattern matching involves computing the Euclidean distance between the sample acquired and the template of the claimed identity. A threshold test is applied to the computed value.

During enrollment, which takes approximately 30 seconds, the user places a hand in the reader three times. The unit's internal processor and software generate the 9-byte template, an average of the three readings taken during enrollment. Interestingly, our hands tend to be mirror images of one another, so many people can enroll with the right hand and use the left hand, turned upside down, for verification.

Figure 3-4 shows the top image from a hand geometry reader in black and white to enhance the silhouette effect that makes segmentation easy to perform.

Biomet Partners' technology is similar to RSI's, but it draws on the shape and characteristics of the index and middle fingers from either hand, and not the entire hand itself. The data is saved as a 14- to 20-byte template that permits identification searches for small populations as well as verification of claimed identity. This system has two pins that separate the index and middle fingers sufficiently to be able to measure them individually. No side view image is captured, as the thickness of the fingers is not measured.

Figure 3-4
A hand
geometry image

Uses of Hand Geometry

Hand geometry systems provide improved security, accuracy, and convenience for many applications such as access control, time and attendance, metering the use of a resource, and facilitating border control. Some typical applications are discussed next, while Chapters 16 and 18 also provide examples of hand geometry use.

- **Access Control** Many nuclear power stations employ RSI scanners to verify the identities of people seeking access to controlled areas. In these applications where security is paramount, the threshold is turned much tighter than in applications such as time and attendance.

- **Time and Attendance** Tens of thousands of time clocks use RSI scanners to verify the identity of people punching in. This is a cost effective way to eliminate so called "buddy punching." In these cases, the threshold for matching a score can be set to a medium level as the worst case loss needs to be balanced with getting all the rightful employees through rapidly at shift change time.

- **Metering Resource Use** The University of Georgia uses hand geometry to reduce food fraud—preventing students from loaning their meal cards to their friends, while still permitting multiple trips to the cafeteria per student. This case study is discussed greater detail in Chapter 18.

The largest application by far is a hand geometry system at Disney World in Orlando, Florida. Disney was initially faced with a vulnerability. Locals can purchase season passes at a dramatic savings compared to the price for multiple daily passes. When friends and relatives would visit, these paper passes could be used interchangeably by one and all. A larger vulnerability emerged. Tour operators could purchase these passes and then issue them for single-day use by their clients and pocket the daily fee. Disney decided to employ a biometric to reduce the unmeasured fraud rate.

The challenge was to find a biometric that could be used quickly with no training and no preenrollment. Since a parent might purchase four tickets for the family, Disney could not mandate that all of the family members be there at time of purchase. Disney also had to deal with the fact that their clients could not necessarily read English signs for the instructions. In fact, they have many customers from around the world who cannot speak or read any of the major languages.

Today Disney uses BioMet Partners' two-finger geometry system. The first use constitutes an enrollment session. If a group of cards are sold to a family, the cards are cross-linked in the access control computer so that each member of the family can use any of the cards after that initial use. Average transaction time from inserting the paper pass to a green light is about 11 seconds. Disney has spent many hours on operations research, human factors, and biometrics tuning to get that type of throughput time with a low false reject rate.

Facilitating Border Control

One of the great challenges governments face is dealing with the sheer number of border crossers. The United States has a peak of about 50 million people entering the country each July and each August. That comes out to more than 1.6 million people per day or an average of 18 per second, 24 hours per day. In the 1990s, the INS experimented with biometrics to reduce the contact time for frequent border crossers. People could apply for a card that would permit them to bypass the INS inspection lines by verifying their identity with a biometric. One such program was the INS Passenger Accelerated Service System (INSPASS).

Applicants would submit a fingerprint card that would be used as part of a background check. Those who passed the check would have their right hands enrolled and be issued an INSPASS card. When they arrived at a U.S. INS checkpoint at certain airports, they could use the card and their right hands to enter the U.S. without an interview and without standing in line.

Other countries used this same approach; among them were Canada and Bermuda. The system was successful from the user perspective, but a study showed that it was using more INS resources to enroll people than was saved by not having to interact with them at the border. Today its use is minimal, but INS is looking at what can be done to make it more effective and efficient.

Robustness, Expected Accuracy

Since only two finger or hand geometry vendors exist, no international or other independent comparison test results have been published. The most recent hand geometry test in the public domain is the 1991 Sandia National Laboratories test that showed error rates below one half percent equal error rate.

Tests have been run for Disney and the INS, but the results have been withheld from the public. In the case of Disney, the results have proprietary business and security implications. In the INS case, the implications are that the results are good enough to use the systems to control access to our country but too sensitive to share.

Vulnerabilities

The obvious vulnerability is that a person could purchase one of the time clock versions of this technology and experiment until they find a hand that is "close enough" to the hand of a legitimately enrolled person. At that point, they could have the false person get a meal, substitute for a friend at the time clock, visit Disney World, or enter the U.S illegally. What they would not know is what threshold setting was employed in each of these applications. As in other biometrics, threshold settings are an important consideration that has to be based on desired security level and population size (if the users are under observation, and so on).

Hand geometry enjoys the largest installed base of any biometric by unit number and by dollar volume if one omits the high-priced AFIS systems. They are easy to use, reliable, and less likely to suffer from presentation errors than other biometrics. While expensive to purchase and taking up a large amount of space, they can handle high volume use and do not require calibration or ambient light adjustments like some other biometrics.

Chapter 4

Facial and Voice Recognition

By Nicholas Orlans

Computer facial recognition is a complex and fascinating software accomplishment. The question, "Can a machine recognize faces at least as well as humans?" is a challenge problem that dates back to early machine vision research in the 1970s, and the problem continues to intrigue and attract researchers from across many disciplines. We inherently know that people look different, and as humans, we have the ability to recognize hundreds of faces: family, friends, acquaintances, and public figures. Humans recognize faces automatically with no conscious effort, and children at an early age can readily recognize familiar faces of parents, siblings, and others that shape the world around them. While we don't question that individuals exhibit a wide range of differences in appearance, those differences are always something we know exactly how to quantify. In other words, what features might a computer program use to recognize or differentiate individuals based solely on appearance?

Despite much research activity on the matter, there is no single over arching agreement on what the most significant visual differences are that enable us to distinguish individual appearance. Thus it comes as no surprise that there is no unified theory on how best to encode and quantify significant facial features for computer matching. Multiple computer techniques have been explored as candidate solutions, and many have contributed research and partial solutions to the problem. All techniques attempt to compare faces in a fundamental manner such that comparisons are invariant to position, pose, expression, facial hair, or eyeglasses, but are somehow sensitive to the core differences that establish individual identity. The current state of the art for computer facial recognition results from contributions from machine vision, machine learning, image processing, and the cognitive sciences. Although other types of biometrics are known to be more robust and distinctive for identification accuracy, facial recognition remains popular (and also somewhat controversial). The technology is both liked and disliked for the same reason. Namely, because it is one of the most passive, natural, and noninvasive types of biometrics. And with the prevalence of low-cost digital cameras and video, the basic potential inputs for the technology are certainly familiar to everyone.

Facial Recognition Applications

Most uses for facial recognition broadly fall under either identification and authentication applications or surveillance and monitoring. Identification and authentication applications involve verifying identity for access control, either physical or computer based. Surveillance applications, discussed later in more detail, are perhaps the more interesting, challenging, and controversial uses of the technology. Surveillance applications scan faces in public areas or at checkpoints and compares faces against a watch list database to see if a felon or other "bad person" is present. Other uses of the technology include identity fraud prevention where one-to-many matches are exhaustively conducted against a database of identities in an attempt to find and remove duplicate (fraudulent) identities. If this function is performed on any sizable population (say even over 500 faces) the face matching is best done in conjunction with other reliable identity attributes such as gender, age, height, and weight. This permits additional filtering and effectively reduces the search space. The additional attributes allow for multi-attribute comparisons that are necessary to help interpret ambiguous results. Facial recognition also has found some niche and novel uses. It has been used to support video search and indexing applications. For example, facial recognition software could search hundreds of hours of news video to find all occurrences of a political figure or known individual. And as facial recognition and other technology improves, it is possible that future applications will increasingly make use of facial recognition in cell phones, videoconferencing applications, robots, interactive games, and "smart home" appliances.

Facial Recognition Technology

As with all image-based biometrics, the correct detection, isolation, and registration of the subject within the image frame is a critical and necessary step before the recognition processing can occur. The face detection and background removal steps are also referred to as the segmentation process. With facial recognition at even a nominal distance, especially in crowd surveillance, the face segmentation process tends to be more challenging than other techniques, as there is greater potential for variation. The camera's location, field of view, and background setting can introduce considerable variation in how faces occur within the frame and how easy or hard it is to automatically locate and separate the face from the nonface parts of the image frame. Location and size differences, if not too extreme, can be corrected once the face is detected and the eyes are located. Face detection is accomplished according to shapes and features in the image. Most software attempts to find "face-like" regions of the image by starting from the center and progressing outward. The output of the face detection process is location and registration information, consisting of a minimum bounding box for the face, the coordinates of the eyes, and perhaps also the location of the bottom of the nose and the center of the mouth.

Thresholds for expected intraocular distances can be used to aid the detection process (although that distance varies according to horizontal face rotation). Also, in the case of video sequences, motion information can be used to help locate candidates' faces. Face detection performance has become very good for single-face images—even rotated, off-center faces can be detected and registered for encoding. However, the problem is significantly harder when generalized to crowd environments. Crowd scenes can contain multiple faces and large variation in distance, camera angle, and pose. Additional background motion (noise) can compound the problem further, making face detection performance in these environments much less reliable than in simpler, more controlled, single-face environments. Even under less than ideal conditions, reasonable results can be achieved if the software is correctly calibrated and tuned, and cameras are strategically placed in the target environment. Some, but by no means all, of the software calibrations necessary for a particular environment can be configured by knowledgeable operators and system integrators. More dedicated calibration efforts could involve modifying the software or adding custom markers in the environment. Markers provide depth queue information to the otherwise flat images and can also help disambiguate some occlusion problems that arise in crowd situations.

The commercial face recognition techniques discussed here are all designed to work best on straight 2D frontal images, or "mug shots." Plausible approaches to the problem were researched and explored by universities during the 1980s, and the first generation of moderately successful approaches began to surface in academic literature in the late 1980s and early 1990s. These first examples of the technology operated in minimally constrained environments and only performed well on a small number of individuals and a limited set of images. 1996 was an important year for facial recognition, as it was the year of the first government FacE REcognition Tests (FERET).[1] The 1996 FERET tests were sponsored by Army Research Laboratories and designed and orchestrated by

---

[1]　P. J. Phillips, P. Rauss, and S. Der, 1996, "FacE REcognition Technology (FERET) Recognition Algorithm Development and Test Report," ARL-TR-995, United States Army Research Laboratory.

Dr. Jonathan Phillips. The tests compared performance of several different face recognition algorithms against the same gallery of images. The test images, collected over a three-year period by Dr. Phillips and Dr. Harry Wechsler, were later expanded and used as part of the more elaborate Facial Recognition Vendor Test 2000 (FRVT2000)[2] tests. The 1996 FERET tests were significant because they encouraged and stimulated technology development in the 1990s, setting performance standards for improvement. Most of the first companies to bring facial recognition to the commercial market were university spin-offs comprised of FERET participants who used their prevailing algorithms as the basis for the company.

Even with additional years of refinements and improvements, today's techniques work best under controlled environmental conditions to capture suitable, consistent, frontal-face images. As camera angles are allowed to vary or crowd conditions are considered, the problems of face detection and encoding are compounded and performance degrades as a result. Although there are a multitude of variations and differences within each approach, three classes of algorithms emerged from the 1996 FERET tests: neural networks, eigenfaces, and local feature analysis. Template sizes vary somewhat within these three main approaches and across different vendor implementations, but in general, they are less than 100 bytes. Prominent industry vendors report their templates to be approximately 86 bytes.

Neural network solutions represent a broad class of pattern recognition algorithms, here applied to facial image patterns, that in one way or another use neural networks as the locus for recognition decisions. In broad terms, neural networks are based on simple processing units, or nodes, that are organized in layers and connected by weighted links. The number of input nodes corresponds to the number of features, and today's networks typically use one or more intervening layers before data is passed to the output layer. The output layer corresponds to (or may be greater than) the number of classes. For facial recognition applications, the number of classes is the population of enrolled individuals being considered for recognition. This organization provides a technology that allows computers to learn to perform classification tasks based directly on patterns in data. Although the functions of the basic processing units used in neural networks were biologically inspired by the basic properties of neurons, computer neurons do not fully adhere to the behavior of their biological counterparts. Logically they accept multiple weighted inputs (akin to the synaptic strength of their biological brethren), perform simple additions to determine an activation level, and in turn provide that as output. They do not capture time delays and other intricate functions of the biological neuron. Nonetheless, the re-

---

[2]   P. J. Phillips, et al., 2000, "FRVT 2000 Evaluation Report," Department of Defense Counterdrug Technology Development Program Office, http://www.frvt.org/FRVT2000/documents.htm.

sulting networks exhibit certain traits that mimic human intelligence. For instance, they can generalize well, allowing them to match against incomplete data or data with naturally occurring variations.

Neuron models were first developed in the 1950s and 1960s. While many individuals contributed to their development, Marvin Minsky is most notably associated with the first generation of neural networks and, interestingly, also in subsequently establishing some of their shortcomings (Minsky 1969). As a computing paradigm, there is an enormous range of processing architectures that can be called neural networks. Many details in the feature selections, weightings, and error correction schemes have led to many variations of the basic theme, each with subtle differences in behavior or benefits for certain data. While the exploration has enriched the study of neural networks, the diversity also means that different vendor implementations may produce different results from the same data. And that is a potential drawback for some security applications.

Eigenfaces is the term used to categorize a second broad class of algorithms that represent and compare faces on the basis of a palette of facial abstraction images. The development of this technique is associated with Matthew Turk and Alex Pentland, who demonstrated a process for how facial abstraction images, or characteristic eigenfaces, are generated from a collection of images, and then the faces are expressed as a weighted sum of these archetypal faces (Pentland 1991, 71–86). The desired similarity or likeness between faces can then be expressed as a numerical distance on the basis of these weights. It has been argued that this classification technique bears no semblance to the way humans recognize and gauge similarity between faces. Nonetheless, the mathematical properties of the eigenface representation and matching process has been demonstrated to achieve reasonable results in certain minimally controlled environments.

Local feature analysis refers to a class of algorithms that extract a set of geometrical metrics and distances from facial images and uses those features as the basis for representation and comparison (note the local features could be used in conjunction with a neural network). The actual features used in today's commercial products are considered proprietary by the companies and are not made public. Instead they are described only in general terms, and are the things we might expect: the mouth, nose, jaw line, eyebrows, and checks. Local feature analysis must locate and extract these features, and represent their position, size, and general outline shape.[3] Faces can then be compared on the basis of their similarity to their ingredient features. In general, the local feature analysis technique is attractive because it represents faces as less abstract, vector-based features; and the technique has demonstrated that it is one of the better performing tech-

---

[3] P. Penev, J. Atick, 1996, "Local Feature Analysis: A General Statistical Theory for Object Representation," *Network: Computation in Neural Systems*, vol. 7, 477-500. See also T. Choudhury, 2000. "Current State of the Art," http://www-white.media.mit.edu/tech-reports/TR-516/node8.html.

niques. However, local feature analysis may not generalize as well across environments as other techniques because it depends on successful and uniform quality for the location and extraction of all the primary features. Attempts to refine this technique include adjusting the weight of the subcomparisons according to human cognition studies. Alternatively, more pragmatic approaches to optimize performance might attempt to set the weights according to statistical properties of the features as they exist in the enrolled population.

There is no single error rate for the technology, as performance depends on the environmental factors and the data presented. However, government testing has illustrated the detailed effect of these factors on performance and shown that technology vendors are capable of delivering 75–80 percent accuracy under certain simulated operational conditions, and higher (90–98 percent) under ideal conditions.[4] Nonetheless, critics question the effectiveness of the technology in real-world circumstances. The urgency of recently piloted field tests (in airports) has drawn attention and raised expectations, often resulting in hasty, incomplete reporting and bogus conclusions. Some of the recent trial deployments failed to put forth the time and effort necessary to properly calibrate the technology into the target environment. And none of the tests seriously considered integrating the technology in with other systems such as travel documents to both boost performance and, more importantly, to help disambiguate the alarms that can and *should* be predicted to occur. Well-integrated and well-calibrated systems, even if they involve some manual control and review, have found the accuracy of facial recognition to be sufficient for casinos to put the technology to use since the late 1990s as a means to help spot and track banned players.

There are image standards that address minimal image quality and desired orientation of mug shots for facial biometrics. The resolution of the database and probe images, measured by the number of pixels across the face or between the eyes, should adhere to these standards if reasonable results are expected. Also, consistent quality for image acquisition and storage is desirable and should be maintained across the application.[5] As discussed earlier, there currently are no standards for what face features should be used, how they should be weighted for comparison, or how they can be stored in a generalized format conducive to interchange and interoperability. All the details of the image processing, feature selection, isolation, extraction, and representation are proprietary and vendor specific. As a result, there is a range of performance and specialization present in today's commercial face recognition applications.

---

[4] P. J. Phillips, et al., 2000, "FRVT 2000 Evaluation Report." Department of Defense Counterdrug Technology Development Program Office, http://www.frvt.org/FRVT2000/documents.htm.

[5] National Institute of Standards and Technology, 2000, "Data Format for the Exchange of Fingerprint, Facial, and Scars Marks and Tattoo (SMT) Information," ANSI/NIST-CSL 1a-2000 (amendment).

Research and Other Related Technologies

Facial thermography, or imaging the face with infrared sensors, is a related technology that supports (or extends) 2D face recognition based on normal, visible light imaging techniques. Facial thermograms are based on the underlying vascular structure and heat properties of the face and are of interest because they are much less vulnerable to disguises. Also, thermograms can be captured in low ambient light and are less influenced by directional lighting (noise in the visible spectrum). Thermograms have individually distinguishing properties that can be used for recognition; however, their other promise seems to be as a hybrid technology. Infrared cameras can be used in conjunction with normal (visible light) imaging to improve human and face detection performance in surveillance applications. Another potential use of facial thermography is for "detecting subtle, involuntary "flushed face" responses associated with anxiety. However, physiological conditions other than anxiety also correspond with stimulated blood flow in facial regions, including physical exertion, alcohol intoxication, and basic chewing or eating. Some of these hybrid detection techniques have already been tested for military surveillance. Their specialized nature and high cost makes it unlikely they will be a part of commercial applications in the near future.

Although not immediately included in mainstay face recognition applications, there are complementary technologies that bring relevant capabilities to the application space. Some of these related capabilities may play a role in further enabling the technology and improving standardization. In particular, the field of facial animation shares similar underlying capabilities to face recognition. Both applications are driven by similar functions of isolating and representing face features, as well as the ability to track and map them (see Figure 4-1). MPEG-4 is an international standard that includes a standard encoding for facial animation parameters (FAP).

The MPEG-4 model defines a generic face model (representation) in its neutral state with 84 points and provides both low-level and high-level animation action controls.[6] Some of the facial feature tracking capabilities used in the animation industry have already been transferred into manufacturing and automobile safety applications. Those applications are interested in monitoring and tracking human gaze for patterns of fatigue and distraction.

---

[6]   J. Ostermann, 1998, "Animation of Synthetic Faces in MPEG-4," *Computer Animation* (June 8-10, 49-51), Philadelphia, Pennsylvania.

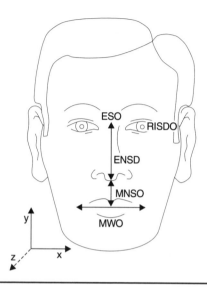

Figure 4-1 MPEG-4 FAP

Voice Verification

Voice verification is a biometric with both physiological and behavioral components. The physical shape of the vocal tract is the primary physiological component. As shown in Figure 4-2, the vocal tract consists of the oral and nasal airways, and the soft tissue air cavities are where vocal sounds originate. The cavities work in combination with movement of the mouth, jaw, tongue, pharynx, and larynx to articulate and control speech production. The physical characteristics of these airways impart measurable acoustic patterns on the speech that is produced. Their shape, length, and volume act as an acoustic filter, influencing the tone, pitch, and resonance. The motion, manner, and pronunciation of words form the basis for the behavioral aspects of voice biometrics. Additionally, free speech analysis, analysis based on speech models with no fixed vocabulary, considers grammatical context, word frequency statistics, idiomatic use, and other rhythmic and intonational aspects of the language for metric comparison and analysis.

Voice verification, also sometimes referred to as *speaker recognition,* is one of several quasi-related speech technologies. *Voice recognition* is a similar but differently purposed technology from speaker recognition. The goal of voice recognition is to understand spoken words and sentences—that is, the content of what is being said. Originally developed to provide voice interfaces to computers, voice recognition is able to support dictation and transcription applications and also is increasingly used to support voice command interpretation in automated telephone call centers. Voice recognition will become increasingly avail-

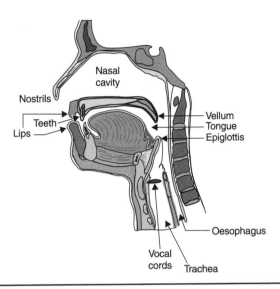

Figure 4-2   Anatomy of speech production

able for a variety of embedded systems that require or could benefit from hands-free, voice interfaces. Potential uses include computers, automobiles, consumer electronics, and even appliances. However, the single goal of voice verification as a biometric is to establish the identity of *who* is speaking—to confirm the identity of an individual using their voice. A user's identification claim is presented with a voice sample (a word or short pass phrase, also known as an utterance). The utterance is captured with an ordinary microphone, and its acoustic properties are verified against the user's previously enrolled sample. If they are sufficiently similar, the user is authenticated.

Verification or identification can be done in either unconstrained or constrained mode depending on the nature and purpose of the application. *Unconstrained* verification means the speech input is free, or text-dependent, conversation. The more commonly used *constrained* mode is able to achieve lower error rates by restricting utterances to predetermined single words or short phrases (text-dependent conversation). By its nature, the unconstrained mode operates on speech inputs of longer duration. Nothing prevents both techniques from being used concurrently, but as a practical matter longer speech inputs are unsuitable for cooperative authentication applications where the user is expecting a response for an access request. The science and engineering focus of voice recognition and speech synthesis applications tends to be on how to parametrically capture, store, and replay voice signals, whereas speaker recognition applications are primarily concerned with the classification of voice signals.

History and Development

Voice verification, voice recognition, and speech synthesis (text to speech) are all speech technologies that were made possible though the study and analysis of human speech production. These technologies coevolved together with the advancement of computer science and digital signal processing. Pioneering research efforts into speech technology were initially interested in voice recognition and speech synthesis. Engineers and researchers sought to understand the mechanics of speech production as a means to synthesize speech. The goal was (and still is) to instruct computers to understand, reproduce, and generate understandable speech—to converse with computers and to have them understand.

Gunnar Fant, a Swedish engineer, published the first physiological model describing the acoustics of speech production in 1960. Fant's well-referenced model was based on a series of diagrams obtained by x-raying the head and vocal tract during the utterance of common vowel sounds and phonemes (components of speech).[7] In the late 1960s and early 1970s Dr. Joseph Perkell, currently a Senior Research Scientist at MIT, extended Fant's models by using x-ray motion pictures to trace outlines of the tongue and jaw.[8]

Other laboratories participated in related projects during the 1960s, all striving to create a speech synthesizer as a computer output device (recall that punch cards were the alternative in those days). Notably, IBM Research Laboratory in San Jose, California, conducted a series of projects known as TASS (Terminal Analog Speech Synthesizer). TASS-II (1961–1967) read phonetically spelled punch cards and mapped them into diphones (vowel-consonant pairs), which were in turn fed to a digital-analog converter for audio output. TASS-III (1967–1970) enhanced the basic functions to include graphic display and online diphone creation. Ultimately, TASS-IV (1980–1985) realized the goal of text-to-speech through the concatenation of diphones.[9]

By 1968, the intellectual underpinnings for realizing the first generation of speech synthesis, speaker recognition, and voice recognition, as depicted by HAL9000 in Stanley Kubrick's *2001 Space Odyssey*, were all in place and starting to come together. (The author acknowledges that HAL's artificial intelligence programming and bad attitude present an entirely different matter.) In 1977, the United States Air Force, in conjunction with The MITRE Corporation, described and tested a prototype speaker recognition access control system developed by Texas Instruments. The evaluation of the prototype system focused on establishing characteristic type I and type II error rates and used

---

[7]   G. Fant, 1960, "Acoustic Theory of Speech Production," Mouton and Co., The Hague, Netherlands.

[8]   Massachusetts Institute of Technology, 2002, "MIT Speech Communications Group: History," http://web.mit.edu/speech/www/history.html.

[9]   D. H. Maxey, ed., 2002, "Smithsonian Speech Synthesis History Project," http://www.mindspring.com/~ssshp/ssshp_cd/ss_ibm.htm#TASS2.

a population of 209 users for testing. The error rates were also considered in light of different enrollment strategies, gender classification, and multimodal access control (speech and signature).[10] Research and development continued on the Texas Instruments system, and it was soon joined by other systems.

The NIST Speech Group, established in the late 1980s, is dedicated to the study and promotion of all speech processing technologies. Today NIST continues to interact with many organizations that implement a wide range of speech processing technologies. NIST has developed an impressive suite of tools, many of which can be accessed from their web site.[11] With assistance from MIT, SRI, and Texas Instruments, NIST publishes a corpus of test data, notably the DARPA TIMIT Acoustic Phonetic Continuous Speech Database. The TIMIT corpus includes phonetic and word transcriptions as well as a 16-bit, 16 kHz speech waveform file for each utterance. These data, as well as other task-specific corpora provide the vital means to measure performance and progress. For example, the Wall Street Journal (WSJ) corpus is intended for testing and developing dictation applications, and the Air Travel Information System (ATIS) was intended to help create automated dialog systems for travel information and improve spontaneous speech recognition. NIST remains the custodian of the TIMIT database, and also provides robust evaluation and benchmark tests to assist the community with measurement and advancement of speech technologies. Lastly, NIST also organizes and conducts the yearly NIST Speaker Recognition Evaluation tests. These important government tests were initiated in 1996 and are of interest to anyone researching or developing text-independent recognition systems.

There is an enormous series of seemingly related patents concerning one aspect or another of speaker recognition. Searching the U.S. patent database for abstracts containing the term "voice" and the term "identification" returns 246 patents. A search for "speaker" and "identification" in the abstract narrows the number of patents down to 62. Among these include several Japanese patents issued in the late 1970s and into the 1980s, notably one issued to Matsimi Suzuki of Fuji Xerox Company in 1977 entitled "Method for verifying identity or difference by voice."[12] While the author is not a patent lawyer, this appears to be the first description of an automated electronic system to compare characteristic parameters of an individual's voice for the purpose of verifying identity.

The increase in the use of cellular phones and the surge of the telecommunications industry in general has produced a number of speaker recognition vendors

---

[10]   A. Fejfar, and W. Haberman, 1977, "Automatic Identification of Personnel Through Speaker and Signature Verification—System Description and Testing." Proceedings of Carnahan Conference on Crime Countermeasures Oxford, United Kingdom.

[11]   National Institute of Standards and Technology, 2002, "NIST Speech Group Home," http://www.nist.gov/speech.

[12]   M. Suzuki, and S. Kitamoto, United States Patent No. 4,054,749 (issued October 18, 1977). Method for Verifying Identity or Difference by Voice, Washington D.C.: U.S. Government Printing Office.

in today's market. With a collected legacy of 30 or more years of research and development (of course, not all implemented or owned by any given vendor), today's vendors offer products and services ranging from low-cost PC login products to large telecommunications infrastructure solutions. A representative, but not exhaustive, list of voice verification vendors follows:

- Persay Inc. (Woodbridge NJ), a subsidiary of Comverse Technology, http://persay.com/
- VeriVoice Inc. (Princeton NJ), http://www.veriVoice.com/
- Nuance Communications Inc., http://www.nuance.com
- T-NETIX Inc., http://www.t-netix.com/
- Sansoft Inc., http://scansoft.com/

Applications

Speaker recognition provides a convenient interface for authentication and identification applications. Most verification applications are text dependent, requiring the user first to enter a user ID by keyboard entry or swipe of a smart card, and then to repeat a predetermined word or short phrase. The user's voice sample is filtered and compared against the previously enrolled voice properties associated with their user ID. To prevent playback attacks, some applications randomly construct a pass phrase for the user to repeat from a small vocabulary of enrolled words and digits. The additional challenge and response thwarts or deters most casual imposters and presents a few more obstacles for the skilled and determined ones. However, overall voice verification is not regarded as one of the most accurate biometric technologies. Performance for text-dependent matching as described is generally expected to have a crossover error rate of about 2 percent, making it (by itself) only a reasonable solution for low-assurance environments. Also, speaker recognition performance is very susceptible to differences in the environment, and some conditioning and training is often necessary. For example, using different handsets or microphones between enrollment and verification will degrade performance, often in unknown and unpredictable ways. Additionally, speaker recognition performance is adversely affected if there are multiple speakers, if there is noise in the environment, or if the technology is used over degraded communication channels. Text-dependent verification performance can be tuned to work quite well in relatively clean, quiet environments, but the technology by itself does not constitute strong authentication. If voice verification is used in conjunction with a four-digit PIN, a 1 in 100 false acceptance rate (FAR) becomes roughly "strengthened" to 1 in 1,000,000.

A more challenging (and less accurate) family of voice identification applications seeks to identify speakers though conversational, text-independent speech. These applications are used to analyze voice communications and also can be used to help scan or search communication channels. For example, banking and accounting businesses may desire a voice check as an additional security measure before discussing private information with telephone callers. A second potential use scenario is searching broadcast news. A political analyst may want to review all public speeches made by an opponent or by a certain leader. Rather than manually listening to weeks or months of general archives, the analyst could use speaker recognition to help locate the relevant sections. And of course the ability to match and identify speakers is of keen interest to law enforcement. Linking voices to identities on wiretap data is an essential tool for law enforcement to understand how many suspects are involved in a particular investigation.

How Speaker Recognition Works

Voice signals are rich in information content, but also tend to be redundant. Depending on the implementation, the size of voice templates is about 70 or 80 bytes for each second recorded. Storage requirements for voiceprints are large when compared to other biometrics, but are quite manageable for small applications that use short, single-word passwords. Template size is an issue for applications with a large population of users or for collection and analysis of long, text-independent samples and associated reference data.

Voice samples are a waveform with time on the horizontal dimension and loudness on the vertical, as shown in Figure 4-3. The frequency of the wave refers to the number of complete cycles per second that the wave oscillates back and forth. Conventional analog phones transmit electromagnetic waves that cycle about 3,000 times per second. This frequency is normally expressed as 3,000 Hertz (Hz), or 3 kHz. When sound or voice waveforms are converted into digital representations, the signals are sampled over many small time intervals (T). This allows the original signal to be represented at multiples of the sampling period, as $x(nT)$. Digital signals are technically superior to analog because they operate at higher speeds, have clearer voice quality, and fewer errors. Digital telephone lines operate at 8 kHz; however, most nontelephony applications of voice verification prefer voice signals sampled at 12 kHz or 16 kHz. For comparison, standard digital audio for compact discs (CDs) is sampled at a rate of 44.1 kHz.[13]

Voice verification considers the quality, duration, pitch, and loudness of the signal and compares these characteristics to the previously enrolled utterance. Although the phonetic content or meaning of the utterance is not directly relevant for verification, phonetic features or segments can be used as additional features for comparison. Phonetic units of the language, such as vowels and consonants, are typically of short duration (measured in milliseconds); however, there are methods for marking and extracting this information from speech.

Although they are accomplished in a variety of different ways, there are four basic steps to speaker recognition. The first step is the digital acquisition of speech data. The second step is feature selection and extraction. The third step

---

[13] Tina-Louise Burrows, 1996, "Speech Processing with Linear and Neural Network Models," Cambridge University Engineering Department, Cambridge, United Kingdom.

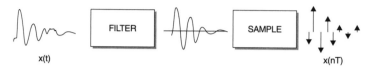

Figure 4-3   Speech digitization

is feature clustering and saving the clustered representation in a database. The last step is pattern matching new voice data against the database for decision making. Various methods and acoustic models exist for determining features and grouping them for subsequent template comparisons. A technique called vector quantization (VQ) maps large vector representations of voice signals containing many thousands of values into a small number of regions, on the order of 100–200. This small set of regions forms the basis for determining speaker-specific features. A VQ lookup table is constructed for each speaker based on a series of training samples. Then, during the recognition phase, the similarities and differences are accumulated over time to determine the most probable match. The crux of word recognition and template matching depends on the proper alignment and normalization of utterances in the time dimension, and a well-known technique for performing temporal registration and scaling is called dynamic time warping (DTW).

Stochastic-based models are also now a popular (and preferred) technique for speaker recognition, and have mostly replaced template matching based on accumulated averages for speaker identification. The most popular stochastic model is the Hidden Markov Model (HHM). Stochastic models are used in the pattern-matching process to measure the likelihood of an observation given a particular speaker model. Such models are constructed by establishing a set of discrete observations and linking them together according to the probabilities of sequenced transitions between the observations.[14] The current state of the art for text-dependent verification consists of applying an HHM model to the entire phrase. This yields an equal-error rate of about 2–3 percent for verification.

VeriVoice is an example of a commercial voice verification system. Its intended use includes phone security, access control, and PC login. Voice enrollment consists of the users voicing digits to the system: "zero," "one," "two," and so on. One of the dialogs used in the enrollment process is shown in Figure 4-4. The entire process takes about three minutes and results in a voiceprint template that is 2–5 KB large.

After enrollment is complete, access control events are verified in a matter of two to three seconds. VeriVoice reports the equal error rate of its system to be

---

[14]   R. Cole, et al., 1997, "Survey of the State of the Art in Human Language Technology," Web Edition, Cambridge University Press and Giardini.

Figure 4-4   VeriVoice Enrollment dialog

1.7 percent,[15] which of course could be adjusted to reduce either false accepts or false rejects (each at the expense of the other).

Other Related Software Resources and Technologies

The maturation of and commercial interest in speaker recognition and companion speech processing technologies is evident by a broadening base of software tools and resources. Microsoft Office XP now comes with support for voice command interfaces and dictation capabilities for the office product line.[16] Microsoft's technology is supported by its Speech Application Programming Interface (SAPI), which was designed to help developers utilize voice input in other software applications. IBM has a long commitment to speech processing and related research. It maintains and supports a suite of consumer voice recognition products called ViaVoice.[17] Apple Computers has integrated speech recognition and text-to-speech capabilities into its current line of operating systems. When enabled, human speech can be used to invoke items placed in the speakable items folder, and can be used to respond to basic OK and Cancel dialog boxes. For output, dialog boxes and error messages are recited in a variety of different voices.

VoiceXML (Voice eXtensible Markup Language) is a recently developed interchange technology that promises to expand the application base of voice technologies on the Web. The basis of VoiceXML is voice recognition, and the primary purpose of voice recognition is the interchange and conversion of voice commands into structured, tagged, text-based descriptions. In conjunction with voice

---

[15] The author is unaware of testing methods used in determining this accuracy rate but acknowledges VeriVoice for including this important information as part of their published technical specification.

[16] Microsoft Corporation, 2001, "Office XP Speaks Out: Voice Recognition Assists Users," http://www.microsoft.com/PressPass/features/2001/apr01/04-18xpspeech.asp.

[17] International Business Machines, 2002, "IBM ViaVoice," http://www-3.ibm.com/software/speech/.

recognition and speech synthesis, VoiceXML documents describe voiced prompts and response selections (output audio files), dialog and telephony control (call transfer and hang up), and recording functions. These tagged descriptions can subsequently be transported and interpreted by conventional text-based processing systems that could, for example, return an appropriate account balance or describe current weather conditions. The definition of VoiceXML was lead by a mini-consortia of telecommunications companies, including AT&T, Lucent, and Motorola.[18]

Research Challenges

Voice processing research and development has been actively pursued for over 30 years, so the technology is well developed by most accounts. And since the mid-1980s, the NIST Speech Group has provided data and methods for measuring the many accomplishments, improvements, and milestones that have occurred. Despite the enormous accomplishments, speaker and voice recognition techniques are not robust enough for all purposes. That is, voice patterns are not highly repeatable by nature, and individuals exhibit these differences in ways that are sometimes problematic. Aside from colds (clogged nasals) and sore throats that may affect performance, the existence of certain statistical *animals* has been noted for speaker recognition. The animal terminology is used by George Dottington to describe individual statistical differences in identification performance. Sheep are the main herd. They are well behaved, and their voices are regularly accepted. However, certain individuals are simply more prone to be rejected (goats), and others have a voice that is more likely to be impersonated than others (lambs). The critters that are exceptionally good at impersonating others are wolves.[19]

Like other somewhat less-robust biometrics such as signature recognition, speaker recognition provides valuable additional information for authentication purposes. However, by itself, speaker recognition is not an absolutely conclusive determination of identity. Secure environments might use speaker recognition in conjunction with conventional numerical personal identification numbers (PINs) or passwords. Noisy environments and applications that are not telephone based may favor using a different biometric.

While the overall techniques for speech processing are quite functional, current research seeks to address some of the remaining challenge areas. As mentioned earlier, robustness is a known issue. While technology won't change individual differences in speech, it may provide a greater ability to suppress

---

[18] The VoiceXML Forum, 2002, "VoiceXML Forum Page," http://www.voicexml.org/.

[19] G. Dottington, et al., 2002, "Sheep, Goats, Lambs and Wolves: An Analysis of Individual Differences in Speaker Recognition NIST Speech Group," http://www.nist.gov/speech/tests/spk/1998/icslp_98/sld001.htm.

background noise from adverse environments. A related goal is to extend the operational range of the technology to operate on voice inputs from degraded communication channels. Voice processing and speaker identification is computationally one of the more expensive biometrics, so there naturally also is a desire for faster, more computationally efficient processing methods.

Other voice processing research seeks to enhance the ability to train speech generators to convincingly mimic, or impersonate, a particular voice. And all voice recognition applications continue to strive for the ability to handle different languages and larger vocabularies. The ability to handle speech that falls outside of known vocabularies (for example, names, scientific terms, and slang) is an area of particular interest because it continues to be one of the main causes of errors. Other niche application efforts seek to automatically classify characteristics of the language or of the speaker; these include identification of the language, particular dialects, stress, and the attitude and emotional state of the speaker.

Chapter 5

Eye Biometrics: Iris and Retina Scanning

By Nicholas Orlans

The intricate nature of the human eye provides two of the most accurate biometrics. The iris and retina, located on the front and back of the eye, respectively, are individually distinguishing structures. The iris is the ring of colored tissue surrounding the pupil. It is the rich textured patterns of the iris that form the basis for iris identification systems. The retina is located on the back of the eye and normally is not visible, but it, too, possesses distinguishing features. The geometrical arrangement of the retinal blood vessels forms the basis for retinal recognition systems. Iris and retinal analysis techniques were developed independently by different researchers, developers, and private companies. Retinal recognition became commercially available in the early 1980s, preceeding commercial availability of iris recognition systems by about five years.

Iris Scanning

According to *Webster's New World Dictionary*, the iris is "the round pigmented membrane surrounding the pupil of the eye, having muscles that adjust the amount of light entering the eye." The iris is layered beneath the cornea and has patterns that are intricate, richly textured, and composed of many furrows and ridges. Iris identification technology is the acquisition, analysis, and comparison of these patterns. The human iris is controlled by two muscles, the dilator and the sphincter, that allow it to adjust its size and control the amount of light entering the eye. When the iris is fully constricted, its tissue mass becomes thicker and the size of the pupil and amount of light entering the eye is increased. When the iris is expanded, the reverse occurs and less light is allowed to enter the eye. In addition to direct adjustments in response to changes of light in the environment, the two muscles of the iris are also linked to the autonomic nervous system and thus are affected by internal physiological responses. Sympathetic responses, also known as "flight and fright" conditions, stimulate the dilator, causing the iris to constrict and the pupil to dilate. Parasympathetic responses, also known as "rest and relaxation" conditions, stimulate the sphincter, enlarging the iris and reducing the size of the pupil.

Ophthalmologists first noted the distinctive features of the iris and observed the patterns to be different between the left and right eye. They postulated further that all irises are unique with no detectable or known genetic dependencies. Irises are randomly formed prior to birth and under normal health conditions remain stable from early childhood till death. Together these two characteristics, distinctiveness and stability, make irises an excellent choice for biometric identification.

Ophthalmologists Leonard Flom and Arin Safir were awarded a patent in 1987 for describing methods and apparatus for iris recognition based on visible iris features.[1] Dr. John Daugman of Cambridge University later developed the algorithms, mathematical methods, and techniques to encode iris patterns and compare them in an efficient manner. All commercial applications currently implement Daugman's elegant, patented techniques[2] and are currently licensed and marketed through Iridian Technologies, Inc. of Moorestown, New Jersey, and Geneva, Switzerland.

Hollywood movies have provided indelible images of eyeballs being modified or eviscerated, and then presented to identification systems for someone to bypass security or make an escape from a villain's compound. While perhaps not the best advertising for biometrics, and certainly not the most common of real-world exploits, these spectacular images do challenge security designers to understand and account for all possible system attacks, however unlikely they may seem. Iris 'spoofs' attacks have been reported by journalists, and while the eye is an instinctively protected organ, it is not immune to injury and disease. Albeit quite rare, iris melanoma is a degenerative disease that affects (and alters) the iris. Melanoma's presence in the iris causes elevated lesions ranging

---

[1] L. Flom and A. Safir, United States Patent No. 4,641,349 (issued February 3, 1987). Iris Recognition System. Washington D.C.: U.S. Government Printing Office.

[2] J. Daugman, United States Patent No. 5,291,560 (issued March 1, 1994). Biometric Personal Identification System Based on Iris Analysis. Washington D.C.: U.S. Government Printing Office.

from nearly colorless to brown and is normally detected during routine eye examinations.

Fascination with the eye and its rich colors and detailed patterns is not confined solely to biometrics. An alternative therapeutic health science known as *iridology* branched off from early medical studies and perhaps culminated in the late 1800s (a period when the observation-based sciences lacked modern magnifying equipment and apparently had too much spare time) with the publication of an iris chart. The iris chart is a detailed mapping of various regions of the iris to internal human organs and heath conditions, and others expanded on this concept to include personality traits and characteristics such as athletic performance. The assumption that changing health conditions can actually be diagnosed from iris patterns suggests the iris, too, must be dynamic and subject to change. This belief contradicts the premise for iris recognition that the iris is in fact a stable, constant, and highly distinguishable structure (that is, randomly formed, and the patterns are unrelated to health or environment). Dr. Daugman has gathered references from medical journals from experts who have evaluated and rejected iridology. He quotes Berggren (1985) as follows: "Good care of patients is inconsistent with deceptive methods, and iridology should be regarded as a medical fraud."[3]

Iris Recognition Technology

Iris recognition uses a near infrared light and is designed to operate with cooperative subjects at close range. Some customized research systems with specialized cameras claim to operate at a significantly longer operational range, 5–10 meters and beyond.[4] However, the longer ranged systems are prototypes and their capabilities are not available in commercial products. Commercial iris scanning works at a focal distance of about 3 to 7 inches. The images are scanned and processed as grayscale values (not color). As shown in Figure 5-1, the image is segmented to locate and isolate the iris. Size and contrast corrections are performed on the image to counterbalance naturally occurring contractions and expansions. The result is a size-invariant representation.

As described by Dr. Daugman in 1998 in "How Iris Recognition Works" the key image operations and computation time as executed on a 300 MHz Sun workstation are reproduced in Table 5-1. (For more information, go to http://www.cl.cam.ac.uk/users/jgd1000/irisrecog.pdf.)

---

[3]   J. Daugman, "John Daugman's Webpage, Cambridge University, Computer Laboratory," 1999-2002, http://www.cl.cam.ac.uk/~jgd1000/; see also Iridology at http://www.cl.cam.ac.uk/users/jgd1000/iridology.html.

[4]   Defense Advance Research Projects Agency, "Iris Recognition at a Distance" (IPTO Project with Sarnoff Corporation), 2001.

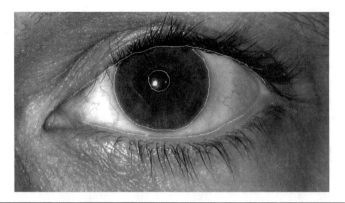

Figure 5-1   Isolation of iris image

Based on Dr. Daugman's initial performance observations with optimized, integer-base code, he estimated a single search engine performs about 100,000 comparisons per second and also concluded:

> "The mathematics of the iris recognition algorithms make it clear that databases the size of entire nations could be searched in parallel to make a confident identification decision, in about 1 second using parallel banks of inexpensive CPUs, if such large national iris databases ever came to exist."

The actual comparison of two IrisCodes reduces to a series of efficient, low-level XOR operations. XOR, also called *exclusive OR*, is the bit-wise operation that accepts two binary inputs and returns true (or 1) whenever the inputs differ and false (or 0) whenever the inputs match. Thus, the extent to which two IrisCodes differ is the number of mismatched bits, or the Hamming distance between the two IrisCodes. Dr. Daugman's analysis documents originally describe a 256-byte IrisCodes representation and explain how distances are measured

Table 5-1

Speeds of Various Stages in the Iris Recognition Process

Operation	Time in msec
Assess image focus	15
Scrub specular reflections	56
Localize eye and iris	90
Fit pupillary boundary	12
Detect and fit both eyelids	93
Remove lashes and contact lens edges	93
Demodulation and IrisCode creation	102
XOR comparison of two IrisCodes	10

for those code lengths. However, perhaps additional header information or changes have since been added to the process as Iridian now describes the iris as being processed into a 512-byte IrisCode. (For more information, go to http://www.iridiantech.com/.) Regardless of the code size, the theory and technique are unchanged.

Hamming distance can also be expressed as the fractional difference between two binary sources of equal length. Dr. Daugman's mathematical analysis of IrisCode comparisons shows iris recognition to have a very low error rate. The odds of two different irises generating a sufficiently similar code to produce a false match is theoretically 1 in 1.2 million.[5] In practice, iris recognition systems perform extremely well. A recent real-world technology test with 200 subjects reported iris recognition performance as almost flawless. Iris recognition performed better than the fingerprint, hand geometric, voice, and face systems involved in the test. There were no decision errors (no false accepts or rejects), and the single error reported for iris recognition was one of the subjects failing to enroll due to a blind eye.[6]

Applications

Initial commercial markets for iris scanning were mostly geared toward physical access applications. These applications are characterized by having a relatively small population of enrolled users and fairly infrequent identification events. Thus, a single modern PC easily provides sufficient processing power and storage capacity to support them. An access control unit produced by IrisScan is shown in Figure 5-2.

With growth in security markets, equipment manufacturers and security integrators have aggressively pursued the broader space of authentication and identification applications, including desktop authentication, secure banking, biometrics on access cards, passenger screening, and even remote surveillance. In 2000, the Charlotte/Douglas International Airport in conjunction with EyeTicket of McLean, Virginia, piloted iris recognition for pilot access and passenger screening. (For more information, go to http://www.eyeticket.com.)

As with any biometric, the advantages and disadvantages of iris identification depend heavily on the application and the intended target environment. From a pure technology standpoint, iris representation and matching techniques are elegant and refined and the systems have been well tested in a variety of environments ranging from cozy offices to ship decks in the military. Iris identification is a known accurate technique with transaction time for trained

---

[5] J. Daugman, 1998, "How Iris Recognition Works," University of Cambridge, http://www.cl.cam.ac.uk/users/jgd1000/irisrecog.pdf.

[6] Tony Mansfield, 2001, "Biometric Authentication in the Real World," The National Physical Laboratory (NPL) Center for Mathematics and Scientific Computing, Middlesex, United Kingdom.

Figure 5-2 Access control with iris scanning

users, being as fast as 4 seconds, and the majority of that time is spent by the subject aligning his or her eye. Once the image is captured and processed, the actual computer matching is fast, on the order of micro-seconds. Recent tests observed average transaction time for iris verification to be about 10 seconds, where that time also included entry of a four-digit PIN.[7]

From the standpoint of the trait itself, it is an advantage that the iris is visible (hence, readily scanned) but also a naturally protected part of the eye. While eyelids, eyelashes, contact lens, size variation, and natural movements present challenges for isolating iris samples from images, processes to accommodate these difficulties have been worked out for most environments. The natural motion of the iris is said to be the basis for liveness detection, although this has not been established through independent testing. The small size of the iris and its curved surface are easily accommodated for in cooperative access control applications using short-range frontal scans. However, the small size of the iris presents significant challenges for longer range, noncooperative surveillance applications where image resolution, camera angles, occlusion, and isolation and tracking increasingly become factors.

---

[7] Tony Mansfield, et al., 2001, "Biometric Product Testing Final Report," The National Physical Laboratory (NPL), Center for Mathematics and Scientific Computing, Middlesex, United Kingdom.

Retina Scanning

Retina biometrics distinguishes individuals by using the patterns of veins occurring in the back of the eye. A 1935 study by Drs. C. Simon and I. Goldstein first observed the individually distinguishing characteristics of retinal vascular patterns.[8] Automated techniques to capture and process retinal patterns for recognition were developed in the 1970s along with the first wave of other early pioneering efforts in digital imaging. Established in 1976, EyeDentify of Baton Rouge, Louisiana, made retinal scanning commercially available for access control in the early 1980s.

Retinal scanning is accomplished by illuminating the retina with a low-intensity infrared light and imaging the patterns formed by the major blood vessels. As the retina is located on the back of the eye, the process requires a high degree of cooperation (and a certain amount of agility) from the user to ensure proper illumination and alignment. Although there are small capillary features and other intricate smaller features contained in the retina, retina recognition technologies are based on the vascular patterns formed across the scan circle of the annular region, as shown in Figure 5-3. Templates of aproximately 96 bytes are created from the circular image band by unfolding the band into a linear structure similar to a bar code. The digital block encoding of the vein patterns can then be efficiently stored and compared by computers.

An example image of a retina's blood vessels converging around the optic nerve is seen in Figure 5-4. The patterns of the vascular network are thought to be created by a random biological process; thus, there is no propensity for genetic likeness and these patterns are believed to be one of the most individually distinguishable features that humans possess. The author is not aware of any scientific studies addressing long-term stability of vascular patterns, but like fingerprints and irises, retinal patterns are understood to be stable and remain unchanged throughout life.

Common sense suggests that retinal vascular patterns will not be willingly altered or disfigured by any human subject. Of course, as is the case with any human physical attribute, the features can be altered as a result of injury or certain diseases. Eye injuries such as a detached retina or severe impact to the eye could result in hemorrhaging, blotching, occlusion, or otherwise damaging or disrupting the vascular network. Glaucoma and diabetes are common diseases that also can affect the retina. Drainage problems and excess fluid pressure in the eye and on the retina are characteristics of glaucoma that can cause deformations, constricting blood vessels on and around the optic nerve. When diabetes affects the retina, the eye disease is called diabetic retinopathy. The disease is progressive and is marked by abnormal blood flow and leakage in the retina that can degrade vision or lead to blindness. Although no studies have established

---

[8]   University of Albany Library, 1988, "Finding Aid for the Carleton P. Simon Papers, 1881–1952, 1956 (APAP-073)," http://library.albany.edu/speccoll/findaids/apap073.htm.

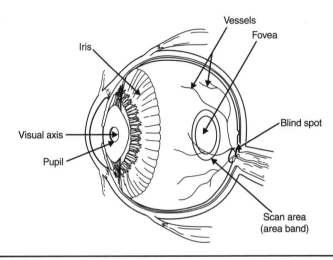

Figure 5-3 Retinal recognition scan area

conclusively these eye diseases degrade recognition performance, both diseases affect the retina and therefore may over time have a degenerative effect on recognition, particularly if templates are never updated.

Because the retina is a protected, internal organ, the scanning process requires close focal distance and users must be compliant and cooperative with the process for the technology to work. Traditionally, retinal scanning is deployed as a wall unit and used for door access, securing entry into facilities and controlled areas. As users approach the door, they must position themselves about 2 to 3 inches from the scanner, align an eye into the lens, and remain still for the 1 to 2 seconds it takes the scanner to illuminate, focus, and capture a retinal image. Even though the technique provides accurate results, some people consider the scanning process inconvenient and somewhat intrusive. Without a breakthrough in sensor technology or a swing in public opinion, retina scanning

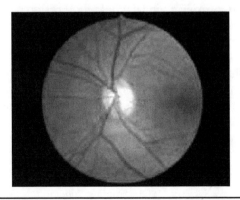

Figure 5-4 A retina's blood vessels converging around the optic nerve

is likely to continue to be regarded as being more cumbersome than other techniques.

At present, the mainstay market for retinal scanning continues to be for door access control. The high accuracy achieved by these systems makes them ideal for military and special purpose government use. The somewhat limited use (relative to other biometrics) resulted in retinal scanning being one of the more expensive biometrics with per unit costs of $2,000 to $2,500. However, EyeDentify has started to offer less costly scanners intended for desktop and general use. And in 2001 a new company, Retinal Technologies (Boston, Massachusetts) joined the market, striving to broaden the applications for retinal scanning into more general authentication and identification markets by offering portable, inexpensive scanner technology. (For more information, go to http:// www.retinaltech.com/.)

EyeDentify's Icam scanners use a low power (approximately 7mA) light source to gently illuminate the retina. The lighting must be sufficient to penetrate the eye and provide consistent imaging with a full range of contrast, but it should not be so bright as to be distressing to the user. The light source provides some visible light but mostly consists of near infrared light (890nm wavelength). Infrared light is necessary because the retina is transparent to these wavelengths. The scanner captures the entire retinal and subsequent image segmentation and the isolation and registration of the portion of the image necessary for recognition, locates the optic nerve, and samples an area band around it. This process creates a 96-byte template for each enrolled individual.

The EyeDentify stand-alone identification systems have an advertised storage capacity for 3,000 individuals. The devices provide both Wiegand and serial (RS232) interfaces. The Wiegand interface allows the device to communicate with door systems, and the serial interface enables communication to computers and networks. These basic interfaces make the device a powerful access control system for stand-alone, single door applications and also provides integrators the opportunity to use the device as part of larger networked security applications. An example of a larger networked application might be the security of an entire campus or large facility with hundreds of doors.

Accuracy

Except for a 1990 report by the Orkand Corporation[9] there is not a great deal of independent assessments or test results available on retina scanning. However, none of the experts doubt that retina scans are a good, accurate form of identification. Positive matches are highly conclusive and false accept rates are

---

[9] Orkand Corporation, "Personal Identifier Project: Final Report," April 1990, State of California Department of Motor Vehicles Rept. DMV88-89; reprinted by the U.S. National Biometric Test Center.

anecdotally said to be close to zero. False rejects that do occur are likely attributed to user unfamiliarity and eye alignment issues. Humans are instinctively protective of the eye and initially respond with some hesitation and trepidation when first using eye biometrics. With practice, however, presentation and alignment of the eye is less problematic. Summaries of the 1990 Orkand report indicated public acceptance of retinal scanning was similar to iris scanning (cited to be 94 percent).

The protected, internal, and unexposed nature of the retina that causes retinal scanning to be awkward and cumbersome in some applications also offers major advantages to others. Unlike faces (and to a lesser extent irises) that are permanently visible and fingerprints that are readily left behind (on various surfaces), retinas are presented only when and where a person chooses. These properties make retinal scanning ideal for applications with high security demands that use relatively small private databases. Moreover, as the retina is protected, fixed tissue inside the body it is less susceptible to environmental changes that add variability to the presentation of other biometrics. Other biometrics such as irises and fingerprints require additional software techniques (and complexity) to insure image quality and compensate for size variations or, in the case of fingerprints, fluctuations due to skin conditions, pressure, and sensor characteristics.

Perhaps because the retina is an internal organ, or perhaps in part because of heightened sensitivities from recent "big brother" privacy debates, there is a misconception that retina scans for identification purposes also reveal personal medical information. This had led some to believe that retinal scanning biometrics are inherently more prone to privacy abuse than other biometrics, which is not actually the case. The confusion may stem from biometric retinal scanning being incorrectly associated with a different process of retinal imaging used for medical diagnostic purposes. The medical retinal scanning process is angiography, an accepted diagnostic method within the medical community that, by design, does reveal particular health information.

Both angiography and retinal scanning for identification image the fascinatingly beautiful patterns of the retina, but that is perhaps the extent of the similarity. Angiography captures hundreds of dye-enhanced images over time and is concerned with investigating the details of blood circulation over the entire retinal surface. Scanning for recognition captures only a few images (one good one is all that needed) and is interested in only a relatively small band of pattern information around the optic nerve. Angiography uses an orange or green dye that is physically injected into the subject's eye prior to the procedure. The dyes amplify and accentuate details of blood circulation over time, revealing the presence of fluid leaks or degenerative conditions in the retinal tissue. Retinal scanning for recognition involves no such injections and no dyes are used. Only a few images are quickly taken and only a relatively small circular band of the image is ever processed or stored.

Angiography captures images of the entire retina for 5 to 10 minutes and retains all the images as the sequence information is necessary to reveal and understand circulatory rhythms. So with perhaps the exception of revealing conditions of complete blindness, retinal scanning for identification arguably contains no medical information. And because of the delicate registration requirements for retinal (and iris) scanning, blind persons are unfortunately precluded from using these systems in the first place.

While iris scanning has drawn recent attention for being the most accurate, "super" biometric, both biometrics of the eye are regarded as highly accurate. Albeit products are still evolving and changing, both techniques are based on well developed, mature technologies. While Dr. Daugman has published his patented iris analysis techniques, retinal scanning lacks publicly available mathematical models to estimate and compare its ultimate strength of function. (Although no formal comparative analysis exists, relative template sizes and intuitions on feature density suggests the information space of a retina encoding is less than an iris encoding.) Both techniques are essentially single-vendor, proprietary implementations that are known to function well for access control applications. So which is better? No biometric by itself is ever a magic solution to identification applications. The advantages of scanning the eye's internal surface as opposed to the external, visible surface are a matter of application, purpose, and user preference. Cost, initial costs, as well as installation and integration may also weigh in as determining factors.

Chapter 6

Signature Recognition and Keystroke Dynamics

By Nicholas Orlans

Signature recognition and keystroke dynamics are both behavioral biometrics in that they measure how an individual does something—how an individual signs and how an individual types. Signature verification uses a digitizing tablet to record signatures electronically, including a full trace of how the signature was produced. Keystroke dynamics are a biometric based on the timing and latency between a key press and key release event on a keyboard. The statistical properties of how we type, particularly how we type known words (especially passwords) or phrases—is measurable. These measured patterns are repeatable and can be used with modest accuracy to distinguish one person from another. Unlike signature verification (and most every other biometric), keystroke dynamics do not require sensors or equipment beyond a regular keyboard.

Signature Recognition

Signature capture verification technology can be used anywhere conventional signatures are used, such as for business documents and check signing. Of course the technology can also be used to improve both the issuance and presentation (use) of identification material, helping to safeguard identification cards, drivers licenses, passports, and travel documents. Additional applications seek to use signature verification to strengthen the identification process and hence reduce fraud and misuse for electronic commerce applications. These applications include computer sign-on, data access, credit card transactions, and a variety of point-of- sale applications.

Signatures have a different and somewhat elevated stature as a "latent" identifier within our culture. As discussed in Chapter 15, original ink signatures carry legal authority for binding a party to an agreement or business contract. Personal signatures are commonly used to validate or authorize documents, approve purchases and credit card transactions, or otherwise associate an individual to a document of record. A signed letter (or painting) also connotes a sense of authorship and authenticity, characteristics that are often prone to confusion and controversy when transferred to the world of electronic media. Traditional authors and artists remain uneasy with digital "cut and paste" production tools and rapid electronic reproductions (replication). And publishers are naturally fearful of untethered access and duplication of copyrighted digital content. While the transformation to digital media is a complex process and disruptive to conventional business models, digitized signatures (and signature biometrics) could likely play an important role.

How Signature Recognition Works

Signature verification works by considering a variety of factors, including both features of the signature itself (the static product) and details on how the signature is generated (the dynamic process). The signature itself provides geometry, curvature, and shape information of individual characters and complete words. How a signature is generated provides additional information on stroke direction, speed, pen up and pen down events, and pressure metrics. For security applications the dynamic aspects of signature analysis can be combined with a known secret password, making forgery very difficult. Handwritten signatures are electronically captured with a digitizing tablet and stylus. Many signing tablets are commercially available today. They come in a variety of sizes, options, and performance characteristics, as some are intended for graphics applications beyond just electronic signature capture.

Interlink's product line ranges from basic electronic signature acquisition and integration with popular document formats for word processing and electronic publishing to complete enterprise solutions with verification software bundles by alternative third-party vendors:

CIC Sign-It	http://www.cic.com/
Silanis ApproveIt	http://www.silanis.com
Valyd eSign	http://www.valyd.com/

Figure 6-1

Interlinks ePad
digitizers

Interlink's ePad digitizers, as shown in Figure 6-1, have a capture resolution of 300 pixels per inch (ppi) and reports (or samples) 100 times per second. The middle model (VP9515) is also an ink system that is designed to capture both digital and actual signatures, and the high-end model (VP9616) provides a 320-by-240 monochrome LCD for visual feedback. The ePad products support 7-bit (128 values) of pressure sensitivity, an important dimension to the behavioral dynamics of handwriting.

Larger digitizing tablets, normally intended for graphics applications such as electronic sketchpads, digital photograph editing, and computer aided design, also are perfectly able to support signature verification applications. Tablets sold by the Wacom Technology Corporation are available in a full range of sizes and capabilities.

History and Development

According to Gopal Gupta and Alan McCabe, the first published understanding of the individuality of hand written signatures is credited to A. S. Osborn in 1929 (Gupta and McCabe 1997, 2). The basic observation was that individuals possess a characteristic style to their handwriting. The style elements include the formation and shape of characters and common character pairs, as well as evidence of articulated starts and stops. Furthermore, these style elements, or features can be analyzed and compared to help determine authenticity of signatures. The study and understanding of handwriting later came to play an important role in forensic science and criminal justice. Early practitioners developed manual (observation-based) techniques to analyze and match handwriting samples for the purpose of case evidence.

Automated handwriting signature verification systems evolved from implementations of more general character and gesture recognition technologies developed in the companion field of machine vision and Human Computer Interfaces (HCI) in the late 1970s and early 1980s. HCI designers sought to recognize static characters, numerals, symbols, and gestures from electronic handwriting traces so they could interpret the inputs as text strings, graphical elements, or application commands. Machine vision researchers developed working methods for achieving this goal on static inputs by 1977 (Ali and Pavlidis 1977, 537-541).

Signature recognition systems became the next logical challenge for pen computing, and with the availability of the force-sensitive capture techniques, prototype systems were soon realized. Many patents have been issued related to the capture and processing of handwriting. Notably, in 1977, a patent for "Personal identification apparatus" was awarded to Veripen, Inc., of New York, for an apparatus to acquire pressure information.[1] That same year Veripen, Inc., was involved in biometrics testing that assessed the use of early automatic handwriting verification and speaker verification. That testing was conducted by The MITRE Corporation and was done on behalf of the Electronic Systems Division of the United States Air Force.[2] Today, 25 years later, computer techniques to process characters and gestures automatically are quite robust and well developed. (Hand-written character recognition was in fact a critical capability for the success of the Palm Pilot and Win CE stylus-based personal digital assistants.)

Although highly cursive text is still not fully machine-readable, a number of good implementations of dynamic signature verification techniques are commercially available. As with most biometrics, the implementations are not based on any standard prescribed features; thus performance and particular match results will differ to some extent across different vendor solutions.

Implementation Studies

With modern electronic capture that includes pressure and the ability to report 100 to 200 times per second, the basic dimensions for dynamic analysis of signatures are position, pressure, and time. The descriptive features outlined by

---

[1] A.G. Boldridge, and R.W. Freund, United States Patent No. 4,035,768 (issued July 12, 1977). Personal Identification Apparatus. Veripen Incorporated, New York, New York.

[2] A. Fejfar, and W. Haberman, July 1977, "Automatic Identification of Personnel Through Speaker and Signature Verification—System Description and Testing," Proceedings of Carnahan Conference on Crime Countermeasures, Oxford, United Kingdom.

Gupta and Rick Joyce used the following six features as a basis for engineering experiments:

■ Total time

■ Number of velocity sign changes in the X direction

■ Number of velocity sign changes in the Y direction

■ Number of acceleration sign changes in the X direction

■ Number of acceleration sign changes in the Y direction

■ Total pen-up time

The significant conclusion from the Gupta and Joyce study was that their relatively simple proposed features (that did not include pressure) could be used to distinguish forgeries (Gupta and McCabe 1997, 12). Although their testing was not extensive, it did involve participants who were practiced at forgery. Gupta and Joyce noted the forged feature values for total time, the number of acceleration sign changes, and the pen-up time were usually far off from the reference values (originals). The differences were as much as 50 standard deviations off the average reference value (expected value). So, in other words, the forgers were able to duplicate the static signature but had no bearing on how to duplicate the manner in which it was produced.

Other more elaborate parameters have been described and implemented. Crane and Ostrem (1983) proposed a set of 44 features, and then after performance testing reduced the features to a subset of 23 best features (Gupta and McCabe 1997, 29). Although the feature selection strategy was not explicitly discussed, it is an important topic both for system optimization and for establishing standard representations. They did observe that the same feature set was not universally prominent for all users, and they suggested features could be over-collected for the training examples and then personalized, selecting only the best features for each person on an individual basis.

Many promising markets for automatic signature verification exist in the business world: document signing, approvals, checking and commerce, and enhancements to time and attendance recording. In addition, of course, the technology is also available for PC authentication. Cyber SIGN, of San Jose, California, founded in 1997 as a subsidiary of CADIX (Tokyo, Japan), offers a low-cost screen saver that comes bundled with Wacom digitizing tablets. Other Cyber SIGN products include document signing plug-in technology and server-based solutions for larger networked applications.

Limitations

In that signature verification technology and its related underpinnings have been actively studied and developed for nearly three decades, it is arguably a mature technology. Being reasonably mature, however, does not mean that signature verification is perfect and without limitations. Ostensibly it is used for verification (one-to-one) matching.

Despite at least one vendor comparing signatures to the individuality of DNA, there is absolutely no basis for such claims. Signatures are behavioral traits and different signatures collected from the same person can exhibit considerable variation. As a result, signatures alone are not likely to distinguish individuals reliably from among medium- to large-sized populations, and when signatures are a part of identification applications, invariably they are used in conjunction with other administrative or biographical data such as addresses and phone numbers.

Certain environmental factors and characteristics of the signature capture apparatus are known to affect robustness (how repeatable the signature trait is) and hence performance. The physical characteristics of the signature equipment, such as pen weight, diameter, and surface friction, add variation to the process. Additionally, fatigue and psychological context are human factors that play a role in repeatability. A person may sign important documents such as job applications and home loans more carefully, slowly, and deliberately, for example, than they sign routine, boring documents such as phone bills and office memorandums that are hastily scrawled out with no hesitation and forethought to the process.

Keystroke Dynamics

Unlike signature verification (and most every other biometric) keystroke dynamics are somewhat unique in that they do not require special sensor equipment beyond a regular keyboard. The keystroke dynamics are captured entirely by software, so the technique can be applied to any system that accepts and processes keyboard input events.

Keystroke dynamics can be used for single authentication events or for continuous monitoring. Continuous monitoring is not normally done in commercial biometrics products; however, it has been proposed as a legitimate and reasonable means to help prevent unauthorized use of unattended terminals. For example, if an authorized user leaves their terminal unattended and another user attempts to use it, the change in keystroke dynamics could be detected. The presence of the different user's keystrokes (which is by definition an unauthorized intruder in some environments) could then automatically trigger a request for reauthentication. Continuous monitoring for the purposes of establishing identity is a different process from keyboard logging or monitoring for auditing or eavesdropping purposes.

Keystroke monitoring is the unsophisticated, yet surprisingly easy way to achieve logging of every key pressed by a user. While many have argued the potential for abuse far outweighs any legitimate use of the process, keystroke monitoring is sometimes used to provide auditing and security information that may be required in certain sensitive environments. Such systems should be marked with banners and notices to inform users that their use is monitored. The more nefarious use of keystroke monitoring, also sometimes known as *spyware*, is to eavesdrop on others. The software can capture work, e-mail, chat sessions, and of course passwords. Spyware is inexpensive, simple to use, and once installed (deliberately or otherwise), is extremely invasive.

History

The canonical analysis and assessment of using keyboard characteristics to establish identity was a 1980 RAND report[3] funded by the National Science Foundation. The RAND report used a digraph representation for the keystrokes (discussed later in this chapter) and conducted experiments on a small population of users.

A relevant general patent was issued that same year to Robert Salem of General Electric Company in New York. Although not directly applied to keyboards and user identities, the patent describes a tap-actuated lock and a method of actuating the lock based on tap sequences.[4]

In the early 1980s, a feasibility study was conducted by Stanford Research Institute, and the idea and application of keystroke characteristics was later studied and advanced by many others, notably Leggett and Williams (1988) and Joyce and Gupta (1990). The first patent to apply keyboard patterns specifically for the purpose of identification was entitled "Method and apparatus for verifying an individual's identity" and was issued to James Young and Robert Hammon of International Bioaccess Systems Corporation of New York.[5] Filed in 1985 and issued in 1989, the abstract from the patent is quoted here:

> A device and method for verifying the identity of an individual based on keystroke dynamics comprising a keyboard for the inputting of data in the form of alphanumeric characters by keystrokes, a timing encoder coupled to the keyboard for timing periods between keystrokes, a CPU coupled to RAM and to the timing encoder for generating a template for the individual, the template comprising a first plurality of features based upon a first set of time periods between keystrokes from a first set of keystrokes of the individual and the CPU determining a plurality of extracted features based upon a second set of time periods from a second

---

[3] R. Gaines, W. Lisowski, S. Press, and N. Shapiro, 1980. "Authentication by Keystroke Timing," RAND Report R-256-NSF. RAND Corporation.

[4] R. Salem, United States Patent No. 4,197,524 (issued April 8, 1980). Tap-acuated Lock and Method of Actuating the Lock. Washington D.C.: U.S. Government Printing Office.

[5] J. Young, and R. Hammon, United States Patent No. 4,805,222 (issued February 14, 1989). Method and Apparatus for Verifying an Individual's Identity. Washington D.C.: U.S. Government Printing Office.

set of keystrokes, and comparing the template to the plurality of extracted features such that the identity of the individual may be verified.

Application

The most natural application for keystroke dynamics is to "harden" passwords. The keystroke dynamics of each user is used to augment existing passwords by requiring that the password be entered in a manner consistent with the intended user. For this purpose, the technique is relatively straightforward to apply and is one of the least expensive biometrics. No additional devices need to be purchased, installed, or integrated, and the software itself is reasonably priced.

The principal disadvantage is that it is not always easy to quantify the security benefit and weigh that benefit against the software cost and the newly introduced possibility of rejecting authorized users. A certain percentage of authorized users will experience rejects because they bruised their finger, or because they are weary, ill, or stressed, or they otherwise happen to be having a bad typing day. Even so, keystroke dynamics is an elegant addition to system security and increasingly will be available as an option, either as determined by user preference or as part of an organization's security policy. In the near future, operating system vendors might well choose to incorporate keystroke dynamics biometrics into their systems to augment existing built-in password policy options.

Conventional password hardening policies used in some of industry and in many secure environments call for passwords to be selected and administered with some (or all) of the following additional properties:

- Passwords shall be at least six characters in length.

- Passwords shall include at least one special character (non-alphabetical).

- Passwords shall not contain or be a dictionary word (English implied).

- Password shall be changed periodically (frequency can vary).

- Upon each periodic password change, the new password must be different from last five passwords used.

These factors do force users to select passwords that are less easy to guess; however, in doing so they also tend to increase the likelihood of users forgetting passwords. Users typically respond to forced password rotations by devising a family of similar passwords to circumvent the annoyance of having to remember five different passwords, particularly if they are all used for the same system. Conventional password policies operate by placing additional burdens on administrators and (presumably) valid users, and in some cases the extra burdens have no measurable benefit. While it is obviously desirable to change the password for a user whose password is *known* to have been compromised, the benefit of changing passwords for *all* users on apparently arbitrary calendar cycles is much less clear. Along with any benefit, the practice certainly also causes an increase in administration, forgotten passwords, and locked accounts. By comparison, biometric hardening of passwords seems to provide a quantifiable additional layer of security and more importantly the extra assurance is accomplished without putting an extra burden on the user.

Although many research prototypes have been developed, studied, tested, and used, BioPassword appears to be the primary commercial implementation available. BioPassword is owned by Net Nanny, Inc., and is part of the Net Nanny's Internet safety software (filtering and security software). BioPassword has also recently been licensed to Musicrypt.com, a provider of digital music. BioPassword runs on most Wintel platforms with Internet Explorer installed. Individual users enroll by typing 15 training samples of their password using the dialog shown in Figure 6-2.

The product allows the matching threshold to be relaxed or constrained using the dialog shown in Figure 6-3. A security setting of 10 is the most constrained matching (permits the least variance), and a security setting of 1 is the most forgiving setting (allows the greatest variance). As keystroke dynamics need more

Figure 6-2
BioPassword
Enrollment
dialog

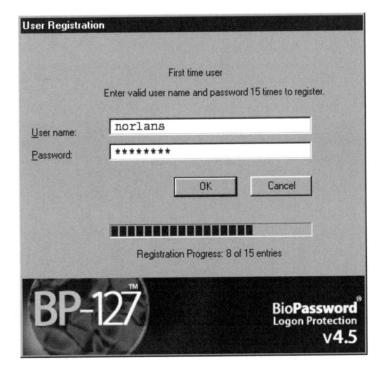

Figure 6-3
BioPassword
Configuration
utility

than a few timing measurements to establish a distinguishable pattern, the software requires passwords that are at least eight characters in length.

The author is not aware of independent performance tests of commercial keystroke dynamics. However, as summarized by Ord and Furnell and shown in the following table, published research findings show a range of system accuracy (Ord and Furnell 1999, 2).

Authors	False Acceptance Rate	False Rejection Rate
Gaines et al. (1980)	0%	4%
Legget & Williams (1988)	5%	5.5%
Joyce & Gupta (1990)	0.25%	16.67%
Bleha et al. (1990)	2.8%	8.1%

The error rates listed in the table reflect different assumptions, test data, and procedures, and they do not necessarily mean that Gaines had a more accurate system for all purposes. The Gaines experiment was more focused on the method and analysis, and the testing involved just six professional typists and used three specially prepared full-page texts for generating test data (akin to a typing test), whereas other research focused their analysis more on single passwords and considered larger populations.

As is true for all behavior biometrics, the disposition of the user and his or her environment affects results. The user's disposition includes his or her state of mind, current level of stress, rest, and distraction. Environmental factors could include the user's posture and type of equipment (laptop keyboard versus a more ergonomic desktop environment). Keyboard layout and user comfort, training, and familiarity with the device are certainly also factors. Individual patterns are not at all likely to transfer well across radically different keyboard types, such as the hinged keyboards or different palm rest arrangements. Keypad layout and size affect use patterns as well. Standard numeric keypads for telephony have a reversed layout from computer keypads (1-2-3 row on the bottom versus on the top for phones). The size of the keys, the separation between them, and the general form factor (particularly if the keypad is part of a mobile handset) all influence how humans handle and use the device. Ultimately, these factors also influence the characteristic keystroke patterns.

Digraph Representation

The actual timing traces used for pattern matching can be represented various ways; however, the normal representation is a series of digraphs. A *digraph* is an adjacent pair of characters in a typing sequence and the associated time delay between the pressing of the first key and pressing of the second key. Alternative measurements are possible as for any given digraph, six alternative measurements are produced, as shown in Figure 6-4. In addition to digraphs, certain common character sequences and words could potentially be represented as trigraphs or tetragraphs (for example, *ing* and *tion*) or word-graphs.

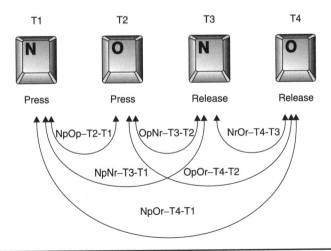

Figure 6-4   Digraph latencies for *no*

The data is kept as a table of time stamps containing key-down and key-up events. The resulting features are expressed as dwell time (time that key is depressed) and flight time (latency between key down events) for the various digraphs. While all systems are based on the same general idea, there are no agreed standards for keystroke representation. Some systems treat the shift key and the space key differently or may chose to ignore punctuation keys. Password hardening systems would acknowledge every keystroke, but may selectively use trigraphs and tetragraphs.

Keystroke dynamics have also been studied and tested for use with numeric keypads. Such systems, if effective, could have an enormous application area for phone systems, automated teller machines (ATMs), or even cash registers. Numeric keypads differ from keyboards in that most people use keypads in a pecking fashion with a single finger and hand. As a result, keypad dynamics do not contain the same neuromuscular information present with two-hand keyboard dynamics.

A recent study of user authentication on keypad-based devices put keystroke dynamics to the test. The study tested 14 users using a common six-digit personal identification number (PIN), and processed the data through three classification techniques: a neural network, minimum distance, and Mahalanobis distance (Ord and Furnell 1999). For the test data, the neural network provided the best results but still had a false acceptance rate (FAR) of 9.9 percent with the corresponding false rejection rate (FRR) arbitrarily set to 30 percent (assumed to be human patience threshold for being incorrectly rejected).

An 11-digit PIN (10 latency measurements) provided better results than did the 6-digit PIN, but of course the increased number of digits becomes too long for most people to commit to memory. The authors conclude that the error rate of keystroke authentication is too high for use in ATM or phone applications. Even with a generously imposed FRR of 30 percent, the FAR was still 9.9 percent, meaning that if a six-digit PIN is lost or stolen, the system would allow unauthorized use of the PIN 1 out of 10 times. As multiple attempts would have to be allowed (as the FRR was set to 30 percent), the net result is that the system would just add inconvenience to authorized users and still would not be able to prevent unauthorized access.

Other Uses

A related use of keystroke dynamics is for human typing detection. That is, keystroke patterns can be used to help determine the difference between man and machine (live human typing vs. scripted programs). The presence of scripted interfaces in certain conditions, namely brute-force access attempts (password guessing), is undesirable and should be prevented. Although scripts can be modified to introduce latencies (to mimic human typing), the technique is a useful countermeasure against most scripted attacks. Recent studies have shown that subtle keystroke timing information can even be reconstructed from network traffic without the use of local software. By eavesdropping on network traffic from strongly encrypted Secure Shell (SSH) sessions, it was demonstrated that keystroke timing information could be reconstructed and used to infer certain common character sequences. These character sequences were then used in turn to improve the efficiency of password guessing programs by a factor of 50.[6]

Which Biometric Is Better?

While neither signature recognition nor keystroke dynamics by themselves are "ultimate identifiers" for individuals, they both are reasonably mature technologies that offer distinct benefits to certain applications. The variation between different instances of the same signature (or keystroke sequence) is too large for either technique alone to be useful for strong authentication. However, signature biometrics are likely to play an increasingly important role as more documents of record and business processes migrate to electronic media. Keystroke dynamics are the only biometric designed to work directly with (and on) conventional passwords. Marketing claims continue to repeat the assertion that biometrics are better than passwords and should replace them (you forget passwords but not your biometrics); however, the reality is that there are still unknowns and risks with most biometrics. The integration effort and lack of common administration tools remain as significant obstacles for large deployments (even if passwords are maintained). Thus keystroke dynamics are a natural biometric to consider if the goal is simply to augment password-based authentication.

---

[6]   D. X. Song, D. Wagner, and X. Tian, 1999. "Timing Analysis of Keystrokes and Timing Attacks on SSH," University of California, Berkeley (for DARPA contract N6601-99-28913).

Chapter 7

Esoteric Biometrics

**By John D. Woodward, Jr. and Nicholas Orlans,
with Julius Gatune**

Whether the result of an evolutionary process or a divine hand, each human is unique in many ways. Thus, the number of possible physical characteristics or personal traits of a human is only limited by our imagination and our ability to measure the characteristic or trait. Previous chapters discussed mainstream biometrics or biometrics that are commonly available or commercially viable. This chapter focuses on *esoteric biometrics* or biometrics that are still in the early experimental and development stages. Research efforts have started to tackle some of the more esoteric biometrics and it is reasonable to expect this: as algorithms improve and computing power gets cheaper, some of these will move from esoteric to mainstream. At least some of today's esoteric biometrics will become tomorrow's commercial-off-the-shelf technologies (or so-called COTS products). In the meantime, realists must evaluate today's esoteric biometrics with a skeptical eye, in part because of the lack of empirical testing to substantiate vendors' claims about the technology.

Vein Pattern

The *vein pattern* biometric relies on measurement of the vascular pattern made by the blood vessels on the back of the hand. Vein patterns are developed before birth and differ even between identical twins. Apart from their overall size,

115

which grows from birth to adulthood, these patterns persist throughout life, well into old age.

Using vascular patterns as a means of automated human recognition has successfully been accomplished with at least one other body part. Specifically, as discussed in Chapter 5, retinal scanning is an example of a biometric based on the vascular pattern of the back of the eye that is known to be quite accurate.

Take a moment and look at the back of your hands. You can easily see the bluish tree-like patterns formed by the veins. A special camera combined with an infrared light captures a much better image of these blood vessels. This captured image gets digitized and converted to a binary template as small as 300 bytes. There are two representation methods: one takes image bands (or cross sections) at key areas of the back of the hand, representing the vein pattern into something like a barcode. The second method marks the location of vein junctions, creating a representation somewhat akin to minutiae points, with directional vectors (for example, ridges and bifurcations) in a fingerprint.

Vein patterns have some advantages: they are universal, in that everyone has this feature, although it is not certain what the failure to enroll rate would be over a large population. Because the veins are an internal trait protected by the skin, the biometric is not so susceptible to damage, compared to biometrics without this protection. The vascular pattern apparently remains robust, even in the face of such activities as bricklaying and gardening, and in the face of scars, cuts, and moisture. Moreover, the vascular pattern is hard to disguise and alter. Drugs, exercise, mental health, and medical conditions that affect blood flow can consequently also enhance or diminish images of vascular patterns. However, such affects on recognition performance are uncertain.

Vein patterns, as a biometric, have not yet won full mainstream acceptance; however, the idea of vein measurement as a unique identifier is not new. European scholars published several papers on the subject in the early part of the twentieth century, but interest waned as fingerprints became universally accepted for identification purposes. For many practical applications, vein measurement holds promise and products are already available on the market. One such product is VeinCheck, by Nuesciences of the United Kingdom, proudly marketed with the slogan, "Know people like the back of your hand." (For more information, go to http://www.neusciences.com/biometrics/Bio-index.htm.) At the other end of the globe, NEXTERN, a South Korean company, also markets a Vein Recognition System. (For more information, go to http://www.etechkorea .info/articles/20020310002.php.)

Scientific and technical issues remain with vein pattern measurement. According to Dr. L. John A. Di Dio, a leading anatomist and professor emeritus of the

Medical College of Ohio, "there has not yet been a definitive study proving the reliability for precise identification of the dorsal patterns of the human hand."[1]

Dr. Di Dio's comment is a fact well-worth emphasizing because it applies to the entire realm of esoteric biometrics and many of the mainstream biometrics as well. That is, there is a paucity of test data sets for biometrics with the recent exceptions of face, fingerprint, and voice.

Another technical issue is the cost of vein pattern systems, in part, because the required infrared (IR) cameras tend be specialized and, thus, more expensive than conventional ones used for imaging (for example face). At least one vendor admits as much "because of the complexity and cost of the technology, it has limited usage."

Active research is currently being undertaken, especially in Europe and Asia. The European Union government has provided funding for vein pattern research. In Asia, several scholars at the Korea University in Seoul are conducting vein pattern research for biometric applications and have published their findings, most recently in the *Journal of the Korean Physical Society,* in March 2001. The researchers' goal is to develop "a new, low-priced, biometric identification system using hand vein patterns."

The nonintrusive nature of vein pattern authentication makes this esoteric biometric an attractive one, but it must compete with more established technologies, such as hand geometry, fingerprints, and others that offer similar authentication functions. However, vein patterns could be an attractive alternative when concerns exist about environmental conditions, like surface contamination, because no contact is required—unlike hand geometry and fingerprint readers.

Instead of competing with these more-established biometric technologies, a more complementary approach could be considered, using multimodal biometrics. In other words, the case can be made that vein pattern biometrics will augment and enhance the more conventional, established biometrics and not replace them. For example, adding vein pattern biometrics to hand geometry readers might make good sense for adding more information as an enhancement to existing technologies. Such an addition of vein patterns could also add an impressive liveness "test" capability to the system.

Facial Thermography

Facial thermography refers to the pattern of facial heat caused by the distinctive flow of blood under the skin. IR cameras capture this heat to produce a thermal pattern. Because the vein and tissue structure of an individual's face is

---

[1]   John D. Woodward, Jr., "Biometric Scanning, Law and Policy: Identifying the Concerns—Drafting the Biometric Blueprint," *University of Pittsburgh Law Review* 59.97 (1997), 108.

distinctive, the infrared image is also distinctive. The thermal data is analyzed to yield anatomical information, which is converted to a template. The process is based on this principle: while the underlying vein and tissue structure is stable, the dynamic nature of blood flow causes fluctuations, as well as the appearance and disappearance of secondary patterns. Thus, the image itself is not as stable as environmental conditions (for example, ambient temperature) and the introduction of certain agents (for example ingestion of alcohol, drugs) can cause it to change. The image (data) captured can then be processed and used to discern the subject's condition to answer such questions as: Is she present or absent; alive or dead; attentive or inattentive; physically rested or fatigued; relaxed or anxious? With respect to this last question, evidence exists that associates the blood flow in the face, particularly the regions around the eyes, with anxiety (thus adding a whole new twist to the phrase "bloodshot eyes").

On the technical side, extensive testing of infrared imagery and facial thermography has not yet been done. Collecting solid data is costly and complicated because conditions like ambient temperature, wind, and metabolic processes of the subject need to be taken into account. However, preliminary tests conducted by Andrea Selinger and Diego A. Socolinsky in 2001 indicate that TR imagery is better than visible imagery in some situations. Specifically, this research, performed for Defense Advanced Research Projects Agency (DARPA)'s "Human Identification at a Distance" program, has demonstrated that thermal images can provide more distinctive queues for face detection in images, particularly in low or unevenly lit environments.[2]

Another challenge is that despite efforts, no COTS facial thermography products are currently available. Some companies have announced that products are under development. For example, in the mid-1990s, Technology Recognition Systems tried to commercialize a product, but abandoned the effort; IRID Inc.[3] is now trying to bring a product to the market.

Challenges remain, starting with a most basic one: user acceptance. The questions facial thermography seeks to answer can provoke concern. For example, thermal data, according to one vendor, IRID Inc., might reveal information about one's health condition to include respiration rate, heart rate, sites of infection, internal bleeding, swelling, broken bones, as well as other systemic and local medical conditions.[4] Times could occur when this information might be

---

[2] Andrea Selinger and Diego A. Socolinsky, "Appearance-Based Facial Recognition Using Visible and Thermal Imagery," available at http://www.equinoxsensors.com/publications/andreas_face.pdf.

[3] IRID Inc., (Infrared Identification Incorporated), available at http://www.iridinc.com and http://www.sarcon.com/news_&_info/oakridger080201.htm.

[4] IRID Inc., "Basics of Infrared Imaging," February 14, 2002, available at http://www.iridinc.com/IR%20Imaging.htm.

highly desirable; however, many potential users could deem it far too intrusive because it reveals too much about them, causing problems of user acceptance at least among the general populace.

Depending on one's perspective, facial thermography has an advantage or downside compared to other biometrics precisely because it can provide information on the medical condition of a person. Such a capability would be extremely useful in situations where the physical condition of the person being identified also needs to be determined. Such callings as law enforcement and security personnel, air traffic controllers, commercially licensed drivers, and surgeons, among others, come immediately to mind. For example, in controlled environments (for example, indoors, with no exertion), facial thermography can provide indications of alcohol use. Thus, in a real-world application, facial thermography would not only authenticate the identity of an airline pilot or school bus driver, but it could also help make certain that a person was sober and fit for duty. On the other hand, this capability to report a person's medical information could cause problems of user acceptance, as well as legal challenges. While society fully expects a municipal bus driver behind the wheel to be sober, we might not hold bus passengers to such a high standard.

Another major advantage of this biometric is that the infrared camera is not affected by visible illumination (that is, 400–700 nanometers). In other words, it can work in darkness or in light, overcoming some of the recognition problems caused by differences in directional lighting with visible light cameras. This capability is extremely useful in surveillance applications, especially when it is necessary to identify people (for example, terrorist threats, unauthorized personnel) in dark places or at night. Dovetailing nicely with the surveillance capability is the fact that the image is unaffected by visible, external disguises. Thus, high military, law enforcement, and counterterrorism interest would exist in such a technology.

As Selinger and Socolinsky have explained, historically, the low level of interest in infrared imagery compared to other biometrics, such as facial recognition, has been based in part on the following factors:

- The much higher cost of thermal sensors versus visible video equipment
- The lower image resolution
- The higher image noise
- The lack of widely available data sets to ensure rigorous testing.

Continuing advances in IR technology are making IR cameras cheaper and improvements are being made in the other areas.

As the technology improves and becomes more readily available, infrared thermography will likely become a more common form of identification in some domains. Moreover, facial thermography will offer a complementary, multimodal approach to biometrics. Adding facial thermography to facial recognition systems can provide additional information, as well as liveness testing. Thus, facial thermography is likely to be used in specialized applications to extend and enhance optical facial recognition techniques.

DNA

DNA, the acronym for deoxyribonucleic acid, carries the genetic information of a cell and encodes the information to form proteins. Since 1953, thanks in large part to the work of James Watson and Francis Crick, scientists have recognized that the chemical structure of an individual's DNA encodes information about that individual's inherited characteristics. As *DNA Identification in the Criminal Justice System,* a May 2002 white paper of the Australian Institute of Criminology has explained:

> The DNA in a human cell is unique, the product of sexual reproduction that combines half of the mother's DNA and half of the father's DNA. Every cell in an individual's body is the result of cellular division, which copies the DNA in the newly fertilized cell into every other nucleic cell. As a result, DNA in a cellular nucleus is identical throughout a human body but variable between any two humans, making it a natural alternative to artificial human identifiers, such as names or tax-file numbers. The notable exception is identical twins, which develop from a single fertilized cell and hence have identical nuclear DNA.

In 1985, Alec Jeffreys and his colleagues in Great Britain first demonstrated the use of DNA in a criminal investigation. During the rape-homicide investigation of two girls, Jeffreys used DNA in two ways: first to exonerate one suspect and later to show that another man had a DNA profile matching that of the sperm in the evidence samples from the girls. Since that time, DNA has become generally accepted by the scientific community, the legal system, and the public as a high-integrity identifier. By 1996, a National Research Council study in the United States determined: "The state of [DNA] profiling technology and the methods for estimating frequencies and related statistics have progressed to the point where the admissibility of properly collected and analyzed data [in courts of law] should not be in doubt."

In the United States, the United Kingdom, and elsewhere around the world, DNA is regularly used for law enforcement or forensic purposes, sometimes referred to as "DNA profiling" or "DNA fingerprinting." For example, in a rape case, the goal is to match the DNA of the criminal suspect with any DNA he might have left in the blood, semen, or hair taken from the crime. Alternatively, the goal could be to match the victim's DNA with the DNA found on a suspect's personal effects (for example, the victim's hair on the suspect's clothing). DNA might also be used to investigate paternity in cases involving incest or rape. Another application involves forensic identification to identify missing persons or the deceased, a technique used to identify many of the victims of the September 11, 2001 terrorist attacks. DNA is attractive to use for these applications because of its accuracy of typing, relative ease of use, and high levels of polymorphism. To be clear, the parts of the DNA that are used for law enforcement and forensic purposes are located in those parts of the chromosomes without known functions or, if part of a gene, not in the part that produces a detectable effect. The use of this so-called "junk DNA" is, in part, done to protect individual privacy.

In the United States, this acceptance of DNA has led to the establishment of databases of DNA samples. For example, "The DNA Identification Act of 1994" (Public Law 103-322) provided the Federal Bureau of Investigation (FBI) with the authority to establish a national DNA index for law enforcement purposes. Based on this statute, the FBI operates the Combined DNA Index System (CODIS) that enables federal, state, and local crime labs to exchange and compare DNA profiles electronically. CODIS provides investigators with leads in crimes where a DNA sample is recovered from the crime scene.

CODIS is implemented as a distributed database with three tiers—local, state, and federal. The National DNA Index System (NDIS), the highest level in the CODIS hierarchy, enables the laboratories participating in the CODIS program to exchange and compare DNA profiles on a national level. DNA profiles originate at the local level (for example, when the local police obtain a DNA sample from a crime scene or, when upon conviction, a criminal is required by law to give up a DNA sample), and then go on to the state and national levels.

NDIS relies on two databases to operate—the Forensic Index and the Offender Index. The *Forensic Index* contains DNA profiles from crime scene evidence. The *Offender Index* contains DNA profiles of individuals convicted of sex offenses (and other violent crimes), with many states now expanding legislation to include other felonies. As of August 2002, the Forensic Index contained 39,096 profiles and the Offender Index contained 1,119,127 profiles. All but six states participate in this system. In Virginia and in many other states, on conviction of a felony, an individual must provide a DNA sample to the state.

As the FBI explains it, "Matches made among profiles in the Forensic Index can link crime scenes together possibly identifying serial offenders. Based on a match, police in multiple jurisdictions can coordinate their respective investigations and share the leads they developed independently." Any match(es) that are made between the Forensic and Offender Indexes provide the authorities with the identity of the perpetrator(s). The CODIS system has digital representations for the DNA profiles (templates) and performs automated matching. For example, when DNA is found at a crime scene, it can be searched against the DNA database for a possible match. Matches are regularly made because a large number of criminals are recidivists. As a National Institute of Justice working group concluded in 2000, "The scientific foundations of DNA are solid.

Any weaknesses are not at the technical level, but are in possible human errors, breaks in the chain of evidence, and laboratory failures."

The Department of Defense also maintains a DNA database to identify the remains of personnel. Chapter 16 discusses this database in depth.

The question is frequently asked, "Is there a DNA biometric?" The lawyerly answer is: "It depends." The technical answer is "No," or, perhaps, "Not yet." This is because DNA is not an automated method or process of providing for human recognition. No current DNA biometric exists in the sense that a person provides a "finger friction rub" on a platen or an expectoration sample into a spittoon sensor and is immediately recognized by the system. Nonetheless, scientists and engineers are working on it. For example, *The Future of Forensic DNA Testing: Predictions of the Research and Development Working Group,* a National Institute of Justice study published in 2000, confidently opined, "Methods of automation, increasing the speed and output and reliability of [DNA] methods, will continue. In particular we expect that portable, miniature chips will make possible the analysis of DNA directly at the crime scene. This can be telemetered to databases, offering the possibility of immediate identification."

DNA has the advantage of being distinctive (except for identical twins) and robust (for example, it does not change over the lifetime of an individual). However, challenges remain. At present, DNA testing is relatively costly and time-consuming—making it unsuitable for automatic identification or verification purposes. Moreover, the perception is widely shared that additional secondary information can be gleaned from a DNA sample, such as the presence of hereditary factors and medical disorders, which raises privacy concerns and emotion levels not so much associated with other biometric technologies. Again, this is why law enforcement applications, such as CODIS, use "junk DNA" that does not contain secondary information.

Current processes for obtaining DNA samples are also quite intrusive, requiring some form of tissue, blood, or other bodily sample. Less-intrusive methods for extracting DNA from samples of hair or skin are in development. DNA research is active in many locations, though not all research objectives are focused on automated human recognition. As the National Institute of Justice reported, efforts are underway to create a "lab-on-chip" product that will cut the processing time dramatically and make portable DNA identification devices a reality in forensic and law enforcement applications. Japanese researchers at Nippon Telegraph and Telephone (NTT) and Chuo University recently published an article on "Biometric Personal Authentication Using DNA Data" in the *Information Processing Society of Japan Journal.* In their paper, Mssrs. Itakura, Nagashima, and Tsujii propose a public-key encryption method incorporating DNA data into a private key and authenticating individuals according to the public key encryption scheme. Similarly Japan's NTT Data Corporation has announced two DNA-based authentication products, one of which incorporates "Smart Card with Registered Seal."

DNA has been called the "ultimate identifier," but as Raj and Samir Nanavati of the International Biometric Group have made clear, DNA differs from conventional biometrics in important ways as shown in the following table:

DNA	Conventional Biometrics
Requires an actual physical sample	Uses an impression, image, or recording
Not done in real-time; not all stages of comparison are automated	Done in real-time; "lights-out" automated process
Does a comparison of actual samples	Uses templates or feature extraction

The intrusiveness of collection and the wealth of data it could provide lead to user acceptance issues. Moreover, in light of the other biometric options, DNA might be considered overkill for the purpose of authentication in normal daily activities. At any rate, even if perceptions of intrusiveness and information content could be overcome, barriers remain in the form of cost, timeliness (for example, how automated can it become?), and lack of convenient nonclinical sensors.

Sweat Pores

Sweat pores literally are responsible for latent fingerprints or prints left behind (for example, at a crime scene). Anil Jain and Sharath Pankanti have explained that "constant perspiration exudation of sweat pores on fingerprint ridges and intermittent contact of fingers with other parts of human body and various objects leave a film of moisture and/or grease on the surface of fingers." In touching an object (for example, a glass), the film of moisture and/or grease could be transferred to the object and leave an impression of the ridges thereon. This type of fingerprint is called a latent fingerprint.

Based on their research, Jain and Pankanti, citing research done by A. Roddy and J. Stosz, determined that "[t]he location and densities of the minute sweat pores have been found to contain information helpful for distinguishing individuals." Sweat pores as an esoteric biometric are based on the premise that the distribution of sweat pores is distinct for each individual and their distribution remains the same throughout life. As for distinctiveness, it must be noted that this premise is based purely on anecdotal evidence and has not been tested against even modestly sized test populations. In one such approach, a finger is placed on a sensor and computer software records the location of the sweat pores, storing their position relative to the area of the finger. Software is capable of converting the image captured to a binary measure, digitizing the data and storing it in a template. This template then forms the basis of future authentication.

In operational terms, the data collection is not considered intrusive or invasive. Sweat pore biometrics encounter some of the same problems as fingerprint analysis—for example, unsuitability in dusty or dirty environments. To date, attempts to utilize the pattern of sweat pores as a biometric identifier have not been fully successful. In some cases, the image resolution required to capture sweat pores consistently is high. Thus, the problem is that scanners designed for capturing ridge information might not offer enough resolution (for example, image information) to distinguish and locate the sweat pores.

A promising application of the sweat pore biometric is in the context of multimodal biometrics, which utilize a combination of biometrics to provide better security. For example, a fingerprint or hand geometry pattern could be combined with sweat pore analysis. Such multimodal biometric approaches could soon be in greater demand in light of the fact that liveness testing remains a hot issue within the biometric community. For example, Professor Matsumoto of Yokohama National University recently demonstrated that at least some fingerprint readers can be fooled or "spoofed" by the use of "Gummi fingers," or artificial fingerprints made from gelatin (discussed in Chapter 8).

Stephanie Schuckers, Larry Hornack, and other researchers at the Center for Identification Technology Research at West Virginia University (WVU) are actively researching the incorporation of sweat pores analysis as a liveness test for fingerprints. This research is based on the fact that the contact techniques for fingerprint acquisition are naturally prone to large variations in moisture conditions. In other words, your live finger should contain some element of moisture (from perspiration) when you put it on the sensor. The WVU's researchers' working hypothesis is that a live finger, as opposed to a cadaver finger or spoof finger (for example, gummi finger), demonstrates a specific changing moisture pattern because of perspiration. Using a capacitive fingerprint scanner, they capture the same fingerprint twice over a five-second time frame, and they then extract the temporal perspiration pattern of the skin. Using these features, the algorithm makes a decision about the liveness of the print. They have discovered that "in live fingers, perspiration starts around the pores and spreads along the ridges, creating a distinct signature of the process."

Hand Grip

Did you ever notice how different people shake hands in different ways? The *hand grip* biometric is premised on the notion that each individual has a distinctive grip. Two approaches are possible with this type of biometric. In one approach, infrared light is used to illuminate and analyze subcutaneous tissue and blood vessel patterns of a hand presented in a gripped position. According to one vendor, the subcutaneous patterns that lie approximately three millimeters beneath the skin are unique for an individual.[5] These patterns are then analyzed

---

[5] This claim is made by the manufacturer, Advanced Biometrics Inc., available at http://www.livegrip.com/livegrip.htm.

to produce an individual "hand signature." This signature is then converted to a template that is used for future authentication. Future scans are matched against the stored information to verify identity. A method to determine dermal properties for IR absorption is already a patented component for liveness.

A second approach utilizes the uniqueness of the pressure applied when an object is gripped. As every orthopedic surgeon knows, the human hand has 19 bones, 19 joints, and 20 muscles with 22 degrees of freedom—offering considerable scope for biometrics to distinguish between humans on the basis of neurophysiological control of finger, hand, and wrist motion. A pressure sensor captures and digitizes the individual signature to create a template for future mapping.

Challenges remain. As is the case for all esoteric biometrics, the argument for distinctiveness is not supported by any empirical study, but rather by assumptions. As for robustness, ambient temperature and the condition of the subject will impact infrared sensing devices. It is reasonable to expect that age and health status of the subject will impact how one grips an item.

In operational terms, hand grip technology is not intrusive; however, it might prove unpopular with those who are concerned about hygiene or in cultures where hand gripping is not common. For example, in certain Asian countries, such as Japan, it is not customary to shake hands. A bow of the head is preferred (which might lead to "head bow" biometrics).

Researchers at the University of Twente in the Netherlands, including Pieter Hartel, Cees Slump, and Raymond Veldhius, aim to develop "Smart Objects,"[6] which will identify their owners from their owner's grip. Such hand-held Smart Objects might include the controls of aircraft, vehicles, and dangerous machinery, firearms, and military weapon systems. The New Jersey Institute of Technology (NJIT) is also looking at grip biometrics as one way of securing a gun.[7] The NJIT study focused on three of the most promising biometrics:

- Fingerprint recognition systems that can be captured from a handgun's normal grip

- Static grip detection; a hand measurement

- Dynamic grip detection, the way a user squeezes a handgun's handle immediately before firing

---

[6] University of Twente, Department of Computer Science, "Distributed and Embedded Systems Research Group—Research," available at http://wwwhome.cs.utwente.nl/~pieter/projects/smartobjects.pdf.

[7] New Jersey Institute of Technology, "Section 4: Technology Assessment," Personalized Weapons Technology Project Progress Report With Findings and Recommendations, April 15, 2001, available at http://www.njit.edu/pwt/reports/VolumeI/11Sect4-Technologies.htm#Biometric.

The NJIT study team determined that with respect to gripping a handgun, the three most influential variables were the horizontal placement of the ring finger and the vertical position of the middle and pinkie fingers. Research continues.

The natural use of this kind of biometric would be for doors, handles, and many hand-held objects. A particularly compelling use is for handguns—law enforcement officials have expressed interest for such "smart guns" because of the large number of law enforcement officers who are shot by their own guns wrested from them by criminals. Other promising applications include deterring terrorists from taking controls of aircraft or other sensitive equipment. In terms of multimodal biometrics, hand grip measurements could be used to augment or enhance the more established hand geometry biometrics.

Fingernail Bed

On the skin underneath your fingernails are parallel lines that constitute "a unique longitudinal, tongue-in-groove spatial arrangement of papillary papillae and skin folds arranged in parallel rows producing a kind of personal barcode unique to an individual."[8] These parallel lines serve as the basis for research and development of the *fingernail bed* biometric. If the pattern can, in fact, be isolated and the image captured, software will digitize it. The underlying assumption is these patterns are unchanged over one's lifetime. However, nail beds can be damaged by accidents, chemical exposure, and occupational hazards. To date, no solid empirical data exists to support claims of the nail bed pattern as biometric identifier.

AIMS Technology Inc., located in South Carolina, markets itself on the Internet as developing the technology, although it does not advertise any specific commercial products for sale at this time.

Developers claim that because the nail bed structure is fairly simple, the image processing is not computer-intensive. If this argument holds, then nail bed biometrics could be ideal for small portable devices like PDAs, cell phones, and smart guns, among others.

Body Odor

The uniqueness of an individual's *body odor* has long been used to track humans, with dogs, like bloodhounds, providing the nose work. Each unique human scent is composed of approximately 30 chemical substances, known as *rolatiles*. The idea behind this biometric is this: an electric "nose" can be built, consisting of a number

---

[8] Janet J. Barron, "Knock, Knock. Who's There? Will the Science of Biometrics Replace Passwords and PINs?" *High Technology Careers,* February/March 2000, Vol. 17, no. 1, available at http://www.hightechcareers.com/doc100/biometrics100.html

of chemical receptors that generate a difference in voltage when a particular chemical substance is present. With the help of neural networks, it is possible to distinguish specific scent patterns[9] and, thus, recognize an individual.

Current approaches use neural networks in which the artificial nose is trained to smell, rather than digitize, scents. Chemical sensors are a related technology that has been getting recent attention. These sensors operate at the molecular level and can be quite accurate; however, they are unable to cope with the dynamic range that real olfactory systems possess. Hence, these sensors can be fooled by different (higher) concentrations of other substances.

Challenges remain. Body odor is greatly affected by factors such as diet and emotional state. Moreover, inconsistencies in chemical composition as a result of hormonal or emotional changes are also a problem. These effects on recognition are unknown because the distinctiveness of body odor has yet to be demonstrated empirically. However, ample precedent exists from the animal kingdom to believe it could be useful. As Roger Caras has aptly noted, going back to the days of ancient Rome, "hounds of enormously sophisticated scenting ability" were found throughout the Mediterranean region. These dogs were ancestors to the modern-day bloodhound.

An operational concern is odor masking, a significant industry in itself (far bigger than the biometric industry), and the common use of perfumes could have an impact on the operational feasibility of such a biometric. Body odor can reveal other sensitive information, like health status or hygiene, which might be considered intrusive. However, it is doubtful that many people would raise a stink over this biometric.

Research efforts to replicate the olfactory process of the nose have been ongoing for the past decade or so, mainly in Europe, though the bulk of research today is done in the United States. Some of the institutions active in this area include University of Warwick, University of Southampton, Tufts University, California Institute of Technology (Caltech), University of California (Riverside), and the Massachusetts Institute of Technology (MIT). Research is focused on developing a nose in a particular domain, rather than a generalized artificial nose. The United States Department of Defense and National Institutes of Health have funded some of this research.

A number of artificial noses are under development and some are available. No biometric product has been produced yet. *Wired* reports that a British developer, Mastiff Electronic Systems Ltd., makes a new sensor called Scentinel, but Senior Engineer Stephen McMillan says the product won't be ready for another three years. Thus, it is a largely unknown business case.

---

[9]   Registratiekamer, "At Face Value—On Biometrical Identification and Privacy," September 1999, available at http://www.cbpweb.nl/documenten/av_15_At_face_value.htm.

The number of possible applications is so large that even the mention of use for human recognition is absent in many publications. Already application-specific products are gainfully employed in all kinds of environments. One such application supposedly recognizes fruits and vegetables at a supermarket check out.[10] The broad spectrum of potential applications for an artificial nose include detecting land mines, monitoring air quality, surveilling for bio-terrorism agents, enabling remote medical diagnosis, as well as applications in the cosmetic, food, and beverage industry, and the future human parts replacement industry. Within the realm of human recognition, body odor biometric could be used clandestinely—that is, the data subject would not necessarily know that he or she is being monitored. Thus, the esoteric biometric might be of interest for law enforcement, computer assisted tracking, or surveillance applications.

The challenges of producing a general-purpose application are huge, given how difficult it is to train a neural network to recognize only a handful of specific odors.

Ear

Ear shape has been considered a unique identifier since Alphonse Bertillon, revered in some quarters as the pioneer of human identification "sciences," pronounced its uniqueness, "It is, in fact, almost impossible to meet with two ears which are identical in all their parts."[11] An American law enforcement professional, Alfred V. Iannarelli, described as "perhaps the foremost American advocate of ear print identification," has researched and published a book on ear identification, which is based on the ridges of ear tissue, as well as the ear's overall shape and geometry.[12]

In the Netherlands, the United Kingdom, and some states of the United States, evidence based on *ear prints* and *ear images* has been deemed admissible in various courts and has been used to convict criminals.[13] However, in the United States, a Washington state appellate court has ruled that ear print identification is not a generally accepted method of identification.[14] In *State v. Kunze* (Court of Appeals of Washington, 1999), David Kunze appealed his convictions for aggravated murder and other crimes. At his trial, Kunze was convicted, in part, on a latent ear print found on a wall at the home of the victim. The main issue for the court was whether the State's witnesses could offer testimony, based on the relationship among some of the anatomical features of the external ear, that

---

[10] University of California, Berkeley, "The Berkeley Initiative in Soft Computing," 2002, available at http://www-bisc.cs.berkeley.edu/BISCSIG/Rtec.htm.

[11] A. Moenssens, "Forensic-Evidence.com: Alphonse Bertillon and Ear Prints," 2001, available at http://www.forensic-evidence.com/site/ID/ID_bertillion.html.

[12] A. Moenssens, "Forensic-Evidence.com," 2001.

[13] BBC News, "U.K. Ear Print Catches Murderer," December 15, 1998, available at http://news.bbc.co.uk/1/hi/uk/235721.stm.

[14] A. Moenssens, "Forensic-Evidence.com," 2001.

Kunze was the probable and likely source of a latent ear print discovered at the crime scene. The law of Washington State, known as the *Frye* test, requires that novel scientific, technical, or other specialized knowledge may be admitted or relied upon in court only if generally accepted as reliable by the relevant scientific, technical, or specialized community. In this case, the court found that "twelve long-time members of the forensic science community stated or implied that latent ear print identification is not generally accepted in the forensic science community." Moreover, the court found that the "FBI does not use latent ear print identification—which the FBI would surely do if the forensic science community had generally accepted latent ear print identification." Thus, the court did not permit the expert testimony on ear print identification, Kunze's conviction was overturned, and a new trial was ordered.

Distinguishing between ear print identification and ear identification from photographic evidence is important. Identifying an ear from photographs could offer more meaningful opportunities for investigation because ear prints, consisting of pressure distortions left on a hard surface, are less amenable to side-by-side comparison. Nonetheless, evidence has been given in both forms of ear identification.

Only recently, research has been undertaken on automatic identification by ear. In at least one graduate thesis by Carreira-Perpinan and others writing at the Technical University of Madrid, Spain, in 1995, the ear has been advocated as having advantages over the face in automatic identification because of

- The ear's smaller surface, which enables work with images of reduced spatial resolution (higher ratio of information to image area)

- The ear's more uniform distribution of color, which allows almost all information to be conserved when converting to gray-scale image, whereas eye color is lost when facial images are converted

- The ear's relatively fixed shape and appearance, which does not change with facial expression

The ears do not change significantly after the subject reaches maturity. However, the issue of the ear's distinctiveness is still an untested hypothesis, though some evidence has been obtained to support it (Hoogstrate et al. 2002). It has been claimed the ear has more identification richness than the face (Carreira-Perpinan 1997), but no empirical exists to support the premise that ears of human beings are so different that an exact shape is never duplicated.[15] Efforts to collect such data are currently being undertaken by the National Training Center for Scientific Support to Crime in the United Kingdom,[16] which

---

[15] *State v. Kunze*, Court of Appeals of Washington, Division 2, 97 Wash. App. 832, 988 P.2d 977.

[16] BBC News, "Police Play It by Ear," January 2, 1999, available at http://news.bbc.co.uk/1/hi/sci/tech/246713.stm.

is developing a database of ear photographs. British authorities are reported to already have over 1,500 images.

The ear can be hidden or covered, or the suspect could engage in activities and actions that make it impossible to get a good photo or print. The lighting and camera angles are important in capturing the necessary details. Given the size of the ear, a good camera is required to capture an image that can provide distinguishable characteristics. Fashion styles such as ear piercing, which are common in some cultures and among some age groups, might impact the ear shape.

According to a Dutch government report prepared by the Registratiekamer in 1999, ART Technique has developed an *Optophone,* which incorporates an ear shape verifier into the ear part of a telephone. While this is mentioned in literature, scant details exist regarding the extent of this project.[17]

Little doubt exists that as the search for surveillance products continues, increased interest will occur in ear identification as it offers covert search capabilities. If combined with facial recognition systems, the two methods can compliment each other as multimodal biometrics.

Gait

William Shakespeare told us all we need to know about this esoteric biometric. In *The Tempest*, Ceres shouts, "Great Juno comes; I know her by her gait." The theory behind *gait* biometrics is this: just as each person has a distinctive voice or fingerprint, each person also has a distinctive walk. The trick lies in translating body motion into numbers that a computer can meaningfully recognize.[18] A person's gait derives from his or her physical build and body weight, but it is also affected or altered by factors including shoe type, heel height, clothing, illness, injury, emotional state, environment, and so forth. Ample anecdotal evidence exists about people being recognized by their gaits. Medical research also helps support the view that, if all gait movements are considered, an individual's gait is unique.

Two approaches have been used to model gaits. The first approach models the gait as a simple harmonic motion (SHM) (for example, a pendulum motion of the legs). The *gait signature* is one's deviation from a given standard SHM. In the second approach, the motion of the whole body is modeled by capturing images of the body as it moves. Principal Component Analysis (PCA) uses statistical techniques to compress the frames and a canonical analysis is performed to produce a signature (Little 1998).

---

[17] Registratiekamer, 1999.

[18] David Cameron, "Walk This Way," *MIT Technology Review*, April 23, 2002, available at http://www.technologyreview.com/articles/print_version/wo_cameron042302.asp.

Challenges remain. In terms of measurability, this is accomplished by software once an image is captured, but no standard measure exists—measures are still being developed. Pure video-based techniques are subject to differences in clothing that could obscure the legs and feet. An individual's gait can change because of illness, aging, weight gain or loss, injury, and other factors (such as inebriation or use of a prosthetic device—remember how General DeGaulle's would-be assassin disguised himself as a war amputee in *Day of the Jackal*). Also, people can be taught to walk differently. Only anecdotal evidence suggests that gait is truly distinctive. The techniques are not likely ever to be strong identifiers, however, the information could be helpful for related segmentation and classification tasks, such as finding human motion in surveillance video (for example, is that a human or a deer in the restricted area of the nuclear power plant?) or attempting to determine behavior (for example, running, walking, carrying heavy objects, and so forth).

Gait is nonintrusive and, thus, desirable. However, the question of whether gait is unique has yet to be fully resolved. As Mark Nixon, a gait researcher said to *MIT Technology Review*, "[F]or now, it looks encouraging, but before we go to application, we have to ask, what support is there for gait as a basic biometric?"[19] And, as the editor of *MIT Technology Review* duly notes, "As the Bard would say, that is the question."

This area has recently attracted great interest, and a number of algorithms and approaches have been developed.[20] Previous studies were based on a small number of test subjects and it is not clear how the results scale to larger databases. Therefore, generalizing the findings is difficult. As such, data collection and testing efforts need to be intensified. Active research exists and DARPA has supported many such projects as part of its "Human ID at a Distance" initiative. Institutes of higher learning actively involved in gait recognition research include the University of Southampton, Carnegie Mellon University, Georgia Institute of Technology, Massachusetts Institute of Technology (MIT), the University of Maryland, and University of Southern Florida. For example, at the University of Maryland, Chiraz BenAbdelkader, Ross Cutler, and Larry Davis are studying an "EigenGait" approach that treats gait much like the Eigenfaces technique, discussed in Chapter 4, treats a face image, using PCA to reduce the dimensionality of the feature space, and then applying a supervised pattern classification technique in the reduced feature space for recognition.

On a related research note, some cross-fertilization might exist from the field of biomechanics for sports, medical, and rehabilitation analysis. These techniques

---

[19]   Cameron, "Walk This Way," 2002.

[20]   For example, James Little and Jeffrey Boyd, "Recognizing People by Their Gait: The Shape of Motion," 1998, available at http://citeseer.nj.nec.com/little96recognizing.html.

use actual markers to describe and understand performance characteristics of various human motions (for example, running, jumping, and golf swings).

Interest in human identification at a distance will fuel research in this area. The widespread use of surveillance cameras (for example, CCTV) calls for new products to increase their utility further and gait recognition is one such application. Gait recognition is particularly applicable to covert surveillance and detection, as the active participation of the human subject is not required. Gait recognition also does not require high resolution, and it can complement facial and ear recognition. Beyond surveillance and security applications, gait recognition systems can be integrated into customer relationship systems to identify loyal customers. Thus, "big spenders" will be recognized as they walk from their car in the parking lot to the entranceway of the store.

However, there are huge challenges in efforts to model the gait. For starters, recovering the full three-dimensional model of human motion is difficult. This is because the human body is composed of a large number of parts that can move nonrigidly and the process must be insensitive to clothing or any other features specific to an individual.

Skin Luminescence

Human skin, with its dermal thickness and subcutaneous layers, creates a *skin luminesense,* or distinctive signature of reflections when light is shown through it. Medical researchers discovered this fact serendipitously when they were looking for noninvasive ways to monitor patients.[21] The distinctive signature of reflections is because of individual characteristics of human skin, consisting of multiple layers and different structures, which affect the different wavelengths of light, allowing a possibility that the distinctive signature can work as a biometric.

The developer of the technology, Lumidigm, claims the measure is relatively stable—pregnant women were tested in each trimester and subtle changes in body chemistry did not affect accuracy. The developer also claims that, to date, they have tested approximately 1,000 people multiple times, with results supporting the biometric's distinctiveness and robustness. Lumidigm's commercial product, known as *LightPrint,* is a dime-sized system containing two electronic chips—one chips illuminates the skin using light emitting diodes (LEDs) and collects the reflected rays and the second chip processes the signal to create a "light print" signature, which can be compared to an authorized set of signatures. In operational terms, the technology is nonintrusive.

The technology was developed at a commercial research laboratory, so strong motivation exists to provide favorable test results. No independent tests have

---

[21]   David Cameron, "Skin Chips," *MIT Technology Review,* August 8, 2002, http://www.technologyreview.com/articles/wo_cameron080802.asp.

been done to substantiate the claims. This is still a relatively new technology and more testing is required to determine its biometric capabilities.

Light processing, as opposed to the image processing of other biometrics, requires little computing power, making it ideal for portable devices like smart cards, handguns, and cell phones. Smith and Wesson, the makers of American firearms, is developing a smart gun to be secured by Lumidigm Technology.[22] As a multimodal biometric, skin luminescence could be an excellent way to ensure liveness testing for biometrics such as fingerprints, where detecting real skin as opposed to facsimiles is critical.

Brain Wave Pattern

Laura Guevin, in a short article, "Picking Your Brain in The Name of Security," published on August 19, 2002, has explained what "brain fingerprinting" or what is more properly known as "computerized knowledge assessment" is all about: In the 1990s, the United States Intelligence Community apparently provided research funds for Emanuel Donchin, a psychologist, and his student, Lawrence Farwell, to expand on a standard EEG test, which measures fluctuations in electrical potential caused by patterns of brain activity. (EEG is an acronym for encephalogram, or brainwaves.) According to Guevin:

> Donchin specialized in a characteristic bump in the EEG scan called the P300, which occurs approximately a third of a second after the subject being tested recognizes something significant. Farwell continued testing the viability of using P300 for criminal cases, and ended up patenting the Farwell Brain Fingerprinting method. The system basically works by flashing words or pictures relevant to a crime on a computer screen, along with irrelevant words and pictures. Electrical brain responses are measured through a patented headband equipped with sensors. Farwell discovered that a memory and encoding related multifaceted electroencephalographic response (MERMER) was elicited when the brain processed noteworthy information it recognized. Therefore, if details of a crime only a perpetrator would know about were presented, a MERMER would be emitted by the brain of the perpetrator—but not by the brain of an innocent suspect.[23]

Farwell advocates using brain fingerprinting for security applications, such as screening airline passengers. His theory is that people could be screened

---

[22]   Cameron, "Skin Chips," 2002.

[23]   Laura Guevin, "Picking Your Brain in The Name of Security," August 19, 2002, available at http://www.tmcnet.com/tmcnet/columns/laura081602.htm.

without revealing their names, through the use of biometrics. As the brain wave test is given, the passenger's biometric (for example, fingerprint or iris scan) would be gathered to link the subject to his/her identity. The test subject would then put on a headset and watch video images on a standard computer monitor for a short while. The test would be used to present information with which terrorists are familiar. Brain fingerprinting supposedly works by determining whether a stimulus (such as a video clip of a terrorist camp or crime scene) has been previously seen by a subject.

Similarly, William Lawson has explained, "While it is true that a person has the ability to alter most of their own brain wave patterns, they cannot alter what is referred to as their baseline brain-wave pattern. So, it occurred to us that an individual's baseline brain-wave pattern has the ability to be recognized as the newest undiscovered biometric solution. This is a solution we like to refer to as an 'EEG Fingerprint.' "

According to John Polich, writing in the *Journal of Clinical Neurophysiology* in 1998, clinical factors can affect the results generated by the P300 bump, including heavy use of alcohol and marijuana.[24]

At first thought, brain wave patterns seem to be the basis for a science fiction blockbuster. After more reflection, the technology, if true, has great potential in law enforcement and counterterrorism applications. One could easily see how brain wave fingerprints would replace the polygraph as the investigator's technology of choice to determine whether someone has knowledge of a crime that only the criminal would have. One could also envision how the technology could be used in countless applications, such as background investigations, trusted traveler programs, and many others. Civil libertarians will vociferously object to its use.

Footprint and Foot Dynamics

Footprints as a form of identification date back to ancient China, where they were used to help identify children—a practice still common today when a newborn baby's footprints are taken at the hospital. And as the old Western films make clear, lawmen and Indian scouts used footprints to track, a well-established technique, but not exactly a biometric. Two approaches to footprint biometrics exist. One approach measures the static features, such as the footprint ridges, just like fingerprint or palm prints. The other approach attempts to measure the foot dynamic of a footstep as one walks.

---

[24]   John Polich, "P300 Clinical Utility and Control of Variability," *Journal of Clinical Neurophysiology,* January 15, 1998, 15(1): 14-33.

Static	Dynamic
Foot size	Step size
Foot shape	Pressure analysis
Foot geometric	Timing
Footprint ridges (dermatoglyphics)	Friction

A significant challenge is the lack of a standardized way to measure foot-prints. Even though dermatoglyphic patterns of the footprints may be robust and distinctive, like fingerprints, the foot's dynamic features will be affected by weight, type of shoes, injuries, age, and so forth. Although, arguably, a lack of empirical evidence exists, the high distinctiveness of footprint patterns is generally accepted in both the scientific community and courts.[25] On the other hand, the distinctiveness of footprint pressure is an untested hypothesis.

In operational terms, the use of footprint ridges as a measure is likely to be cumbersome and intrusive because it requires one to remove shoes for the ridges to be scanned. But the approach that measures foot dynamics as one walks or runs is passive and readily acceptable. Data and testing are required to establish footprints as a viable biometric for automatic recognition. Research is being conducted at several locations, including the National Institute of Longevity Sciences (NILS) in Japan. Scientists at NILS have measured the footprint pressure distribution using a pressure-sensitive mat and claim an 85 percent recognition rate.

Footprint identification (pressure distribution) has a covert capability and can serve to complement gait recognition. But one would have to somehow direct the person to walk on the pressure-sensitive mat. A need exists to understand better how footwear and other pertinent factors impact pressure distribution.

The Future

The number of potential biometrics is as great and diverse as the number of the body's measurable parts. The realm of esoteric biometrics adds new meaning to the phrase, "Your body as password." As the challenges plaguing particular esoteric biometrics are resolved, some of these technologies will become more mainstream or establish themselves more securely into niche applications, and researchers will head on to explore additional esoteric biometrics. Some of the biometrics we could soon see in research laboratories include brain wave pattern,

---

[25] A. Moenssens, "Forensic-Evidence.com: Validating Friction Ridge Examination Techniques Proposals Solicited," available at http://www.forensic-evidence.com/site/ID/ID_fpValidation.html.

analysis, lip prints, knee creases, elbow creases, and so forth. Today's esoteric biometric will become tomorrow's mainstream choice.

At least some of these esoteric biometrics will become part of a biometrics-based paradigm that will be used to identify ourselves to whatever authorities or objects require an unequivocal avowal as to who we are. Envisioning a situation where a person naturally carries a variety of biometrics, each activated as the need arises, is not hard. With wearable computers becoming a reality, we could soon have clothes with biometric capabilities that can cautiously announce to all and sundry who we are (who we were from past biometrics) by collecting our sweat, reading our knee prints, our soles, and so forth. For example, biometric devices on my soles will announce my presence (and shoe size) as I walk by a shoe store, and, for that matter, order new shoes for me as well. Maybe a biometric on a driver's license will not only identify the driver, but also his or her state of sobriety and make an appropriate decision as to whether he or she is fit to drive. The biometric could conceivably be implemented into automobile ignition systems that refuse to operate until the driver became sober. The Transportation Security Administration will read my brain wave pattern before I board the commercial airliner.

And a handshake will be as good as a legal seal. And, a person's word can finally become a person's authenticated word.

Part III

Issues Involving Biometrics

place index finger in window

Chapter 8

Biometric Liveness Testing

By Valorie S. Valencia, Ph.D.[1] with Christopher Horn

Recent reports have shown that biometric devices can be spoofed using a variety of methods. Articles published in *The Atlantic Monthly, c't* magazine, and *Network Computing* have described relatively simple procedures that can regularly fool biometric devices. The security provided by biometric devices—that is, the level of confidence in the user's identity—is diminished if the devices can be readily circumvented. Liveness detection, among other methods, has been suggested as a means to counter these types of attacks. As you can imagine, these disclosures have pushed liveness testing into the limelight. Something you might be surprised to hear, however, is that liveness testing has been around for a long time. Chapters 1 and 2 briefly discussed liveness testing; this chapter explains why liveness testing is done, how it is done, and how it should be done.

Biometric liveness tests are automated tests performed to determine if the biometric sample presented to a biometric system came from a live human being—not just any live human being, however, but the live human being who was originally enrolled in the system—the "authentic live human being," if you will.

---

[1] This chapter is based, in part, on a recent speech the author gave: Valorie S. Valencia, April 25, 2002, "Biometric Liveness Testing." Briefing presented at the CardTech SecurTech Conference, New Orleans, LA.

Why Test for Liveness? Why Not?

Why should we test for liveness? Because we know that if a system is made by man, it can be defeated by man. One way to defeat a biometric system is to substitute an artificial or simulated biometric sample for the biometric sample of the "authorized live human being." As such, liveness testing is a technique used to maximize our confidence that individuals are who they claim to be, and that they are alive and able to make the claim.

Sometimes liveness testing is not a sophisticated process. Depending on the system, liveness testing can be as simple as having an observer supervise the capture of the biometric sample. Take, for example, this true story set in South Africa and reported in the *Eastern Province Herald* newspaper: "At first, nothing seemed untoward," Postmaster Dawie Bester related. "I was manning the post office counter, which is used to serve illiterate people when a young man and woman arrived, holding an older man between them."[2]

In South Africa, pensioners can use a fingerprint to claim their monthly pension check. The young man and woman explained that the older man was their uncle and said, "he is very lazy, he cannot be bothered to stay awake to claim his pension. He may be drunk. He is ill." All the same, Postmaster Bester started to become suspicious when he noticed the old man's eyes were completely closed and still. Then, when he noticed the way the young man was maneuvering the old man's hand on the counter for fingerprint-taking, the postmaster told them that pension claimants have to be in full control of their bodies and minds to get their cash, and he would summon his supervisor.

At that point, the couple shouted at the postmaster, and then abruptly ran off, leaving the old man to fall to the ground. Postmaster Bester explained: "When I got around to the other side of the counter, I discovered that the old man was ice cold and had obviously been dead for many hours, so I called the police. In all my 29 years working in this post office I have never known such a thing. We have had several people die while waiting in the queue but never a dead person trying to claim."

This "Stupid Crimes" article illustrates one situation where biometric liveness testing could have inhibited a bogus authentication attempt. Luckily in this situation, the postmaster was observant enough to sense something wasn't quite right. Had this been an unsupervised process, akin to withdrawing money from an ATM, the criminals might have been able to succeed.

Like any other security technology, biometrics have inherent weaknesses that can reduce the security of the system, especially in unsupervised applications. Biometrics are not a silver bullet for authentication security. In fact, a typical biometric system has many points that are vulnerable to circumvention. By successfully circumventing key points in the system, it is possible for an adversary to gain unauthorized access to a protected physical or logical area, or appear

---

[2]   The account is sourced to the *Eastern Province Herald,* Port Elizabeth, South Africa, in an article first published on November 23, 1999.

as if he or she isn't already registered in the system. One of the most susceptible points in the system is the user-data capture interface. This *user-data capture interface* is particularly important from a security perspective because the capture device is often readily observable by and available to the user, as well as to any potential adversary.

One of the major threats to capture devices is the use of simulated or artificial biometric specimens or samples. Several excellent papers published in the open literature document this threat.

For example, Professor Tsutomu Matsumoto and his colleagues at Japan's Yokohama National University have recently detailed two methods of creating an artificial biometric specimen in the form of fake fingerprints.[3] Both of Matsumoto's methods use gelatin to re-create a person's finger. Gelatin is readily available at most grocery stores and is a major component of Gummi Bears, the well-known goodie.

In the first method, Matsumoto takes a live finger and makes a plastic mold from that finger. He then pours liquid gelatin into the mold and lets it harden. This fake "gummy" finger can be used to fool both optical and capacitive fingerprint detectors.

The second method is more sophisticated and is used to generate gummy fingers from latent fingerprints. Matsumoto first takes a fingerprint left on a piece of glass and enhances it with a type of super glue known as *cyanoacrylate adhesive*. He then photographs that enhanced latent fingerprint with a digital camera and uses photo-editing software to improve the contrast and quality of the image. Next, the image is printed on to a transparency sheet and used in conjunction with a commonly available photo-sensitive printed circuit board (PCB) to etch the fingerprint into the copper of the PCB, making a three-dimensional representation of the fingerprint. Finally, the gelatin is poured on the PCB to create the gummy finger. Gummy fingers are particularly flexible in that they can fool sensors being watched by guards. All the adversary needs to do is form the gelatin mold over his or her own finger and, effectively, new fingerprints are created! After using the gummy finger to gain illicit access, the adversary can then eat the evidence.

Researchers from West Virginia University have also performed similar experiments using molds made from dental material. They showed that Play-Doh and clay molds could be verified against enrolled, live fingers for all fingerprint technologies tested (capacitive and optical). In addition, they were also able to scan, enroll, and verify fingerprints from cadaver fingers.

In an article in *Network Computing* by David Willis and Mike Lee, entitled "Six Biometric Devices Point the Finger At Security," the testing team reports that they were able to fool many of the optical scanners they tested using lifted

---

[3] T. Matsumoto, H. Matsumoto, K. Yamada, and S. Hoshino, 2002, "Impact of Artificial Gummy Fingers on Fingerprint Systems," Proceedings of SPIE Vol. #4677, Optical Security and Counterfeit Deterrence Techniques IV.

latent prints and silicone fingers.[4] To lift the latent prints, the team first dusted the prints with toner from a laser printer cartridge, and then lifted them using adhesive tape. Next, they transferred the adhesive images to transparency material using a photocopier. By wetting the ink side of the transparency and placing it on the scanning platen, they were able to break into a couple of the devices they were testing. The silicone fingers were made using a wax mold and a thin layer of silicone.

Finally, *c't* magazine's article, "Body Check: Biometrics Defeated," outlines even more methods to outfox the latest commercial biometric systems.[5] In addition to spoofing fingerprints with water-filled plastic bags, the team used short video clips played back on a laptop to fool facial recognition software. They also managed to fool iris recognition software using a simple printed image of an iris with a small hole cut out for the real pupil of the adversary.

These aren't new threats and they have been acknowledged and addressed in the United Kingdom and Department of Defense Common Criteria biometric protection profiles as potential threats to biometric systems.

Important to realize, however, is that biometric systems are no more vulnerable than other authentication technologies. For example, bar codes, magnetic stripes, and plastic photo identification cards are all imperfect as well. An advantage of biometric authentication technologies is that we can do something about it—we can incorporate automated liveness tests to minimize the effectiveness of artificial or simulated biometric specimens.

What Is Liveness Testing?

Exactly what is biometric liveness testing? Specific methods vary, but all methods fall into three broad categories. The first category is to look at the intrinsic properties of a living body. The second category is to analyze involuntary signals generated by a living body. The third category is to measure a bodily response to a stimulus—in other words, a challenge-response method. This challenge-response method can look for either voluntary (behavioral) or involuntary (reflexive) responses.

While the first two types of liveness testing are largely self-explanatory, the third requires elaboration. In a voluntary challenge-response test, the user provides a logical response to a prompt generated by the system. The stimulus can be tactile, visual, or auditory in nature. With a tactile stimulus, the user is instructed

---

[4]   David Willis, and Mike Lee, "Biometrics Under Our Thumb" (Sidebar), *Network Computing,* June 1, 1998, available at http://www.networkcomputing.com/910/910r1side1.html#bio.

[5]   Lisa Thalheim, Jan Krissler, and Peter-Michael Ziegler, "Body Check: Biometrics Defeated," *c't* magazine, November 2002, available at http://www.heise.de/ct/english/02/11/114.

to say or do something in response to feeling something (for example, a thermal, electrical, or physical impulse). A tactile example is "Touch Button A if the platen is hot or touch Button B if the platen is cold." In the same vein, visual and auditory cues require the user to respond to either seeing or hearing something, respectively.

In an involuntary challenge-response test, the user's body automatically provides the response with a physiological change or reaction to a stimulus. Examples include the response of muscles to electrical stimulation, known as electromyography (EMG), the response of the eye's pupil diameter to varying light levels, the dynamic change in the color of skin when pressure is applied, the rapid movement of a hand when shocked, and the reflex of a knee when struck.

The following tables summarize the categories and provide examples of each property for each.

Intrinsic Properties of a Living Body

Physical/Mechanical
   weight, density, elasticity

Electrical
   capacitance, resistance, impedance, dielectric constant

Visual
   color, opacity, appearance and shape of features

Spectral
   reflectance, absorbance, transmittance, fluorescence

Body Fluid
   oxygen, blood constituents, DNA (deoxyribonucleic acid)

Involuntary Signals Generated by a Living Body

Pulse

Blood pressure

Heat

Thermal gradients

Corpuscular blood flow (plesythmographic) signals

Skin exudation (shedding of dead skin cells)

Transpiration of gases

Body odor

Perspiration

Electrical signals generated by the heart (ECG or EKG)

Brain wave signals (EEG)

Responses to a Stimulus by a Living Body (Challenge-Response)
Voluntary (behavioral)
Tactile–respond to feeling something
Visual–respond to seeing something
Auditory–respond to hearing something
Involuntary (reflexive)
Electromyography (EMG)
Pupil dilation
Reflex of a knee when struck

As you might have guessed, all biometric modalities are, in and of themselves, liveness tests. Fingerprint sensors measure the intrinsic properties of a living body, such as index of refraction, capacitance, and acoustic impedance. Hand, iris, and facial biometrics measure visual properties of a living body. Speaker recognition uses challenge-response to obtain a sample of the voice. However, we typically consider these to be "weak" liveness tests: weak because they are vulnerable to simulated biometric specimens. The goal of liveness testing is to incorporate a robust test for liveness into a biometric sensor—a test that yields results distinct from the biometric measurement.

Some biometric technologies, such as facial thermogram, vein pattern in back of hand, gait, and keystroke, may be considered stronger tests for liveness. Some would consider these biometric identifiers more difficult to simulate artificially. However, these technologies are not widely implemented and will need to be validated as reliable biometric identifiers.

Described below are a few examples of liveness testing products or methods that are currently in use in the biometric marketplace. The first is the Sony Fingerprint Identification Unit (FIU-500), which tests for liveness by measuring the intrinsic properties of a living finger. An optical fingerprint scanner, the FIU-500 incorporates a sensor that claims to measure the capacitance of the skin. If the measurement is within norms for skin, the finger is assumed to be real, and the optical scan of the fingerprint is accepted for processing.

The second example demonstrates an approach to analyzing involuntary signals generated by a living body. Developed at West Virginia University by Reza Derakhshani, Stephanie Schuckers, and others,[6] this approach captures the time-varying perspiration pattern on a fingertip using a capacitive fingerprint sensor, see Figure 8-1. Because of perspiration, the specific values of a person's finger capacitance vary with time. This variance is shown in the following line plot; the two plotted lines are the capacitance plots across a ridge of the finger,

---

[6] R. Derakhshani, and S. A. C. Schuckers, "Determination of Vitality From A Non-Invasive Biomedical Measurement for Use in Fingerprint Scanners," *Pattern Recognition* (forthcoming).

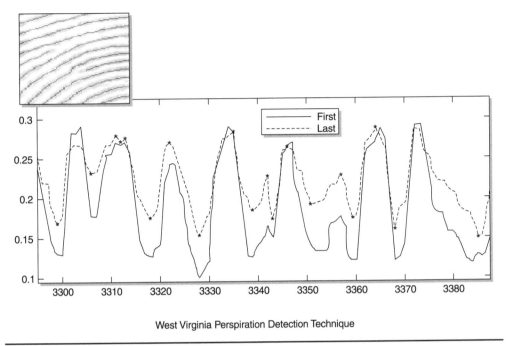

Figure 8-1   Fingertip perspiration pattern

measured five seconds apart. The local maximums in the plot represent the pores in the fingerprint ridge that are saturated with moisture. As indicated by the sensor readings (solid = initial reading, and dashed line = reading after five seconds), the areas between the pores tend to fill up with perspiration over time as the moisture spreads across the ridges. Thus, if the capacitance plots do not indicate the perspiration effect over time, the finger can be assumed to be fake or dead.

A patent for another interesting method to measure involuntary bodily signals was filed in mid-1998 by SmartTouch LLC. The patent, entitled "Anti-Fraud Biometric Scanner that Accurately Detects Blood Flow,"[7] describes how to use two light emitting diodes (LEDs) and a photo-detector to determine whether blood is flowing through the finger or whether the finger is being artificially moved to simulate a pulse. The device also checks to see if the background light

---

[7]   Lapsley, et al., United States Patent 5,737,439 (issued April 7, 1998). Anti-fraud Biometric Scanner that Accurately Detects Blood Flow, Washington D.C.: U.S. Government Printing Office.

level is above a threshold to determine if an external light source is being used to fool the device.

This liveness test basically implements what is known as pulse oximetry. *Pulse oximetry* is used in the medical field to determine the oxygen content of a patient's blood. In this test, however, the blood oxygen content information is ignored, while the pulse information is used.[8]

The following describes what is taking place in the device: "Current pulse oximeters measure the differential absorption of two wavelengths (colors) of light projected through the finger or other tissue. It is based on two physical principles: that different colors of light are absorbed differently by oxygenated hemoglobin and deoxygenated hemoglobin; and the fluctuating volume of arterial blood between the source and detector, which adds a pulsatile component to the absorption. Tissue, bone, and venous blood absorb a relatively constant amount of light, producing an unknown, but constant, background absorption. Each time the heart beats, a pulse of arterial blood flows to the tissue. The influx of blood increases the absorption at both wavelengths. The ratio of absorption at these two wavelengths varies with the oxygen saturation."[9]

The fourth example covers voluntary responses to a stimulus. A rather simple test, at least one speaker verification system prompts a user to speak a random set of digits. If the digits are not spoken in the right order, then the validation attempt is assumed to be a recording or some other form of deception. Similarly, a facial recognition product prompts its user to blink or smile. Software detects this change in expression, and then checks the face as usual.

A fifth and final example is a test for an involuntary response to a stimulus. In the patent "Detector for recognizing the living character of a finger in a fingerprint recognizing apparatus,"[10] Peter Kallo and others lay out a method for measuring the dielectric response, as a function of frequency, of a finger to a small impulse current applied to the finger. In this instance, the current is the challenge, and the finger's electrical reaction to the impulse is the involuntary response. If the signals returned by the finger are outside predefined norms for human tissue, the finger is assumed to be a fake. Guardware Systems Ltd. has incorporated this patented liveness technique in their product line.

---

[8]   Robert W. Phelps, "Pulse Oximetry and Its Advances," November 1999, available at http://www.anesthesiologynews.com/specreps/an/sr0001/02report.htm.

[9]   E. Hill, and Stoneham, "Practical Applications of Pulse Oximetry," available at http://www.nda.ox.ac.uk/wfsa/html/u11/u1104_01.htm.

[10] Kallo, et al. United States Patent 6,175,641 (issued January 16, 2001). Detector for Recognizing the Living Character of a Finger in a Fingerprint Recognizing Apparatus, Washington D.C.: U.S. Government Printing Office.

Difficulties with Liveness Testing

In early 1998, about the time the *Network Computing* article documenting artificial fingerprint techniques was published, two patents were filed that dealt with incorporating liveness testing into fingerprint systems. The first, a United States patent entitled "Biometric, personal authentication system,"[11] described a system known as the 3M Blackstone. The *Blackstone* used an optical fingerprint sensor and measured electrocardiograph signals (EKG), blood oxygen levels, and pulse rate. Unfortunately, the user had to hold still in the position shown in the figure at the right for six to eight seconds. This is quite a long time for a person to remain motionless, and the long wait wreaks havoc with throughput rates. If the user moved during the time the EKG sensor was synchronizing, the measurement was disrupted and the user had to start over. For this and other various reasons, the Blackstone liveness testing project was discontinued.

The second patent, filed a short while later by SmartTouch, was previously described. What was not mentioned, though, is that a breadboard prototype was developed, demonstrated, and then dismantled. At the time, vendors did not perceive a market for liveness testing and, quite frankly, a market for liveness testing did not exist at that time. Times have changed, however, and vendors are now actively seeking new ways to enhance the robustness of their products.

As the Blackstone illustrated, liveness testing is not easy. Their technology required a user to remain motionless for six to eight seconds. For normal applications, this is an unacceptably long delay. Incorporating liveness testing into a biometric system often runs the risk of making that system solution less appealing. Liveness tests have the propensity to increase the "time to acquire," the "false rejection (or false nonmatch) rates" and costs, as well as inconvenience for the users of the device.

Technology aside, liveness testing faces other obstacles—importantly, the lack of open discussion of liveness testing. James Cambier, vice president of research at Iridian Technologies Inc., outlines the problem in an e-mail[12] to Valorie Valencia [repeated here with permission]:

> "One problem with liveness testing is that most biometric vendors,
> Iridian Technologies included, do not publicly disclose information
> about their countermeasures because of the security risk associated
> with that disclosure. We are not yet to the point in liveness testing
> where the techniques are so reliable that detailed knowledge of their

[11]   Osten, et al. United States Patent 5,719,950 (issued February 17, 1998). Biometric, Personal Authentication System, Washington D.C.: U.S. Government Printing Office.

[12]   Based on a personal e-mail from James L. Cambier to Valorie S. Valencia (March 7, 2002).

functionality does not give the hacker an advantage, as is the case with encryption techniques.

That said, all commercially available iris recognition products contain some level of liveness testing. The sophistication and effectiveness of those countermeasures are directly related to cost and the degree of user inconvenience that can be tolerated in a particular application. In general we take measures that attempt to prevent the use of photographs, contact lenses, and artificial eyes in either enrollment or recognition or both. This is an ongoing R&D effort, which we expect to continue indefinitely."

While the lack of open discussion surely slows development of new liveness tests, personal prejudices also interfere with development. Some only consider tests that measure signals produced involuntarily by a living body to be true "liveness" tests, as opposed to "realness" tests that measure intrinsic properties of a living body. Furthermore, some consider voice-based challenge-response to be a classic example of liveness testing, while others argue that such voluntary challenge-response techniques, in general, test only for the *presence* of a human as opposed to testing for the *liveness* of the biometric being measured.

Best Approaches to Liveness Testing

The robustness of a liveness technique depends more on how the test is implemented than on what liveness indicator is measured. The best liveness tests measure or challenge the liveness of the biometric feature simultaneously with the capture of the biometric data (that is, same time, same place). They are also relatively difficult to deceive.

One approach to achieving robust integration of liveness detection is to implement "living" techniques that evolve and improve over time. This "moving target" helps to stay one step ahead of would-be adversaries. The credit card industry's anticounterfeit model uses this approach of continually implementing new countermeasures to stay one step ahead of experienced credit-card defrauders.

Another approach minimizes the effectiveness of artificial or simulated biometric specimens by combining biometrics with other authentication methods. Such methods include (1) things a person has (tokens such as physical keys, photo ID cards, proximity cards, magnetic stripe cards, and smart cards), (2) things a person knows (such as passwords and PINs), and (3) manned supervision of biometric stations. In addition, multimodal biometric systems also place additional hurdles in that a potential criminal would have to spoof multiple biometrics.

The most important point to remember, though, is that liveness testing is only a means to *minimize* the effectiveness of artificial or simulated biometric specimens. Liveness testing is *not* a guarantee that the biometric specimen belongs to the authentic live human being. *If man can make it, man can break it!*

The take-home message here is this: liveness testing can improve the security integrity of biometric systems—if it is designed and implemented appropriately. No security technology can ever provide 100 percent security. All we can ever hope to do with biometric liveness testing, or any security technology advance, is to "raise the bar" for potential foes.

Liveness tests can, and are, being implemented in biometric systems to increase our confidence that only alive, originally enrolled individuals are authenticated by biometric systems. The best liveness testing is performed simultaneously with the biometric data capture—at the same time and at the same place. This ensures that the liveness data being collected is of the same source as the primary biometric sample. The best liveness tests must also be carefully and robustly designed. Careless implementation of a good idea is worthless.

While not infallible, liveness testing "raises the bar" to would-be adversaries by decreasing the chances that an artificial or simulated biometric specimen will be accepted as real. The security posture of biometric systems can also be improved by supervising biometric stations and combining biometrics with other authentication technologies, such as tokens possessed by the user and data memorized by the user. The actual combination of authentication methods used for a given application is selected based on the requirements of that application. Care also needs to be taken to address threats at other points in the biometric system, where liveness testing cannot help. Doing so ensures that balanced, system-wide protection is achieved.

Chapter 9

Biometrics in Large-Scale Systems

By Peter T. Higgins

The procurement of large-scale biometric systems can be daunting. This chapter presents a structured approach to the problem. It is based on the activities associated with the procurement of several large-scale systems over the past 10 years. The unfortunate reality is that there is no one-size-fits-all answer to any questions. Your problem is more likely than not to be different in enough respects from other people's that you will have to understand it well enough to manage it yourself or hire an expert to help you tailor a commercial solution to your problem.

Getting Started

The first question that is typically asked in any large-scale biometric systems procurement is "which biometric?" Since there is no one-size-fits-all biometric, this is an important question. A structured approach can be taken to answer this question.

Before that question is addressed, you must define your need for a biometric. What is its purpose and how will it add value? If you cannot articulate a crisp answer to those underlying questions, it is too early to be thinking of selecting a biometric. Remember that the biometric is rarely, if ever, an end to itself. Most biometric systems are installed for one of four reasons:

- Providing greater convenience for users
- Reducing business costs (for example, reducing help desk staffing to deal with forgotten passwords)
- Reducing fraud
- Increasing the strength of a security access control system

Once you understand your reasons for needing a biometric, you can use the following steps to choose which biometric is appropriate:

1. Determine whether the problem you are trying to solve is a previously solved problem. In other words, do not reinvent the wheel. For example, for a problem such as welfare fraud control, studies and experiences have already established that fingerprints are an acceptable form of identification. Now you only need to see how others' solutions can be tailored to fit your problem.

2. Determine whether the subjects of interest are already linked through a biometric to a set of relevant records. A good example is the Immigration and Naturalization Service's Passenger Accelerated Service System (INSPASS), where all applicants are checked using fingerprints because that is the biometric linked to criminal records. Successful applicants are then issued a card linked to their hand geometry for day-to-day use.

3. Identify the type of application and then eliminate any biometric that is not capable of performing your function (such as surveillance, identification, or just verification). For example, hand geometry cannot perform a surveillance function.

4. Identify any location-of-use constraints. Use outdoors in adverse weather or lighting conditions can degrade performance of many biometrics. For example, extremely cold weather inhibits users of outdoor hand geometry readers without provision of an environmental covering and some heat source.

5. Identify any constraints such as population size and age range. Extremely large populations limit the number of biometrics to the one successfully demonstrated to work with tens of millions of records—fingerprints. Populations that include very young persons and persons over 55 years of age can pose performance problems for many biometrics.

6. Consider the availability of decision makers in case of a false claim or challenged results and understand the anticipated numbers of false rejects and false matches that a biometric would likely have on your population and transaction rates. The fallback must be well thought out

since people cannot differentiate most biometric samples (even the accuracy of facial comparisons by people has been shown to be less than 90 percent). Thus, secondary check personnel will have to rely on alternative biometric technology, identity documentation, or other information to resolve challenged results.

7. Determine the sensitivity of failures. Biometric performance rates and threshold settings will depend on the purpose of your system. If you are controlling who gets a meal at a college cafeteria, for example, your threshold of pain is lower than if you are controlling access to a nuclear power plant. While both can employ the same biometric, the threshold will be set quite differently. You can tolerate the occasional unauthorized student getting falsely accepted into the cafeteria and getting a "free lunch." You cannot tolerate an unauthorized person gaining access to nuclear materials.

8. Understand which requirement (that is, convenience, business costs, fraud, or security) is your driver. Analyze your performance expectations in light of independent test results, not manufacturers' claims.

9. If none of the above considerations leads to a conclusion, one should follow the "Best Practices" document and run a cross-technology fly-off of different biometrics. This could involve benchmarking existing sites or funding prototypes or pilots. See the Biometric Consortium web site (www.biometrics.org) for a link to the most recent release of the UK Best Practices document.

Table 9-1 provides a graphical representation of the functionality of mainstream biometrics.

The next question: What is the complexity of the system to be "biometricized"? From experience, we know the problem scope and the current environmental baseline (that is—is the current system automated or not, is it secure, an so on) drive complexity. A set of complexity codes (1 through 3 with lower numbers indicating a higher degree of complexity) can help categorize the problem and then help you determine the level of formality required to manage a biometric project. Table 9-2 shows the classification of complexity.

Biometric	Verification of Claim (Positive ID)	Identification, If Known (Negative ID)	Surveillance
Face	↑	↓	↑
Finger	↑	↑	↓
Eye	↑	↑	↓
Hand	↑	↓	↓
Voice	↑	↓	↓

Table 9-1 Applicability Table

Nature of Change	Access Control	Tactical	Strategic: Civil	Strategic: Law Enforcement
Added Functionality	3	2	2	2
System Upgrade	2	3	3	3
New System	2	1	1	1

Table 9-2   Complexity Matrix

Following is an explanation of the codes in the complexity matrix:

1. **Highest degree of complexity**   Requires selection of standards and operational concepts, and a full set of interface, functional, and performance requirement specifications. Has the most impact on stakeholders, infrastructure, and business operations.

2. **Medium complexity**   Updated or new concept of operations that has some impact on users, infrastructure, and workflows.

3. **Low degree of complexity**   Changes are usually transparent to users, but interface specifications and performance requirements need technical details.

Documenting the Procurement Process

The key to procuring a system successfully with a biometric component is to approach it in the same disciplined and structured way successful Information Technology (IT) procurements are managed. The first document to be prepared should be an "Acquisition Strategy," which should cover topics such as these:

- Concept of operations or statement of need (see next section for scope)
- Funding sources
  - Legislation
  - Grants
  - Fiscal year constraints
  - Out year cost of ownership
  - Any fee for services
- Activities and schedule
  - Approval for procurement
  - Solicitation release

- Proposal preparation
- Proposal evaluation and contract award
- Operational dates
- Roles and responsibilities
  - Project manager
  - Contracts shop
  - Finance officer
  - User manager
  - Training organization
  - Information technology shop
  - Facilities manager
  - Consultants
- Procurement approach
  - Competition
  - Sole source

The acquisition strategy will be useful for satisfying the need for information for management, finance, security, contracts, and the user population. The level of detail and the scope of the contents will depend on the complexity of the system.

Specifying the Systems

The requirements should flow from the "concept of operations" and serve as a communications vehicle among the system owners, users, contractors, or in-house organization that will develop and integrate the system. If the work is to be contracted out, a Request for Proposals (RFP) or a similar vehicle must be prepared and approved. The details and approval process will be determined by the degree of complexity and "local policy."

The typical concept of operations should contain the following types of information:

- Purpose and complexity
  - **Purpose**   Refer to the list in beginning of this chapter for an explanation
  - **Timeframe**   For need and anticipated period of use
  - **Locations to be supported**   Environmental and maintenance considerations

- **Functionality** Biometric, administrative, and IT
- **Clients** Users, administrators, and others
- **Staffing levels** Required to use and maintain the system
- **Hours** Of operations and locations
- **Work loads** Per hour/day/year and response time
- **Interfaces** To other systems and services
- Biometric and other services and how they will be used
  - **Workflows** To include biometric services
  - **Customers supported** By service
  - **Administrative modes** Normal backup, recovery, file management, and threshold settings
  - **System and biometric performance** Error rates, response time, capacity, and availability

The typical RFP should contain multiple sections, each of which is used to convey specific information to the potential vendors and integrators. The following list reflects the typical contents—local policy will dictate the actual contents. (Details are provided in the section that follows in the form of specifics for an Automated Fingerprint Identification System (AFIS) procurement.)

- Terms and conditions
- Proposal preparation instructions
- Statement of work (SOW)
- Work breakdown structure (WBS)
- Requirements specification
- Vendor qualifications
- Source selection process overview
- Acceptance testing criteria or process

Sample AFIS RFP Overview

An overview of the major sections of a typical RFP for an AFIS is provided in this section. Further details of how to prepare an RFP can be found on the web at a Department of Defense web site, http://web2.deskbook.osd.mil/default.asp, as well as at other sites.

Terms and Conditions (Ts & Cs)

This section is often referred to as "boilerplate." It provides a compilation of various mandatory state or federal procurement laws and policies to include payment terms, social clauses, and other similar information. The following list is a sample of typical Ts & Cs topics:

- Americans with Disabilities Act compliance
- Minority and small business contracting rules and incentives
- Audit rules
- Drug testing policies
- Personnel and integration facility security requirements
- Insurance requirements
- Blacklisted companies
- Government options (such as termination for cause)

Proposal Preparation Instructions

The proposal preparation instructions ensure that all proposals will contain similar information organized in roughly the same way. They permit the procurement managers to dictate what information will be provided as a minimum. The instructions are used to separate the technical and management material from the cost data. The following list is a sample of typical proposal preparation instruction topics:

- Due date and location
- Number of volumes and their contents as well as any page limitations (see next section for details)
- Number of copies—both paper and CD-ROMs or other storage media
- Any mandatory oral presentations
- Any benchmarks or mandatory demonstrations of functionality
- Requirements Traceability Matrix (RTM) to permit evaluators to determine where in a proposal each and every requirement is addressed

Executive Summary Instructions

The Executive Summary should provide an overview of the vendor's capabilities and its approach to solving your problem. The intended audience is the executive team responsible for the procurement—on the assumption that they will not have time to read the full proposals but will need to get a "feel" for the proposals. The following list is a sample of the type of material that should be provided:

- **Vendor background**   Size, ownership, and so on
- **Teammates**   If any
- **Brief statement of problem**   To be addressed with emphasis on key challenges and approaches—biometric specifics and their assessment of complexity
- **Outline of proposed solution**   To include biometric specifics
- **References (2 or 3)**   To include benchmark sites (if required)

Management Volume Instructions

The Management Volume should explain who the vendor is and how they will plan, staff, and manage your project. The Management Volume can be combined with the Technical Volume on small and medium procurements. For projects with high complexity or multiple years of performance, it is often cleaner to request that the management information be broken out in a separate volume. The following list is a sample of the type of material that should be provided; note the overlap between this list and that of the Executive Summary:

- **Vendor background**   Including size, ownership, financial condition, and so on
- **Teammates and key vendors**   Roles and relationships
- **Management approach to be used**   Design reviews and documentation, development, integration, installation
- **Biometric-related environmental and user-results-challenge considerations**   Considerations for weather, lighting, and dealing with false nonmatches
- **Testing**   Factory Acceptance testing (FAT) and Site Acceptance testing (SAT) strategy
- **Training**   Scope, approach, number of courses, and training material to be provided
- **Detailed schedule**   Meetings, reports, factory events (such as integration tests), and deliveries
- **Key personnel**   Resumes with relevant experiences
- **Reference clients**   To include benchmark sites (if required)

Technical Volume Instructions

The Technical Volume should describe the proposed solution to your problem and why it is appropriate. Bidders should show how they will address each of your requirements in the proposed system. Their response can be as simple as a matrix of your requirements with an appropriate length response for each requirement. The responses will range from "yes, we will do that" for simple requirements such as "solution shall include an operational copy of Adobe Acrobat software" to more complex responses for requirements such as "system shall dynamically set thresholds based on vendor selected parameters."

In the Technical Volume, the bidder must address items such as these:

- Concept of Operations, as understood by the vendor
- Description of proposed solution
  - Architecture, design, and any standards to be used
  - Performance in terms of throughput, response time, and biometric error rates
  - Work flows, such as enrollment, verification, maintenance, as well as queue management
- Storage and retrieval of fingerprint images, templates, features, and transaction history
- Interfaces with other systems, such as communications systems and other AFIS systems at state or federal level
- Reliability, availability, Mean Time Between Failures (MTBF), and so on
- Bill of material in a sortable and searchable spreadsheet
  - Hardware items with model numbers
  - Software items with version numbers
  - Matrix of hardware to software relationships

Cost Volume Instructions

The Cost Volume should detail what the proposed solution will cost and why. It should be organized in a fashion that supports evaluation and unambiguous understanding. The normal constituents are as follows:

- Costs by fiscal year
- Costs for bill of material
- Costs decomposed for WBS elements
  - Initial delivery
  - Future upgrades
  - Options
  - Training
  - Operations and maintenance

Oral Presentation Instructions

For projects of complexity factors 1 and 2 (see Table 9-2), it is worthwhile to solicit oral presentations by the vendors. This permits you to assess the vendor team and to ask clarifying questions. The typical list of evaluation criteria to be followed is shown next—this will focus the vendor on the correct outline. The logistics, to include time and location, must be provided in the RFP and should include the number of people that the vendor is permitted to bring. Oral presentations should last no more than four hours. After a suitable break, the purchasers can ask clarification questions.

- Depth and relevance of experience in meeting similar needs for other clients
- Depth of understanding of your needs and intended use of the technology
- Familiarity of the vendor's personnel with the proposed technology and standards
- Completeness of the proposed technical solution to show design and compliance with standards and with requirements using a specific workflow as a model
- Appropriateness of the project management approach and schedule to the degree of complexity and size of your project

Statement of Work (SOW)

The SOW reflects the scope of the work to be performed under the contract. Many agencies use the SOW to convey the functional, performance, and other requirements. The SOW should include the full scope of work to be performed and for each task it should offer a paragraph or two of explanation, as well as a list of any deliverable for that task. The deliverables are known as "contract data requirements," and the list of all of them is known as the Contract Data Requirements List (CDRL, pronounced *see drill*). The CDRL list should include the following types of deliverables:

- Design documents
- Hardware and software
- Facility modifications (as required)
- Furniture (as required)
- Systems (numbers, locations, and so on)
- Manuals (users and administrators)
- Training courses
- Reports
- On-site support

- Licenses for commercial software products
- Certifications of standards compliance

The SOW describes in clear and understandable terms what products are to be delivered and what services are to be performed by the contractor after award of a contract. Preparation of an effective SOW requires an understanding of both the products and services that are needed to satisfy a particular requirement. A SOW prepared in explicit terms will facilitate effective contractor evaluation after contract award. The SOW becomes the standard for measuring contractor performance.

In preparing the SOW for a system acquisition, the use of a standardized Work Breakdown Structure (WBS) as a template will help streamline the process. (The WBS definition is addressed in the next section.) Use of the WBS will also provide a convenient checklist to ensure that all necessary elements of the program are addressed.

The typical SOW tasks include design, procurement, integration, installation, training, testing, and other relevant information. A sample SOW task and related CDRL is provided next. Note that some tasks are marked as *M* for *mandatory* (that is, those to be addressed in the proposal in a pass/fail manner) and others are marked as *R* for *rated* (to be evaluated and scored as part of the proposal evaluation). Also note the inclusion of three CDRL documents for this one task.

Sample SOW Task   Take the following steps to perform the design review and documentation task:

1. The contractor *shall* document the design and present it at a design review to be held at the purchaser's headquarters no later than 90 days after award of contract. *(M)*

2. The contractor *shall* provide the following documentation in initial draft (in contractor format and at a level of specificity appropriate to that point in the effort) with their proposal and an updated version three weeks prior to the design review:

   - **Requirements traceability matrix**   Requirements allocation to system components in both the design specification and the bill of materials, phases, and test plans. *(M)*

   - **Workflow document**   Allocation of tasks for tenprint, latent and administrative use for remote users, local tenprint users, forensic (latent) users, and system administrators to include backup and restore of the system and its databases and the latent case management subsystem. *(R)*

   - **System design**   To document design particulars to include, but not be limited to, components, communications links, inter and intra site or configuration item communication loads, databases, security features, hardware, software, any binning and filtering algorithms, number of fingers matched, normal operations and lights-out decision algorithms, feature-matching algorithms, name-search techniques, and feature dataset distribution across storage devices (for example, distributed randomly or based on classification). *(R)*

Work Breakdown Structure (WBS)

The WBS provides a framework for specifying the work processes required for the SOW, and it is the reporting structure for schedule and cost data. Each element of the WBS provides a way for assessing technical accomplishments and for measuring the cost and schedule performance achieved in execution of the tasks in the SOW. The WBS should be aligned with any internal reporting requirements (such as procurement costs versus operations and maintenance costs) so the project managers can use contractor data with a minimum of reformatting and recalculation to satisfy their own internal reporting requirements.

If the contract is firm-fixed priced, the WBS can provide the basic structure in the SOW and it will form the cost structure for the proposal and the schedule structure for performance reporting.

If the contract is a cost-plus type (frequently used in the federal government for engineering contracts), the WBS is used to allocate SOW tasks to contractor organizational elements. Then as resources are employed and work progresses on the tasks, current technical, schedule, and cost data are reported against the WBS structure. The task data may then be summarized to provide successive levels of management with the appropriate reports on planned, actual, and current projected status of all elements for which the contractor is responsible.

A WBS is developed in levels where each level has more tasks with more details than the previous level. When the tasks are integrated across any level, they cover all the effort required to deliver a system. The first level has one element – the system to be delivered. At the second level the typical elements would be: design effort, development and integration effort, quality assurance effort, installation effort, and user training effort. At the third level the elements under the design effort would be: requirements analysis effort, system engineering effort, COTS product selection effort, and so on.

A typical WBS for an AFIS project would look like the following at the second level. More details would be available at the third and subsequent levels. An example of a fourth-level task is provided following the second-level list.

Here's a sample of an AFIS procurement WBS structure:

1.0 AFIS Project

1.1 Card conversion

1.2 Design and document

1.3 Interface development

1.4 New software development and integration of Commercial-off-the-Shelf (COTS) products such as Adobe Photoshop software.

1.5 Pre-ship testing (FAT)

1.6 Delivery

1.7 Installation

1.8 Transition planning and support

1.9 Training

1.10 On-site testing (SAT)

1.11 Maintenance

Here's a sample of a fourth-level WBS element:

1.1 Card conversion

1.1.2 Quality assessment of scanned cards

1.1.2.1 Provision of verification equipment

Fourth-Level WBS Deliverable   Workstation and software to inspect image samples from converted cards. (Note: Cost volume will have cost data for this fourth-level WBS element and the master schedule will show when it will be installed. The related SOW Task and the Requirements Specification describe what the workstation is to do and when and where it is to be installed.)

Requirements Specification

You specify what the delivered system or services are to be capable of doing, how many are to be delivered, how fast they must work, and other similar information in the requirements specification. It covers a multitude of requirement types. An example of a requirement is provided after the following list of requirement types:

- Functional
- Interface
- Standards
- Performance
- Reliability, maintainability, and availability

Here's a sample interface requirement:

- **Requirement Specification Paragraph # 3.1.4.1, Exchange EFTS messages**   The AFIS server *shall* be able to exchange (both receive and send) FBI EFTS transactions, with live scans, card scanners, IAFIS, other AFIS systems, and other ANSI NIST servers using frame relay, fast Ethernet, and dial-up modem communications. *(M)*

Source Selection Process Overview

Source selection is usually the single area that is most reflective of local policy and experience. The process itself is relatively uniform—the implementation and scope of the steps can vary significantly. Normally, one tries to balance technical merit, management approach, past performance, and cost in selecting a contractor. Focusing on just one of these factors can lead to systems of high quality but unreasonable price or attractively priced systems of dubious quality. The process is not dissimilar to purchasing police cars. A fleet of Mercedes just costs too much to own and operate while a fleet of Yugos will not be on the road long enough to provide adequate service, even though you'll have cash left after the purchase.

The following list is a recommended sequence of steps for source selection:

1. Select evaluation criteria and relative weights
2. Document process in a handbook or handout
3. Establish team
4. Distribute handbook
5. Produce forms
6. Perform evaluation (see next section for outline of process)
7. Recommend winner to source selection authority
8. Select and notify successful vendor

Source Selection—Evaluation Process

The evaluators should perform the following steps at a minimum:

- Contracts checks for mandatory Ts & Cs, page counts to limit sections of the proposal to a readable number, and so on.
- Management and tech teams verify all mandatory requirements—biometric specifics.
- Rated requirements are compared to the standards and scored—results must be well documented.
- Cost team evaluates cost criteria for accuracy and reasonableness—results must be integrated with management and technical evaluations for a complete picture.
- Weighted values are computed and significant comments are documented—for the legal record.
- Source Selection Board evaluates results and recommends winner to Source Selection Official (SSO). SSO makes decision.

It often seems like all of the energy spent in getting to the award of a contract means the hard part is behind you. Unfortunately, the second challenge—managing the contract—brings a whole new set of challenges. Keep firmly in mind that you are paying to have something unique built and that means it is likely that you, the users, and the vendor have different images of the finished product in your minds. The rule of thumb is that the value of written documentation and structured design reviews cannot be overemphasized.

Chapter 10

Biometric Standards

By Jeff Stapleton

In general terms, a *standard* is a published document, developed by a recognized authority, which defines a set of policies and practices, technical or security requirements, techniques or mechanisms, or describes some other abstract concept or model. Many standards and many recognized (and not so recognized) authorities exist. Some authorities are formal in nature and have obtained worldwide acceptance as a standards body, others are more informal, and still others are relegated to private consortia. Specifically, biometric standards are published documents (or works in progress) that define requirements, provide technical specifications, or establish common file formats for the interchange of biometric information between two or more authentication systems.

Biometric Implementation

Several fundamental processes must be taken into consideration when biometric technology is integrated into an application as the authentication mechanism. Figure 10-1 shows the relationship between a typical application for biometric verification, consisting of Data Collection, Signal Processing, Matching, Decision and Storage.

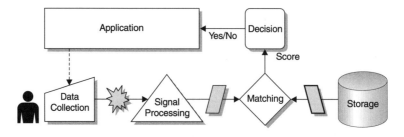

Figure 10-1 Biometric authentication processes

The application initiates the following series of biometric processes:

1. The Data Collection process, which captures the individual's biometric data using a physical biometric reader (for example, a fingerprint scanner, an iris or facial camera, or a microphone) and sends the unprocessed biometric data (shown by the irregular shape) to Signal Processing.

2. Signal Processing refines the unprocessed biometric data and sends the biometric sample (shown by the parallelogram) to the Matching process.

3. The Matching process compares the biometric sample with the individual's template and sends a Score to the Decision process.

4. The Decision process, shown separately from the application in this example, determines whether the Score is above or below some preestablished thresholds, and it sends the final Yes or No to the Application.

Biometric standards should enable high-level interoperability of the Data Collection and Storage processes, and provide a common approach to securing a biometric authentication system, independent of the underlying biometric technology. Other biometric standards should enable lower-level interoperability of Signal Processing and Match within similar types of biometric technology. The development of biometric standards is well underway in the U.S. with both formal and informal organizations, and, in fact, several American National Standards have already been published. Internationally, lesser progress has been made, but the United States is attempting to lead the way.

Formal Standards Organizations

The term "standard" often means different things to different people, depending on their predisposed viewpoints of technology. Standardization processes also differ from one organization to another. The formal term for a *standard* is a document developed by consensus and approved through a public review process by a national or international accredited organization. One such well-established organization is the International Organization for Standardization, or ISO.

International Organization for Standardization (ISO)

Many people are confused by the false assumption that ISO is an acronym, which it isn't. According to the ISO web site (www.iso.ch) the organization name "ISO" is a word derived from the Greek "isos" meaning "equal," which is the root of the prefix "iso-" that occurs in many terms. Established in 1947, ISO currently hosts over 150 member bodies active in over 200 technical committees. These committees range from TC1 for Screw Threads to TC215 for Health Informatics. ISO standards are formal in the sense that in each participating member body vote, formal balloting rules are followed and each member body must have a national standards body to represent itself.

The ISO Technical Committee 68 (TC68/SC2)

The ISO Technical Committee 68 for Banking, Securities, And Other Financial Services (www.tc68.org) has established Subcommittee 2 (TC68/SC2) to address Security Management and General Banking Operations for the international financial services industry. This subcommittee is considering developing a standard for the management and security of biometric information.

ISO has also established a Joint Technical Committee (JTC1) with the International Electrotechnical Commission (IEC) to address information technology standards (www.JTC1.org). JTC1 has over three dozen subcommittees, including the following three subcommittees that are also looking at biometric standards.

ISO/IEC JTC1 Subcommittee 17 (JTC1/SC17)

This subcommittee focuses on Identification Documents, and has several working groups developing standards for passports, international driver's licenses, and smart cards.

ISO/IEC JTC1 Subcommittee 27 (JTC1/SC27)

This subcommittee focuses on Information Security, and has established a liaison relationship with both TC68/SC2 and JTC1/SC37 to coordinate the development of security standards regarding the use of biometric authentication systems.

ISO/IEC JTC1 Subcommittee 37 (JTC1/SC37)

This subcommittee was established in 2002 for the standardization of generic biometric technologies to support interoperability and data interchange between applications and systems. Generic biometric standards include common file formats; application programming interfaces; biometric templates; template protection techniques; and related application/implementation profiles, as well as methodologies for conformity assessment.

American National Standards Institute (ANSI)

In the United States, the central standards body is the American National Standards Institute (ANSI). According to the ANSI web site (www.ansi.org), ANSI itself does not develop American National Standards. Instead, ANSI facilitates development by establishing consensus among qualified organizations. ANSI ensures that its guiding principles of consensus, due process, and openness are followed by its accredited organizations. Of the more than 150 accredited standards bodies, two important organizations for biometrics are the Accredited Standards Committee X9 Incorporated for the Financial Services Industry and the International Committee for Information Technology Standards (INCITS).

The X9 Committee

The X9 Committee is the United States Technical Advisory Group (TAG) to TC68/SC2 and currently has four subcommittees:

- X9A focuses on Retail Banking.
- X9B focuses on Check Processing.
- X9D focuses on Securities.
- X9F focuses on Information and Data Security.

X9F has five active working groups:

- X9F1 deals with Cryptographic Tools, and has developed several digital signature and encryption algorithm standards.
- X9F3 deals with Cryptographic Protocols.
- X9F4 deals with Application Security. The X9F4 working group developed the American National Standard X9.84-2001, Biometric Information Management and Security. This standard was synchronized with the BioAPI Specification (version 1.0) and the NISTIR 6529 Common Biometric Exchange File Format (CBEFF). X9.84 is undergoing revision to enhance its capabilities and align it with other recent biometric standards.
- X9F5 develops application standards for Public Key Infrastructure (PKI) applications.
- X9F6 focuses on Cardholder Authentication for Retail Banking applications.

The International Committee on Information Technology Standards (INCITS)

INCITS has almost three dozen Technical Committees, addressing such topics as computer media formats, computer languages, and multimedia protocols. Many of the Technical Committees are also U.S. TAGs to various subcommittees in JTC1.

The B10 Technical Committee The B10 Technical Committee on Identification Cards and Related Devices is the U.S. TAG to JTC1/SC17. B10 was developing a new ANSI standard for Driver's License and Identification (DL/ID) that supported the use of biometrics and referred to the X9.84 standard for security.

However, opposition to the requirements for Track 3 magnetic stripe data and two-dimensional bar codes (currently the retail banking industry uses Track 1 or Track 2 and one-dimensional bar codes) caused the DL/ID standard to fail its initial ballot in 2001. The ANSI ballot process requires that such issues be resolved and, if needed, might necessitate changing the DL/ID standard. Apparently, these issues weren't successfully resolved and the standard seems to have disappeared from the B10 work list. Meanwhile, another version of the same document has been published by the American Association of Motor Vehicle Administrators (AAMVA) that served as the B10 Secretariat. The legal disposition of the original DL/ID standard and its copyright with the AAMVA have been put in question.

The purpose of the AAMVA DL/ID Standard is to provide a uniform means to identify issuers and holders of driver's license cards within the U.S. and Canada. The standard specifies identification information on driver's license and ID card applications. In the high-capacity technologies, such as bar codes, integrated circuit cards, and optical memory, the AAMVA standard employs international standard application coding to make additional applications possible on the same card. The standard specifies minimum requirements for presenting human-readable identification information, including the format and data content of identification in the magnetic stripe, the bar code, integrated circuit cards, optical memories, and digital imaging.

The AAMVA DL/ID standard specifies a format for fingerprint minutiae data that would be readable across state and province boundaries for driver's licenses. DL/ID-2000 is intended to be compatible with the BioAPI Specification and the Common Biometric Exchange File Format (CBEFF) specification. The standard also refers to the X9.84 standard for guidelines regarding the secure management of biometric information.

The M1 Technical Committee on Biometrics Established in 2002, M1 is the U.S. TAG to JTC1/SC37. It has since published ANSI/INCITS 358-2002 BioAPI Specification (version 1.1), which was adopted from the BioAPI Consortium. M1 continues to foster new work items.

Informal Standards Organizations

Informal standards organizations are typically self-defined groups. They frequently are technology focused and might publish a technology "specification" versus a formal standard. Although often vital and well accepted by a given industry or market, these groups are not accredited or recognized by formal standards organizations. Furthermore, the membership and balloting rules will vary from group to group. Many such examples exist, including the Internet Engineering Task Force (IETF) and the Word Wide Web (W3C) Consortium.

The BioAPI Consortium

BioAPI was formed in 1998 to develop a widely available and widely accepted Application Programming Interface (API) that would serve for various biometric technologies and vendors. Unification efforts resulted in a single industry standard for biometrics, in part, because two separate groups joined forces with the BioAPI Consortium. The BAPI group folded efforts into BioAPI in December 1998. The HA-API group merged with BioAPI in March 1999 and all further work following the HA-API version 2 specification was folded into the BioAPI Specification.

Version 1.0 of the BioAPI Specification was approved by the membership and published in March 2000.

Version 1.1 of the specification and a reference implementation was released in March 2001, and version 1.1 was submitted to the INCITS M1 Technical Committee in January 2002.

The Biometric Consortium (BC)

The Biometric Consortium serves as the United States government's focal point for research, development, test, evaluation, and application of biometric-based personal identification/verification technology. The BC developed the CBEFF, which was published in cooperation with the National Institute for Standards and Technology (NIST) as NISTIR 6529 in January 2001.

Since that time, the Biometric Consortium created the Biometric Interoperability, Performance, and Assurance Working Group to broaden the utilization and acceptance of biometric technologies, and to facilitate and encourage further exchange of information and collaborative efforts between users and private industry. The Biometric Consortium has essentially become an incubator for new work items to INCITS M1.

OASIS

The Organization for the Advancement of Structured Information Standards (OASIS) is a not-for-profit, global consortium that drives the development, convergence, and adoption of e-business standards. OASIS boasts over 500 companies and individual members in over 100 countries. The primary focus of OASIS is geared toward the adoption of Extensible Markup Language (XML) implementations, including the XML Common Biometric Format (XCBF) Technical Committee.

The XCBF Technical Committee is defining a common set of XML encodings in accordance to the NISTIR 6529 CBEFF and with the security schema defined in ANS X9.84-2001, Biometrics Information Management and Security.

Standards Development

In 1993, the existing biometric standards were focused on the use of fingerprints that were part of the Automated Fingerprint Identification System (AFIS) for law enforcement. Some of the earlier documents include the following standards:

- American National Standard for Information Systems, Data Format for the Interchange of Fingerprint Information, ANSI/NIST – Computer System Laboratory (CSL) 1-1993

- Criminal Justice Information Services, WSQ Gray-Scale Fingerprint Image Compression Specification, 1993

In 1995, a Mugshot and Facial Image Standards Workshop was held to discuss issues related to the capture and interchange of mugshot or facial image data. The workshop expanded the scope to include Scar, Mark, and Tattoo (SMT) information and agreed to expand the ANSI/NIST-CSL 1-1993 standard to include a specific logical record structure for processing mugshot, facial, and SMT image data. The National Institute for Standards and Technology (NIST) revised its earlier 1993 standard and published a newer standard in 1997:

American National Standard for Information Systems, Data Format for the Interchange of Fingerprint, Facial & SMT Information, ANSI/ NIST – Information Technology Laboratory (ITL) 1a-1997   In September 1998, another Fingerprint Data Interchange Workshop was held that revised, redesignated, and consolidated ANSI/NIST-CSL 1-1993 and ANSI/ NIST-ITL 1a-1997. The newer standard specifies a common format to be used to exchange fingerprint, facial, scars, mark, and tattoo identification data effectively across jurisdictional lines or between dissimilar systems made by different manufacturers. NIST published the document as NIST Special Publication SP 500-245.

ANSI/NIST-ITL 1-2000 and NIST Special Publication SP 500-245   Over the course of the next several years, newer biometric technology became commercially available, including real-time fingerprint verification and identification, and many other biometrics, such as facial recognition, voice recognition, retinal and iris scanning, hand geometry, keystroke analysis, and many others too numerous to mention. Each vendor created proprietary algorithms and unique application programming interfaces (APIs) with similar but different functions and parameters. The biometric vendors soon realized this proliferation of APIs only slowed the adoption of biometric technology and a common approach was necessary, so application programmers and system integrators would only need to adopt a single API. The BioAPI Consortium was formed in 1998 and published an industry specification in March 2000: BioAPI Specification, version 1.0, 2000.

At around the same time the BioAPI Consortium began its work, two other initiatives began, one led by NIST and another by the Accredited Standard Committee X9 (ASC X9) to develop other biometric standards. All three organizations—the BioAPI Consortium, the Biometric Consortium, and ASC X9—cooperated in the development of their various standards.

In 1999, the Information Technology Laboratory (ITL) of NIST and the Biometric Consortium sponsored a workshop to discuss the potential for reaching industry consensus in a common fingerprint template format. As a result of the workshop, the participants agreed to develop a technology-neutral biometric file format to facilitate handling different biometric types, versions, and biometric data structures in a common way. Working in cooperation with the BioAPI Consortium and ASC X9, NIST published its report in January 2001: NISTIR 6529, Common Biometric Exchange File Format (CBEFF), 2001.

Meanwhile, the price of biometric technology was becoming more affordable and its reliability was increasing such that the financial industry determined an X9 security standard for biometric was needed. The new work item was assigned to the X9F4 working group in early 1999. The resulting X9.84 standard successfully completed its ballot in December 2000 and was finally published in March 2001:

American National Standard X9.84-2001 Biometric Information Management and Security   X9.84 defines the requirements for managing and securing biometric information (for example, fingerprint, iriscan, voiceprint) for use in the financial industry (for example, customer identification, employee verification). Furthermore, the standard identifies techniques (for example, digital signatures, encryption) to provide integrity and maintain privacy of biometric data. The standard also provides a comprehensive set of control objectives to validate a biometric system, suitable for use by a professional audit practitioner.

The standard purposely avoids any technology or vendor-specific issues, such as countermeasure technology that might test for liveliness of the individual. This is considered part of the vendor's "value add."

The standard also identifies the International Biometrics Industry Association (IBIA) as the Registration Authority for Object Identifiers (OID) intended to be kept synchronized with the BioAPI Format Owners and Format Types values. In March 2002, there were 13 registered CBEFF format owners; at present (October 2002) there are approximately 21 registered format owners. (For more information, go to http://www.ibia.org/cbeffregistration.htm.)

The BioAPI Consortium continued to refine its work and a revised specification was published a year later in 2001.

BioAPI Specification, version 1.1, 2001   The interplay of the three standards is rather subtle. The BioAPI specification defines an API that provides a set of high-level abstractions (for example, Enroll, Verify, Identify), a set of primitive functions, (for example, Capture, Process, Match, Create Template), and a common data structure called the Biometric Information Record (BIR) used by an application as the input and output to the Biometric Service Provider (BSP).

The X9.84 standard defines a set of mandatory requirements to manage biometric information securely, provides optional techniques that satisfy the management and security requirements, and offers a rich set of Biometric Validation Control Objectives for use by a qualified professional to assess the compliance of an biometric authentication system. The techniques in X9.84 define a Biometric Object that is compatible with the BIR, but significant differences exist in the actual data representation and features of the standards:

1. The BioAPI Specification defines an API and the underlying function calls, whereas X9.84 does not.

2. The BioAPI Consortium provides a Reference Implementation, whereas X9.84 does not.

3. X9.84 focuses on security, whereas the BioAPI Specification does not explicitly address security.

4. X9.84 provides a set of Biometric Validation Control Objective to assess compliance, whereas the BioAPI Specification does not address this issue.

5. The X9.84 Biometric Object is a variable-length data structure defined using Abstract Syntax Notation One (ASN.1) and some of the same data fields are optional, whereas the BioAPI's BIR is a fixed-length data structure defined in 8-bit octets and all the data fields are mandatory.

6. X9.84 was synchronized with the BioAPI Specification Version 1.0 and is, therefore, slightly out of date with ANSI/INCITS 358-2002 BioAPI Specification (version 1.1).

Figure 10-2 depicts the relationship among the three standards. The three dark-shaded boxes in the center and the right of the figure show the BioAPI components consisting of the BioAPI Framework, the Biometric Service Provider, and the Biometric Information Record (BIR). The two shaded boxes show the X9.84 components consisting of the X9.84 layer and its Biometric Object. The single background box shows how CBEFF recognizes both the BioAPI's BIR and the X9.84 Biometric Object as instances of a Common Biometric Exchange File Format. The single box to the left side of the figure is the Cryptographic Service Provider (CSP) module that X9.84 assumes is available.

The BioAPI Specification is missing an interface between the BioAPI Framework and CSP, and is, therefore, not compatible with the security requirements in X9.84. Therefore, using the standards as they are today, an implementer would most likely layer the X9.84 security on top of the BioAPI Framework (as shown), and the cryptographic security functions in the X9.84 layer would need to interface directly to a CSP, or an implementer could add a CSP interface to the BSP.

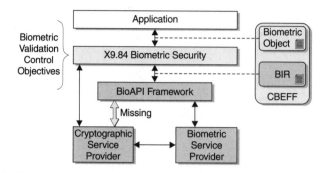

Figure 10-2   X9.84, BioAPI, and CBEFF: The Relationship of Three Standards

Following the publication of X9.84 in early 2001, ASC X9 (United States national standards body) submitted the new ANSI standard ISO TC68/SC2 (international standards body) for a fast-track ballot as Draft International Standard (DIS) 21352. Eight countries (Canada, Denmark, Finland, France, Germany, Italy, the Netherlands, and Sweden) of the twelve voting member bodies of SC2 voted negative, citing two repetitive comments:

■ The voting member body disapproved of the ISO fast-track process. The normal standards process is a five-stage approval program consisting of a working draft, a committee draft, a draft international standard, a final draft international standard, and, finally, an international standard. The member bodies felt the standard beginning at the DIS stage would not allow any technical issues to be addressed or resolved and, therefore, wanted the full five-stage development program.

■ The voting member body felt the biometric standard was not specific to the financial services industry and, therefore, that its five-stage development should be assigned to ISO/IEC JTC1/SC17. This position was further advanced by none other than the SC17 chair, who issued a letter encouraging all SC2 voting members to vote negative on the DIS 21352 ballot.

As noted earlier, because ASC X9 is the U.S. TAG to ISO TC68, the submission of X9.84 to TC68/SC2 was a natural choice and, in fact, ASC X9 does not have a relationship to any of the JTC1 subcommittees. Consequently, ASC X9 has not, and for all practical purposes, cannot submit the X9.84 standard to any other international body.

To promote the standardization of biometric technology further, INCITS established the M1 Technical Committee in November 2001. As its first item of work, INCITS balloted and published ANSI/INCITS 358-2002 BioAPI Specification (version 1.1).

The issue with the failed DIS 21352 ballot did not go unnoticed in the ISO community and, in July 2002, the new Subcommittee 37 on Biometrics was established by JTC1 and M1 was designated as the U.S. TAG to SC37.

X9.84 Standard

Meanwhile, ASC X9 announced in July 2002 an early revision of the X9.84 standard. Not scheduled for revision until 2004, ASC X9 has the goal to prepare an update of this key standard—X9.84—by the close of this year. ASC X9 is the national standards-setting body for the financial services industry and is accredited by ANSI.

"Since its publication in March 2001, the ASC X9 standard has been widely accepted by the financial community both in the U.S. and internationally," said Richard Sweeney, Chairman of X9F, the group responsible for developing and managing the biometric standard, X9.84. "The standard posts requirements, techniques, and interoperability to securely managed biometric information that may be sent over open networks like the Internet and World Wide Web. The X9.84 is most suitable for use in applications where small message size and efficient encodings are need, like with smart cards, wireless, and remote devices," explained Sweeney.

Biometrics involves the use of such personal items as fingerprints, iris scans, and voice prints to help secure transactions. For the financial industry, biometric information provides help in identifying customers and the verification of transactions.

When first developed, the standard—X9.84—relied on cryptographic messaging that did not include today's fast-growing XML-language applications. Since that time, biometric application development experiences have shown the need for tamper-resistant and tamper-evident security module solutions compatible with new technology. The security requirements for these types of devices are not addressed in X9.84.

The revision of X9.84 will align the standard with the needed formats that promote interoperable exchange among all standards necessary for biometric transactions. Additional requirements will be added to the revised X9.84 to offer support for tamper-resistant and tamper-evident security modules.

The X9F working group is seeking technical participation to ensure successful completion and adoption of the ASC X9.84 standard. Others interested in the revision process can contact X9 at www.x9.org.

Cooperation is the key to any successful standard-setting process. "The original standard was developed in conjunction with other organizations, including the BioAPI Consortium, the National Institute of Standards and Technology (NIST), Information Technology Laboratory's Common Biometric Exchange File Format (CBEFF) imitative, and the International Biometric Industry Association (IBIA). It is hoped that revisions will be conducted with the cooperation of these same organizations, as well as any new groups that want to contribute.

ASC X9 has expressed its intent to resubmit the revised X9.84 standard to ISO TC68/SC2 as a new work item for the full five-stage ballot program, in cooperation with a similar new proposed work item in ISO/IEC JTC1/SC27. No other ANSI biometric standards have been published since February 2002; however, M1, in cooperation with the Biometric Consortium, continues to generate new work items relating to biometrics, including the following:

- Augmentation of NISTIR 6529—A Common Biometric Exchange File Format (CBEFF)

- New work item on Biometric Performance Testing and Reporting

- New work item on Application Profiles—Interoperability and Data Interchange—Biometrics-Based Verification and Identification of Transportation Workers

- Proposed new work item Template Protection and Usage

- Proposed new work item Application Profile for Point-of-Sale Biometric Verification and Identification

- Proposed new work item Information Technology—Iris Image Interchange Format

- Proposed new work item Information Technology—Finger Image-Based Interchange Format

Clearly, the days of proprietary biometric solutions, inoperable data formats, and nonstandard message protocols are quickly drawing to a close. With the establishment of the INCITS M1 Technical Committee on Biometrics, its influence in the newly formed ISO/IEC JTC1/SC37, the partnership between JTC1/SC37 and JTC1/SC27, and the liaison relationships between JTC1/SC27 and ISO TC68/SC2, and, finally, the influence of ASC X9 in TC68/SC2 dynamic worldwide synergy has hopefully been created that should usher biometric technology into a new era.

The evolution of biometric standards covers the wide range of biometric technology specific to generic requirements and techniques. Table 10-1 provides a quick guide to the current suite of biometric standards.

Clearly, the earlier standards dealt with technology-specific topics, particularly fingerprint technology due to law enforcement efforts. Early standards also proceeded widespread adoption of digital acquisition techniques. Consequently, most of the image quality standards assumed that digital scans were created from ink prints or photographs, not from live digital prints. With the turn of the century, standards began addressing multiple biometric technologies, but were still focused on low-level biometric processes. The more recent standards are generic and intend to be applicable for any biometric technology. They also deal with higher level issues, such as the management and security of biometric data.

Biometric Standard	Sensor Traits and/or Data Quality	Compression	Feature Representation	Exchange Format	Feature Functionality	Data Management and Security
ANSI/ NIST-CSL 1-1993	fingerprint	fingerprint	fingerprint	fingerprint		
FBI WSQ 1993 Image Compression	fingerprint	fingerprint		fingerprint		
CJIS- RS-0010 FBI Appendix F & G	fingerprint	fingerprint		fingerprint		
ANSI/NIST ITL 1a-1997	fingerprint facial	fingerprint	fingerprint	fingerprint		
ANSI/NIST ITL 1-2000 SP 500-245	fingerprint facial	fingerprint	fingerprint	fingerprint		
AAMVA DL/ID-2000	fingerprint facial hand signature	fingerprint facial hand signature	fingerprint			
BioAPI-2000 Specification Version 1.1					generic	
NISTIR 6529-2001 Common Biometric Exchange File Format				generic		
ANS X9.84-2001 Biometric Information Management and Security				generic		generic
ANSI/ INCITS 358-2002 BioAPI Specification Version 1.1					generic	

Table 10-1　Quick Guide to Current Biometric Standards

State of the Industry

Most of the biometric vendors and other interested parties have been focusing on gaining compliance to the INCITS 358 BioAPI Specification over the last several years, with one notable and notorious exception. Microsoft announced its adoption of BAPI prior to the publication of the BioAPI Consortium's version 1.1 specification and of the INCITS 358 standard. Microsoft has not publicly announced its biometric technology strategy. Furthermore, no formal certification program is in place to verify compliance with INCITS 358, so most vendors' claims are based on trust.

Many of the biometric vendors are only now looking at the X9.84 standard for security, although a few have already begun to implement security methods to protect biometric information. On the other hand, many federal and state government requirements reference both the INCITS 358 and X9.84 standards, and some even require CBEFF compatibility. Regarding compliance, the X9.84 standard does provide control objectives to validate the deployment of a biometric authentication system. To date, no deployed biometric systems have been examined; however, several biometric vendors have had assessments of their biometric products, with the goal of passing an X9.84 examination sometime in the near future.

Microsoft has been silent on the subject of biometric security; however, not all hope is lost. Microsoft currently requires that a Certification Authority (CA) that wants to have its root public key certificate included in Internet Explorer, must undergo a WebTrust for CA audit, whose PKI control objectives are based on the American National Standard X9.79-2000, PKI Policy and Practice Framework. The X9.84 biometric control objectives are based on the previous work in the X9.79 PKI control objectives.

The Future of Biometric Standards

Biometric technology is traversing the typical acceptance curve that any significant technology has similarly undergone: through the early adopters, up the slope of preposterous hype, down into the trough of despair, and, finally, crawling up the slope of enlightenment. The early adopters were historically the law enforcement market segment, which has now created legacy systems that are understandably noncompliant to the newer biometric standards. The marketing hype consisted of outrageous claims that biometrics were infallible and the next best thing that generated numerous start-up companies. The economic failure of many start ups and the inevitable merger that accompanies most high-tech markets have now passed through the trough of despair.

The generation and adoption of the newer standards by the biometric vendors has started the industry up the slope of enlightenment and will make the integrator's and implementer's development easier. In turn, this will result in more deployed biometric systems that eventually will undergo security assessments and compliance examinations.

Already the financial services industry is beginning to migrate its numerous biometric pilots to production systems and although the healthcare industry is launching pilot projects, it lags several years behind the financial industry. The United States Government has been conducting biometric pilots for many years, and the Department of Defense, with congressional support, has established the Biometrics Fusion Center with a primary mission of biometric testing and evaluation. Furthermore, as more international standards on biometrics are established, the U.S. influence will migrate to the world and large corporations will begin worldwide implementation of biometric authentication systems.

Chapter **11**

Biometric Testing and Evaluation

By Nicholas Orlans

Why test biometric systems? Manufacturers, vendors, and integrators are eager to explain the benefits and virtues of their products. They will tell you how well the products work, how easy it is to use them, and all the different environments they can be used. Such information is a good first step toward understanding products and services, as well as scenarios for their intended operational use.

Software vendors and system integrators are generally quite good at producing glossy papers with details on product features, platform specifications, and compatible devices—and, of course, performance claims. And, as industry authentication solutions increasingly involve integration of more than one biometric, once exclusively vertical markets are now merging or depicting each other's technology as, perhaps, complementary. Most vendors make a diligent effort to provide balanced, relevant information about biometric products to the community. However, for a consumer attempting to compare products or understand relative performance in a meaningful way, the information is often hard to sort through. Information from different vendors and sources, is likely to use different notations, and almost always is presented differently.

Even under ideal circumstances, vendor information is seldom complete, fully objective, or meaningful for all environments. In the worst cases, vender information can be little more than a series of unverified claims. Anyone looking to apply the promise of biometrics is faced with challenging and costly decisions, particularly if the performance of their systems affects the security of critical resources or public safety. Where do they turn for honest information and what should they do?

In a competitive market environment such as we have, the majority of vendors have neither the resources nor the incentive to conduct elaborate performance tests themselves. From a marketing perspective, most software vendors become cautious when the subject of testing is before them. They don't necessarily *like* to be measured. Product testing results can damage sales and harm reputations if a product performs poorly. Testing can also serve to acknowledge that other companies with similar products have equal footing. Nonetheless, independent testing is the ultimate means consumers have to gauge the maturity of products and objectively to understand how they perform under different conditions or relative to each other. At a minimum, no one in government or industry should purchase or deploy biometrics systems before considering the evaluation methods and reports discussed in this section.

Who Tests and Who Benefits?

Solid, repeatable testing is expensive. It requires careful planning, data collection, execution, and documentation. Everyone wants the answers, but few have the resources and patience to produce them. For the sake of credibility, evaluations must be organized and conducted by an independent party. Because of the high cost of obtaining data and tools for testing, the number of comprehensive independent test projects continues to be relatively limited. The training and expertise necessary for testing is also a major limiting factor. Only a relatively few organizations are motivated, equipped, and capable of planning, funding, staffing, and performing independent tests.

Who Tests?

Government organizations and universities, as well as some government laboratories and research centers, are often in the best position to orchestrate or participate in testing programs. The following discusses an overview of the history of biometric testing and recent noteworthy test programs. The overview is by no means exhaustive, but it will help familiarize the reader with the state of biometric testing.

One of the first independent assessments of a biometric system was done in 1977 by the MITRE Corporation (Fejfar and Haberman 1977). The seven-page engineering report describes systems for signature and voice recognition that were prototypes at the time. The intended use, experimental procedures, timing statistics, and observed error rates were presented, along with discussion and analysis of how multiple biometric decisions can be combined (at the binary, accept or reject, decision level). In 1980, the RAND Corporation published an excellent assessment of a prototype keystroke dynamics system. By the mid 1980s, the NIST speech group established a test program for voice processing technologies (including speaker verification). In 1996, Dr. Jonathan Phillips, a leading biometrics authority, conducted facial-recognition algorithm tests—FacE REcognition Technology (FERET) (Phillips, Rauss, and Der 1996)—under the auspices of the Army Research Laboratory (ARL). The FERET tests are significant and are also mentioned later in this section. The National Institute of Standards and Technology (NIST) has supported testing by publishing tools, methods, and results. NIST has also helped reduce entry costs by compiling, maintaining, and distributing data sets to include faces, fingerprints, and voice utterances. (For more information, go to http://www.nist.gov/speech.)

University research and test programs have made major intellectual contributions to biometric testing. Notably the National Biometric Test Center was established in 1994 at San Jose State University. Under the direction of Dr. James Wayman, the center has been active in testing and exploring biometric systems and sciences. In 2000, the University of Bologna, Italy, in conjunction with San Jose State University and Michigan State University, conducted Fingerprint Verification Tests (FVT). (For more information, go to http://bias.csr.unibo.it/fvc2000.)

The University of Bologna has also developed a Synthetic Fingerprint Generator (SfinGe) that can be used to rapidly create large databases of fingerprint images. Large biometric data sets are costly and time-consuming to collect, and for testing purposes, privacy concerns can also be an issue. (For more information, go to http://bias.csr.unibo.it/research/biolab/sfinge.html.) A synthetic generator that can produce 10,000 realistic fingerprints in about ten hours is noteworthy. Collecting that number of prints from volunteers is a much longer and more costly undertaking. Synthetic generators for faces exist for nonbiometrics applications but, as yet, have not been applied to biometric testing. Existing synthetic generators for face and voice could play an increased role in biometric testing. Generators can support isolated, parametrically driven feature testing and help substantiate statistical models for large data sets. Synthetic generators for irises and other biometrics could be developed and could likely find niches in future testing.

Who Benefits?

The short answer is this: everyone benefits. Testing and evaluation of biometrics seek to advance the science and state of the art; however, such testing also clearly has an element of *Consumer Reports* to it as well. Naturally, this information is of high value to government purchasing programs and to small industry consumers alike. In addition to informing consumers, the testing of biometric systems gives the development community vital insights on how next-generation products and systems might be enhanced. Integrators, researchers, and developers rely on test results to help them remove weaknesses or to improve certain features. Developers are interested in both what failed and the characteristics of how it failed. For example, did the product fail suddenly (system crash or deadlock) or did it degrade gradually (increased errors as a function of some variable, such as distance). Testing and test results are also valuable to integrators. The information helps them appropriately deploy, calibrate, and operate systems. Security objectives are far more likely to be met if systems are carefully fielded into known, tested environments. For vendors, consumers, and integrators alike, disciplined testing is the final word on characterizing the behavior of biometric products and systems.

The Three Bears Principle

Dr. P. J. Phillips uses the "three bears" principle to introduce audiences to testing concepts contained in his face recognition tests (Phillips 2000). The basic idea of three bears testing is if products are to be tested, the most informative tests to run are those that are neither too easy nor too hard. The tests should be somewhere in the middle or "just right." If a test is too easy, all products pass; if a test is too hard, none is able to pass. The desired "just right" happy medium is achieved when test objectives are chosen to produce a range of results so distinctions can be drawn between products. The most valuable tests are always those that reveal distinctions or separation between test subjects. Of course, the relative scale of the separation must be also considered in the context of an application. As has happened in recent pilots and field tests, application performance expectations can fall outside the range of meaningful product separation. When this is the case, the situation is similar to having a test that is too hard. Even if one product is observed to outperform others under certain test conditions, all products might fail with more or less equal misery if the new target application is too hard (or otherwise inappropriate).

Best Practices for Biometrics Testing

Diversity and originality, while desirable attributes in the workplace, do not always contribute to the greater cause of testing biometric systems. Currently, a wide variety of testing and evaluation activities exist, ranging from small PC reviews to multimillion dollar test programs. The differences in methods and purposes can, at times, produce seemingly conflicting results, claims, and conclusions. Diverse methods are hard to combine, compare, or contrast. They generally fail to capture repeatable characteristics accurately and might prompt uninitiated audiences into drawing false conclusions.

"The Best Practices for Biometrics Testing" is a canonical paper that outlines, as the title suggests, the best practices for evaluating and testing biometric systems. Published in 2002 by Her Majesty's Communications-Electronics Security Group (CESG) in the United Kingdom, "Best Practices" was authored by an impressive international working group of biometrics experts, including Dr. James Wayman and Dr. Tony Mansfield of the United Kingdom's National Physical Laboratory. The authors make a convincing case for the use of common vocabulary, methods, and measures for presenting, and, hence, comparing test results. Common terminology and reporting enables sharing of test data, methods, and results across universities, government laboratories, and industry. The paper also summarizes common types of testing and outlines the general rationale and criteria that should be considered. Salient performance criteria for testing and evaluation of biometric systems are discussed in the next section. (For more information about "Best Practices for Biometric Testing," go to http://www.cesg.gov.uk/technology/biometrics/index.htm.)

Testing Criteria

The common test criteria used to characterize biometric systems are outlined here. These criteria are based on those presented in "Best Practices," and they are increasingly reflected in community dialog. The concepts behind the criteria form the language by which we understand, explain, and compare biometric systems.

Match Decision Accuracy

It should be no surprise that most biometric testing centers around measuring the correctness, or accuracy, of system decisions—determining experimentally how often they are right. Biometric systems all ultimately produce a binary decision output. By definition, the output is yes or no (accept or reject). For each output, a corresponding error can occur. These are classically referred to as type I and type II errors. *Type I errors* occur when the positive hypothesis (true condition) is incorrectly rejected—the system should have said yes, but instead returned no. *Type II errors* are when the negative hypothesis (false condition) is incorrectly accepted—the system should have said no, but instead returned yes.

Biometric testing literature discusses accuracy in terms of the likelihood of these types of errors; however, current terminology refers to type I errors as the False Reject Rate (FRR) and type II errors as the False Accept Rate (FAR). To keep the biometric cognoscenti on their toes, a third notation is also used. FRR is sometimes called False Non-Match Rate (FNMR) and, likewise, FAR is sometimes referred to as False Match Rate (FMR). (And to completely confuse anyone remotely interested in biometric testing, but to make our list of error-rate terms complete, False Alarm Rate is sometimes used for False Accept Rate.)

The FRR and FAR for a biometric system always depend on the match threshold and are always inversely related. The *match threshold* is an empirically determined value such that all match scores greater than or equal to this value are considered positive matches for a given system. As the match threshold is increased, it becomes less likely an imposter will be falsely accepted. At the same time, however, the likelihood that valid users will be falsely rejected increases. For a given system, it is not possible to reduce both error rates simultaneously. The improvement of one is obtained only at the cost of the other.

Depending on the purpose of the system, one type of error might be preferred over the other. The best setting is a result of balancing user convenience (few false rejects) with security objectives (few false accepts), and *carefully* considering the costs and risks of each error type in context.

Crossover Error Rate

Best practices suggest that match decision error rates be presented as plots characterizing the error trade space because the threshold might be varied over its entire range for that system. The relationship between the match rate and the false match rate (or alarm rate) is the system's receiver-operating characteristic (ROC). These are the fundamental plots used in signal detection theory. An example is shown in Figure 11-1. The point where the plot crosses the equal error rate line is its *crossover error rate*. In Figure 11-1, the crossover error rate is 20 percent. In reality, most systems calibrate their match threshold to operate at either end of the curve; however, the crossover error rate is a useful reference point for comparing systems.

Failure to Enroll Rate

The *failure to enroll rate* is the probability that, for whatever reason, an individual is unable to enroll. Good reporting practices should describe the main causes that produced such failures. These might include user injuries, image-quality problems, or positioning problems. Failure to enroll rates for most systems are normally quite low. Enrollment problems for large populations tend to result from logistical and programmatic issues more than from isolated "technical difficulties."

Failure to Acquire

The *failure to acquire rate* measures the probability that a system is unable to capture or locate an image. This usually is not a major problem for contact sensors (fingerprints) unless positioning is a factor. This can be an issue for other optical systems, however, such as face systems that are being operated in nonoptimal (noisy) environments. Other contributing causes could include users not being well habitualized from infrequent use and personal injury.

Multiple Attempt Error Rates

Similar to password-based authentication systems, most biometric systems are designed to enable users to make more than one attempt for system access. While the statistical properties of successive password attempts do not necessarily relate to successive biometric-based authentication attempts, a three-

Figure 11-1
Sample
ROC curve

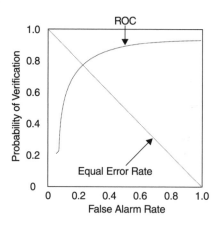

attempt limit is commonly suggested for both. (Security policies seem arbitrary at times, but perhaps baseball's concept of a fair turn at bat is a suitable starting point.) *Multiple-attempt error rates* refers to the inclusion of the effects of a "best of three" (or best of N) decision policy into the fundamental error rates.

User Throughput

User throughput is the number of users that can be processed (or authenticated) per unit time for a given system. User throughput is also expressed in terms of total transaction time for a single user. This includes the time to present the biometric (acquisition time), processing time, and, optionally, might include entry of a PIN or user identifiers. The reporting should indicate minimum, maximum, and average times, and if the time includes other nonbiometric authentication chores (PINS, user identifiers, passwords, card swipes, or tokens). An example of user throughput reporting is shown in the following Table 11-1. The table format and values are from the "Biometric Product Testing Final Report," done by Dr. Tony Mansfield and others (Mansfield 2001).

While isolated transactions that take 15 seconds might be acceptable in some environments, this could be less than ideal for processing a large number of individuals. Understanding user throughput values in light of goals for user convenience and system loading is important. As a point of comparison, passwords take about three to five seconds to enter. Smart cards and proxy cards transactions can be accomplished in approximately one second.

Matching Algorithm Throughput

Matching algorithm throughput is the number of comparisons that can be processed per unit time. Match algorithm throughput is also expressed as the raw execution time for unit quantity, say 1000, biometric comparisons. This metric is most important for systems processing batches of one-to-many matches against a large database. For verification systems, however, matching algorithm throughput times are insignificantly small relative to the time required for presentation, image segmentation, and feature extraction.

Biometric System	Transaction Time (Seconds)			Time Includes Entry of PIN?
	Maximum	Median	Minimum	
Face	15	14	10	Excluded
Fingerprint–Optical	9	8	2	Excluded
Fingerprint–Chip	19	15	9	Excluded
Hand	10	8	4	Included
Iris	12	10	4	Included
Vein	18	16	11	Included
Voice	12	11	10	Excluded

Table 11-1   User Throughput

Performance Differences by User and Attempt Type

These metrics provide a fine-grained view of performance differences on a per-user basis for each attempt type. Statistical evidence exists that users exhibit individual performance differences in match rates and nonmatch rates. A reasonably calibrated system could perform well against most of the population, but a few select users might experience a disproportionate number of false rejects (the goats). Some users are more prone than others to be impersonated (sheep). Others have a higher propensity to impersonate others (wolves). If data is collected on individual performance differences, in theory, the system decision threshold can be adjusted on a per-user basis to compensate for these differences.

Types of Testing

Although not necessarily exclusive or independent of each other, four general families of biometric tests are discussed in this section: algorithm tests, technology tests, scenario tests, and vulnerability tests. One might also hear mention of "biometric pilots" or "field tests." Pilots and field tests are certainly important, however, we will treat them as being somewhat similar to scenario tests. *Pilots* are basically limited deployments that operate on a limited scale in a real-target environment.

Algorithm Testing

Algorithm testing is concerned with understanding and comparing software techniques for acquiring, processing, and comparing biometric data. The primary focus is usually the pattern-matching techniques used for comparing biometric data. These tests study different classification and matching methods, with the goal of evaluating them on efficiency, speed, and performance. However, algorithm testing might also consider related processing capabilities, such as techniques and implementation details on how biometric images are enhanced and segmented—how features are isolated and extracted. Other related support-processing capabilities that affect match performance include signal-processing techniques for quality control and feature enhancement. Last, algorithm tests could also include discussion and analysis on feature selection, describing which features are used, how many are used, and how they are best represented mathematically.

Algorithm tests normally do not involve live human subjects. To assess and compare algorithms in a repeatable fashion, processing prepared data offline is more convenient. A corpus of common test enrollment data is used to establish representative benchmarks for each process being investigated. Even if these data are relatively small, they provide an important basis for the various techniques to be compared meaningfully against each other. If live subjects are used, they tend to be a small group of local volunteers and their role is mostly to support a plausible application context and to help demonstrate the utility of the algorithms.

Technology Testing

Technology tests refer to a family of end-to-end system-level tests or tests of complete software products and devices. These tests are interested in establishing the operating characteristics of the technology and are designed to compare or rate one or more systems under controlled conditions against a similar set of inputs. The FERET tests done by the government are an excellent example of both algorithm and technology testing. Initiated under the ARL in conjunction with the Defense Advanced Research Projects Agency (DARPA) in 1996,[1] and then continued again in 2000.[2] The 1996 FERET tests were algorithm tests, which sought to identify, understand, and compare the most promising software techniques.

The subsequent Face Recognition Vendor Tests in 2000 (FRVT 2000) were technology tests. (For more information, go to http://www.frvt.org/FRVT2000/default.htm.) FRVT 2000 performed an expansive series of technology tests to understand how well the software capabilities (algorithms) have matured into workable products that can be integrated into working systems. Taken together, these tests provide valuable information to characterize the state of the art and the operational range for commercial face recognition. The success of the FERET tests has lead to a recently announced third series of tests: Face Recognition Vendor Test (FRVT) 2002. (For more information, go to http://www.frvt.org/FRVT2002/default.htm.) Under the continued leadership of Dr. Jonathan Phillips (and others), FRVT2002 has involvement or sponsorship from 16 organizations, including defense agencies, federal government, and international partners. Vender participation includes 14 vendors. By comparison, the tests conducted in 2000 were funded by three Department of Defense organizations and had participation from five vendors.

Legal considerations and good business practices are key ingredients for fair and impartial technology testing. All vendors and participants should be clearly informed of stated objectives in advance of testing. Ideally, the test data set should not be known or be available to the test participants before testing. Information on test data typically is a categorical description and an interface specification. And information made available to one participant must be made equally available to everyone. This precludes the possibility (or the perception) that prior knowledge of test data was used to skew results. Test participants should also be fully informed of the intended distribution of any final report, and they should be provided a fair opportunity to review and comment on the

---

[1]   P. J. Phillips, P. Rauss, and S. Der, 1996, "FacE REcognition Technology (FERET) Recognition Algorithm Development and Test Report, ARL-TR-995," United States Army Research Laboratory.

[2]   P. J. Phillips, et al., 2000, "FRVT 2000 Evaluation Report," Department of Defense Counterdrug Technology Development Program Office, http://www.frvt.org/FRVT2000/documents.htm.

findings. Technology testing is impossible to do without cooperation of skilled developers, integrators, and vendors. So, ultimately, the results should help support and accurately describe their achievements.

Scenario Testing

Scenario testing is primarily concerned with the integration of biometric systems into existing business processes and real-world human transactions. A scenario test is the final information point for how well the technology works in the context of the target environment. The target operational environment can be simulated but, if so, it must be as realistic as possible. The objective is to understand and evaluate how the technology impacts workflow *in that environment*. Similar to pilot deployments, ideally, real users and administrators are involved in scenario tests. This serves as early training and generally helps raise overall awareness of the technology. User reactions and comments provide information on usability, human factors, and ultimate acceptance.

For whatever reason, if users don't accept the technology in the proposed scenario, the technology will fall short of its intended benefits. Sometimes, usability factors can be more important than raw performance for certain scenarios, especially if the application has high throughput requirements and a diverse, unpredictable use population. Scenario tests should describe details relevant to the user transactions and capture timing measurements in terms of throughput. This helps identify queuing problems so they can be avoided or accounted for in final installations. Transactions should also be described in light of system purpose and work flow. For example, if the system is for PC login, are login events available to be used only for authentication or does the information also support time and attendance reporting?

Human factors and user acceptance ultimately reflect a prevailing attitude toward the system. Observations on how people use the system in the target environment (and even the occasional complaint) help us relate better to human issues and exceptions, and, more important, force us to consider ways of addressing them. Even if somewhat anecdotal in nature, such observations can reveal areas for improvement or places where small modifications to the environment could have a large impact. For example, simple ergonomic adjustments often improve throughput and user acceptance.

As the environment can be an important part of biometric systems, this information can be captured in the form of facility diagrams. Diagrams are a natural and easy means to communicate quickly the location of biometric devices, and to show how they are approached and used. In the case of cameras, range, lighting, and potential occlusions can also be documented. Conclusions for usability testing could depend heavily on the environment and user population. While we all desire biometrics to be used in nonintrusive, nondiscriminatory ways, these concepts mean different things to different people in different environments.

Vulnerability Testing

Vulnerability tests have the goal of understanding how systems can be defeated or how they fail on their own. While the topic is not new, recently published fingerprint spoof exploits have escalated concerns. No conclusive industry metrics are available on the matter; however, a reasonable assumption is that biometric systems are most susceptible at the sensor level. This is the primary point of interface for humans and the point where biometrics are presented to the system. Replication attacks, or spoofs, can be either impersonation attempts (disguises) or the presentation of bogus artifacts. Other high-level classes of vulnerabilities include database attacks (exchanging or corrupting templates), tampering with threshold settings, and network-based attacks. Network attacks are not necessarily unique to biometrics. They include the usual gambit of eavesdropping, playback, and denial of service (DOS) attacks. Vulnerability testing is the practice of finding weaknesses and exploiting them. Exploits are classified according to type, and estimates are made as to the level of expertise and resources needed by an adversary to take advantage of the various exploits. For example, improved liveness checking is a crucial countermeasure needed to protect systems against replication attacks. Please also refer to Chapter 8 where this topic is discussed in greater detail.

Vulnerability tests also involve statistical studies to assess risks and to estimate the ultimate strength of function for a given system. Strength of function arguments are statistical models developed to define the attack space for the identifier. That is, the probability a suitable identifier can be generated (or manufactured) or a second identifier elsewhere in the population is sufficiently similar (a false accept). Determining the theoretical attack space for a particular biometric trait involves establishing formal definitions on similarity. Unlike passwords that are matched exactly, biometrics matches are approximate. Next, the attack space analysis must model the biometric features and estimate how many distinguishable configurations are possible. This part of the analysis is not well understood for all biometrics, mostly because the matching algorithms are proprietary and standards are not yet available to address feature-level representations. Noteworthy analytical models have been presented for irises and fingerprints (by Dr. John Daugman[3] and Dr. Anil Jain,[4] respectively). However, rigorous theoretical models to describe feature space, distinguishablity measures, and attack spaces for other biometrics remain an open research topic.

---

[3]   J. Daugman, 1994. United States Patent No. 5,291,560 (issued March 1, 1994). Biometric Personal Identification System Based on Iris Analysis, Washington D.C.: United States Government Printing Office.

[4]   Anil Jain, Sharath Pankanti, and Salil Prabhakar, 2001, "On the Individuality of Fingerprints," Michigan State University, IBM Research Center, Digital Persona Inc.

Certification

To many people, the desired outcome of testing and evaluation is certification. A stamp of approval should given to products that pass all the right tests or perform above some minimum standard. And good precedent exists for this expectation within industry and government acquisition programs. Underwriters Laboratories rates and certifies products for fire safety and other performance factors. Their ratings are, in turn, widely used within the manufacturing and construction industries. (For more information, go to http://www.ul.com.) Acquisition programs within the Department of Defense require information assurance products to comply with National Information Assurance Partnership (NIAP) certification. Biometrics, as an enabling technology for information assurance, must look forward to yet more testing to achieve eventual NIAP certification. At present, certification requirements are not published and, hence, no products are certified under this program.

Because of the large number of variables and factors affecting biometrics, we see that testing systems and the conclusions drawn from test results are not always a simple, straightforward process. Test results can be skewed or rendered meaningless if quoted out of context. Care must be taken to understand exactly what is being testing and what is not being tested, who did the testing and why, and under what assumptions and conditions. For all the test types we have discussed, there still can be a number of critical (and potentially expensive) integration and deployment factors that remain out of scope or are not adequately covered in technology or scenario tests. Compliance with emerging standards is also an important factor for government systems yet, to date, standards compliance can't be tested by automated procedures. The community lacks automated test suites and the standards are still shifting somewhat. Manual review, integration trial and error, and vendor claims are currently the only means available to determine if products really comply with standards.

Integration factors include basic platform support, especially the availability of device drivers for different operating systems (OSs). Because many biometric products are relatively new in the commercial market, companies seek to establish market share in the larger PC (Wintel) desktop market first, prior to investing development and support labor to other platforms (UNIX, Linux, or Mac OS). Details surrounding the ease of installation and interoperability with pre-existing user account management tools, such as Active Directory, Novel, or database accounts, can also be an important consideration. Integration of biometrics authentication into environments with diverse OSs, applications, and databases, as typically found in a mid-size company, is nontrivial. Resource management and authorization processes (access control and user permissions) must be wired into biometric authentication for the promise of biometrics to become a reality.

Part IV

Privacy, Policy, and Legal Concerns Raised by Biometrics

place index finger in window

Chapter 12

Biometrics and Privacy

By John D. Woodward, Jr.

On May 18, 1997, in his commencement address at Morgan State University, President William J. Clinton stated:

> The right to privacy is one of our most cherished freedoms. As society has grown more complex and people have become more interconnected in every way, we have had to work even harder to respect privacy, the dignity, the autonomy of each individual.... We must develop new protections for privacy in the face of new technological reality.

It is doubtful that President Clinton had biometrics specifically in mind as one of these "new technological realities" during that Sunday speech. However, the Administration of his successor, President George W. Bush, has focused much attention on this emerging technology. For example, on January 7, 2002, the Office of Homeland Security, headed by former Pennsylvania Governor Thomas Ridge, announced its "Specifics of Secure and Smart Border Action Plan," which lists "biometric identifiers" as its first priority. Following up on this announcement, President Bush made a veiled reference to biometrics in his State of the Union Address on January 29, 2002, when he said "We will...use technology to track the arrivals and departures of visitors to the United States."

On May 14, 2002, President Bush became the first U.S. president not only to refer to biometrics, but to endorse its use by government. In his official remarks at the signing of the Enhanced Border Security and Visa Entry Reform Act, President Bush explained that this legislation, part of the U.S. response to the terrorist attacks of September 11, 2001, would, among other things, require all foreign visitors seeking entrance into the United States to carry an official travel document containing, as he phrased it, "biometric identification—that would be fingerprints or facial recognition—that will enable us to use technology to better deny fraudulent entry into America."

Promoted in the aftermath of the September 11 attacks as a means to improve homeland security, biometrics is clearly emerging as a "new technological reality." Biometrics relies on "the body as password," as a *Wired* article put it, improving the speed and accuracy of human recognition and in turn providing better security, increased efficiency, and improved customer service. While not yet enjoying the media stature and public controversy associated with such high-tech issues as genetic cloning and cyberspace, the increasingly extensive use of biometrics in both the public and private sectors will force the public to take notice and to confront the accompanying legal and policy challenges. As the technology becomes more economically viable, technically perfected, and widely used, biometrics could become the passwords, PINs, and tokens of the twenty-first century. In the process, biometrics could refocus the way Americans look at the brave new world of personal information.

History teaches us that new technologies invented by engineers and scientists can spark new law and cause old legal doctrines to be rethought, rekindled, and reapplied by the nation's law and policy makers. Technology seems to move quickly, getting deployed and put into use while the legal order struggles to catch up—thus, the perception that "technology is fast and the law is slow." However, sometimes the legal order moves with surprising celerity with respect to technology. In fact, new technology can cause a creative reshaping of existing legal doctrine when, for example, the judiciary embraces a technology more quickly than the legislature, the executive branch, or even the actual users or marketplace for the technology.

An example from the law casebooks helps to illustrate this point. Even in our current age of sophisticated weather forecasting tools and state-of-the-art communication equipment, vessels at sea are still at the peril of Mother Nature. Early on, radio emerged as an effective way to transmit weather reports. Yet, even as late as 1928, no law or regulation in the United States required that coastwise seagoing carriers equip their tugboats with radio receiver sets. Moreover, no such custom or practice existed in the maritime industry, despite the fact that such sets could easily be used by tugs at sea to receive storm weather warnings.

In the landmark legal case of *The T. J. Hooper*,[1] Judge Learned Hand, one of the great American jurists, deemed that tugboats without radio receiver sets were unseaworthy because "a whole calling may have unduly lagged in the adoption of new and available devices." By accepting a new technology—in this case, wireless communications—more quickly than the legislative and executive branches or even the affected industry, Judge Hand, in effect, creatively re-shaped the law. No longer would strict adherence to local custom and industry practice offer a guaranteed defense against charges of negligence when a readily available technology could result in greater utility to society. In effect, a federal appeals court judge moved much more quickly than an entire industry. In other words, in the case of radio receivers, "the law was fast and the end users slow."

Similarly, today's new technological reality of biometrics should force us to explore from the law and policy perspectives what, if anything, is required to safeguard the public interest and to ensure optimal results for society. Engineers and scientists should not be excluded from this law and policy examination. Indeed, the law and policy concerns raised by biometrics are far too important to be left solely to politicians and lawyers.

This part of the book examines these law and policy concerns. As a first step, we must examine what "privacy" is. This chapter focuses largely on the elusive concept of privacy. Privacy is defined here in the context of biometrics and is examined from the perspective of the specific privacy concerns that the use of biometrics implicates. Critics of biometrics make various arguments as to how biometrics is privacy's foe: Biometrics poses a threat to privacy because its use leads to loss of individual autonomy; provides the state with a powerful ability to monitor the citizenry; and raises cultural, religious, and philosophical objections. At the same time, we must also pay attention to the opposite side of the coin—the ways in which biometrics can be perceived as privacy's friend: Biometrics is privacy's friend because, for example, it can be used to help protect information integrity and to deter identity theft. The government, whether at the federal, state, or local levels, or by the legislative, executive, or judicial branches, can play a positive role in regulating and thereby promoting public acceptance of this new technology by, for example, regulating ways that biometric information may be collected or disclosed.

This chapter also speculates about the biometric future, contending that "biometric diversity," or the use of multiple biometric technologies deployed for multiple applications, provides greater privacy protections than does biometric centralization, or the use of one dominant biometric technology for multiple applications.

---

[1]   *The T. J. Hooper*, 60 F.2d 737 (2d Cir.) cert. denied, 287 U.S. 662 (1932) (Hand J.).

What Is Privacy in the Context of Biometrics?

The issue of privacy is central to biometrics. Critics complain that the use of biometrics poses a substantial risk to privacy rights. Proponents claim that biometrics protect privacy. Evaluating these arguments requires, in the first instance, an understanding of what privacy means. In this chapter we explore the definition of privacy in general.

Working Definition of Privacy

We all might have strong subjective ideas about what privacy is. Yet, the word "privacy" is hard to define, in part because the meaning depends greatly on the situation, culture, environment, and moment. In the immediate aftermath of September 11, for example, many Americans welcomed more intrusive governmental measures to increase public safety, even though that meant their privacy could suffer. As one New Yorker put it, "I want Big Brother on my shoulder, looking out for me." Pre-September 11, a frequent question asked at "Introduction to Biometrics" seminars was, "What about the privacy concerns?" Post-September 11, the more frequently asked question became, "What about the security aspects?"

Privacy scholar Ruth Gavison sees privacy as consisting of three parts: secrecy, anonymity, and solitude. She offers what is perhaps the extreme privacy model: "Privacy is a limitation of others' access to an individual.... In perfect privacy no one has any information about X, no one pays any attention to X, and no one has physical access to X" (Gavison 1980, 428).

Robert Ellis Smith, the editor of *Privacy Journal*, defines privacy as "the desire by each of us for physical space where we can be free of interruption, intrusion, embarrassment, or accountability and the attempt to control the time and manner of disclosures of personal information about ourselves" (Smith 2000, 6/ Smith 2002, 1–8). This definition hints at three types of privacy recognized by U.S. courts: physical, decisional, and information privacy.

Based on her survey of the extensive privacy literature, however, Professor Lillian R. Bevier concluded that "privacy is a chameleon-like word, used denotatively to designate a range of wildly disparate interests—from confidentiality of personal information to reproductive autonomy—and connotatively to generate goodwill on behalf of whatever interest is being asserted in its name" (Bevier 1995, 458).

Most important from the standpoint of biometrics, privacy includes an aspect of autonomy—as various scholars have expressed it: our control over information about ourselves, control over who can sense us, or control over the intimacies of personal identity. This control over information about us, or what is termed "information privacy" (or "informational privacy"), lies at the heart of the privacy concerns raised by this new technological reality. Individuals have an interest in determining how, when, why, and to whom information about themselves, in the form of a biometric identifier, would be disclosed.

What Privacy Concerns Does the Use of Biometrics Implicate?

With this working definition of privacy in mind, we next discuss the privacy concerns implicated by the use of biometrics. These concerns relate to identification and invasiveness.

The Individual Gives Up a Biometric Identifier

To determine the specific privacy concerns implicated by biometrics, we must first focus on what exactly is disclosed when biometric data is collected. Regardless of whether an individual voluntarily provides a biometric identifier or is forced to surrender it as part of state action or government-required scheme, he is giving up information about himself. When biometrics, like fingerprinting, iris recognition, or retinal scanning is used, he discloses robust and distinctive information about his identity. When other biometrics, such as hand or finger geometry, are used, at a minimum, he discloses accurate information about who he is. Depending on the biometric, he is giving information about himself that could be used to identify him over large-scale databases.

Invasive Aspects of the Information

Beyond this fundamental disclosure, invasive implications might also be related to privacy concerns that stem from the biometric identification information disclosed. These invasive implications for privacy are essentially three-fold:

- The invasive effects of a secondary market, defined as disclosure of the biometric identification information to third parties

- Any invasive information that might be additionally obtained as part of the biometric identifier

- The invasiveness that might be associated with actual physical harm caused by the technology

Invasive Secondary Market Effects   Once a biometric identifier is captured or collected from an individual in the primary market, and even if it is captured only once, the biometric identifier could easily be replicated, copied, and otherwise shared among countless public and private sector databases. This sharing in a secondary market could conceivably take place without the individual's knowledge or consent. Indeed, biometric identifiers could be bought and sold in a secondary market much the way names and addresses on mailing lists are currently bought and sold by data merchants.

An example illustrates the secondary market effect: I give my face and fingerprints to my local sports club so I can access the club and keep better track of my workouts. I do this by presenting my face to a camera whenever I enter and by touching my finger to the computer display on the treadmill and other equipment. I get a detailed monthly fitness report. The sports club conveniently enrolled both of my index fingers so I don't even have to remember which pointer finger to use. After a while, I start receiving marketing information telling me to show up at the local grocery store, retail outlet, and so on, because I am already preregistered and biometrically enrolled in their systems. That's because, along with my facial photograph, the sports club kept my raw data, or file images, in addition to the fingerprint templates, and sold the information to others.

Later, while shopping in the mall, sales associates insist on selling me athletic gear, protein supplements, and diet aids because their facial recognition system identified me as a failed jock from the sports club. Later, the police are confronted with the grisly homicide of the sports club manager in his office, where the only evidence is a single latent print left on the murder weapon. After no matches are made against the FBI's criminal master file, the new sports club management readily agrees to turn over the file images of fingerprints of all its members, including mine, so the latent print can be searched against them.

Particularly with respect to the private sphere, where the conduct of private actors has traditionally been given a large degree of freedom of action from government interference, few current legal limits exist in the United States on the use of biometric information held by private actors. This observation is not meant to suggest that the federal or state governments would not be able to regulate the use of biometric information held by private actors; rather, it emphasizes what the present regulatory baseline is with respect to the regulation of biometric information: Until regulatory action has been taken by government, the use of biometrics is left to the market. The legal situation is very different in the European Union, where a comprehensive privacy protection framework exists.

Invasive Information Is Obtained   In addition to the identification information associated with the biometric, invasive information threatening privacy could conceivably include three other types of concerns. First, biometric identifiers could be used extensively for law enforcement purposes, as raised in the sports club example. Fingerprints have long been used by law enforcement, and electronic finger images—or what are in effect the next generation of fingerprints—are presently being used by various law enforcement agencies as part of their databases, such as the FBI's Integrated Automated Fingerprint Identification System (IAFIS).

Second, it is possible (and this point needs to be stressed: *only* possible) that some biometrics might capture more than just mere identification information. Information about a person's health and medical history might also be incidentally obtained. Recent scientific research, while the subject of controversy, suggests that fingerprints might disclose such information about a person. For example, Dr. Howard Chen, in his work on dermatoglyphics, or the study of the patterns of the ridges of the skin on parts of the hands and feet, notes that "certain chromosomal disorders are known to be associated with characteristic dermatoglyphic abnormalities," specifically citing Down syndrome, Turner syndrome, and Klinefelter syndrome as chromosomal disorders that cause unusual fingerprint patterns in a person. Certain nonchromosomal disorders, such as chronic, intestinal pseudo-obstruction (CIP) (described in the next paragraph), leukemia, breast cancer, and Rubella syndrome, have also been implicated by certain unusual fingerprint patterns.

Dr. Marvin M. Schuster, the recently retired director of the division of digestive diseases at Johns Hopkins Bayview Medical Center, has discovered a "mysterious relationship" between an uncommon fingerprint pattern, known as a digital arch, and a medical disorder called CIP that affects 50,000 people nationwide. Based on the results of a seven-year study, Dr. Schuster found that 54 percent of CIP patients have this rare digital arch fingerprint pattern. In comparison, arch fingerprints appear in only seven percent of the general population. Schuster's discovery suggests a genetic basis to the disease. Schuster explained that in the case of CIP, "the more digital arches there are in the fingerprint, the stronger the correlation [to the condition]. The majority of CIP patients possess at least one digital arch. This discovery offers an important clue in diagnosing CIP, and it suggests that the disorder is congenital. It could potentially save people with CIP from multiple needless operations" (Hancock and Hendricks 1996).

While still extremely controversial within the scientific communities, several researchers report a link between fingerprints and homosexuality. For example, psychologists at the University of Western Ontario report that homosexual males are more likely than their heterosexual counterparts to show asymmetry in their fingerprints. "What we found is a statistically significant difference between groups of heterosexual and homosexual men," researcher Doreen Kimura said (Associated Press 1994). While this research is far from conclusive, the availability of such information with its possible links to medical and related information again raises concern about privacy and can create misperceptions.

From examining the retina or iris, an expert can determine that a patient may be suffering from common afflictions such as diabetes, arteriosclerosis, and hypertension; furthermore, a medical professional can also detect unique diseases of the iris and the retina. Moreover, the onset of certain diseases (such as diabetes) and conditions (such as pregnancy) may cause the retinal pattern to change; are the changes enough to cause a previously enrolled user to be rejected by a system because the user's biometric is no longer recognized by the system? Although both the iris and retina contain medical information, it is by no means obvious that the biometric data taken of the iris or retina implicates privacy concerns related to the disclosure of medical information. A necessary area of further technical inquiry is whether the computerized code taken of the iris or retina actually contains any medical information or if the information captured is sufficient to be used for any type of diagnostic purpose.

Much research remains to be done; however, a biometric identifier with any possible links to medical information will raise lingering questions about the privacy aspects of the information disclosed. More important, the mere perception that such sensitive information may be disclosed could dissuade people from using potentially beneficial biometric systems.

Actual Physical Harm; Physical Invasiveness   Part of the "urban legend" surrounding biometrics holds that retinal scanning "shoots a laser beam into the eye." This is not the case, but urban legends die hard. Anecdotally, certain aviators, who are extremely proud of their 20/20 vision, supposedly had a hard time accepting retinal scanning devices in an experimental program because at least some of them feared the devices would adversely affect their perfect vision. Other users feared that diseases, such as conjunctivitis, may result from having to come into close proximity with a binocular-like device that strangers had touched. Some users of biometrics have complained that hand geometry systems dry their hands. Such fears, even when unfounded, can negatively affect the system because dissatisfied users will go out of their way not to cooperate with the system; some may even actively engage in acts of sabotage to prevent its use.

Documented cases of biometrics causing actual harm to a person are difficult, if not impossible, to find, but many of the technologies are fairly new. And to date, no enterprising plaintiff's attorney has brought a class-action lawsuit for personal injury on this biometrics-induced harm basis. The bottom line is that any liability resulting from any proven actual physical harm caused by biometric systems would be addressed by the individual state's tort liability regimes. On a related note, eventually, the judiciary will also have the opportunity to decide the admissibility of biometric identification as scientific evidence using the prevailing standards articulated by the Supreme Court in *Daubert v. Merrell Dow Pharmaceuticals* in 1993.

Biometrics as Privacy's Foe: Criticisms of Biometrics

This section discusses the "foe" side of the coin: the criticisms of biometrics leading to loss of anonymity and autonomy and the "Big Brother" scenario, including the danger of function creep and degradation of the individual's reasonable expectation of privacy.

The Loss of Anonymity; the Loss of Autonomy

A basic criticism of biometrics is that we, as individuals, risk losing our anonymity and autonomy whenever biometric systems are deployed. Part of controlling information about ourselves includes our ability to keep other parties from knowing things about us, like who we are. While we all know that a determined party—whether the government or a private party—can learn our identity (and much more about us), the use of biometrics makes it clear that our identity is now fully established within seconds. As Roger Clarke explains, "The need to identify oneself may be intrinsically distasteful to some people.... They may regard it as demeaning, or implicit recognition that the organization with whom they are dealing exercises power over them" (Clarke 1994).

Robert Ellis Smith agrees, noting that, "In most cases, biometric technology is impersonal" (Smith 1996). At the same time, as the technology improves, its use may become more ubiquitous, and individuals may find that they are required to provide a biometric identifier in unexpected, unwelcome, or unforeseen circumstances. Moreover, you cannot simply "make up" a biometric as you can a name, an address, or a phone number. In this sense, perhaps, the loss of anonymity leads to an inevitable loss of individual autonomy.

Biometrics should not really be blamed for the fact that there is less individual anonymity in society today than in decades or centuries past, however. Rather, far larger economic, political, and technological forces have been at work. America's transformation from an agrarian to industrial to post-industrial service (or "information age") economy, combined with the massive growth of government since the New Deal of the 1930s, have put a greater premium on the need for information about individuals and organizations. At the same time, technical advances have made it much easier and more convenient to collect, compile, and keep extensive information on individuals. This information-centric trend takes place because in the Information Age information has great value as a commodity. The computer, the enabler of "info-centrism," has helped make information a valuable commodity because it can process large amounts of personal information from large numbers of people in little time and at low cost.

While a biometric identifier is an accurate identifier, it is not the first nor the only identifier used to match or locate information about a person. Names and numerical identifiers such as social security numbers, account numbers, and military service numbers have long been used to access files with personal information. Moreover, the impressive search capabilities of computer systems with their abilities to search, for example, the full text of stored documents, make identifiers far less important for locating information about an individual.

We also should not lose sight of the fact that there is usually a good reason why individual recognition in the form of identification or verification is needed. Balancing the equities involved and depending on the case, the benefits—to the individual as well as to society—of establishing a person's identity generally outweigh the costs of losing anonymity. For example, given the massive problem of missing and abused children, many citizens would eagerly support the idea of day care providers using biometrics to make certain that our children get released at the end of the day to a parent or guardian whose identity has been verified. However, reasonable people can disagree as to the cost-benefit analysis.

Similarly, to consider a "pocketbook" example, the world's financial community has long been concerned about growing problems of ATM fraud and unauthorized account access, estimated to cost $500 million a year, check fraud at least $2 billion, and credit card fraud about $1.5 billion per year. The financial services industry believes that a significant percentage of these losses could be eliminated by the use of biometrics, by ensuring that only the authorized account holder could access the account. MasterCard, for example, has been evaluating various biometrics since 1995 and believes fingerprint technology is the best technology to reduce credit card fraud. According to Joel Lisker, the company's senior vice president of security and risk management, "We estimate that a fingerprint system, fully implemented, could save the financial services industry billions of dollars" (Haapaniemi 1998).

Critics give too much credit to biometrics' alleged ability to erode anonymity without giving enough attention to the market's ability to protect privacy in response. It is not obvious that more anonymity will be lost when biometrics are used. Public and private sector organizations already have the ability to gather substantial amounts of information about individuals by tracking, for example, credit card use, consumer spending, and demographic factors.

A parallel to the financial services industry might be helpful. Despite the existence of many comprehensive payment systems such as credit cards, which combine extreme ease of service with extensive record-keeping, many Americans still prefer to use cash for transactions—a form of payment that leaves virtually no record. An individual who wants anonymity might have to go to greater lengths to get it in the biometric world, but the ability of the marketplace to accommodate a person's desire for anonymity should not be so readily dismissed. Moreover, as explained next, the ability of biometrics to serve as privacy enhancing technologies should not be discounted.

The Biometric-Based "Big Brother" Scenario

Aside from the alliterative qualities the phrase possesses, critics of biometrics seem to inevitably link the technology to "Big Brother." Biometrics, in combination with impressive advancements in computer and related technologies, would, its critics argue, enable the State to monitor the actions and behavior of its citizenry. In this vein, concern has been expressed that biometric identifiers will be used routinely against citizens by law enforcement agencies. As Marc Rotenberg of the Electronic Privacy Information Center has succinctly explained, "Take someone's fingerprint and you have the ability to determine if you have a match for forensic purposes" (American Banker 1996).

This "Big Brother" concern, however, goes beyond normal police work. Every time an individual used her biometric identifier to conduct a transaction, a record would be made in a database that the government, using computer technology, could then match and use against the citizen—even in ways that are not authorized or meet with our disapproval. To borrow the reasoning of a 1973 report on national identity card proposals, the biometric identifier, in ways far more effective than a numerical identifier, "could serve as the skeleton for a national dossier system to maintain information on every citizen from cradle to grave" (U.S. Department of Health, Education and Welfare 1973).

Roger Clarke has perhaps offered the best worst-case *1984*-like scenario:

> Any high-integrity identifier [such as biometrics] represents a threat to civil liberties, because it represents the basis for a ubiquitous identification scheme, and such a scheme provides enormous power over the populace. All human behavior would become transparent to the State, and the scope for nonconformism and dissent would be muted to the point envisaged by the antiutopian novelists (Clarke 1994).

At least one example exists from U.S. history of supposedly confidential records being used in ways never likely intended. In November 1941, almost two weeks before the Japanese attack on Pearl Harbor, President Franklin D. Roosevelt ordered a comprehensive list made to include the names and addresses of all foreign-born and American-born Japanese living in the United States. To compile the list, staffers used 1930 and 1940 census data. Working without the benefit of computers, staffers compiled the list in one week. Following the attack, President Roosevelt issued Executive Order 9066, authorizing military personnel to detain and relocate persons of Japanese ancestry. By the spring of 1942, the U.S. government forced persons of Japanese descent, including U.S. citizens, to relocate from their homes on the West Coast and report to relocation centers. An estimated 120,000 people, many of whom were U.S. citizens, were held without judicial review. John Miller and Stephen Moore, two libertarian scholars, contend, "The history of government programs indicates that privacy rights are violated routinely whenever expediency dictates" (Miller and Moore 1995).

Function Creep

The biometric-based "Big Brother" scenario would not happen instantly. Rather, when first deployed, biometrics would be used for limited, clearly specified, sensible purposes—to combat fraud, to improve airport security, to protect our children, and so on. But consider what Justice Louis Brandeis (of "right to privacy" fame) warned in his famous *Olmstead v. United States* dissent of 1927:

> Experience should teach us to be most on our guard to protect liberty when the Government's purposes are beneficent. Men born to freedom are naturally alert to repel invasion of their liberty by evil-minded rulers. The greatest dangers to liberty lurk in insidious encroachment by men of zeal, well meaning but without understanding.

What would inevitably happen over time, according to civil libertarians, is a phenomenon known as "function creep" or "mission creep": identification systems incorporating biometrics would gradually spread to additional purposes not announced or not even intended when the identification systems were originally implemented.

The classic example of function creep is the use of the Social Security Number (SSN) in the United States. Originated in 1936, the SSN's sole purpose was to facilitate record-keeping for determining the amount of Social Security taxes to credit to each contributor's account. In fact, the original Social Security cards containing the SSN bore the legend, "Not for Identification." By 1961, the Internal Revenue Service (IRS) began using the SSN for tax identification purposes. By 2002, countless transactions from credit to employment to insurance to many states' drivers licenses require a Social Security Number and countless private organizations ask for it even when it is not needed specifically for the transaction at hand. From "Not for Identification," the SSN has become virtual mandatory identification.

Moreover, given the consequences of function creep, the size, power, and scope of government will expand as all citizens get their biometric identifiers thrown into massive government databases by the "men [and women] of zeal, well-meaning but without understanding" about whom Justice Brandeis warned. In effect, an old Russian proverb aptly identifies the danger of biometrics for freedom-loving Americans: "If you are a mushroom, into the basket you must go."

Reduction of the Individual's Reasonable Expectation of Privacy

Just as function creep implies that biometrics will gradually (and innocently) grow to be used by zealous, well-meaning bureaucrats in numerous, creative ways in multiple forums, function creep will also enable the government to use the new technology of biometrics to reduce further over time the citizenry's reasonable expectations of privacy.

Analogies can be drawn from previous cases in which the government has used cutting-edge technology to intrude in an area in which the private actor had manifested a subjective expectation of privacy. For example, the Environmental Protection Agency (EPA), in an effort to investigate industrial pollution, used "the finest precision aerial camera available" mounted in an airplane flying in lawful airspace to take photographs of Dow Chemical Company's 2,000-acre Midland, Michigan, facilities. Fearful that industrial competitors might try to steal its trade secrets, Dow took elaborate precautions at its facility. Despite the precautions the company took to ensure its privacy, the Supreme Court, in a 5–4 vote handed down in 1985, found that Dow had no reasonable, legitimate, and objective expectation of privacy in the area the EPA had photographed. The dissent noted that, by basing its decision on the method of surveillance used by the government, as opposed to the company's reasonable expectation of privacy, the Court ensured that "privacy rights would be seriously at risk as technological advances become generally disseminated and available to society" (*Dow Chemical Co. v. United States,* 476 U.S. 227 (1986)).

Some contend that biometrics is precisely the kind of technological advance the *Dow* dissenters warned about. Citizens no longer would have a reasonable expectation of privacy any time they use a biometric identifier because the government's use of biometrics and computer matching would be merely utilizing commercially available technologies.

Cultural, Religious, and Philosophical Objections

Other criticisms of the use of biometrics originate on cultural, religious, and philosophical grounds. These objections might not be shared by large numbers of people, but to the extent those who advocate them have sincerely held beliefs, they merit discussion.

Cultural: *Stigma and Dignity*

Simon Davies of Privacy International notes that it is no accident that biometric systems are being tried out most aggressively with welfare recipients. The British scholar contends that they are in no position to resist the State-mandated intrusion. Interestingly, in the 1995 GAO Report on the use of biometrics to deter fraud in the nationwide Electronics Benefit Transfer (EBT) program, the U.S. Department of the Treasury expressed concern over how finger imaging would impact on the dignity of the recipients and called for more testing and study.

While stigma and dignity arguments tied to the less fortunate elements of society have a strong emotional appeal, the available empirical data from Connecticut suggests that the majority of entitlement recipients actually support the use of biometrics. Some have criticized such surveys as flawed because the recipients could be reluctant to provide their true opinions because of retaliation fears.

Religious Objections

Several religious groups criticize biometrics on the ground that individuals are forced to sacrifice a part of themselves to a godless monolith in the form of the State. For example, certain Christians interpret biometrics to be a "mark of the beast," an objection based on language in the New Testament's "Revelation":

> [The Beast] causeth all, both small and great, rich and poor, free and bond, to receive a mark in their right hand, or in their foreheads: And that no man might buy or sell, save that he had the mark, or the name of the beast, or the number of his name.... And his number is six hundred, threescore, and six (Revelation, 13:16–18).

Certain Christians consider biometrics to be the brand discussed in Revelation and biometric readers as the only means of viewing these brands. For example, stressing that "the Bible says the time is going to come when you cannot buy or sell except when a mark is placed on your head or forehead," fundamentalist Christian Pat Robertson has expressed doubts about biometrics and has noted how the technology is proceeding according to scripture. And at least one religious group has complained that the hand geometry devices used by California were making "the mark of the beast" on enrollees' hands.

Private sector end users of biometrics have to consider customer reaction to its use. In this sense, end users have to be ready to answer customer concerns and assuage customer fears about the technology. While only a small number of people voice religious objections to the use of biometrics, they can be vociferous and they're hard to ignore. Thus, the end user should be poised to deal with such objections so that a public relations disaster is avoided. While theological discussion is beyond the scope of this chapter, it should be pointed out that Revelations is one of the most controversial parts of the Bible, subject to many different interpretations. Moreover, rather than being a "mark of the beast," biometrics may be seen as demonstrating humankind's God-given individuality since biometrics help prove that we are all unique.

Philosophical: Biometric-Based Branding

Biometrics also receives criticism on the grounds that a biometric identifier is nothing more than biometric-based branding or high-tech tattooing. There is an understandably odious stigma associated with the forced branding and tattooing of human beings, particularly since branding was used as a recognition system to denote property rights in human slaves in the eighteenth and nineteenth centuries and tattooing was used by the Nazis to identify concentration camp victims in this century. More than just the physical pain of the brand or tattoo accounts for society's revulsion. Analogizing from these experiences, biometric identifiers have been described as the equivalent of a brand or tattoo that the State will impose on its citizens for nefarious purposes. Under this view, biometrics are just another example of the State using technology to impair individuality and autonomy.

Comparisons of biometrics to brands and tattoos appeal to the emotions. Essentially these arguments are the ultimate form of the "Big Brother" concerns outlined earlier. Slave owners and Nazis forced branding and tattooing on victims who had absolutely no choice. In the private sector realm, however, citizens are making voluntary choices to use or not to use biometrics; these citizens are not defenseless victims. When biometrics is used in the public sector in the U.S. and many other countries, the legitimacy of its use is overseen by democratic institutions.

Biometrics as Privacy's Friend: Support for Biometrics

Here we look at biometrics as privacy's friend. Biometrics serve in a "privacy friendly" role when they are used to safeguard identity and integrity, limit access to information, serve as a privacy enhancing technology, as well as provide other benefits.

Biometrics to Protect Privacy by Safeguarding Identity

While critics of biometrics contend that this new technology is privacy's foe, the opposite side of the coin also must be examined: biometrics can be a friend of privacy whether used in the private or public sector. Biometrics proves itself as privacy's friend when it is deployed as a security safeguard to prevent identity theft and to provide identity assurance.

Let's consider an example drawn from the financial services industry but applicable to almost any fraud-prevention scenario: It is well known that criminals eagerly exploit weaknesses with present access systems, which tend to be based on passwords and PINs, by clandestinely obtaining these codes. They then surreptitiously access a legitimate customer's account or ATM. The honest citizen effectively loses control over her personal account information. Her financial integrity is compromised and her finances are gone because a criminal has gained unauthorized access to the information. In effect, she has suffered an invasion of her privacy related to her financial integrity. With biometric-based systems, identity theft, while never completely defeated, becomes more difficult for the criminal element to perpetuate. Biometrics means less consumer fraud, which means greater protection of consumers' financial integrity.

Biometrics Used to Limit Access to Information

Biometrics becomes a staunch friend of privacy when it is used for access control purposes, thereby restricting unauthorized personnel from gaining access to sensitive personal information. For example, biometrics can be effectively used to limit access to a patient's medical information stored on a computer database. Instead of relying on easily compromised passwords and PINs, a biometric identifier is required at the computer workstation to determine database access. The same biometric systems can be used for almost any information database (including databases containing biometric identifiers) to restrict or compartment information based on the "need to know" principle.

Biometrics also protects information privacy to the extent that it can be used, through the use of a biometric logon, to keep a precise record or audit trail of who accesses what personal information within a computer network. For example, individual tax records would be much better protected if an IRS official had to use his biometric identifier to access them, knowing that an audit trail was kept detailing who accessed which records. Far less snooping by curious bureaucrats would result.

Biometrics as Privacy Enhancing Technology

Beyond protecting privacy, biometrics can be seen as actually enhancing privacy. Several newly developed biometric technologies use an individual's physical characteristics to construct a digital code for the individual without storing the actual physical characteristics in a database. According to George Tomko, this "biometric encryption" could use a person's fingerprint as one's private encryption or coding key. "We could use your fingerprint to code your PIN for accessing your bank machine. The coded PIN has no connection whatsoever to the finger pattern." Tomko explains the privacy enhancement by noting, "What is stored in the database is only the coded PIN. The finger pattern only acts as the coding key of that PIN, any PIN. The fingerprint pattern, encrypted or otherwise, is not stored anywhere during the process. It stays on your finger, where it belongs" (Tomko 1998).

The applications of this type of anonymous verification system are extensive. Most notably, such a biometric-based system would seem to provide a ready commercial encryption capability. Moreover, rather than technological advances eroding privacy expectations as we saw, for example, with the EPA's use of a special aerial camera in *Dow*, biometrics, as used to create an anonymous encryption system, would provide for privacy enhancement.

Many of the criticisms of biometrics are flawed. They either miss the mark in that they should really be aimed at the explosive growth of contemporary information systems that are the result of economic, political, and technological change, or the criticisms fail to acknowledge the countervailing benefits of accurate identity verification. As explained next, the use of biometrics might provide for even further individual privacy protections through a phenomenon known as *biometric diversity*.

Other Benefits of Biometrics

While biometrics is an important technological achievement, its use should be kept in perspective: "Big Brother" concerns implicate far more than biometrics. The broader underlying issue is not controlling biometrics but rather the challenge of how law and policy should control contemporary information systems and the data they hold. As one scholar has explained, computers and the matching they perform permit "various fragments of information about an individual to be combined and compiled to form a much more complete profile. These profiles can be collected, maintained, and disclosed to organizations with which the individual has no direct contact or to which the individual would prefer to prevent disclosure" (Mell 1997). Biometrics should be viewed as an appendage or footnote to this enormous challenge.

Critics also overlook the many legitimate reasons why the government needs to use biometric applications. Biometric applications related to national security and prison management are easy to grasp; for example, all of us want solid guarantees that only the appropriate personnel can access nuclear materials and that serial killers do not slip out of prison by masquerading as someone else. These same concerns related to the use of false identity really apply across the board; for example, the government has a legitimate purpose in preventing fraud in the programs it administers.

For example, fraud is a significant issue in public sector programs. A persistent problem of entitlement programs is fraud perpetrated by double dippers—individuals who illegally register more than one time for benefits using an alias or otherwise false information about themselves. Many experts believe that fraud in entitlement programs, such as welfare, can be as high as 10 percent, which translates in dollar terms to more than $40 billion a year in potential savings.

To the extent critics have concerns about function creep, two points need to be made: First, as explained, the critical and key function creep issue is controlling information systems, not controlling a nine-digit number or an x-byte numerical template used as a biometric identifier. Second, issues specifically related to biometrics can be addressed within our present legal and policy framework. We do not need a new "Law of Biometrics" paradigm; the old bottles of the law will hold the new wine of biometrics quite well. In this regard, legislative proposals, particularly at the federal level, should be considered and studied, particularly if the threat of function creep or the emergence of an undisciplined secondary market is real. With respect to private sector use of biometrics, viable options exist for our national and state policymakers.

Biometric Centralization vs. Biometric Diversity: Which Protects Privacy Better?

It is important to address whether a specific biometric technology will come to dominate biometric systems. In other words, will the biometric future feature centralization, whereby one biometric would be used for multiple applications, or will we see biometric diversity or biometric balkanization where multiple biometrics are used for multiple applications? At present, fingerprinting has an early lead in terms of industry presence with an estimated one-third of the biometric market. The popularity of fingerprinting is explained primarily by its distinctiveness or individuality, the fingerprint's long acceptance by the public, and the extensive competition in the finger imaging market leading to rapidly decreasing user costs, among other factors.

For example, with regard to public acceptance of fingerprinting, a survey of 1,000 adults revealed that 75 percent of those polled would be comfortable having a finger image of themselves made available to the government or the private sector for identification purposes. This high acceptance is arguably underscored by more than half of those surveyed saying they had been fingerprinted at some point in their lives. Only 20 percent thought that fingerprinting stigmatizes a person as a criminal.

Despite this early lead, however, it is not clear that fingerprinting will emerge as the biometric of choice. It is tempting to predict that fingerprinting will dominate or that another biometrics will come to monopolize the market because of its perceived advantages. However, this view overlooks one of the great strengths of the current biometric market: it offers many technologies that allow maximum choice for users. A more likely outcome is that biometric diversity will result: multiple biometrics will be deployed not only by various public and private sector actors but multiple biometrics will also be deployed by the same actor depending on the specific mission.

Arguably, this biometric diversity can take on a sinister spin. Individuals will be forced to give up various identifying "pieces" of themselves to countless governmental and corporate bureaucracies. In an Orwellian twist, the retina, the iris, the fingerprints, the voice, the signature, the hand, the vein, the tongue, and presumably even the body odor will all be extracted by the State and stored in databases. The State will then use this biometrics to monitor our lives and degrade our anonymity and autonomy.

Yet biometric diversity offers at least two key advantages for the protection of privacy. First, biometric diversity offers maximum flexibility to the private or public end user that will use the technology. The actor can tailor a specific biometric program to meets its own unique mission within its resource constraints. Depending on the situation and the degree of accuracy in identification required, the optimal biometric for that use can be selected. For example, the best biometric used to verify access to a government entitlements program might differ from the best biometric used by a university to ferret out undergraduate examination fraud, which in turn might differ from the best biometric needed in a prison environment where hostile users will go to extreme lengths to foil identification efforts. Similarly, voice verification might be ideal for determining account access over the telephone, while signature dynamics might be better suited for the tax authorities monitoring returns.

Second, biometric diversity might actually mean a synergy of the actor's interest and the individual's concerns. Consider, for example, the public sector use of biometrics: Government agencies basically want dependable, workable biometrics to achieve their primary purpose—verifying or identifying an individual. The individual essentially wants the same thing, plus protection of private information. If different technologies are used for different situations, citizens will not face the necessity of reporting to the government's "biometric central" for enrollment. By allowing the agencies maximum choice of biometric technologies, the individual gains greater protection for private information.

Biometric diversity could also lead to the safeguard of biometric compartmentation that would be achieved through the use of different biometric identifiers. For example, an iris pattern used for ATM access would be of little use to the Connecticut Department of Social Services that uses fingerprinting, just as a finger geometry pattern captured at Disney World would be of little value to tax authorities investigating phony signatures on fraudulent tax returns from the Sunshine State.

From the privacy enhancement perspective, biometric diversity is the equivalent of being issued multiple identification numbers, PINs, or passwords with the important difference that biometric-based systems provide better security and greater convenience.

On balance, however, the greater threat to privacy will likely not arise from the use of advanced technology to monitor but rather from sloppiness in database management—that is, where the human factor enters the scene. The potential for a breach in database security increases greatly as shortcuts are taken, budgets are slashed, trained personnel are few, and leaders do not draft and implement a plan to safeguard biometric identification information for which they are responsible. Organizations considering the technology need to practice "safe biometrics;" moreover, government might have an important role to play in ensuring that privacy concerns are addressed. Accordingly, limited government regulation should be viewed as biometric technology promoting and not biometric technology opposing.

Chapter 13

Legal Considerations of Government Use of Biometrics

By John D. Woodward, Jr.

The public sector, particularly U.S. government agencies, is increasingly interested in using biometrics for a variety of applications. Indeed, since the terrorist attacks of September 11, 2001, both the Administration and the Congress have identified biometrics as a tool for improving homeland security. In light of this high-level interest, this chapter discusses the privacy protections afforded by law in the context of government or public sector use of biometrics. What happens, for example, when an individual must provide a biometric identifier to receive an entitlement or benefit from the U.S. government? What legal rights, if any, does an individual providing a biometric have, and what legal responsibilities, if any, does the government agency collecting the biometric owe with respect to the data taken? Can a citizen refuse to provide a biometric identifier? To begin to answer these questions, we first must look to the United States Constitution.

Constitutional Law Considerations

Because the U.S. Constitution is the highest law of the land, there is something to be said for starting at the "top" with our legal discussion. The following sections describe how biometrics and the U.S. Constitution interact. We start with analyzing what the right to privacy means based on the judiciary's interpretation of the Constitution.

The Right to Privacy

The American concept of privacy has changed over the centuries as America has changed—reflecting the idiom that "law mirrors the society that creates it." Prior to the birth of the nation, the American colonists essentially recognized a strong right of physical privacy centered in the home, where a person could be free from contact with others. For example, as part of his famous courtroom defense against British-imposed general search warrants in 1761, James Otis, a leading Boston attorney, said: "Now one of the most essential branches of English liberty is the freedom of one's house. A man's house is his castle; and while he is quiet, he is as well guarded as a prince in his castle" (Flaherty 1972). While Otis lost his case before the ill-disposed crown court, his argument eventually carried the day. The colonists' intense dislike of the general warrants, whereby a person and his effects could be searched without probable cause, added fuel to the fires of the American Revolution and led to the establishment of the Fourth Amendment in the Bill of Rights, discussed in the following section.

Since colonial times, jurists and legal scholars have grappled with defining privacy and explaining what the right to privacy should encompass. By the second half of the nineteenth century, the judiciary and academia focused more attention on privacy rights, moving beyond privacy of place to privacy of person. In 1879, Judge Thomas M. Cooley, in his classic treatise on torts, included "the right to be let alone" as a class of tort rights, contending that "the right to one's person may be said to be a right of complete immunity" (Hixson 1987; Goldberg 1994).

Echoing and popularizing Cooley's phrase, Samuel D. Warren and Louis D. Brandeis, in their landmark law review article, "The Right to Privacy," written in 1890, articulated their view of privacy as a "right to be let alone." (They also appropriately cited Cooley's previous work.) Brandeis, as a Supreme Court Justice, later used this phrase,[1] declaring in 1928 that the Founding Fathers "conferred, as against the Government, the right to be let alone—the most comprehensive of rights and the right most valued by civilized men" (Goldberg 1994).

Privacy as the "right to be let alone" has a positive appeal and commendable simplicity; however, privacy scholars such as Ellen Alderman and Caroline Kennedy criticize the phrase in that "legally, it offers no guidance at all. Coveting an indefinable right is one thing; enforcing it in a court of law is another" (Alderman and Kennedy 1995).

Constitutional Background

The Constitution regulates government action; however, it generally provides no protection from actions taken by private individuals. As constitutional law scholar Laurence H. Tribe has explained, "the Constitution, with the sole exception

---

[1] *Olmstead v. United States*, 277 U.S. 438, 478 (1928).

of the Thirteenth Amendment prohibiting slavery, regulates action by the government rather than the conduct of private individuals and groups."[2] Although Tribe should have included the Eighteenth Amendment prohibiting the manufacture, sale, or transportation of intoxicating liquors along with the Thirteenth, his legal point is unassailable. The Constitution provides citizens with protections from actions taken by government.

The word *privacy*, like the word *biometrics*, is nowhere to be found in the text of the U.S. Constitution. An obvious point needs stating: Just because something is not in the text of the Constitution does not mean that it is outside the Constitution's authority or protection. After all, no one supposes that Congress is without power to fund and regulate the Air Force simply because the Constitution refers only to land and naval forces. Therefore, it makes sense that without making explicit reference to privacy, the Constitution can nonetheless protect certain privacy interests, or "zones of privacy," to use Justice William Douglas's term. Justice Douglas used "zones of privacy" in his opinion in *Griswold v. Connecticut*, a landmark 1965 Supreme Court case holding unconstitutional a state statute that criminalized the sale of contraceptives to married couples.[3]

With the founding of the republic, the Constitution, without making explicit reference to privacy, protected privacy interests. The Bill of Rights, or the first ten amendments to the Constitution, reflects these "zone of privacy" protections in the First Amendment rights of freedom of speech, press, religion and association; the Third Amendment prohibition against the quartering of soldiers in one's home; the Fourth Amendment right to be free from unreasonable searches and seizures; the Fifth Amendment right against self-incrimination; the Ninth Amendment's provision that "the enumeration in the Constitution, of certain rights, shall not be construed to deny or disparage others retained by the people," and the Tenth Amendment's provision that "the powers not delegated to the United States by the Constitution, nor prohibited by it to the States, are reserved to the States respectively, or to the people."

What, then, is the constitutional right to privacy and how does it affect biometrics used in government mandated applications? The answer to the first part of the question is legally fuzzy. As a federal appellate court has observed, "While the Supreme Court has expressed uncertainty regarding the precise bounds of the constitutional 'zone of privacy,' its existence is firmly established."[4] So while the federal courts have made it clear that there is a zone of privacy, they have not done such a thorough job of mapping it.

The roots of most modern constitutional privacy interests are found in the Due Process Clause of the Fourteenth Amendment. This clause provides that no

---

[2]   Laurence H. Tribe, "The Constitution in Cyberspace," 1991, http://www.epic.org/free_speech/tribe.html.

[3]   *Griswald v. Connecticut*, 381 U.S. 479, 484 (1965).

[4]   *In re Crawford*, U.S. App. LEXIS 24941, *7 (9th Cir. 1999) (citing *Whalen v. Roe*, 429 U.S. 589, 599-600 (1977); *Griswold v. Connecticut*, 381 U.S. 479, 483 (1965)).

State shall "deprive any person of life, liberty, or property, without due process of law."

For more than 100 years, the Supreme Court has interpreted these words as containing a substantive protection that "bar[s] certain government actions regardless of the fairness of the procedures used to implement them."[5] In other words, the Due Process Clause bars the government from doing certain things to us.

Three Forms of Privacy Under Law

The Supreme Court has emphasized "there is a realm of personal liberty which the government may not enter." This realm, or zone of privacy, consists of rights that are "fundamental" or "implicit in the concept of ordered liberty"[6] or as the Court would later phrase it, "deeply rooted in this Nation's history and tradition."[7]

These terms may read well, but they have been criticized for lack of clarity. For example, Robert H. Bork, a former federal judge, believes "the judge-created phrases specify no particular freedom, but merely assure us, in sonorous phrases, that they, the judges, will know what freedoms are required when the time comes" (Bork 1990).

Accordingly, it is difficult to determine precisely what is protected. In what specific areas of the zone of privacy is the government forbidden entry? In its consideration of privacy interests, the Supreme Court has implicitly categorized privacy as taking three distinct forms. These three forms of privacy, or what can be viewed as three slices of the privacy pie, are physical, decisional, and information.

Physical Privacy

This form of privacy is also known as freedom from contact with other people or monitoring agents. Physical privacy enjoys its greatest constitutional protection under the Fourth Amendment, which governs searches and seizures conducted by government agents. The amendment provides that "the right of the people to be secure in their persons, houses, papers, and effects, against unreasonable searches and seizures, shall not be violated."

Decisional Privacy

This form of privacy is also known as the freedom of the individual to make private choices, without undue government interference, about the personal and intimate matters that affect him or her. In 1992, the Supreme Court emphasized

---

[5] *Planned Parenthood of Southeastern Pennsylvania v. Casey*, 505 U.S. 833, 846 (1992) (quoting *Daniels v. Williams*, 474 U.S. 327, 331 (1986)).

[6] *Griswold v. Connecticut*, 381 U.S. 479, 500 (1965) (Harlan, J., concurring), (quoting *Palko v. Connecticut*, 302 U.S. 319, 325 (1937)).

[7] *Moore v. City of East Cleveland*, 431 U.S. 494, 503 (1977).

that the individual is constitutionally protected in "personal decisions relating to marriage, procreation, contraception, family relationships, child rearing and education."[8]

In determining the commonality of these personal decisions and why they deserve constitutional protection, the Court, through Justice Sandra Day O'Connor's opinion in *Planned Parenthood v. Casey*, explained that:

> These matters, involving the most intimate and personal choices a person may make in a lifetime, choices central to personal dignity and autonomy, are central to the liberty protected by the Fourteenth Amendment. At the heart of liberty is the right to define one's own concept of existence, of meaning, of the universe, and of the mystery of human life. Beliefs about these matters could not define the attributes of personhood were they formed under compulsion of the State.[9]

One of the most controversial Supreme Court cases of the twentieth century, *Roe v. Wade*, concerning a woman's right to have an abortion, may be thought of as a decisional privacy case. It focused on an individual's freedom to make a private choice about a personal and intimate matter without undue interference from the government.

Informational Privacy

This form of privacy is also known as the freedom of the individual to limit access to certain personal information about him or herself. The Court of Appeals for the Ninth Circuit has defined this phrase as "the individual interest in avoiding disclosure of personal matters...."[10] In his classic 1967 study, *Privacy and Freedom*, scholar Alan Westin defines it as "the claim of individuals...to determine for themselves when, how, and to what extent information about them is communicated to others."[11] Similarly, Professor Lawrence Lessig, drawing heavily

---

[8] *Planned Parenthood of Southeastern Pennsylvania v. Casey*, 505 U.S. 833, 851 (1992).

[9] *Planned Parenthood v. Casey*, 505 U.S. at 851.

[10] *Doe v. Attorney General*, 941 F.2d 780, 795 (9th Cir. 1991) (quoting *Whalen*, 429 U.S. 599-600). As the Supreme Court has not yet ruled definitively on the issue, there is not a unified view in the federal judiciary as to whether there is a constitutionally protected right to informational privacy. The majority of circuits considering this issue (the Second, Third, Fifth, and Ninth Circuits) find that there is. See, e.g., *Doe v. City of New York*, 15 F.3d 264, 267 (2d Cir. 1994) (concluding there is "a recognized constitutional right to privacy in personal information"); *Fadjo v. Coon*, 633 F.2d 1172, 1175-76 (5th Cir. 1981); *United States v. Westinghouse*, 638 F.2d 570, 577 (3d Cir. 1980), and *Roe v. Sherry*, 91 F.3d 1270, 1274 (9th Cir. 1996); *Doe v. Attorney General*, 941 F.2d 795-96. A minority conclude there is not. See *J.P. v. DeSanti*, 653 F.2d 1080, 1090 (6th Cir. 1981).

[11] Alan F. Westin, *Privacy and Freedom,* 337 (Atheneum 1967) (citing Scott, W. and M. Jarnagin, *Treatise Upon the Law of Telegraphs, Appendix,* 457-507 (Little, Brown & Co. 1868)).

on the scholarship of Ethan Katsh, has defined privacy in this context as "the power to control what others can come to know about you."[12] As Lessig explains, others can acquire information about you by monitoring and searching. Monitoring refers to that part of one's daily existence that others see, observe, and can respond to. Searching refers to that part of one's life that leaves a record that can later be scrutinized. Noting both quantity and quality aspects to informational privacy, a federal appellate court has phrased it in terms of, "control over knowledge about oneself. But it is not simply control over the quantity of information abroad; there are modulations in the quality of knowledge as well."[13]

U.S. government biometric programs could potentially require government employees, along with many others, such as citizens, and taxpayers, to be compelled to provide biometric identification information to a government agency for collection, maintenance, use, and dissemination in government-controlled databases. Such government-mandated use of biometrics implicates physical and informational privacy concerns and, to a lesser extent, decisional privacy concerns.

Physical Privacy and Biometrics

Public sector biometric applications could implicate Fourth Amendment considerations when biometrics, like fingerprints, are used in noncriminal contexts or when they are used in a criminal justice context. The courts have decided many Fourth Amendment cases involving individuals having to provide physical characteristics or personal traits, such as fingerprints or voice samples, to the State. Accordingly, analysis of the state of the law in the noncriminal and criminal justice areas may be instructive.

Constitutional Challenges to Fingerprinting in Noncriminal Context

The overwhelming majority of government biometric applications will fall into the noncriminal context, for such matters as logical or physical access control, fraud prevention, and other business processes. While the federal courts have not had occasion to rule on the government-mandated use of biometrics, many decisions have established that an individual has minimal constitutional privileges concerning his fingerprints or similar physical characteristics and personal traits.

Moreover, the courts have upheld numerous federal, state, and municipal requirements mandating fingerprinting for employment and licensing purposes, provided that the government has a rational basis for requiring fingerprinting. In the federal context, the so-called *rational basis test* means that Congress must show that the fingerprinting requirement bears a rational relationship to a legitimate government objective or interest. The rational basis test is a lesser

---

[12] Lawrence Lessig, *Code and Other Laws of Cyberspace* 143 (Basic Books 1999). (citing M. Ethan Katsh, *Law in a Digital World* 228 (Oxford University Press 1995)).

[13] *United States v. Westinghouse Elec. Corp.*, 638 F.2d at 577 n.5.

standard of judicial scrutiny than the compelling state interest test. Courts apply the compelling state interest test when state action affects the exercise of a fundamental right, such as political speech. Accordingly, using the rational basis test, courts have upheld government-mandated fingerprinting for employment and licensing purposes in connection with the taking of fingerprints for spouses of liquor licensees, male employees of alcoholic beverage wholesalers, taxi drivers, cabaret employees, bartenders, dealers in secondhand articles, all employees of member firms of national security exchanges registered with the Securities and Exchange Commission, and all individuals permitted unescorted access to nuclear power facilities.

For example, in *Utility Workers Union of America v. Nuclear Regulatory Commission*, decided in 1987, a union representing some 5,170 utility workers in nuclear power plants challenged as unconstitutional that part of a newly enacted federal statute requiring that these workers be fingerprinted. The Utility Workers Union claimed the fingerprinting requirement violated the workers' Fourth Amendment and privacy rights. The federal district court in the Southern District of New York disagreed and upheld the fingerprinting requirement. Citing a long string of cases, the court noted that in noncriminal contexts, the judiciary has "regularly upheld fingerprinting of employees."[14]

As for the union's constitutional right to privacy claim, the court quoted from a leading federal appellate court case, *Iacobucci v. City of Newport*:

> Whatever the outer limits of the right to privacy, clearly it cannot be extended to apply to a procedure the Supreme Court regards as only minimally intrusive. Enhanced protection has been held to apply only to such fundamental decisions as contraception...and family living arrangements. Fingerprints have not been held to merit the same level of constitutional concern.[15]

Moreover, in applying the rational basis test, the federal district court noted Congressional concern over an incident of sabotage at a nuclear power plant in Virginia and concluded that "using fingerprints to verify the identity and any existing criminal history of workers with access to vital areas or safeguards information is a rational method of clearing these workers."

Similarly, in a 1969 case involving a challenge to a New York state regulation requiring fingerprinting of all employees of national stock exchanges, a federal district court found that "possession of an individual's fingerprints does not create an atmosphere of general surveillance or indicate that they will be used for

---

[14]   *Utility Workers Union of America AFL-CIO v. Nuclear Regulatory Commission*, 664 F.Supp. 136, 138-139 (S.D.N.Y. 1987). The union directed its challenge to Section 606 of the Omnibus Diplomatic Security and Anti-Terrorism Act of 1986, codified as section 149 of the Atomic Energy Act of 1954, 42 U.S.C. § 2169 (1986). 10 C.F.R. § 73.57 implements the statute.

[15]   *Utility Workers Union of America*, 139 (quoting *Iacobucci v. City of Newport*, 785 F.2d 1357-58).

inadmissible purposes. Fingerprints provide a simple means of identification no more." The court in *Thom* observed that as long as the government had a "valid justification...for the taking of the prints under reasonable circumstances, their use for future identification purposes even in criminal investigations, is not impermissible."[16]

Constitutional Challenges to Fingerprinting in Criminal Justice Context

What will happen when government authorities want a biometric identifier from someone whom they suspect has committed a crime? Capturing the biometric identifier in this context should not run afoul of the Constitution. The Fourth Amendment governs searches and seizures conducted by government agents. The amendment makes clear that the Constitution does not forbid all searches and seizures, only "unreasonable" ones. The Supreme Court defines a search as an invasion of a person's reasonable expectations of privacy. To evaluate whether providing a biometric identifier in a criminal justice context constitutes a search, the judiciary focuses on two factors. First, the court examines the nature of the intrusion. Actual physical intrusions into the body, such as blood-drawing, breathalyzer testing, and urine analysis, can constitute Fourth Amendment searches. Second, the court examines the scope of the intrusiveness paying close attention to the "host of private medical facts."[17]

In the criminal justice context, the Supreme Court has examined the issue of whether acquiring information about an individual's personal characteristics constitutes a search. It has found that requiring a person to give voice exemplars is not a search because the physical characteristics of a person's voice, its tone and manner, as opposed to the content of a specific conversation, are constantly exposed to the public, such that no person can have a reasonable expectation that others will not know the sound of his voice.[18]

Using the same reasoning, the Court has ruled that requiring a person to give handwriting exemplars is not a search.[19] It has also described fingerprinting as nothing more than obtaining physical characteristics constantly exposed to the public,[20] and that fingerprinting involves none of the probing into an individual's private life and thoughts that marks an interrogation or search.[21]

In cases where provision of a biometric identifier might be found to constitute a search (such as in the hypothetical case of a physically intrusive, DNA-based biometric that would reveal extensive private medical facts about the individual), "the ultimate measure of the constitutionality of a governmental search is

---

[16]   *Thom v. New York Stock Exchange,* 306 F.Supp. 1002, 1010 (S.D.N.Y. 1969).

[17]   *Skinner v. Railway Labor Executives' Ass'n,* 489 U.S. 602, 617 (1989).

[18]   *United States v. Dionisio,* 410 U.S. 1, 93 (1973).

[19]   *United States v. Mara,* 410 U.S. 19, 93 (1973).

[20]   *Cupp v. Murphy,* 412 U.S. 291 (1973).

[21]   *Davis v. Mississippi,* 394 U.S. 726-727.

'reasonableness.' "[22] To make this determination, a court must balance the "intrusion on the individual's Fourth Amendment interests against its promotion of legitimate governmental interests."[23] In the criminal context, a search is "reasonable" only if the law enforcement agency has probable cause or reasonable suspicion of criminal activity.

Decisional Privacy: A Hypothetical

Decisional privacy involves a person's decisions relating to intimate matters such as marriage, procreation, contraception, and so on. Biometric applications will not likely involve decisional privacy, although the following hypothetical example might illustrate how decisional privacy concerns could be implicated by a biometric scheme.

In response to growing concerns about missing children, a state legislature decides to require all children attending private day care programs to be biometrically scanned for identification purposes. Parents object on the grounds that they are fully satisfied with the less-intrusive security already offered at the private day care program and that the biometric scanning will unduly traumatize their children. Educational zone of privacy considerations are possibly implicated. As the technology advances and its use becomes more widespread, however, decisional privacy concerns may increase.

Information Privacy—Whalen v. Roe

Why is a Supreme Court case decided more than 25 years ago still required reading? Because while the Information Age has drastically changed our lives since 1977, the Supreme Court's articulation of information privacy is still firmly anchored to its 1977 decision in *Whalen v. Roe*.[24]

The Supreme Court's 1977 decision in *Whalen v. Roe* "began the process of identifying the elements of an American constitutional right of informational privacy."[25] In 1999, a federal court cited *Whalen* for the proposition that "the

---

[22] *Vernonia Sch. Dist. 47J v. Acton*, 515 U.S. 646, 652 (1995).

[23] *Vernonia Sch. Dist. 47J v. Acton* 515 U.S. at 652 (quoting *Skinner*, 489 U.S. 619) (internal quotation marks omitted).

[24] *Whalen v. Roe*, 429 U.S. 589 (1977). Unless otherwise footnoted, all quotations in this section are sourced to this case.

[25] Paul M. Schwartz, "Privacy and Participation: Personal Information and Public Sector Regulation in the United States," 80 *Iowa Law Review* 553, 574-575 (1995). Other scholars have interpreted the significance of *Whalen v. Roe* slightly differently. See, e.g., Allen, "Legal Issues in Nonvoluntary Prenatal Screening in AIDS," 181 ("The Court has come closest to recognizing an independent right of information privacy in *Whalen v. Roe*."); Michael P. Roch, "Filling the Void of Data Protection in the United States Following the European Example," 12 *Santa Clara Computer & High Technology Law Journal* 71, 89 (1996) ("[I]n *Whalen v. Roe*, the court [sic] recognized in dicta that there may exist a right to protect against improper disclosure of personal data."); see also Fred H. Cate, *Privacy in the Information Age* 63 ("[H]aving found this new privacy interest in nondisclosure of personal information, the Court...applying a lower level of scrutiny, found that the statute did not infringe the individual's interest in nondisclosure.");

Constitution protects an individual's privacy right to avoid disclosure of personal information."[26]

Whalen involved the constitutional question of whether the state of New York could record and store, in a centralized computer database, "the names and addresses of all persons who have obtained, pursuant to a doctor's prescription, certain drugs." While technology has changed greatly since 1977, the legal reasoning in *Whalen* is still relevant, particularly for biometrics and more important for the government mandated use of biometrics. *Whalen* is instructive because it demonstrates the federal judiciary's approach to deciding some of the major constitutional law issues likely to be raised by government-mandated biometric applications. Accordingly, the facts of the case, the holding and the judicial reasoning deserve detailed examination.

Facts   In 1970, the New York state legislature, disturbed about the growing drug problem, established a state commission to evaluate the state's drug control laws. After study, the commission made recommendations to correct perceived deficiencies in these state laws. Following up on these recommendations, the state legislature amended the New York Public Health Law to require that all prescriptions for Schedule II drugs had to be prepared by the physician on an official state-provided form. The statute classified potentially harmful drugs in five schedules, which conformed to relevant federal law. Schedule II drugs included the most dangerous of the legitimate drugs. Examples of such drugs would include opium, methadone, amphetamines, and methaqualone, all of which have accepted medical uses. The statute also provided for an emergency exception. The completed form identified:

- The prescribing physician
- The dispensing pharmacy
- The prescribed drug and prescribed dosage
- The name, address and age of the patient

The statute required that a copy of the completed form be forwarded to the Bureau of Controlled Substances, Licensing and Evaluation (BCSLE), New York State Department of Health in Albany. Albany received about 100,000 Schedule II prescription forms each month. There the government agency recorded the information on magnetic tapes for eventual processing by computer. Based on his study

---

Peter L. Strauss et al., *Gellhorn & Byse's Administrative Law: Cases & Comments* 874 (1995) ("A requirement that information of arguable utility to a lawful regulatory program be collected or submitted is unlikely to fall beyond the constitutional power of either federal or state government.").

[26] *Wilson v. Pennsylvania State Police*, CA 94-6547, 1999 U.S. Dist. LEXIS 3165 *5 (E.D. Pa. Mar. 11, 1999) (U.S. Mag. Judge Hart) (citing *Whalen v. Roe*, 429 U.S. 599-600). See also *In re Crawford*, 1999 U.S. App. LEXIS 24941 *16.

of other states' reporting systems, the commission's chairman found that this comprehensive government-mandated database would serve two purposes: it would be a "useful adjunct to the proper identification of culpable professional and unscrupulous drug abusers" and it would enable the authorities to have a "reliable statistical indication of the pattern of [the state's] drug flow" to help stop the diversion of lawfully manufactured drugs into the illegal market.

Patient, doctor, and physician associations challenged the New York state statute in the federal courts. The evidence offered before the federal district court, where *Whalen v. Roe* was first heard, included testimony from:

- Two parents who "were concerned that their children would be stigmatized [as drug addicts] by the State's central filing system"
- Three adult patients who "feared disclosure of their names" to unauthorized third parties
- Four physicians who believed that the New York statute "entrenches on patients' privacy, and that each had observed a reaction of shock, fear and concern on the part of their patients"

The parties thus advanced two related privacy concerns that eventually reached the Supreme Court's consideration: "the nondisclosure of private information" or information privacy, and an individual's "interest in making important decisions independently" or decisional privacy.

Holding   In his opinion for the Court, Justice John Paul Stevens, joined by the Chief Justice and five other justices, found that "neither the immediate nor the threatened impact of the [statute's] patient-identification requirements...on either the reputation or the independence of patients ...is sufficient to constitute an invasion of any right or liberty protected by the [Due Process Clause of the] Fourteenth Amendment." With these words, the Supreme Court rejected the privacy claim. In sum, the nation's highest court ruled that a government's centralized, computerized database containing massive amounts of extremely sensitive medical information about citizens passed constitutional muster.

Judicial Reasoning   What factors influenced the Supreme Court's reasoning? First, the Court seemed impressed by the fact that the New York state legislature had created a specially appointed commission, which held numerous hearings on and conducted a thorough study of the state's drug problem. The commission consulted extensively with authorities in other states that were using central reporting systems effectively. In other words, a commission empowered by the legislature had done its homework in an attempt to help solve the menacing problem of drugs. The Court concluded that the statute was "manifestly the product of an orderly and rational legislative decision." In other words, there was a rational basis for the legislative action.

Arguably, the New York statute had not had much of an impact on the "war on drugs." For example, 20 months after its enactment, examination of the database led only to two investigations involving illegal use of drugs. As a kind of political process check, the Court explained that the state legislature, which gave this patient identification requirement its legal life, can also sound its death knell if it turns out to be an "unwise experiment."

In its analysis of the information privacy concerns raised, the Court paid close attention to what specific steps the state agency had taken to prevent any unauthorized disclosures of information from the centralized database. In particular, the Court noted that:

- The forms and the records were kept in a physically secure facility.
- The computer system was secured by restricting the number of computer terminals that could access the database.
- Employee access to the database was strictly limited.
- There were criminal sanctions for unauthorized disclosure.

Thus, the *Whalen* court scrutinized the technical and procedural protections in place to safeguard the information. A lot has changed in 25 years. Perhaps a contemporary court will examine technical protections and look for such things as firewalls, encryption, and biometric access control. But it's safe to predict that even a contemporary court will be impressed with procedural safeguards in the form of criminal sanctions for unauthorized disclosure.

The Court took a somewhat practical approach to the way personal information is used in the contemporary age. It accepted the view that disclosure of such medical information to various government agencies and private sector organizations, such as insurance companies, is "often an essential part of modern medical practice even when the disclosure may reflect unfavorably on the character of the patient. Requiring such disclosures to representatives of the State having responsibility for the health of the community does not automatically amount to an impermissible invasion of privacy."

In addressing decisional privacy issues, the Court acknowledged genuine concern that the very existence of the database will disturb some people so greatly that they will refuse to go to the doctor to get necessary medication. However, given the large number of prescriptions processed at Albany, approximately 100,000 prescription forms for Schedule II drugs monthly, the Court concluded that the "statute did not deprive the public of access to the [legal] drugs."

The Court's opinion concluded with a cautionary note that still echoes loudly today:

> We are not unaware of the threat to privacy implicit in the accumulation of vast amounts of personal information in computerized data banks or other massive government files.... The right to collect and use such data for public purposes is typically accompanied by a concomitant statutory or regulatory duty to avoid unwarranted disclosures.

The New York statute and its related implementation showed "a proper concern with, and protection of, the individual's interest in privacy." The Court, however, limited the effect of its decision by reserving for another day consideration of legal questions which could arise from unauthorized disclosures of information from a government database "by a system that did not contain comparable security provisions."

Justice Brennan's Concurring Opinion   In his concurring opinion Justice William Brennan, more so than his colleagues, expressed his concern over the potential erosion of information privacy in the face of emerging technologies. "The central storage and easy accessibility of computerized data vastly increase the potential for abuse of that information, and I am not prepared to say that future developments will not demonstrate the necessity of some curb on such technology." While this specific "carefully designed program" did not "amount to a deprivation of constitutionally protected privacy interests," Justice Brennan suggested that there is a core right to informational privacy and stressed that future programs might be subjected to a compelling state interest test or strict scrutiny by the court of the government action.

Justice Stewart's Concurring Opinion   Justice Potter Stewart, in his concurrence, took issue with what he implicitly viewed as Justice Brennan's expansive privacy approach as well as with his brethren's view of constitutional privacy interests. According to Stewart, there is no general right of privacy in the Constitution. Moreover, in Stewart's view, privacy concerns are matters left largely to the individual states.

Cautionary Note   The *Whalen* Court expressed its concern about "unwarranted disclosures" from government databases. As Professor Lillian Bevier has explained:

> The fact that the government collects such great quantities of data gives rise to concern...that the data will be inappropriately disseminated, within government or to outsiders, or that it will be otherwise misused or abused. Recent advances in computer technology, which permit data to be manipulated, organized, compiled, transferred, distributed, and retrieved with hitherto unimaginable ease, exacerbate such concern.[27]

With the exception of Justice Stewart, all of the justices adopted a prospective approach. That is, by intensely focusing on the facts of *Whalen*, the Court left itself with ample judicial wiggle room to find that government-mandated use of

---

[27] Lillian Bevier, "Information About Individuals in the Hands of the Government: Some Reflections on Mechanism for Privacy Protection," *William & Mary Bill of Rights Journal*, vol. 4, no. 455 (1995): 458.

new technologies combined with powerful computer systems might lack necessary constitutional safeguards. Since the *Whalen* decision is tied so intimately to the specific facts of *Whalen*, a future Court could easily distinguish the facts of a future case from the facts of *Whalen* to reach a different result. Professor Steve Goldberg of Georgetown University Law Center has explained that when a Supreme Court opinion offers broad pronouncements and little factual analysis, it is a sure sign that the Court is on comfortable turf. However, when the opinion deals with intense factual scrutiny, the Court is less sure of itself, and thus is keeping its options open for the long run.[28]

In sum, a lesson to take away from *Whalen* is that a future Court might find an informational privacy right violated unless the government agency collecting the information had made clear its need and purpose in collecting the information and had taken strong and effective measures to prevent unwarranted disclosures from its databases. In other words, if the government agency ignores these steps, the Court's cautionary note of *Whalen* could turn into a clear-sounding constitutional alarm bell in the future.

Recent case law suggests that the federal judiciary accepts the informational privacy concept articulated in *Whalen*. In 1999, for example, the Court of Appeals for the Ninth Circuit explained that one of the constitutionally-protected privacy interests of *Whalen* is "the individual interest in avoiding disclosure of personal matters...."[29] Moreover, the Ninth Circuit, like the *Whalen* court, found that the right to information privacy is not absolute, but must be balanced with the governmental interest.

In *In re Crawford*, the court held that federally required public disclosure of social security numbers (SSN) of certain paralegals does not violate any constitutional or statutory rights of these individuals. The federal law at issue requires a bankruptcy petition preparer (BPP), a type of paralegal, to include his SSN on all documents filed with the federal bankruptcy courts. By law, these documents are public records that can be accessed by anyone. Jack Ferm, a BPP, refused to provide his SSN on bankruptcy documents he had filed with a bankruptcy court in Nevada. He feared disclosure of his SSN would make him particularly vulnerable to the crime of identity theft. When the court fined him for refusing to provide his SSN, Ferm filed a lawsuit in federal court, claiming the disclosure of his SSN violated his privacy rights.

While the court sympathized with Ferm's "speculative fear," it noted that an SSN, "unlike HIV status, sexual orientation or genetic makeup" is "not inherently sensitive or intimate information, and its disclosure does not lead directly to injury, embarrassment or stigma." The court balanced Ferm's interest in nondisclosure of his SSN with the governmental interests. The many factors the court considered included:

---

[28]   Steve Goldberg, interview by author, September 1996.

[29]   *In re Crawford*, U.S. App. LEXIS 24941 *7-8. pg. 16

The type of record requested, the information it does or might contain, the potential for harm in any subsequent nonconsensual disclosure, the injury from disclosure to the relationship in which the record was generated, the adequacy of safeguards to prevent unauthorized disclosure, the degree of need for access, and whether there is an express statutory mandate, articulated public policy, or other recognizable public interest militating toward access.[30]

The court found that the disclosure requirement serves the Bankruptcy Code's "public access" provision that is rooted in the traditional right of public access to judicial proceedings. After weighing the many relevant factors, the court concluded:

The speculative possibility of identity theft is not enough to trump the importance of the governmental interests [requiring public disclosure]. In short the balance tips in the government's favor. Accordingly we cannot say that Congress transgressed the bounds of the Constitution in enacting the statutes at issue here.[31]

In re Crawford is just a recent example that the Supreme Court's approach in *Whalen* remains firmly in place with the federal judiciary. It is prudent for prospective government users of biometrics to study *Whalen* closely, to explain the need for biometrics and to have database safeguards in place.

Other Constitutionally Based Considerations of Biometrics

As explained in Chapter 12, some limited segments of American society have expressed religious objections to the use of biometrics. Although these religious-based concerns may not on the surface appear to implicate privacy issues, the constitutionally protected right to the free exercise of religion can be understood to vindicate privacy-related values. Some individuals oppose being compelled to participate in a government program that mandates the provision of a biometric identifier.

These religious-based refusals raise a sensitive issue, in which the intrusion on the free exercise of religion must be carefully weighed. Some "real-world" cases provide guidance as to how the law reacts to such refusals. For example, the New York Department of Social Services and the Connecticut Department of Social Services (DSS) have encountered legal challenges based on religious concerns from entitlement program recipients who refused to provide a biometric

---

[30]   *In re Crawford,* *11 (citing *Doe v. Attorney General*, 941 F.2d 796 (quoting *Westinghouse*, 638 F.2d 578)).

[31]   *In re Crawford,* *16. The court did, however, "encourage the Bankruptcy Courts to consider enacting rules to limit the disclosure of BPP SSNs."

identifier. Based on these objections, other government agencies might encounter a similar legal challenge to its mandated use of biometrics. Accordingly, the New York DSS and Connecticut DSS experiences might offer useful insight to how the legal system reacts.

New York Experience

Liberty Buchanan, a New York resident, received Aid to Families with Dependent Children (ADC) and Food Stamps for herself and her four minor children. In 1996, New York DSS informed her that she would be required to participate in an automated finger imaging system (AFIS). New York law required participation in AFIS as a condition of eligibility for ADC and other entitlements. Buchanan refused to participate in AFIS. She based her refusal on her religious convictions, grounded in part on her interpretation of the "mark of the beast" language in the Book of Revelations. Because she refused to provide a fingerprint, DSS discontinued the Buchanans' entitlement benefits. After a DSS agency hearing, the State Commissioner of Social Services affirmed the DSS decision, finding that Buchanan did not demonstrate a good cause basis for exemption from the finger imaging requirement. Buchanan then appealed to the New York Supreme Court. After a hearing, in 1997, the New York Supreme Court Appellate Division, Third Judicial Department, in *Buchanan v. Wing,* found that Ms. Buchanan had failed to "set forth any competent proof that the AFIS actually involved any invasive procedures marking them in violation of [her] beliefs."[32] Accordingly, the court upheld the DSS decision.

Connecticut Experience

Similarly, in Connecticut, John Doe, his wife and minor children, recipients of Temporary Family Assistance (TFA), refused to submit to the Connecticut DSS digital imaging requirement. ("John Doe" is an alias used to protect the true identity of the individual out of respect for his and his family's privacy.) Beginning in January 1996, DSS, pursuant to state law, began requiring all TFA recipients to be biometrically imaged for identification purposes by providing copies of the fingerprints of their two index fingers. In April 1996, Mr. and Mrs. Doe objected based on their religious beliefs. DSS exempted them from the requirement in April 1996 and October 1997. In July 1998, however, DSS reviewed its policy and determined that the Does would have to comply with the digital imaging requirement. Doe requested a DSS hearing.

At the August 1998 hearing, he testified as to his objections to providing a biometric identifier. He based these objections on his religious beliefs. Specifically, Doe testified that the Book of Revelations discusses the "mark or number of the beast" that the "beast" tries to make all people receive on their hand or forehead.

---

[32] *Buchanon v. Wing*, New York Supreme Court, Appellate Division, Third Judicial Department, December 4, 1997, 79343: 21

According to Doe, those who accept the mark "shall drink of the wine of the wrath of God" and be condemned. By submitting to digital imaging and allowing himself to be marked in this way, he would violate his religious convictions. He therefore requested a "good cause" exception to the digital imaging requirement as provided in the DSS regulations. According to the relevant regulatory guidance from the *Uniform Policy Manual*, "Good cause is considered to exist when circumstances beyond the individual's control reasonably prevent participation in the Digital Imaging Process."

In November 1998, the hearing officer ruled that Doe, "although having strong religious beliefs, some of which he interprets as a barrier for him to be digitally imaged, does not have as a result of this religious belief a circumstance beyond his control which prevents him from being digitally imaged."[33] Doe appealed from this final DSS decision to the Connecticut state court. While his case was pending, the DSS Commissioner decided to vacate the hearing decision and grant the Does an exception from the digital-imaging requirement. Rather than fight the Does in state court, in a legal battle that attracted the interest of civil liberties groups, the Commissioner took an easier way out—the Does got their exception from the biometric requirement; the state of Connecticut avoided potentially controversial litigation, and we are left wondering what the higher courts would have done.

Goldman v. Weinberger

While the U.S. Supreme Court has not yet decided any legal challenges involving religious objections to biometrics, it has decided one landmark case involving an individual's objections to military regulations based on an individual's religious beliefs, which may provide some indication of how the Court would deal with a similar complaint related to biometrics. One of the best-known legal challenges brought against the military on this basis is the case of *Goldman v. Weinberger*, decided by the Supreme Court in 1986.

S. Simcha Goldman, an Air Force officer and ordained rabbi of the Orthodox Jewish faith, was ordered not to wear his yarmulke while on duty and in uniform, pursuant to Air Force regulations. Goldman brought an action in federal district court, claiming that the application of the Air Force regulation to prevent him from wearing his yarmulke infringed upon his First Amendment freedom to exercise his religious beliefs. The District Court agreed with Goldman and permanently enjoined the Air Force from enforcing the regulation against him. The Court of Appeals reversed and Goldman appealed to the Supreme Court.[34]

The Supreme Court held that Goldman's religious objections, grounded in the First Amendment's free exercise of religion clause, did not prohibit the challenged regulation from being applied to Goldman, even though its effect is to

---

[33] State of Connecticut Department of Social Services, Office of Administrative Hearings and Appeals, *Notice of Decision*, November 10, 1998.

[34] *Goldman v. Weinberger*, 475 U.S. 503 (1986).

restrict the wearing of the headgear required by his religious beliefs. The Court found that the First Amendment does not require the military to accommodate such practices as wearing a yarmulke in the face of the military's view that such practices would detract from the uniformity sought by dress regulations. In his majority opinion, then Justice Rehnquist explained that, "when evaluating whether military needs justify a particular restriction on religiously motivated conduct, courts must give great deference to the professional judgment of military authorities concerning the relative importance of a particular military interest."[35]

Congress reacted to the *Goldman* decision by passing a statute effectively eviscerating the Court's ruling. In 1987, Congress amended the U.S. Code to permit a member of the armed forces to "wear an item of religious apparel while wearing the uniform of the member's armed force," with two exceptions: when "wearing of the item would interfere with the performance of the member's military duties," or if "the item of apparel is not neat and conservative."[36]

In 1990, the Supreme Court decided another important case involving religious beliefs. In *Employment Division, Department of Human Resources of Oregon v. Smith* (referred to as *Smith*), Alfred Smith and Galen Black brought suit against the Oregon State Employment Division after it refused their claims for unemployment compensation. Their employer had discharged them from their jobs on "misconduct" grounds because they had ingested peyote, a hallucinogen, as part of the sacramental observances of their Native American religion. Under Oregon law, peyote is a controlled substance and thus prohibited.

In *Smith*, the Supreme Court held that the First Amendment's free exercise of religion clause does not require exemption from a religiously neutral law for those whose religious beliefs preclude them from complying with the law. *Smith* holds that the legislature is free, however, to grant religious exemptions to the neutral laws if it so chooses. Thus, in *Smith*, the First Amendment's free exercise clause did not prohibit the application of Oregon state drug laws to use of peyote for religious purposes. However, were it so inclined, the Oregon state legislature could create a religious exemption.[37]

Lessons Learned   We can draw several broad lessons from *Goldman*. First, the congressional reaction to the *Goldman* decision demonstrates that Congress is not unwilling to require the military, or other government agencies, to make special allowances for religious objections. Second, a government agency, as an institution,

---

[35] *Goldman,* 475 U.S. at 507 (citation omitted).

[36] See 10 U.S.C. § 774 (1999).

[37] *Employment Division, Department of Human Resources of Oregon v. Smith,* 494 U.S. 889 (1990).

will likely heed directions from Congress. A lesson from *Smith* reinforces a lesson from *Goldman*: While a government agency's requirement for participating in biometric applications, just like the Oregon law prohibiting peyote, will be religiously neutral, the Congress, like the Oregon state legislature, could grant, if it were so inclined, religious exemptions to the neutral requirement. In this sense, government agencies considering the use of biometrics would be wise to have an established policy in place to deal with religious practices.

Statutory and Administrative Law Considerations

In examining the privacy rights recognized by the Constitution, we see that informational privacy is the one most likely implicated by government-mandated use of biometrics. The Court's decision in *Whalen v. Roe* provides a framework for how a future court might address such issues. We have also examined physical and decisional privacy as well as how the court would deal with religious-based objections to biometrics. With this constitutional basis thus established, we next have to examine statutory and administrative law protections. Congress is free to regulate government-mandated use of biometrics. Congress has already passed comprehensive legislation, known as the Privacy Act, affecting how U.S. government agencies must protect personal information. This act also applies to biometric records. For this reason, we next examine the Privacy Act in detail.

The Privacy Act of 1974

The Privacy Act of 1974 (codified at 5 U.S.C. § 552a, as amended) regulates the collection, maintenance, use and dissemination of personal information by federal government agencies.

In broad terms, the Privacy Act gives certain rights to the "data subject," or the individual who provides personal information, and places certain responsibilities on the "data collector," or the agency collecting the personal information. The Privacy Act balances a federal agency's need to collect, use, and disseminate information about individuals with the privacy rights of those individuals. In particular, the act tries to protect the individual from unwarranted invasions of privacy stemming from a federal agency's collection, maintenance, use and dissemination of personal information about the individual.

There are several things the Privacy Act does not do. For example, the Privacy Act does not regulate the collection, maintenance, use, and dissemination of personal information by state and local government agencies. The Privacy Act does not regulate personal information held by private sector entities. The Privacy Act does not apply when the individual, or data subject, is not a U.S. citizen or an alien lawfully admitted for permanent residence.

The Privacy Act's basic provisions include the following:

- Restricting federal agencies from disclosing personally identifiable records maintained by the agencies

- Requiring federal agencies to maintain records with accuracy and diligence

- Granting individuals increased rights to access records about themselves maintained by federal agencies and to amend their records provided they show that the records are not accurate, relevant, timely, or complete

- Requiring federal agencies to establish administrative, technical, and policy safeguards to protect record security

As these basic provisions suggest, the Privacy Act sets forth a so-called "code of fair information practices" requiring federal agencies to adopt minimum standards for collection, maintenance, use and dissemination of records. It also requires that agencies publish detailed descriptions of these standards and the procedures used to implement them.

Applicability to Biometrics

Although the Privacy Act does not specifically mention "biometrics," there is little doubt that the Act can apply to biometrics. As the Act applies to a "record" that is "contained in a system of records," the threshold issue to resolve is whether biometric identification information, whether in the form of an image file or a template file, falls within the Act's broad definition of record. The Privacy Act (5 U.S.C. § 552a(a)(4)) defines "record" as:

> Any item, collection, or grouping of information about an individual that is maintained by an agency, including, but not limited to, his education, financial transactions, medical history, and criminal or employment history and that contains his name, or the identifying number, symbol, or *other identifying particular assigned to the individual, such as a finger or voice print or a photograph....*

The Office of Management and Budget (OMB) *Guidelines* explain that "record" means "any item of information about an individual that includes an individual identifier" and "can include as little as one descriptive item about an individual."[38] In 1992, in the Court of Appeals for the Third Circuit has affirmed the *Guidelines'* definition, finding that "record" includes "any information about an individual that is linked to that individual through an identifying particular."[39] In 1994, the Court of Appeals for the District of Columbia stressed that

---

[38]   See OMB *Guidelines*, 52 *Fed. Reg.* 12, 990 (1987).

[39]   *Quinn v. Stone*, 978 F.2d 126, 133 (3d Cir. 1992).

the Privacy Act protects only "information that actually describes the individual in some way."[40]

Biometrics are distinctive individual identifiers. They are "identifying" and they are "particular" to an individual. Moreover, finger or voice print, two of the examples cited in the Act's definition of "record," are physical characteristics. As such, they fall within the definition of biometrics.

To fall within the Privacy Act, the record must be "contained in a system of records." The Act 5 (U.S.C. § 552a(a)(5)) defines "system of record" as:

> A group of any records under the control of any agency from which information is retrieved by the name of the individual or by some identifying number, symbol, or other identifying particular assigned to the individual....

OMB *Guidelines* explain that a system of records exists when two conditions are met. First, there must be an "indexing or retrieval capability using identifying particulars [that is] built into the system." Second, the agency must "retrieve records about individuals by reference to some personal identifier." Commenting on these OMB *Guidelines*, in 1996, the Court of Appeals for the District of Columbia has explained that a federal agency must not only have "the capability to retrieve information indexed under a person's name, but the agency must in fact retrieve records in this way in order for a system of records to exist."[41]

To determine whether a U.S. government agency's biometric application is a record contained in a system of records, an agency must do a case-by-case analysis of each such application examining how the biometric is used. For some applications, it is possible that the Privacy Act would not be implicated because the record is not contained in a system of records. For example, the U.S. Army's Fort Sill pilot program did not implicate the Privacy Act because while the biometrically protected digital cash card provided to Army basic trainees was arguably a record, the fingerprint template was stored only on the card. It was not contained in any system of records, such as a central database. On the other hand, some applications will implicate the Act. Such an application would include biometric identification information combined with information about an individual that can be retrieved by an identifying particular, like a biometric. In cases where an agency's biometric application implicates the Privacy Act, the agency must make certain that it complies fully with the Act's provisions.

The Privacy Act's major requirements are briefly explained in the following sections.

---

[40] *Tobey v. N.L.R.B.*, 40 F.3d 469, 471-473 (D.C. Cir. 1994).

[41] *Henke v. United States Department of Commerce*, 83 F.3d 1453, 1460 n. 12 (D.C. Cir. 1996). pg. 23

The "No Disclosure Without Consent Rule"

The Privacy Act (U.S.C. § 552a(b)) prohibits a federal agency from "disclos[ing] any record which is contained in a system of records by any means of communication to any person, or to another agency, except pursuant to a written request by, or with the prior written consent of, the individual to whom the record pertains...." This provision is known as the "No Disclosure Without Consent Rule."

While the "No Disclosure Without Consent Rule" applies, the Privacy Act contains 12 enumerated exceptions to this rule.

The "Intra-Agency Need to Know" Exception   This exception applies when officers and employees of the federal agency maintaining the record have a need for the record in the performance of their duties.

The "Required Freedom of Information Act (FOIA) Disclosure" Exception This exception provides that the Privacy Act cannot be used to prohibit a disclosure that the FOIA requires.

The "Routine Use" Exception   As for disclosure of a record, a "routine use" means "the use of such record for a purpose which is compatible with the purpose for which it was collected." The Privacy Act requires that the federal agency publish in the *Federal Register* "each routine use of the records contained in the system, including the categories of users and the purpose of such use." Thus, the federal government agency must satisfy two requirements for a proper routine use disclosure: the routine use must be "compatible" and constructive notice must be given by publication of the agency's routine use in the *Federal Register*.

According to OMB, compatibility encompasses functionally equivalent uses and other uses that are necessary and proper. The federal judiciary has not settled on a uniform interpretation of compatibility. For example, in 1993,[42] the Court of Appeals for the District of Columbia adopted a broadly construed "common usage" requiring only that "a proposed disclosure would not actually frustrate the purposes for which the information was gathered."[43] On the other hand, in 1989, the Court of Appeals for the Third Circuit put forth a narrower construction: a "concrete relationship or similarity, some meaningful degree of convergence, between the disclosing agency's purpose in gathering the information and its disclosure."[44] In cases where the federal judiciary must determine the legality of a federal agency's routine use, the judiciary gives deference to the federal government agency's construction of its routine use.

Two important types of "compatible" routine uses frequently occur in the law enforcement context. First, in the context of investigations and prosecutions,

---

[42]   *United States Postal Serv. v. National Ass'n of Letter Carriers*, 9 F.3d 138, 144 (D.C. Cir. 1993).

[43]   *Britt v. Naval Investigative Serv.*, 886 F.2d 544, 555 (3d Cir. 1989).

[44]   *Britt v. Naval Investigative Serv.*, 1989.

law enforcement agencies may routinely share law enforcement records with each other. Second, agencies may routinely disclose any records indicating a possible violation of law, regardless of the purpose for collection, to law enforcement agencies for purposes of investigation and prosecution.

Because of its "potential breadth," the routine use exception is a controversial provision of the Privacy Act. For example, it has been called "a huge loophole" that has been used by federal agencies to justify almost any use of the data.

Moreover, Congress can always mandate additional new "routine uses" for agencies that the affected agencies must establish as "routine uses." For example, Congress has mandated the establishment of a federal "Parent Locator Service" within the Department of Health and Human Services (HHS) and requires federal agencies to comply with requests from the Secretary of HHS for addresses and places of employment of absent parents.

The "Bureau of the Census" Exception   This exception is for disclosure of information made to the U.S. Bureau of the Census for purposes of planning or carrying out a census or related activity pursuant to statute.

The "Statistical Research" Exception   This exception permits disclosure of information to entities that will use the information for statistical research or a reporting record. The information must be transferred to the entity in a form that is not individually identifiable.

The "National Archives" Exception   This limited exception permits disclosure of records that have sufficient historical or other value to warrant consideration for their preservation by the U.S. government.

The "Law Enforcement Request" Exception   This exception provides for disclosure of information to federal law enforcement agencies and allows an agency, "upon receipt of a written request, [to] disclose a record to another agency or unit of State or local government for a civil or criminal law enforcement activity."

The "Individual Health or Safety" Exception   This exception permits disclosure of information pursuant to a showing of compelling circumstances affecting the health or safety of an individual. For example, dental records on several individuals could be released to identify an individual injured in an accident.

The "Congressional" Exception   This exception applies to disclosure of information to the House of Representatives and the Senate, or, to the extent of matter within its jurisdiction, any committee or subcommittee thereof, any joint committee of Congress or subcommittee of any such joint committee.

The "General Accounting Office" Exception   This exception applies to disclosure of information to the Comptroller General in the course of the performance of the duties of the General Accounting Office.

The "Judicial" Exception   This exception applies to court orders requiring disclosure prevents the Privacy Act from obstructing the normal course of court proceedings, including court-ordered discovery.

The "Debt Collection Act" Exception   The Debt Collection Act of 1982 authorized this disclosure exception. It permits agencies to disclose bad debt information to credit bureaus. Before disclosing this information, however, agencies must complete a series of due process steps designed to validate the debt and to offer the individual an opportunity to repay it.

Under the Privacy Act, rights are personal to the individual who is the subject of the federal agency record. Others cannot assert these rights on behalf of the aggrieved individual.

Agency Responsibilities

The Privacy Act places certain responsibilities on the data collector. Some of these responsibilities include publishing information about the systems of records in the data collector's charge, giving notice to data subjects, and safeguarding data.

Publication   Among the responsibilities the Privacy Act (5 U.S.C. § 552a(e)(4)) places on the data collector, it requires an "agency that maintains a system of records" to "publish in the *Federal Register* upon establishment or revision a notice of the existence and character of the system of records...." This notice is known as a "Privacy Act Systems of Records Notice."

As government agency use of biometrics will likely lead to the establishment of new systems of records and revisions to old systems, the agency must comply with this Privacy Act Systems of Records Notice requirement.

Notice   The Privacy Act (5 U.S.C. § 552a(e)(3)) requires the data collector to give notice—which may be given on the actual form the data collector uses to collect the desired information, or on a separate form that can be retained by the individual—to the data subject informing him of four factors:

- The authority that authorizes the solicitation of the information and whether disclosure of such information is mandatory or voluntary
- The principal purpose or purposes for which the information is intended to be used
- The routine uses that may be made of the information
- The effects on the data subject if any, of not providing all or any part of the requested information

In its biometric applications, the agency will likely comply with the Privacy Act's notice requirement during the biometric enrollment process, when it first collects the biometric identification information from the data subject.

Data Safeguarding   The Privacy Act requires the data collector to "establish appropriate administrative, technical, and physical safeguards to insure the security and confidentiality of records...." Similarly, the Act (5 U.S.C. § 552a(e)(10)) requires the data collector "to protect against any anticipated threats or hazards to their security or integrity which could result in substantial harm, embarrassment, inconvenience, or unfairness to any individual about whom information is maintained."

As this provision of the Act makes clear, the data collector must put in place appropriate safeguards to protect information in its databases. However, as a federal district court has explained, "the Privacy Act does not make administrative agencies guarantors of the integrity and security of materials which they generate." Instead, "the agencies are to decide for themselves how to manage their record security problems, within the broad parameters set out by the Act." Accordingly, the data collectors "have broad discretion to choose among alternative methods of securing their records commensurate with their needs, objectives, procedures and resources."[45]

The Senate Report accompanying the Privacy Act supports this judicial view. It stated:

> The Committee recognizes the variety of technical security needs of the many different agency systems and files containing personal information as well as the cost and range of possible technological methods of meeting those needs. The Committee, therefore, has not required [ ] in this Act a general set of technical standards for security of systems. Rather, the agency is merely required to establish those administrative and technical safeguards which it determines appropriate and finds technologically feasible for the adequate protection of the confidentiality of the particular information it keeps against purloining, unauthorized access, and political pressures to yield the information to persons with no formal need for it.[46]

The Senate Report stressed that data collectors have flexibility in deciding appropriate safeguards:

> The [Privacy] Act...provides reasonable leeway for agency allotment of resources to implement this subsection. At the agency level, it allows for a certain amount of "risk management" whereby administrators weigh the importance and likelihood of the threats against the availability of security measures and consideration of cost.[47]

---

[45] *Kostyu v. United States*, 742 F.Supp. 413, 417 (E.D. Mich. 1990) (holding that alleged lapses in Internal Revenue Service security resulting in disclosure of information to public were not willful and intentional as required to establish Privacy Act violation).

[46] *Kostyu v. United States*, (citing S.Rep. No. 93-1183, reprinted in 1974 U.S. Code Cong. & Admin. News 6916, 6969).

[47] *Kostyu v. United States*, (citing S.Rep. No. 93-1183, reprinted in 1974 U.S. Code Cong. & Admin. News 6916, 6969).

While a breach of database security and confidentiality can be harmful or embarrassing to the data collector, both the agency and the employee responsible for the breach can be found legally liable for a Privacy Act violation. This legal liability can include civil liability for the agency and criminal liability for an agency official. Civil liability for such a breach attaches when "the agency has acted in a manner which was intentional or willful." The federal judiciary has interpreted this phrase "to require a showing of fault 'somewhat greater than gross negligence.' "[48]

Similarly, criminal liability, in the form of a misdemeanor, attaches for such a breach when an "officer or employee of an agency, who by virtue of his employment or official position, has possession of, or access to, agency records [covered by the Privacy Act], and who knowing that disclosure of the specific material is so prohibited, willfully discloses the material in any manner to any person or agency not entitled to receive it...." Likewise, criminal liability can attach when an "officer or employee of any agency willfully maintains a system of records without meeting the notice requirements of [the Privacy Act]."[49]

In implementing any biometric applications that fall under the Privacy Act, the agency must meet all of the Act's many requirements.

Additional Safeguards   The Computer Matching and Privacy Act of 1988 amended the Privacy Act by adding new provisions regulating federal agencies' computer matching practices and placing requirements on the agencies. A computer match is done by using a computer program to search an agency's files for information associated with or indexed by a personal identifier, such as a name or SSN. The information thus obtained can then be compared with information in the databases of another federal agency. In this way, discrepancies and inconsistencies might be discovered that point to fraud in government benefits, for example.

DOD participates in approximately 25 computer matching programs with various different government agencies. For example, DOD has a "Debt Collection" matching program in effect with the Department of Education. The purpose of this program is to identify and locate federal personnel who owe delinquent payments on certain programs administered by Education.

For all of its matching programs, a government agency must meet the Computer Matching Act's requirements, which basically include entering into formal agreements with the exchanging agencies, verifying independently the accuracy of data received before any official action is taken, providing notice in the *Federal Register* prior to conducting or revising a computer matching program, and establishing a Data Integrity Board to monitor implementation and compliance with the Act.

---

[48]   See 5 U.S.C. § 552a(g)(4); *Pilon v. United States Department of Justice*, 796 F.Supp. 7, 12 (D.D.C. 1992); *Kostyu*, 742 F.Supp. 416.

[49]   See 5 U.S.C. § 552a(i)(2). Certain exemptions apply; for example, 5 U.S.C. § 552a(j).

Because a personal identifier in the form of a biometric identifier could implicate the Computer Matching Act, a government agency will need to study the Act closely to determine whether the specific biometric application is implicated.

Administrative regulation is another safeguard. From the administrative regulatory perspective, Congress can follow two well-worn policy paths when dealing with a public policy issue involving a new technology such as biometrics. It can take the direct route and pass legislation regulating a government agency's use of the technology, or it can delegate its authority to the appropriate administrative agencies within government agency. The delegation route is the road most frequently traveled. However, even though the government agencies, in general, are well equipped with expertise, experience, and institutional memory, they still face enormous challenges in designing, formulating, and implementing government policy for biometric applications. In addition, numerous competing groups (many well-organized and some politically influential) will want to press their claims in this public policy process.

Congress, through the legislative process, can require a government agency to satisfy additional conditions related to its biometric applications. For example, Congress could go beyond the Privacy Act and place additional prohibitions on disclosure of biometric identification information and further restrict sharing.

International Law Considerations

Organizations increasingly operate globally. As a result, their overseas activities, international business partners, and foreign customers may be subject to different laws and regulations. These organizations need to make certain that they are in full compliance with these non-U.S. legal norms, such as laws of a foreign nation-state or an institutional framework such as the European Union. These international law considerations are all the more important for organizations managing, processing, and using information across national boundaries. They are discussed in the following sections, with special attention given to the European Union (E.U.) Privacy Directive.

European Union Data Protection Directive

The E.U. Data Protection Directive, or Directive 96/46/EC, took effect on October 25, 1998. By this date, all 15 E.U. member states were required to enact comprehensive privacy legislation requiring organizations to implement personal data policies. After extensive negotiations, the U.S. and E.U. have reached a "safe harbor" agreement for how the directive will be applied to U.S. organizations. This agreement is designed to serve as guidance to U.S. organizations seeking to comply with the "adequacy" requirement of the directive. The "safe harbor" arrangement provides organizations within the safe harbor with a presumption of adequacy and data transfers from the E.U. to them could continue. Organizations would come into the safe harbor by self certifying that they adhere to these privacy principles. As a result of the safe harbor proposal, the E.U. has announced its intention to avoid disrupting data flows to the U.S. by using the flexibility provided for in the directive so long as the U.S. is engaged in good faith negotiations with the E.U.

American Ambassador David L. Aaron, the former Undersecretary for International Trade, has explained the transnational reach of the E.U. privacy law by noting that the Directive allows transfer of personally identifiable data to third countries only if they provide an "adequate" level of privacy protection.[50] Identifying American concerns about the directive, Ambassador Aaron and others have noted that because the United States relies largely on a sectoral and self-regulatory, rather than legislative, approach to privacy protection, many U.S. organizations have been uncertain about the impact of the 'adequacy' standard on personal data transfers from the E.U to the U.S.

Major Provisions

The directive has the potential to be far-reaching. For example, the E.U. personal data policies provide for the following:

- **Transparency**   Data must be processed fairly and lawfully.

- **Purpose limitation**   Data must be collected and possessed for specified, legitimate purposes and kept no longer than necessary to fulfill the stated purpose.

- **Data quality**   Data must be accurate and up to date.

- **Data transfers**   Article 25 of the directive restricts authorized users of personal information from transferring that information to third parties without the permission of the individual providing the data, or data subject. In the case of data transfers across national boundaries, the directive prohibits data transfers outright to any country lacking an "adequate level of protection," as determined by the E.U. Article 25 is a major source of U.S. concern.

- **Special protection for sensitive data**   This provision requires restrictions on, and special government scrutiny of, data collection and processing activities of information identifying racial or ethnic origin, political opinions, religious or philosophical beliefs or concerning health or sex life. Under the directive, such data collection or processing is generally forbidden outright.

---

[50]   David L. Aaron, "The EU Data Protection Directive: Implications for the U.S. Privacy Debate," Testimony before the Subcommittee on Commerce, Trade, and Consumer Protection, U.S. House of Representatives, March 8, 2001, available at http://energycommerce.house.gov/107/hearings/03082001Hearing49/Aaron102.htm.

- **Government authority** Each E.U. member state must create an independent public authority to supervise personal data protection. The E.U. will oversee the directive's implementation and will engage in E.U.-level review of its provisions.

- **Data controllers** Organizations processing data must appoint a "data controller" responsible for all data processing, who must register with government authorities.

- **Individual redress** A data subject must have the right to access information about himself, correct or block inaccuracies, and object to information's use.

Article 1 of the directive requires member states to protect the "fundamental rights and freedoms of natural persons, and in particular their right to privacy with respect to the processing of personal data."[51] In essence, the E.U. has made privacy a fundamental human right.

Applicability to Biometrics

The directive defines personal data as any information relating to an identified or identifiable natural person. An identifiable person is one who can be identified, directly or indirectly, in particular by reference to an identification number or to one or more factors specific to his physical, physiological, mental, economic, cultural, or social identity. While the word, *biometric* is not specifically cited in the text, biometric identifiers will likely be implicated by the directive's definition of personal data.

Other International Law Concerns

Individuals and businesses using biometrics will inevitably be using these systems in a global environment. When operating in an overseas environment, end users obviously do not want to do things that are in conflict with foreign law. Once an end user entity determines exactly what type of biometric application it wants to deploy in an overseas location, therefore, it must also take into account any applicable local laws to determine how best to proceed to ensure compliance with these laws. A case-by-case analysis of each country's law and whether or how it would affect the use of biometrics is beyond the scope of this book and requires competent legal counsel. An excellent starting point for learning about foreign privacy laws may be found in Privacy & Human Rights 2002. For more information go to http://www.privacyinternational.org/survey/phr2002/.

---

[51] Article 1, E.U. Data Protection Directive, or Directive 96/46/EC; see *Article 1* of The European Union Privacy Directive, Directive 96/46/EC.

For example, in France, the Commission Nationale d'Informatique et des Libertes (CNIL), which acts as a government watchdog for data protection, has recently approved the use of finger geometry for junior high school students to access their school cafeteria in the southern French town of Carqueiranne. CNIL accepted finger geometry because the adolescents' hands will grow over time, thus rendering the data eventually obsolete. CNIL had previously rejected the use of fingerprints for similar student access as well as for other access applications involving adults on the grounds that such use poses a potential danger to personal privacy. Similarly, CNIL has been reluctant to endorse iris recognition for access control, although it has made exceptions for places like airports.[52]

---

[52] "Biometrics: French School to Use Biometric System at Cafeteria Following Watchdog Approval," Privacy & Security Law Report, 1:45, November 11, 2002: 1298.

Chapter **14**

Case Study: Super Bowl Surveillance

By John D. Woodward, Jr.

A large spectator event like the Super Bowl presents a prime target for terrorists and also attracts the criminal element. Fearing the potential for such an attack or some other serious criminal incident, law enforcement officials in Tampa, Florida, in 2001 turned for help to a new technology to identify specific individuals: facial recognition.[1] Specifically, surveillance cameras surreptitiously scanned spectators' faces, capturing their images. Using an existing infrastructure of about twenty surveillance cameras, the facial recognition system took pictures of attendees as they entered Raymond James Stadium through the turnstiles at four main gates. Cables carried these images to computers, and the software did its work. Algorithms measured facial features from these images—such as the distances and angles between geometric points on the face like the mouth extremities, nostrils, and eye corners—to digitize the image into a record known as a *template* or what is sometimes called a *faceprint*. This record was then instantly searched against a computerized database of suspected terrorists and known criminals assembled from law enforcement files. A match would have alerted police, in the control booth deep inside the stadium, to the

---

[1]   This chapter draws, in part, on the author's previous work, published in John D. Woodward, Jr., *Super Bowl Surveillance: Facing Up to Biometrics* (RAND 2001), as well as the Virginia State Crime Commission's Facial Recognition Technology Sub-Committee in 2002.

presence of a potential threat. Police officers monitoring this biometric process stood by to visually inspect any computer-generated matches for confirmation and appropriate action. At the end of the day, the score stood at Baltimore Ravens 34, New York Giants 7; computer matches 19, actual arrests 0; true matches, unknown.

The number of true matches is unknown because although the system indicated 19 matches, these could be false matches, also known as false positives or false alarms. In this kind of law enforcement application, a computer match is ideally confirmed as a true match when the police officer, acting on the computer match, arrives on the scene, sees the suspected individual, and confirms the computer match. Because police made no arrests based on computer matches, we do not know the number of true (and false) matches. We should not assume that all 19 matches were false. For example, a ticket scalper, identified as such by the facial recognition system, may have seen the police officers coming in his direction and given them the slip; or the police, not having actually witnessed him in the act of scalping tickets, may have directed him to leave the area, without making an arrest. In 2002, the American Civil Liberties Union (ACLU) examined police records and other relevant information concerning Tampa's use of facial recognition in the Ybor City district. The ACLU concluded that "[t]he system has never correctly identified a single face in its database of suspects, let alone resulted in any arrests" (Stanley and Steinhardt 2002).

This January 28, 2001 incident was the first wide-scale use of facial recognition in the U.S., and it generated nationwide media coverage and much controversy as, in the eyes of many, the Super Bowl became the "Snooper Bowl." The *Los Angeles Times* headline read, "Super Day for Big Brother: The creeping assault against privacy just turned plain creepy this week." *Wired News* reported, "Yes, Big Brother is watching your face." Should we be concerned about the government's use of this technology? One could argue that facial recognition is a standard identification technique that raises no special concerns. After all, we look at each other's faces to recognize one another every day. Police regularly use mugshots to identify criminals. And we think nothing of being asked to display a photo ID to confirm our identity.

On the other hand, the use of a biometric facial recognition system such as that employed at the Super Bowl—or at airports, like Boston's Logan, or at urban commercial districts where facial recognition has been deployed, like Oceanfront in Virginia Beach—is different in certain respects from these more familiar uses and it has the potential to present greater risks as well as greater advantages. Focusing on the risks, demonstrators, public advocacy groups, and at least one influential congressman have reacted to the use of facial recognition. For example, protestors responded to Tampa Police using facial recognition in the Ybor City entertainment district, as the *New York Times* reported on July 15, 2001: "Wearing masks and making obscene gestures at police cameras, about 100 people protested a new security system that scans faces in the night life district … One protester walked by a camera, gestured obscenely and shouted, 'Digitize this!' "

Privacy advocates have also responded, warning of the dangers posed by the technology's use. Phil E. Agre, a member of the Electronic Privacy Information Center's advisory board, lists these dangers on his web page: "Your Face Is Not a Bar Code: Arguments Against Automatic Face Recognition in Public Places." (Agre 2002) The potential risks of facial recognition were highlighted by a leading lawmaker, Dick Armey, then Majority Leader of the U.S. House of Representatives. Armey joined forces with the ACLU, issuing a joint statement in July 2001 declaring: "[W]e are today joining together to call on all state and local governments to stop using these dangerous technologies now before privacy in America is so diminished that it becomes nothing more than a fond memory." Thus, biometric expert James Wayman had good reason to conclude: "The public relations disaster for biometrics [in 2001] was the surreptitious use of automatic facial recognition at the most popular sporting event in the U.S." With this background in place, this chapter describes the concerns raised by the use of biometric facial recognition and discusses how the technology could potentially threaten our right to privacy. It also discusses the technology's countervailing benefits to national security and law enforcement, and concludes by offering policy recommendations to help maximize the technology's utility while minimizing its threat to our privacy.

Privacy Concerns of Current Facial Recognition Uses

Although the concept of recognizing someone from facial features is intuitive, facial recognition, as a biometric, makes human recognition a more automated, computerized process. It is this aspect of the use of biometrics that raises the fear that we are losing our ability to control information about ourselves—that we are losing our right to privacy.

Does the use of this technology violate legally protected privacy rights? Legal rights to privacy may be found in three sources: federal and state constitutions (if the entity invading your rights is a government actor), the common law of torts (if the entity invading your rights is a private actor), and statutory law.

Although the word "privacy" does not appear in the U.S. Constitution, the need to protect citizens against government intrusions into their private sphere is reflected in many of its provisions, discussed in greater detail in the preceding chapters. For example, the First Amendment protects freedom of expression and association as well as the free exercise of religion; the Third Amendment prohibits the quartering of soldiers in one's home; the Fourth Amendment protects against unreasonable searches and seizures; the Fifth Amendment protects against self-incrimination; and the Due Process Clause of the Fourteenth Amendment protects certain fundamental "personal decisions relating to marriage, procreation, contraception, family relationship, child rearing, and education."[2] The constitutional "right to privacy," therefore, reflects concerns not only for one's physical privacy—the idea that government agents cannot barge into one's home—but also concerns less tangible interests such as the idea that citizens should be able to control certain information about themselves (information privacy), and to make certain decisions free of government compulsion (decisional privacy). And in 1977, the Supreme Court cautioned in that it is "not unaware of the threat to privacy implicit in the accumulation of vast amounts of personal information in computerized data banks or other massive government files."[3]

The use of biometric facial recognition potentially implicates physical and these less tangible privacy interests. Nevertheless, law enforcement's use of the technique at the Super Bowl does not appear to run afoul of the protections afforded by the U.S. Constitution. Some civil libertarians argue that the sort of mass, dragnet scanning that took place at the Super Bowl is improper, and that law enforcement must have individualized, reasonable suspicion that criminal activity is afoot before it can "search" a subject's face to see if it matches that of a wanted individual in its database.

Under current law, however, the type of facial recognition used at the Super Bowl would almost certainly be constitutional in light of Supreme Court precedent because it does not constitute a "search" under the Fourth Amendment. The Court has explained that government action constitutes a search when it invades a person's reasonable expectation of privacy. But the Court has found that a person does not have a reasonable expectation of privacy with regard to physical characteristics that are exposed to the public, such as one's facial features, voice, and handwriting.[4] So although the Fourth Amendment requires that a search conducted by government actors be "reasonable," which generally means that there must be some degree of suspicion that the person to be searched is engaged in wrongdoing, the scan of spectators' facial characteristics at the Super Bowl did not constitute a search. And with respect to concerns about information privacy, if law enforcement officials limited their actions to simply comparing scanned images of people entering the stadium with their computer database of suspected terrorists and known criminals, then the kinds of concerns about information privacy alluded to by the Supreme Court would probably not arise, so long as no information about individuals was retained, disclosed, or linked to any other "massive government files" database.

---

[2]   *Planned Parenthood of Southeastern Pennsylvania v. Casey*, 505 U.S. 833, 851 (1992).

[3]   *Whalen v. Roe*, 429 U.S. 589, 605 (1977).

[4]   See, for example, *United States v. Dionisio*, 410 U.S. 1, 14 (1973).

Under our federal system, states are free to provide greater privacy protections in their laws than those afforded in the United States Constitution. When evaluating the use of a specific biometric system, therefore, its legality must be analyzed under state constitutional provisions as well as state statutory law. Some state constitutions contain privacy provisions, like California's and Florida's, for example. At the other extreme, Virginia's constitution is silent on the subject and the Virginia Supreme Court has explained that Virginia has only recognized a right to privacy in limited form by statute. To be clear, this chapter only discusses privacy rights emanating from the U.S. Constitution.

Potential Privacy Concerns as the Technology Advances

As the technology advances, particularly to the point that many facial recognition or other biometric databases become interlinked and shared, the threat to information privacy has the potential to increase significantly. With biometric facial recognition, the loss of informational privacy essentially takes two forms: fears of tracking and fears of clandestine capture. *Tracking* refers to the ability to monitor an individual's actions in real time or over a period of time. In its most extreme incarnation, tracking could become a kind of "supersurveillance" that lets the tracker "follow" a person today, as well as search databases to reconstruct his movements from months ago.

For example, suppose the authorities place me in their "watch list" database. As I go about my many daily tasks, surveillance cameras could capture my face and digitally transmit this biometric information for instantaneous searching against the watch list. As I leave my residence, walk to the station, board the subway on my way to work, enter and exit my office building, stop by the ATM, make purchases in stores, visit my doctor, or attend a political rally or religious service, my face will be matched with information in the database, allowing the State to track my movements. Similarly, the authorities can enter on their watch list the biometric information of all those who attended the political rally with me. The authorities could then "reverse engineer" the identity of these individuals, by searching the database for their previous movements. If such a system were established, it would become possible to compile a comprehensive profile of an individual's movements and activities.

The theoretical possibility that the government could compile such massive databases, and that such databases could be used by law enforcement, raises the specter of "Big Brother" tracking its citizens' every move. The *clandestine capture* of biometric data increases these fears. As the preceding example makes clear, facial recognition systems can surreptitiously track individuals without their knowledge or consent. Moreover, the information from tracking can be combined with other personal data, acquired by other means (through, for example, a social security number), to provide even more information about an individual's private life.

Whether such technological advances as the capability for "supersurveillance" could render certain applications of this technology unconstitutional remains to be seen. If the compilation of information in these databases had a significant chilling effect on First Amendment rights, such as attending a political rally, if it impinged on fundamental rights of decisional privacy, or if the information were insufficiently safeguarded against unauthorized disclosure, then the maintenance of such databases could potentially run afoul of the law.

Given these potential concerns, civil libertarians are correct that we should be mindful of emerging technologies that may invade our privacy, and it is wise to monitor their development to forestall potential abuses. We should, however, also ensure that perceived or potential threats to our privacy do not blind us to the positive uses of biometric technologies like facial recognition.

Benefits of Facial Recognition Technology

At the Super Bowl and other venues, law enforcement used facial recognition as part of its efforts to prevent a terrorist act or other serious criminal incident. Although no suspected terrorists were apprehended, the authorities took prudent steps to identify them if they had chosen to show their faces. The national security community also understands the need for such precautions, and it believes that in addition to helping prevent potential terrorist acts against the public, biometric facial recognition can help it identify and protect against terrorist threats to U.S. forces and our embassies abroad.

As we all know, terrorist attacks have extracted a painful toll. In Saudi Arabia in 1996, terrorists exploded a truck bomb near Building 131 of Khobar Towers. Nineteen U.S. service members died. Hundreds were injured. In 1998, truck bomb attacks destroyed the U.S. embassies in Kenya and Tanzania, taking 224 lives and wounding some 4,600 others. And on October 12, 2000, a terrorist attack on the U.S.S. *Cole* in the Yemeni port of Aden killed 17 sailors and injured 42 more.

In an effort to protect its forces from such attacks, the U.S. military has looked to technologies such as facial recognition. In the wake of the Khobar Towers terrorist attack, the Defense Advanced Research Projects Agency (DARPA) embarked on a $50 million initiative known as "Human ID at a Distance," a major component of which is facial recognition. DARPA's ambitious goal is to help develop biometric technologies, facial recognition prominently among them, that can be deployed to identify a known terrorist before he closes in on his target: identify and intercept the intruder before he can cause harm. In this way, lives can perhaps be saved.

The terrorist attacks of September 11, 2001 refocused America's attention on technologies that can help improve public safety and homeland security. Congress has provided appropriations for the technology's use in this regard. For example, *Government Technology* reported in August 2002, "The effort to deploy facial recognition software in Massachusetts received strong support from Congress last year from the Massachusetts delegation led by Senator Ted Kennedy. The result was a $1 million appropriation to the state's police departments." In July 2002, Steve Cooper, the Chief Information Officer of the Office of Homeland Security, stated that the administration supports using biometric identification technologies, such as facial recognition, to improve security at U.S. borders, in air travel, in federal buildings and other locations.

As for public safety, while facial recognition did not lead to any arrests at the Super Bowl, there is evidence that using such a system can help deter crime. The United Kingdom's experience is instructive. In October 1998, the council in Newham, England, introduced facial recognition software; the police installed 300 surveillance cameras and incorporated facial recognition technology. Data captured are compared against a police database of approximately 100 convicted robbers known to be recently active in the area. According to a November 2001 report of the U.K.'s Parliamentary Office of Science and Technology, street robberies in the Newham city center fell by 34 percent. The report notes, however, that the "system has not led directly to any arrests, which suggests that its effect is largely due to deterrence/displacement of crime." Nonetheless, 93 percent of the residents support its use.[5]

Moreover, the facial recognition system used at the Super Bowl was not physically invasive or intrusive for spectators. In fact, it was much less invasive than a metal detector at a public building or an inauguration parade checkpoint or a shoe search at an airport. In this sense, facial recognition helped to protect the privacy of individuals, who otherwise might have had to endure more individualized police attention.

One potential criticism is that the known criminals (for example, convicted felons) placed in such a database may face heightened police scrutiny once they are identified in a public setting, despite the fact that they have "paid their debt to society." One response to this concern is that known criminals already face heightened police scrutiny. For example, a prior criminal record has long been a standard screening tool when police are developing a list of suspects, and law enforcement routinely checks latent fingerprints found at a crime scene against databases containing fingerprints of those with prior criminal histories.

While there is also the danger that the biometric facial recognition system will make an incorrect match, that danger exists whether one is using facial recognition or traditional methods of identification such as comparing mugshots. Moreover, the potential for error is reduced when matches made by biometric facial recognition are subsequently confirmed by law enforcement professionals. In this sense, the facial recognition system does the screening by

---

[5]   United Kingdom, Parliamentary Office of Science and Technology, 2001, *Postnote*, "Biometrics and Security," Number 165, November. The U.K.'s Parliamentary Office of Science and Technology is an office of both Houses of Parliament.

culling out the best possible matches from a large database, and humans then make the judgment call. As facial recognition technology improves, such misidentifications will likely become rarer.

The technological impartiality of facial recognition also offers a significant benefit for society. While humans are adept at recognizing facial features, we also have prejudices and preconceptions. The controversy surrounding racial profiling is a leading example. Facial recognition systems do not focus on a person's skin color, hairstyle, or manner of dress, and they do not rely on racial stereotypes. On the contrary, a typical system uses objectively measurable facial features, such as the distances and angles between geometric points on the face, to recognize a specific individual. With biometrics, human recognition can become relatively more "human-free" and therefore free from many human flaws.

While realizing that facial recognition has the potential to be misused in ways that could erode individual privacy, we must also acknowledge that this biometric technology has many positive uses as well. The 2001 Super Bowl introduced its potential to help prevent terrorist acts and criminal incidents at high-profile events. Facial recognition can also have beneficial uses closer to home. As just one example, many parents would most likely feel safer knowing their children's school had a facial recognition system to ensure that convicted child molesters were not granted access to school grounds.

Policy Recommendations

While we must remain alert to potential abuses, it would be ill advised to denounce the technology's use under all circumstances. Instead, our efforts should focus on identifying potential dangers and addressing those concerns with specific safeguards. As the preceding discussion demonstrates, one potential danger is "function creep"—that is, databases individually designed for a specific purpose, such as screening for suspected terrorists at a large sporting event, could be easily interlinked with databases designed for other purposes, such as locating those who are delinquent on child support payments or have overdue library books. The interlinking and interoperability of massive databases could lead to several problems. The most serious of these potential problems is that much more private information is collected and revealed to the government entity than is necessary to achieve the purpose of the surveillance. And as a consequence, the damage caused by inadvertent disclosure or unauthorized access to the database is much greater.

To prevent the unnecessary growth and interlinking of databases, specific protocols should be established to govern what information is authorized to reside in the database. At a minimum, the government entity maintaining the database should provide an articulable reason why the information is needed, how long it needs to be retained in the database, and under what conditions the information may be disseminated or shared with others. To ensure the accuracy of the information compiled in the database, a clear set of standards should set forth the criteria for placing someone on a watch list, and the data should be reviewed periodically to purge outdated or inaccurate information.

To prevent unauthorized disclosures, strict controls to safeguard the information should be required. The database should be made secure, access to it should be restricted, and technical measures, such as encryption, should be used to protect against unauthorized access. Records should be made of when, by whom, and for what purpose the database is accessed, and stiff criminal penalties should be available for unauthorized disclosure.

In addition to regulatory controls, it might be useful to explore less-traditional methods for monitoring this technology. For example, as with any new technology, public understanding of its operation and uses may mitigate many of the fears about Big Brother. To that end, the government should be encouraged to use the technology openly, rather than clandestinely. Moreover, transparency is a worthy goal; the government entity using biometric facial recognition should provide as much information as possible to the public about the technology's purposes and capabilities. To push the transparency envelope, communities using facial recognition could consider broadcasting its operation on the local public access channel for all concerned citizens to see. Finally, some form of active oversight—either by the government or a cooperative effort between government officials and private citizens, such as citizen oversight committees—would be useful not only to quell fears about the technology's use but also to ensure that it will not be abused.

Policy Case Study: The Virginia Experience

Recently, the issue of government use of facial recognition confronted policymakers in the Commonwealth of Virginia. As one of the few states considering how and whether to regulate facial recognition technology, the Virginia experience is an instructive case study. Although the Virginia State Police are considering the use of this technology, currently, Virginia Beach is the only municipality in Virginia that incorporates facial recognition technology into its public safety efforts. In 2001, the Virginia Beach City Council approved a measure authorizing the installation of a facial recognition system in the city's Oceanfront tourist area. After testing, the system went operational in late summer 2002.

Located in the Tidewater region, Virginia Beach is a major tourist draw throughout the year, attracting over three million people in 2001. The Oceanfront area, in particular, receives a large concentration of these visitors. Each year, fugitives have been arrested at the Oceanfront, as shown in the following table:

Year	1997	1998	1999	2000	2001	2002*
Fugitive Arrests	17	14	15	11	26	7

*Statistics through July 14, 2002

The Virginia Beach Police Department, the state's third-largest law enforcement organization, tries to maintain a high level of security and safety, particularly given the city's status as a popular tourist site. To that end, the department was interested in deploying a facial recognition system to determine the technology's value as a public safety tool. When the proposal to install a facial recognition system was introduced, however, controversy ensued. Citizen involvement, therefore, became an important factor in evaluating the acceptability of the technology. City leaders organized several town meetings so that citizens' questions could be answered and the public could be educated on this topic. The American Civil Liberties Union (ACLU), city officials, local community leaders, and outside experts participated in these meetings.

A Facial Recognition Program Citizen's Advisory and Audit Committee was formed by a diverse group of citizens drawn from different organizations, including the National Association for the Advancement of Colored People (NAACP), the National Federation of Filipino Americans, the Hispanic Community Dialogue, the Virginia Beach Hotel/Motel Association, and the Council of Civic Leagues. This Committee provided input and aided in preparation of a general order outlining the use and operation of the facial recognition system. The Committee also serves as an auditor of the system to ensure the proper use, storage, and disposal of digital images.

These efforts helped win community support. In August 2001, the police department applied for a Department of Criminal Justice Service grant. The grant was approved for $150,000. After the city council held a public hearing, the council voted to accept the grant and appropriated an additional $50,000 for the project.

Virginia Beach already had a video surveillance system comprised of ten cameras in strategic locations throughout the Oceanfront area. As part of the facial recognition project, the city integrated three new cameras into the existing system. The facial recognition system, however, is housed on a separate, stand-alone computer to minimize unauthorized access.

The facial recognition system's database will contain images of subjects with warrants (for example, felony warrants, misdemeanor warrants involving violence) or reports (for example, missing persons, runaways). In addition, "endangered individuals" such as Alzheimer's patients will be included. The chart below shows the numbers of outstanding warrants and active reports in Virginia as of September 2002:

Felony Warrants	2,215
Misdemeanor Warrants	11,072
Active Runaway Reports (Yearly Average)	41 (1,500)
Active Missing Persons Reports (Yearly Average)	11 (500)

The database will also contain digital images of volunteer subjects—police officers and citizens—in order to test the system.

During the 2002 General Assembly in the Commonwealth of Virginia, Delegate H. Morgan Griffith, the House Majority Leader from Salem, Virginia, sponsored legislation that would set legal parameters for public-sector use of facial recognition technology in Virginia. The legislation, "Orders for Facial Recognition Technology," known as House Bill No. 454, passed the House of Delegates by a vote of 74–25, and was sent on to the Courts of Justice Committee of the Senate while the Virginia State Crime Commission examines it. The Virginia State Crime Commission, a standing legislative commission of the Virginia General Assembly, is statutorily mandated to make recommendations on all areas of public safety in Virginia.

In essence, House Bill No. 454 would establish a "face warrant" requirement. Specifically, any state or local law enforcement agency in Virginia using facial recognition would have to go before a circuit court and request a court order authorizing the placement of facial recognition technology, when the technology may reasonably be expected to provide one of the following:

- Evidence of the commission of a felony or Class 1 misdemeanor
- A match of persons with outstanding felony warrants
- A match of persons or class of persons who are identifiable as affiliated with a terrorist organization
- A match of persons reported to a law-enforcement agency as missing

The order, if granted, could last no more than 150 days including extensions.

Delegate Griffith made it clear in his remarks that he did not introduce House Bill No. 454 because he feared Virginia Beach's actions; rather, his concern focused on how other less-established law enforcement organizations in Virginia might use the technology, if left completely unrestricted. In philosophical terms, he also stressed Virginia's commitment to Jeffersonian ideals of individual liberty.

It is interesting to note that in 2001, the California State Senate passed similar legislation. Specifically, its bill (S.B.169) would have limited the use of biometric facial recognition by:

- Forcing government agencies to get a warrant before using facial recognition
- Restricting the sharing of facial recognition data
- Requiring any data collected that does not match the watch list data to be destroyed

S.B. 169 passed the Senate by a vote of 23–11; however, it died in the California State Assembly.

Senator Kenneth W. Stolle, the Chairman of the Virginia State Crime Commission and a former Virginia Beach police officer, established an eight-member Facial Recognition Technology Sub-Committee to examine the issue of facial recognition technology. The subcommittee met twice in Richmond to listen to briefings, ask questions, and discuss options. Most members of the subcommittee believed that the greatest potential danger posed by facial recognition systems rested with what information is authorized to reside in the database. Accordingly, the subcommittee recommended that legislation be drafted to specify what categories of people could be lawfully placed in such a system's database and to specify penalties for state and local government agencies that failed to follow the specifications. This draft legislation will be considered by the Virginia State Crime Commission and a recommendation made to the legislature.

Chapter 15

The Law and Private-Sector Use of Biometrics

By John D. Woodward, Jr.

This chapter introduces the legal and policy concerns related to private-sector, or nongovernmental, use of biometrics. Although a thick, densely footnoted legal tome would be required for a thorough treatment of this important topic, we discuss the essentials, in a forward-looking way, with particular focus on two areas: how does the law enable private-sector use of biometrics, and how does the law regulate the private-sector use of biometrics with respect to privacy?

To answer the first question, we have to examine how biometrics can be used in commercial or business transactions, particularly in the digital world. In the information age, we are moving closer and closer to the complete transition from "sign on the dotted line" to "no paper, no problem." As the world goes increasingly digital, biometric authentication can play a more important role for transactions, based on contracts and other legal agreements. Ideally, whenever a signature is required on a piece of paper, we could provide our biometric data attached to an electronic document. However, before we replace a manually executed "John Hancock" with a camera-captured iris template, we need to determine the legal and policy concerns related to such use of biometrics.

To answer the second question, we must discuss regulations affecting the use of biometrics that stem from privacy concerns of the technology. If a private entity collects biometrics from individuals, does that private entity have any legal responsibilities or duties to the individuals from whom the biometrics have been collected? Or as information privacy lawyers and public policymakers might phrase it: Does the data collector have any legal duties to the data subject from whom the data is collected? To get these answers, explain how we got them, and add recommendations, the following section discusses law as an enabler for private-sector use of biometrics.

Law as an Enabler for Private-Sector Use of Biometrics

We begin with some background related to e-commerce and e-government that sets the stage for our discussion of how biometrics can be used with legal enforceability in various transactions, much the way manually executed signatures have been used for centuries.

Background on e-commerce and e-government

e-commerce refers to business processes that shift transactions to a computer-mediated network, such as the Internet or some other nonproprietary, Web-based system. More specifically, these business processes involve the transfer of ownership or rights to use goods or services. e-commerce consists of both business-to-business (B2B) transactions and business-to-consumer (B2C) transactions. Prior to the evolution of the Internet, these transactions would normally have taken place by such means as the telephone, postal mail, facsimile, proprietary electronic data interchange systems, or face-to-face contact.[1]

e-commerce has skyrocketed over the past several years and still has a long way to go! For example, in 1995, sales generated by the Web totaled $435 million. In 2000, e-commerce sales reached an estimated $1 trillion.[2] This figure may be broken out by sector:

- Manufacturing: $777 B
- Wholesale: $213 B
- Service Industry: $ 37 B
- Retail: $29 B

---

[1] U.S. Department of Commerce, *The Emerging Digital Economy II*, June 1999. For a discussion of definitions, see Thomas L. Mesenbourg, *Measuring Electronic Business: Definitions, Underlying Concepts, and Measurement Plans*, available at http://www.census.gov/epcd/www/ebusines.htm.

[2] U.S. Department of Commerce, *E-stats,* March 18, 2002, available at http://www.census.gov/eos/www/papers/estatstext.pdf.

e-commerce is expected to grow, with several estimates predicting sales of well over $3.7 trillion by 2004. According to Forrester Research,[3] between 2002 and 2006, online trade growth will look like this (figures in U.S. billions):

	2002	2003	2004	2005	2006
U.S.A.	$1,610.4	$2,527.6	$3,759.7	$5,296.9	$7,091.6
Worldwide	$2,293.5	$3,878.8	$6,201.1	$9,240.6	$12,837.3

Similar to e-commerce, e-government refers to government agencies' use of information technologies, such as the Internet or other nonproprietary, web-based systems, to provide interactions with citizens, organizations, or other government agencies. Although this chapter focuses on private-sector activities, it's also important to consider e-government for two primary reasons. First, the private and public sectors are not isolated; private-sector entities have countless, regular dealings with government, and biometrics may be able to play an increased role in facilitating these transactions. Second, the e-government market, like the e-commerce market, is huge and growing; how e-government embraces biometrics could have a profound influence on how the e-commerce world will use it.

The demand for e-government continues to grow. In a convergence of interests, citizens want it, businesses support it, and government gains by providing it. According to the United States Department of Commerce, as of September 2001, approximately 143 million Americans are currently using the Internet. Just over half of all residences in the nation, 53.9 million U.S. homes, have an Internet connection.[4] Many of these citizens want more online interactions with the government and they expect the quality of online e-government services to be comparable to other ways of interacting with government. As of 2001, the U.S. Government had about 27 million pages of information available online.

Aside from its interest in serving its citizens, the government has a strong economic incentive to provide greater e-government services because of the cost savings involved. For example, the United States Mint reportedly saves $5 per transaction done online. Other government agencies show similar cost savings.[5]

---

[3] Julie Meringer, Forrester Research, "E-Commerce Next Wave: Productivity and Innovation," Programme and Presentations for the Seminar on Revenue Implications of E-Commerce, April 22, 2002, World Trade Organization Committee on Trade and Development, available at http://www.wto.org/english/tratop_e/devel_e/sem05_e/sem05_prog_e.htmPD.

[4] U.S. Department of Commerce, Economic and Statistics Administration, National Telecommunications and Information Administration, "A Nation Online: How Americans Are Expanding Their Use of the Internet," February 2002, available at http://www.ntia.doc.gov/ntiahome/dn/.

[5] Mary Mitchell, General Services Administration, "The State of Federal eGovernment and eBusiness," January 23, 2001, available at http://www.egov.gov/presentations/DigGovMI12001/sld001.htm.

Moreover, as discussed in greater detail later in this chapter in the section "Federal Law: Electronic Signatures in Global and National Commerce Act," Congress has mandated greater use of e-government services.

Analysis

The broad topic discussed here is whether biometrics can play a role as an enabling technology for e-commerce and e-government. More specifically, the analysis focuses on one important aspect of this topic: Whether an electronic signature, in the form of a biometric, can be legally enforceable to the same extent as a conventional, manually executed paper-and-ink signature when the electronic signature is used to enter into agreements. In other words, can a biometric-based electronic signature have legal equivalence to a conventional, hand-written signature?

For many transactions, an individual must provide a manually executed paper-and-ink signature to enter into an agreement—such as to acknowledge receipt of a "widget." Replacing this paper-and-ink signature with a biometric-based electronic signature promises a more effective and convenient way of entering into agreements, particularly in the electronic world. So, instead of signing his name in ink on a piece of paper representing an agreement, an individual would simply be asked to place his fingerprint on a biometric sensor; his fingerprint would be captured and converted into a template unique to that individual; and that template would be attached to an electronic document representing the agreement.

Definitions

The term "electronic signature" refers to any means of "signing" an electronic document in digital form, in which the "signature" is represented in ones and zeroes.[6] Although the terms "electronic signature" and "digital signature" have sometimes been used interchangeably, a *digital signature* is more accurately defined as one particular type of electronic signature; it uses a specific technology—public-key cryptography—to sign a message. An electronic signature, on the other hand, is a technology-neutral term and encompasses many methods of "signing" an electronic record, including the technology at issue here, the use of a biometric-based identifier.[7]

As shown graphically in the "World of Signatures" chart in Figure 15-1, digital signatures are a subset of electronic signatures, which, in turn, are a subset of signatures. In this context, a biometric template is data that represents the individual's biometric. The biometric system creates the template by using an

---

[6] Thomas J. Smedinghoff and Ruth Hill Bro, "Electronic Signature Legislation," 1999, available at http://profs.lp.findlaw.com/signatures/signature_4.html. This paper uses the definition followed by most commentators.

[7] Thomas. J. Smedinghoff, et al., 1999.

Figure 15-1
"World of
Signatures"
Chart

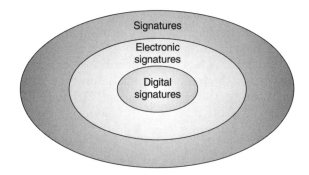

algorithm to extract "features" appropriate to that biometric from the individual's biometric sample as presented. Templates are not an image or record of the actual biometric (such as a fingerprint image or voice recording). Instead, templates are only a record of certain distinguishing features of a person's biometric characteristic or trait. They are numerical representations of key points taken from a person's biometric.

Attributes of a Conventional Signature

The legal enforceability of a transaction often depends on the parties' adherence to certain formalities.[8] Many agreements must be "in writing" and "signed" by the parties to be enforceable. For example, the law has long forbidden the enforcement of certain types of agreements, such as contracts for the sale of land, unless the agreement is in writing and is signed. Similarly, the Uniform Commercial Code (UCC), which seeks to make uniform the various state laws governing commercial transactions, requires a signed writing to enforce a contract for the sale of goods valued at $500 or more. This signed writing requirement is also contained in thousands of other federal, state, and local laws and regulations, covering transactions ranging from the execution of wills and other testamentary dispositions, to adoption and child custody agreements.

The signed writing requirement serves several useful functions:

- Evidentiary
- Cautionary
- Approval
- Efficiency

Let's briefly discuss each in turn: A signed writing serves an *evidentiary* function by providing some proof that the alleged agreement was actually made.

---

[8]   Thomas. J. Smedinghoff, et al., 1999.

Similarly, the act of signing a document serves a *cautionary* function by emphasizing to the parties the significance of entering into a binding agreement and thereby helping to minimize ill-considered or impulsive agreements. The *approval* function refers to the idea that a person's signature, in the context of the document to which it is appended, indicates the signer's approval or authorization of the contents of the document. Finally, a signed document lends *efficiency* to the contracting process by providing clarity and finality as to the scope and terms of the agreement.

The UCC defines a signature as "any symbol executed or adopted by a party with present intention to authenticate a writing."[9] A "writing" is defined to include "printing, typewriting, or any other intentional reduction to tangible form."[10] As these words suggest, the UCC defines "signature" broadly and looks to the intent of the parties. In the context of a conventional paper-and-ink signature, it is relatively easy to understand how this definition—a signature on a piece of paper that the signer intends to authenticate—serves the evidentiary, cautionary, approval, and efficiency functions that underlie the signed writing requirement. The signed document provides a permanent copy that can be stored and referred to later as evidence that the transaction occurred, and the text of the document contains the terms of the agreement to which the signer has promised to be bound. Moreover, the signature is "attached" to the writing in such a way that it's difficult to alter or relatively easy to detect if alteration has been attempted. The signature is unique to the signer, and the signer is identified in the document.

From these principles, legal experts have deduced what general attributes an enforceable signature should have. The American Bar Association (ABA) identifies these attributes as "signer authentication" and "document authentication." *Signer authentication* means that the signature should identify who signed the document and show that the signature should be difficult for another person to produce without authorization. *Document authentication* means the signature should identify what is being signed, such that it would be impracticable to falsify or alter either the signed document or the signature without detection. Accordingly, a signature should identify the person signing, the signature should be unique to the signer, and the signature should be associated with the document is such a way as to indicate the signer's intent and to make it difficult to falsify the document or the signature without detection.

Electronic Signatures

Does an electronic signature have the attributes of an enforceable signature? To satisfy a statute or regulation that requires a transaction to be "in writing" and

---

[9]   UCC §1-201(39).

[10]   UCC §1-201(46).

"signed" requires three elements: (1) a writing, (2) a signature, and (3) shows "intention to authenticate" the transaction. The first question, therefore, is whether an electronic signature contains these elements.

Courts have recognized that many types of "writings" may satisfy this statutory requirement. For example, courts have recognized that a telegram constitutes a writing and have found that a facsimile (or "fax") satisfies the requirement. Courts have also found that data stored on a computer disk can constitute a writing. Provided that an electronic record of the transaction is retained on computer disk or hard drive, therefore, it appears likely that courts would find the writing requirement to be satisfied.

In accordance with the UCC definition that "any symbol" can constitute a signature, courts have recognized that letterhead, trademarks, stamped or printed symbols, or even an "X," can satisfy the signature requirement. Three examples drawn from New York legal history demonstrate that the state law adapted to recognize many signatures. In 1880, the New York courts accepted that any figure or mark may be used in lieu of one's proper name, a legal recognition of the fact that New York attracted many immigrants, not all of whom were literate.[11] By 1911, the courts accepted that a handwritten signature was not required on an agreement, acknowledging that New York's many corporations and service industries could more efficiently use rubber stamps to signify their agreement for many of their standard language contracts, such as those commonly used in the insurance industry.[12] After World War II, the New York state legislature captured what the New York courts had already, in effect, done when it modified the law by broadly defining a signature to include "any memorandum, mark or sign, printed, stamped, photographed, engraved, or otherwise placed on an instrument or writing."[13] The point to remember is that the law adapts to changed circumstances to include demographic, technological, and business advances.

Thus, the restriction on what symbol may constitute a signature is not particularly rigorous because the nub of the requirement is that the signature demonstrate an intention to authenticate the writing. If one party to a transaction places an "X" at the bottom of a contract, the other party (and a court) can reasonably infer that the signer has agreed to be bound by the contract. It may be more difficult, however, to infer such intent in an electronic environment.

Providing a biometric-based electronic signature would seem to constitute a legally enforceable means of entering into a contract. A biometric identifier appended to an electronic record would meet the signature and writing requirements, and the requisite intent by the party to authenticate the transaction could be inferred from the context of the transaction. But such after-the-fact

---

[11]   See, for example, *David v. Williamsburgh City Fire Insurance Co.*, 83 NY 265 (N.Y. 1880).

[12]   See, for example, *Landeker v. Co-op Building Bank*, 71 Misc. 517, 130 NYS 780 (N.Y. Sup. 1911).

[13]   See, for example, *New York General Construction Law*, Section 46 (1947).

determinations may undermine the predictability that is necessary to foster effective and efficient transactions in the e-commerce and e-government arenas. Basically, it's important to know with relative certainty whether the transaction is enforceable before the transaction is performed. The difference in context between the execution of a paper-and-ink signature and an electronic signature raises some doubt about whether simply affixing any electronic symbol to an electronic record embodies sufficient attributes of authentication to warrant enforceability.

Accordingly, to ensure predictability in these transactions and to avoid after-the-fact reliance on proof of "intention to authenticate," lawmakers at both the federal and state levels have addressed the circumstances in which electronic signatures will be valid and enforceable.

Electronic Signature Legislation in the United States

Although each piece of legislation regarding electronic signatures is unique, some general observations about the various legislative efforts are possible. As the previous discussion indicates, signatures must have certain attributes to be enforceable. A legislative drafter may choose to create these attributes in various ways. For example, the definition of an electronic signature could be very broad, whereas the type of transactions for which an electronic signature can be used could be limited. Alternatively, the drafter may attempt to define electronic signature narrowly, ensuring that only those electronic symbols that possess the desired attributes of an enforceable signature will qualify as electronic signatures. The following discussion, which provides an overview of some of the most important legislation governing electronic signatures, illustrates the different approaches adopted to date. It also demonstrates that the law is prepared to recognize a biometric as an electronic signature.

Federal Law: Electronic Signatures in Global and National Commerce Act

A major piece of federal legislation dealing with electronic signatures is the Electronic Signatures in Global and National Commerce Act (E-SIGN Act), signed into law on June 30, 2000 with an effective date of October 1, 2000.[14] Congress passed the E-SIGN Act, in large part, so that "electronic commerce [would] have the opportunity to reach its full potential."[15]

The E-SIGN Act promotes the use of electronic contract formation, signatures, and record keeping in private commerce by establishing legal equivalence between contracts written on paper and contracts in electronic form, and be-

---

[14] The Electronic Signatures in Global and National Commerce Act (E-SIGN Act), P.L. 106-229, 15 U.S.C.A. § 7001 et seq. (2000).

[15] See, for example, Michael H. Dessent, "Digital Handshakes in Cyberspace Under E-SIGN: 'There's a New Sheriff in Town!' " *University of Richmond Law Review*, 35, 943 (January 2002) (footnotes omitted). This article provides a detailed treatment of electronic signature law.

tween pen-and-ink signatures and electronic signatures.[16] The E-SIGN Act applies to any transaction "relating to the conduct of business, consumer or commercial affairs between two or more persons." By its terms, therefore, the E-SIGN Act applies broadly to transactions in e-commerce. Thus, the treatment of electronic signatures under the E-SIGN Act provides useful guidance as to the circumstances under which electronic signatures are enforceable.

The E-SIGN Act defines electronic signature as "an electronic sound, symbol, or process, attached to or logically associated with a contract or other record and executed or adopted by a person with the intent to sign the record."[17] This definition is quite broad, which could allow the formation of an enforceable contract with something as simple as a computer mouse click on a dialog box indicating agreement to specific terms. Biometric data also squarely falls within the E-SIGN Act's definition.

Although the definition of electronic signatures under the E-SIGN Act is broad, the Act also contains numerous exceptions to which the Act will not apply. Among these exceptions are the creation and execution of wills, codicils, or testamentary trusts; family law matters such as adoption or divorce; and court orders and notices. Thus, to generalize, the E-SIGN Act does not venture into affairs of death, affairs of family, and affairs of the judiciary.

The E-SIGN Act is voluntary, requiring the parties to consent to its use. The law does not force individuals to use it. The consumer consent provision of E-SIGN, contained in 15 USC Sec. 7001(c), has been the subject of some concern, and unresolved issues remain about the application of E-SIGN. For example, hackers could attempt to forge electronic signatures on online purchases, requiring the federal or state governments to develop additional consumer protections.

Also, E-SIGN, a federal law, does not replace state law if a state has enacted the Uniform Electronic Transaction Act (UETA) or an equivalent.[18] Since E-SIGN and UETA are not quite identical, it is useful to bear this in mind. The upcoming "State Law" section discusses UETA in detail.

E-SIGN Act Summary

Heart of new law:

- Legal validity of a transaction document is not denied "solely because it is in electronic form."

- "No paper; no problem."

---

[16]   See Office of Management and Budget Guidance on Implementing the Electronic Signatures in Global and National Commerce Act (E-SIGN Act), available at http://www.whitehouse.gov/omb/memoranda/esign-guidance.pdf.

[17]   E-SIGN Act, section 106(5); 15 USC § 7006(5).

[18]   UETA, 15 USC § 7002(a).

Pre-emptive rule:

- Overrules old laws requiring signature in writing and on paper for certain transactions.
- Establishes uniform but voluntary standard.

Applicability to biometrics:

- Definition is broadly written to include biometric data.
- Law is technology neutral, giving flexibility to the parties.

Federal Law: Government Paperwork Elimination Act

The Government Paperwork Elimination Act (GPEA), which took effect in 1998, helps make e-government a reality; GPEA aims to improve the delivery of government services by charging executive agencies with developing procedures to use and accept electronic documents and signatures.[19] The GPEA requires federal agencies, by October 21, 2003, to provide individuals or entities that deal with agencies the option to submit information or transact with the agency electronically, and to maintain records electronically, when practicable. GPEA provides that electronic records and their related electronic signatures are not to be denied legal effect, validity, or enforceability merely because they are in electronic form. It also encourages federal government use of a range of electronic signature alternatives, including the use of biometric-based identifiers.[20] The GPEA defines "electronic signature" as "...a method of signing an electronic message that: Identifies and authenticates a particular person as the source of the electronic message; and indicates such person's approval of the information contained in the electronic message."[21]

The Office of Management and Budget (OMB), in accordance with the requirements of the GPEA, promulgated guidance for GPEA's implementation, and several agencies have promulgated regulations regarding the use of electronic records and signatures. These regulations attempt to duplicate the desired attributes of a paper-and-ink signature, either through the definition of the signature itself or through restrictions on the way the signature is to be used. For example, the Food and Drug Administration defines an electronic signature as "a computer data compilation of any symbol or series of symbols executed, adopted, or authorized by an

---

[19] The Government Paperwork Elimination Act of 1998 (GPEA), P.L. 105-277, Title XVII, codified at 44 U.S.C. § 3504 et seq.

[20] Implementation of Paperwork Elimination Act, Office of Management and Budget, January 26, 2001, available at http://www.whitehouse.gov/omb/fedreg/gpea2.html#iis1.

[21] GPEA, Section 1710(1).

individual to be the legally binding equivalent of the individual's handwritten signature."[22] Although this definition itself is relatively broad, the regulations also ensure that the electronic signature has the equivalent attributes of a handwritten signature by requiring that the electronic signatures be "linked to their respective electronic records to ensure that the signatures cannot be excised, copied or otherwise transferred to falsify an electronic record by ordinary means."[23] The regulations further provide that signed electronic records "shall contain information associated with the signing that clearly indicates all of the following:

- The printed name of the signer
- The date and time when the signature was executed
- The meaning (such as review, approval, responsibility, or authorship) associated with the signature"[24]

State Law

The rapid growth of e-commerce, as well as the desire to increase productivity and efficiency by moving to paperless environments, led many states to enact statutes and regulations governing electronic transactions. One approach, followed by almost one-third of the states, is to define electronic signatures in such a way that the definition itself would embody all the attributes of a valid, enforceable signature. Although the precise wording may differ in various state statutes, those states following this approach require that, to be legally enforceable, an electronic signature must be:

- Unique to the person using it
- Capable of verification
- Under the sole control of the person using it
- Linked to the electronic record to which it relates in such a manner that if the record were changed the electronic signature is invalidated[25]

Other states provide a more general definition for electronic signatures and rely on the context of the transaction to establish the intention to authenticate.

---

[22] 21 CFR 11.3(7) (Definitions).

[23] 21 CRF 11.70 (Signature/record linkage).

[24] 21 CRF 11.70 (Signature/record linkage).

[25] These features were derived in part, from a decision of the U.S. Comptroller General in 1991, which described the rationale for accepting a digital signature as sufficient for government contracts under 31 U.S.C. § 1501(a)(1). For more on this point, *see* Thomas J. Smedinghoff and Ruth Hill Bro, "Electronic Signature Legislation," 1999, available at http://profs.lp.findlaw.com/signatures/signature_4.html.

The Uniform Electronic Transaction Act (UETA) takes this approach. The UETA is the product of a drafting committee of legal scholars established in 1996 under the auspices of the National Conference of Commissioners for Uniform State Laws to draft a uniform statute relating to the use of electronic communications and records in contractual transactions. The object of this endeavor was to draft technology-neutral revisions to general contract law to support electronic transactions. The UETA was approved and recommended for enactment by all the states in July 1999. As of August 2002, 40 states have enacted UETA.[26]

UETA establishes, to the greatest extent possible, the equivalency of electronic signatures and manual signatures. Accordingly, UETA provides that a "signature may not be denied legal effect or enforceability solely because it is in electronic form." UETA defines an electronic signature as "an electronic sound, symbol or process attached to or logically associated with a record and executed or adopted by a person with the intent to sign the record." UETA applies to most transactions, although it does not apply to the extent the transaction is covered by other law, if the transaction is covered by certain portions of the UCC, such as those dealing with secured transactions and negotiable instruments, or if the transaction is the creation of a will, a codicil, or testamentary trust.

UETA also addresses the issue of attribution of the signature, providing that an electronic record or signature is to be attributed to a person if it was the act of the person, and noting that this fact can be established by any relevant evidence, including the use of technology to verify the identity of the signer. The effect of the signature can be determined from the context and surrounding circumstances at the time of the creation, execution, or adoption of the record.

Recommendations

The first recommendation is to contact a qualified lawyer to address and answer any specific legal concerns implicated by the use of biometrics. *This section does not purport to give legal advice and should not be treated as such.* With this disclaimer aside, it should be apparent from the previous discussion that there is not a single specific formula for ensuring that an electronic signature is enforceable.

At a minimum, however, the electronic signature should have the features that are described in the UETA and reflected in the E-SIGN Act and the GPEA. Specifically, the electronic signature should be "attached to or logically associated with the record" and "executed or adopted by a person with the intent to sign the record."[27]

---

[26] Baker and McKenzie, "National Conference of Commissioners on Uniform State Laws (NCCUSL), E-Commerce Legislation and Regulations," *Global E-Commerce Law* available at http://www.bmck.com/ecommerce/nccusl.htm#UETA.

[27] See, for example, E-SIGN Act, section 106(5), UETA Definition of "Electronic Signature," and 21 CFR 11.3(7) (Definitions).

To satisfy these requirements, the parties would have to create an electronic document explaining the transaction (for example, "John Doe on this date has acknowledged receipt of a widget from Jane Roe, for which he paid $500 and has 'signed' for the widget by providing a biometric identifier in the form of his fingerprint template. Jane Roe on this date has acknowledged receipt of $500 for the widget and has 'signed' for the $500 by providing a biometric identifier in the form of her fingerprint template."). The parties' biometric identifiers would be appended to that document, or at least stored electronically in a manner that is "logically associated" with the record. The parties would agree to the purpose of the transaction and the import of providing the biometric—this explanation would help provide the requisite evidence of "intent."

However, to be more certain that the electronic signature will be enforced, a narrower and more specific definition may be desirable. Accordingly, drawing on the principles detailed above and the definitions used in federal and state legislation, an electronic signature used in e-commerce and e-government applications should ideally have the following four elements:

- It should be unique to the person using it.
- It should be capable of verification.
- It should be under the sole control of the person using it.
- It should be linked to or associated with the document to which it relates, such that it would be difficult to falsify the document or the signature without detection.

A biometric-based identifier will easily satisfy the first two requirements. As for sole control, the individual will be in sole control of the biometric itself (for example, his fingerprint, voice, or iris). Once the biometric template is provided to the other party to the agreement, however, that template is no longer in the sole control of the signer. If the other contracting party exercises reasonable care in safeguarding the template to prevent its unauthorized use or its disclosure, and documents its safeguarding procedures, this requirement should be satisfied as well. To provide an additional level of protection, the parties may wish to consider cryptographically binding the biometric template to the message to make it computationally infeasible for that template to be attached to another document without the alteration being detected.

The final requirement would be satisfied so long as the electronic signature is attached to or logically associated with the electronic record. Ideally, this would be accomplished in a way that provides the maximum protection against fraud; that is, the signature should be attached to the record in such a way that the signature cannot be copied or excised and pasted onto another document. This could be accomplished by cryptographically binding the signature to the electronic record. Not all transactions will require this maximum level of protection against fraud, however. In many contexts, so long as the databases containing the biometric template and the electronic record are safeguarded adequately, the signature need only be "logically associated" with the electronic record. This can be accomplished by appending the signature to the electronic record.

As for the electronic record, it should at a minimum:

- Identify the person signing.
- Identify the date and time the signature was executed.
- Identify the meaning associated with the signature (such as acknowledging receipt of a widget).

Finally, as a policy matter, an organization may want to develop a regulatory or policy scheme to delineate how it plans to use biometric-based electronic signatures. Such a scheme would likely incorporate procedures to accomplish the following:

- Clearly inform individuals that electronic records and biometric-based electronic signatures will be acceptable and used for specified purposes
- Set forth the terms and conditions of electronic agreements, or at a minimum ensure that the participants in the transaction understand these terms and conditions
- Minimize the likelihood of repudiation by instituting procedures that safeguard the confidentiality of stored biometric templates and electronic records
- Control and monitor access to these electronic databases to protect against unauthorized alterations to the signature or the record
- Obtain legal counsel during the design of the system to ensure not only that the transactions are legally enforceable, but also that the operation of the system is in full compliance with other laws and regulations, particularly those dealing with privacy and record-maintenance issues

By following these basic guidelines, parties should be able to use biometric-based electronic signatures to enter into agreements, and they should be able to enforce these signatures to the same extent as a manually executed paper-and-ink signature is.

Law as a Regulator of Private-Sector Use of Biometrics: Privacy

In the American legal experience, privacy protections have followed two basic pathways depending on whether the source of the privacy intrusion is a governmental or private-sector activity. By this point, you have learned much about privacy: Chapter 12 discussed privacy in general terms, Chapter 13 surveyed legal scholarship on privacy and examined the "right to privacy" with respect to government use of biometrics, and Chapter 14's case study narrowly focused on the extent to which we have a right to privacy in the face we show in public.

Constitutional Background

When it comes to private-sector actions, the Constitution embodies what is essentially a laissez-faire, or "hands-off" spirit. With respect to the conduct of private individuals, the Supreme Court has not found a constitutional privacy right in personal information given voluntarily by an individual to private parties. This reluctance to find such a privacy right bears on private-sector use of biometrics because biometric identifiers may be categorized as personal information that an individual, or the data subject, gives voluntarily to private parties, or the data collectors. Generally, as a matter of law, a private party in possession of information has the right to disclose it.

Two landmark cases demonstrate the Supreme Court's view. In *Smith v. Maryland*, decided in 1979, the defendant claimed that information in the form of telephone numbers he dialed from his home telephone (which is known as a pen register) could not be turned over to the police without a search warrant. Mr. Smith desperately wanted his pen register records excluded as evidence because they helped establish that he had been stalking a woman. Rejecting this argument, the Supreme Court noted that it "consistently has held that a person has no legitimate expectation of privacy in information he voluntarily turns over to third parties."[28]

United States v. Miller, decided in 1976, involved a bootlegger's private financial records, which his bank gave to United States Treasury agents. Mr. Miller, the bootlegger, failed in his attempt to have this evidence excluded. He wanted his financial records excluded as evidence because the government could use these records to prove that Miller was evading taxes.

The Supreme Court found that the bootlegger had no expectation of privacy in the bank records, reasoning that "The depositor takes the risk, in revealing his affairs to another, that the information will be conveyed by that person to the Government..."[29] The records could not therefore be considered confidential communications because Miller had voluntarily conveyed them to the bank in the "ordinary course of business."

Analogizing to the private-sector's use of biometrics, the Supreme Court's reasoning in *Smith* and *Miller* suggests that the Court would be reluctant to find a reasonable expectation of privacy in biometric identification information provided in connection with a private-sector activity. Rather, the Court would likely view the biometric identification information as having been voluntarily provided by

---

[28]   *Smith v. Maryland*, 442 U.S. 735 (1979).

[29]   *United States v. Miller*, 425 U.S. 435 (1976).

the individual to another party in the ordinary course of business. Thus, the Court would find that, just like the depositor, the individual takes the risk by providing his biometric identification information to another, that the information will be conveyed by that private party to others, including the government.

Despite the Court's likely reluctance to expand individual privacy protections related to private-sector use of biometrics, Congress can have the ultimate word. Again, *Miller* is instructive. Following the *Miller* decision, Congress, in 1976, passed the Right to Financial Privacy Act (12 U.S.C. § 3401 et seq.), which established procedural requirements for financial institutions when disclosing information to the government. Thus, the refusal of the Supreme Court to find a Constitutionally mandated privacy right does not as a practical matter end the debate. Congress is free to act by passing legislation to protect information privacy. Similarly, the states are also free to act by providing for individual privacy protections.

For private-sector intrusions into privacy, the common-law, through its doctrines of contract, tort and property, has, in varying degrees, attempted to provide certain protections for the individual. However, the law has not used these doctrines to protect individual information in private-sector databases.

Accordingly, the private-sector enjoys great leeway as far as what it can do with an individual's information. As Marc Rotenberg, the executive director of the Electronic Privacy Information Center, and Emilio Cividanes, a privacy attorney, have concluded in *The Law of Information Privacy: Case and Commentary*, in 1997: "Except in isolated categories of data, an individual has nothing to say about the use of information that he has given about himself or that has been collected about him. In particular, an organization can acquire information for one purpose and use it for another...generally the private sector is not legislatively constrained."

Policy Background

As discussed in the "Law as an Enabler for Private-Sector Use of Biometrics" section earlier in this chapter, Congress and the state legislatures have taken positive steps to regulate private-sector use of biometrics. The greatest and most impressive part of this regulation at both the federal and state levels has been to encourage the use of electronic signatures to include biometrics. As for privacy policy, we discuss the options next.

Options for Privacy Policy

In balancing the privacy concerns with the benefits biometrics provide in private-sector applications, several options exist for our policymakers. These approaches include the following:

- **Laissez-faire** No government regulation is needed, that is "Hands-off!" "If it ain't broke, don't fix it." This approach would treat biometric data like any other personal information, which generally means that data collectors can do with it what they please. An argument favoring this approach is that because the technology is still emerging, policymakers should not take any quick regulatory action that might impede its deployment. After all, there are no secondary markets for fingerprint templates or hand geometry patterns (yet).

- **Self-regulation**   Based on voluntary industry codes, private-sector entities using biometrics can best determine their own privacy policies and practices. Raj and Samir Nanavati of the International Biometric Group have offered a comprehensive "BioPrivacy's Best Practices" to help institutions determine what steps to take to ensure that biometric deployments do not intrude on individual privacy.[30] Currently, private actors (such as companies or organizations) possessing biometric identification information generally follow a nondisclosure policy—that is, as part of a strategy of building public acceptance for the technology, they do not disclose this information to third parties. This position also has adherents in the International Biometric Industry Association (IBIA), the biometric industry's trade association headquartered in Washington, D.C. The IBIA also has privacy principles its members are obliged to accept.[31] However, such nondisclosure policies are completely voluntary. Critics contend that biometric identifiers, like other personal information, such as names and addresses for mailing lists, might eventually be considered to be part of the public domain. The fear is that the individual will lose ultimate control over all aspects of his biometric identifier.

- **Government regulation**   A presumption that law is needed at the state or federal level. Rather than rely on an end-user's promise or industry goodwill, this approach favors privacy protections under the force of law.

- **Hybrid**   A combination or combinations of the above. For example, an end user with a biometric application in an unregulated state could do what it pleases with biometric data, while another end user could have a voluntary privacy policy in place, and another end user in a regulated state could be subject to the state law and still have a privacy policy giving greater protection to biometric data than what the law requires.

Biometrics is still relatively too new for the Congress or the various state legislatures to have acted from the standpoint of adopting privacy protections specifically

---

[30]   Information about the International Biometric Group and its recommended privacy practices is at www.ibgweb.com.

[31]   IBIA Privacy Principles, available at http://www.ibia.org/privacy.htm.

at private-sector use of the technology. In one of the first steps taken toward understanding private-sector applications of biometrics, Congress held hearings on "Biometrics and the Future of Money" in May 1998. These hearings, before the Subcommittee on Domestic and International Monetary Policy of the Committee on Banking and Financial Services of the U.S. House of Representatives, featured panels of leading technologists as well as policy experts who explained how biometrics can be used for identity assurance and raised law and policy concerns related to biometric use.

In the aftermath of the terrorist attacks of September 11, 2001, numerous congressional hearings examined the role biometrics could play in improving homeland security. For example, on November 5, 2001, Senator John D. Rockefeller IV, Chairman of the Senate Aviation Subcommittee, conducted a hearing at West Virginia University in Morgantown, West Virginia. The Subcommittee heard from witnesses who discussed, among other things, uses of biometrics in civil aviation.

Congress has also enacted legislation requiring government to act to develop this technology to help secure our borders. For example, the USA PATRIOT Act requires, among other things, that the Attorney General and the Secretary of State jointly, through NIST, develop and certify by January 26, 2003, a "technology standard including appropriate biometric identifier standards" that can be used to help ensure that a person has not received a visa under an alias name.

The State Experience

One of the first state attempts to provide privacy protection for private-sector use of biometrics occurred in California. In 1998, Assembly Member Kevin Murray, with the support of the California Banker's Association as well as the Center for Law in the Public Interest, introduced legislation (known as AB 50) in the California State Assembly to promote the responsible use of biometric identifiers to prevent identity theft while preserving the security of consumer information. The bill's key provisions included:

- A prohibition against selling, exchanging, or otherwise providing biometric identification databases to third parties

- A mandate that electronic storage of biometric identifiers be carried out in the same manner as a company's confidential information

- A prohibition on recording someone's voice for biometric identification purposes without their consent

- A prohibition against the discriminatory use of biometric identifiers

Murray's proposed legislation drew opposition from the ACLU, which felt that it did not provide adequate protection to consumers' biometric data. Consumer activist Ralph Nader saw the bill as part of "the banking industry's efforts to invade consumers' privacy through fingerprinting customers."[32] The legislation died in the California State Senate.

More recently, action has shifted from the West Coast to the East Coast, specifically New Jersey. Introduced by Assemblywoman Joan M. Quigley, the Biometric Identifier Privacy Act (Bill No. A2448) provides guidelines for the use and distribution of biometric identifiers and establishes civil penalties for the misuse of biometric information. Specifically, the legislation prohibits a person or government agency that possesses biometric data to sell, lease, transfer, or disclose the information unless the following criteria have been met:

- The individual to whom the biometric data belongs consents to the sale or transfer.

- The sale or transfer completes a financial transaction requested or authorized by the individual.

- The sale or transfer is required or permitted by federal or state law.

- The sale or transfer is made for law enforcement purposes.

In addition, the bill requires that the entity storing the biometric information must protect that data in a manner similar to other confidential information and provides for civil penalties for each violation. The civil penalty provision is not trivial; it would apply to each violation of the act and would not be more than $25,000 for each violation.

On September 12, 2002, the Assembly Homeland Security and State Preparedness Committee approved the bill. On September 23, 2002, the bill passed 75-0 in the New Jersey Assembly. As of this writing, it is pending before the state Senate Judiciary Committee.

Recommendations

Both the California and New Jersey state legislative approaches adopted a privacy enhancing biometric blueprint based on what is known as a Code of Fair Information Practices (CFIP). Such a CFIP-based approach merits consideration because it is arguably an effective way to balance privacy concerns with the benefits of biometrics. As a bedrock premise, a CFIP establishes rights for data subjects and places responsibilities on the data collectors.

Biometric Blueprint

The CFIP consists of five principles: notice, access, correction mechanism, informed consent, and reliability/safeguarding. The CFIP, as the name implies, is

---

[32] Eric Hellweg, "The Security of You," Business 2.0, November 1998, available at http://www.business2.com/articles/mag/print/0,1643,12778,FF.html.

not unique to biometrics but can apply anytime information is at stake. Willis Ware, a leading information privacy scholar at RAND, and public servants from the then Department of Health, Education, and Welfare (including David F. H. Martin who first coined the phrase) came up with the CFIP approach in 1973.

The CFIP-based biometric blueprint for private-sector use should consist of these same five basic principles, along with optional wording, to include:

- **Notice**   The capture of biometric identification information in the private-sector must be accompanied by prominent notice. A more privacy-protective principle would prohibit the clandestine capture of biometric identification information in the private sector; no secret databases should exist.

- **Access**   The individual (or data subject) has the right to access his information in the database. Specifically, the individual must be able to find out if his biometric identification information is in the database and how the data collector is using it. Accordingly, the data collector would be required to disclose its privacy practices.

- **Correction mechanism**   The individual must be able to correct or make changes to any biometric identification information in the database. Since one of the technical advantages of biometrics is that they are based on physical characteristics or personal traits that rarely change over time, this principle would likely not be called into play too often.

- **Informed consent**   Before any information can be disclosed to third parties, the individual must consent. The individual must voluntarily and knowingly provide his biometric identification information to the data collector in the primary market. Once in the possession of the data collector, this information would then be governed by a use limitation principle, which means that the individual has consented that the information she provided would be used in the primary market for a purpose defined by the data collector and known to the individual. The individual must knowingly consent to any exchange, such as buying and selling of his biometric identification information, before it could be traded in a secondary market. Reasonable exceptions can be accommodated as appropriate for academic research, national security, and law enforcement.

- **Reliability/safeguarding**   The organization responsible for the database must guarantee the reliability of the data and safeguard the information. Any data collector that collects and stores biometric identification information must guarantee the reliability of the data for its intended use and must take precautions to safeguard the data. At its most basic level, appropriate managerial and technical controls must be used to protect the confidentiality and integrity of the information. The controls would include making the database and the computer system physically secure. Data collectors should explore the option of encrypting the biometric data to help further safeguard the information from disclosure. (Perhaps, policymakers should consider providing criminal sanctions for willful disclosures, or consider providing for the recovery of civil damages when biometric identification information is disclosed without the consent of the individual.)

Assuming one decides to give this five-prong CFIP-based biometric blueprint or any other approach the force of law, one has to determine who should pass the law. Specifically, if "there oughta be a law," then should Congress or the various state legislatures take action? Federal legislation offers the advantage of providing a uniform standard of privacy protection across the United States. Any organization using biometrics would only need to look to the federal law and its implementing regulations to know what is needed to ensure legal compliance.

On the other hand, some states might move more quickly and provide more extensive privacy protection than Congress, while some states might do nothing. Thus, the various states might take widely divergent approaches to regulation of biometrics, which would require end-users to comply with many different state laws.

Forward-looking Approach

This biometric blueprint admittedly is a forward-looking approach to how the law can sensibly regulate this emerging technology. It presumes that privacy concerns related to biometrics can best be accommodated by legislative enactment of a limited, yet uniform biometric blueprint to provide a framework to address legal and policy issues related to the private-sector's use of biometrics. Not all will agree with this approach. Many will advise that it is not needed; others will claim the time is not right, as the technology is still relatively new. As biometric applications become more common, so too will the law and policy concerns of biometrics become more commonplace.

We are now eyeball to eyeball with a new, exciting technology that can be used in robust ways by the private sector. Congress and the states have encouraged this approach by enacting laws to encourage the use of biometrics as an e-signature in e-commerce and e-government transactions.

With respect to the law as a regulator of privacy, a biometric blueprint based on a CFIP approach can be used to make this dynamic technology even more acceptable and beneficial for private-sector use. It is surely better to have a far-sighted biometric policy that deals with the face of a new technological reality now than to point fingers of blame later.

Part V

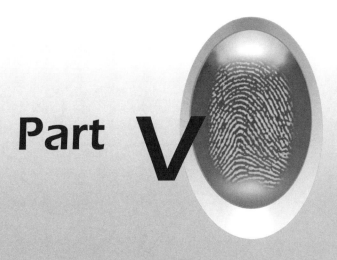

Review of Selected Biometrics Programs

place index finger in window

Chapter 16

Government and Military Programs

By John D. Woodward, Jr.

The public sector has been a major supporter, deployer, and user of various biometric technologies for years. In fact, these public-sector efforts with respect to biometrics have been critical to the success of the technology as well as the biometric industry. In Chapter 3, for example, Peter Higgins explained how law enforcement's need spurred research and development of large-scale automated fingerprint identification systems, like the FBI's IAFIS. The examples that follow in this chapter try to capture the "flavor" of how the government and military are using biometrics.[1]

---

[1] This chapter draws, in part, on the author's previous work, published in John D. Woodward, Jr., Katharine W. Webb, Elaine M. Newton, et al., *Army Biometric Applications: Identifying and Addressing Sociocultural Concerns*, (RAND 2001) in Appendix B: "Program Reports." Julius Gatune provided valuable research assistance.

Social Services[2]

Currently, six states use large-scale biometric applications in social service programs: Arizona, California, Connecticut, Massachusetts, New York, and Texas. Pennsylvania is considering implementing a system.

These various state programs all share the goal of using biometrics to prevent fraud in the form of "double-dipping," or multiple enrollments, defined as having the same person enrolled in a system multiple times using multiple aliases collecting multiple payments. Double-dipping can be prevented by the biometric program's capability of "negative identification," or performing a one-to-many search to make certain that an individual is not already enrolled in the system. By linking identity to the person's biometric, instead of the person's name, a person can only enroll in the system once because all the biometric records of those enrolled in the system will be searched for matches. A new enrollee should not be in the system and when the search is done, no matches should result—the identification comes back negative. Although the biometric cannot prevent someone from initially enrolling in the system in an alias name, it does freeze or fix the person's identity (true name or alias name) by fixing the name to the biometric thereafter.

Los Angeles County AFIRM & California's Statewide Fingerprint Imaging System (SFIS)

In California, the Los Angeles County Department of Public Social Services (DPSS) began the Automated Fingerprint Image Reporting and Match (AFIRM) biometrics program, known as LA AFIRM. LA AFIRM became the "grand daddy" of civil AFIS welfare systems. It has since been superceded by a new statewide system. Owing to its grandfatherly status, it merits discussion.

DPSS used ink-and-paper fingerprints as early as 1986. In 1988, a steering committee approved automated fingerprint matching. By 1991, DPSS launched a pilot program using automated fingerprinting. By the end of 1994, the program had been deployed to 25 DPSS district offices, including 300,000 participants who must be fingerprinted. These include adults receiving AFDC payments, minor parents receiving payments, and adults collecting payments for children. The biometric used consists of templates made from the two index fingers.

DPSS made appointments for enrollment. Those unable to make their appointments were given additional time to comply. After that period, if an adult failed to report for an appointment, adult benefits were cut off, although children's benefits continued. If an adult continued to refuse to enroll, the case was

---

[2]   David Mintie of Connecticut's Department of Social Services generously shared his subject matter expertise with respect to how various states use biometrics in social service programs.

referred to the fraud unit for further investigation. According to a DPSS review, most participants did not feel inconvenienced by the biometric. Rather, they believed the biometric would be effective in reducing fraud, which most thought was a positive step. The DPSS believes that the biometric program saved an estimated $66 million over the first 26 months.

California's Statewide Fingerprint Imaging System (SFIS), which incorporates LA AFIRM, has been implemented statewide since December 2000 to prevent multiple enrollments in the California Work Opportunity and Responsibility to Kids (CalWORKs), Temporary Assistance for Needy Families (TANF), and Food Stamp programs. To date, the SFIS database contains approximately 1.8 million records.

Welfare advocates have challenged SFIS in the courts and in the political process. In the case of *Sheyko v. Saenz*, an August 10, 2001 judgment upheld the department's regulations and policies regarding the use of biometrics, although the department appealed one technical provision of the judgment and the appeal will take time to wind through the courts. On the political front, the California legislature requested an audit of SFIS to be completed by January 2003. This audit will address the amount of fraud detected through the use of biometrics as part of SFIS, whether the system deters any eligible applicant (especially from immigrant populations applying for public benefits), as well as the cost effectiveness of the system. More information about SFIS is available at http://www.sfis.ca.gov/.

Texas Department of Human Services (TDHS)

In 1995, the Texas state legislature mandated implementation of biometrics as part of Texas' initiative to reduce fraud in public assistance programs. Based on TDHS's research of available systems, fingerprint imaging was determined to be the most reliable and affordable technology for identity authentication purposes.

Texas' finger-imaging program, the Lone Star Image System, was developed to deter duplicate participation in the Food Stamp and Temporary Assistance for Needy Families (TANF) programs. A pilot project of the Lone Star Image System began in October 1996 in 10 San Antonio area offices, enrolling more than 85,000 clients.

Based on the success of the San Antonio pilot program, approval for statewide implementation was given in May 1998 and implementation was completed in August 1999.

Adults (over 18 years of age) and minor heads of household receiving food stamps or TANF are required to provide biometric data when they apply or recertify. Fingerprint imaging of two index fingers and a digital photograph of the individual constitute the enrollment record. As of April 2002, the Texas Lone Star System had 1,175,421 recipients enrolled. More than 400 Lone Star Image System enrollment stations can be found throughout the state, including some mobile stations at temporary offices. Enrollments are routinely purged after six months of inactivity.

Although the system has not caught many individuals committing fraud, TDHS estimates that the system saves $6.36 million each year by deterring potential double-dippers. TDHS estimates that the incidence of duplicate participation in the Food Stamp program is about one half of one percent of the total caseload.

In 1997, the Texas legislature instructed TDHS to plan a pilot project allowing clients to provide finger images instead of a PIN at the point of sale when accessing benefits under the Lone Star Card/electronic benefits transfer (EBT) program. This program employs a debit card instead of Food Stamp coupons or paper checks in distributing Food Stamp and TANF benefits. However, in 1999, the Texas legislature did not approve funding for the pilot project, stating that the technology of biometrics at point of sale was not sufficiently mainstream at the time.

Lack of standardization among the various biometric venders is a major problem. For example, DHS has worked with Kroger Supermarkets to develop finger imaging as a point-of-sale joint pilot project. However, interoperability problems—merging TDHS's system with Kroger's existing finger-imaging check authorization program—would require Kroger to use a separate fingerprint scanner, thus adding cost and complexity to the process.

Connecticut Department of Social Services (DSS)

State legislation passed in 1995 funded the study and eventual deployment of a fingerprint biometric to help prevent fraud in Department of Social Services (DSS)-administered programs. Connecticut wanted to create a system that would deter double-dipping, including multiple enrollments in neighboring states. (It is not uncommon for the same person to participate illegally in several states' entitlement programs at the same time through the use of aliases and forged identification documents.) Accordingly, DSS selected a biometric with an eye toward compatibility with the neighboring states of New York and New Jersey; however, the states' fingerprint templates are not compatible, making interstate comparisons somewhat complicated.

Connecticut has 269,000 clients in its system. The biometric program, implemented in 16 regional offices and the DSS Hartford office, uses centralized image storage and retrieval. Enrollees receive a card that can be used in one-to-one verification or one-to-many identification using the network of databases. In addition to the fingerprints stored, each client card and file carries a photograph and signature of the client that can be manually matched by DSS staff to verify the enrollee's identity. DSS estimated its first year operating costs at $2.6 million with an estimated savings (from deterrence) of $7.5 million.

Prior to implementing its program, the DSS conducted an extensive internal education campaign. Despite these efforts, some members of the legislature vigorously opposed the program. In addition, since its establishment, the state has received three refusals to participate made on religious grounds. These cases were resolved by an administrative decision to allow these persons to use alternative means of identification. After implementation, DSS conducted a survey of program participants and found that the majority approve of the Connecticut biometric program—more than 80 percent of respondents stated that they favored the program.

Connecticut's future vision for biometrics includes using the card in Electronic Benefits Transfer (EBT) transactions, point-of-sale devices for disbursement of medical services, and distribution of Food Stamp benefits through food retailers. This vision offers more security and greater convenience for clients because they could use one card safely for multiple transactions affecting their lives. At the same time, the concept of "one card, multiple uses" would also improve DSS record keeping and accountability.

Illinois Department of Human Services

In 1994, the Illinois legislature approved a study of the use of biometrics to detect and deter fraud in programs administered by the Illinois Department of Public Aid. Officials tested retinal scanning and fingerprint imaging. The fingerprint system passed the test while retinal scanning produced dissatisfaction.

In July 1997, a bureaucratic reorganization took place, and the department was partially incorporated into the Illinois Department of Human Services (DHS). This organizational change led to changes in information technology personnel and changes in philosophy. Currently, the system is no longer operational.

Arizona

In Arizona, fingerprint imaging is mandatory for all adults and minor parents receiving TANF, Food Stamps, and state general assistance. As of March 2002, Arizona's database had about 300,000 recipient records; through March 2002, 82 public assistance cases have been closed due to fingerprint matches indicating multiple enrollments.

Refugee Processing, Takhta Baig, Peshawar, Pakistan[3]

As many as 2,000 Afghan refugees per day at the Takhta Baig Voluntary Repatriation Center (VRC) in Peshawar, Pakistan have their irises scanned before receiving a one-time assistance package of money and supplies from the United Nations High Commissioner for Refugees (UNHCR). The UNHCR administration

---

[3]   This example draws heavily on Machiel van der Harst of BioID Technologies, "Keeping an Eye on Afghan Refugee Aid Claims," a presentation delivered at the Biometrics 2002 Conference, November 8, 2002, London, England. Mr. Van der Harst also kindly answered the author's many questions. See also "One Claim Only for Afghans," *Biometric Technology Today*, October 2002.

had expressed growing concern over the "recycle rate" consisting of individuals who enrolled multiple times under different names to get the one-time assistance. Organized crime helped encourage this practice and the UNHCR wanted to ensure that the UNHCR assistance is given only once to a deserving individual. Although staff interviewed claimants to determine their eligibility, the large numbers of refugees processed (an estimated 1.5 million in 2002) made it extremely difficult to catch a multiple enrollee, even when a photograph of such a violator was available.

The UNHCR decided to test a solution—an anonymous enrollment process using iris recognition—to complement its existing procedures. UNHCR officials and the contractors established an iris recognition enrollment center at the VRC, consisting of five enrollment stations, each staffed by an enrollment officer and an assistant. Once a refugee family has been deemed eligible for the assistance package, all members of the family over age 16 have their right irises scanned for negative identification purposes—the system searches all the iris templates for a match. A negative result means they are not already enrolled in the system and are eligible to receive the one-time package. Throughout this process, the refugees remain anonymous as the only personal data that the system records about them is their template.

Several lessons were learned from the test: Because of the conservative religious beliefs of many of the refugees, the staff curtained off the workstations to provide some privacy. Women were used as the enrollment operators and assistants. The staff first explained the iris recognition process to the family patriarch, as the other family members looked on. Once the patriarch gave his consent, he was the first enrolled, with the assistant helping to show him where to look, and reminding him to put his hand over his left eye. The patriarch in turn would allay the concerns of any family members upon their enrollments. Many of the refugees found the equipment fascinating, particularly when it showed the eye of the enrollee on the computer screen. Although some of the refugees (about 35 percent) thought the iris recognition equipment was used for medical purposes (to check the person's vision), 65 percent understood its purpose and word soon spread throughout the VRC. Staff ran controlled tests—in which someone already enrolled in the system would attempt to enroll in alias—daily to ensure performance.

During the 19-day test, the system enrolled 11,500 refugees at five workstations, operating six hours a day. According to the contractors, the failure to enroll rate was very low, (0.9 percent), attributable largely to disease. During the controlled tests, the false reject rate was also 0.9 percent. The actual results, provided to the UNHCR, have not been publicly released.

Immigration and Law Enforcement

Biometrics are becoming more and more common in a wide variety of immigration and law enforcement applications. The studies discussed next highlight the different ways biometrics are being used in these arenas.

Ben Gurion Airport, Israel

At Ben Gurion Airport in Israel, biometrics are used for passport control. Specifically, the biometric system directs its users—Israeli citizens and other frequent travelers—to automated inspection kiosks for fast processing. Users of the program, who have been vetted, are considered low-risk travelers from a security stand point. The biometrically enabled processing allows the authorities to focus their resources on the perceived risky travelers.

Users are first enrolled and the system captures and stores their biographic information and their hand geometry pattern. When they arrive at the airport, they proceed to an entry kiosk where they use their credit cards for initial identification. The system then validates their hand geometry. The system significantly reduces the time required to get through passport control. Before implementation, passengers at peak travel times would often spend up to one hour waiting in passport control lines. Now automated inspection takes less than 15 seconds. The system processes 50,000 passengers a month and has already done more than one million inspections. Users pay an annual fee to enroll.

U.S. Immigration and Naturalization Service (INS)

INS deployed its Immigration and Naturalization Service Passenger Accelerated Service System (INSPASS) in 1993. INSPASS is based on hand geometry. The prototype installations included JFK (New York), Newark, and Pearson (Toronto) International Airports. Additional deployments include Miami, Los Angeles, San Francisco, Dulles (Washington, D.C.), Vancouver, B.C., and other high-volume international airports.

More than 85,000 people are currently enrolled in this frequent international traveler program, and more than 200,000 transactions have been processed since its installation. INS, in cooperation with the Department of State, determines the rules for who may participate in INSPASS. Citizens of the United States, Canada, Bermuda, legal permanent residents of the United States, most landed immigrants in Canada, and citizens of Visa Waiver Program countries, who meet certain visa classifications, may voluntarily enroll in the INSPASS Program. All INSPASS users are first vetted, including a search of their fingerprints against the FBI's Criminal Master File (IAFIS).

Entry into the U.S. using INSPASS typically takes several minutes, while waiting in line for manual passport stamping can take much longer. Travelers who register false reads (false non-match) are sent to an INS inspector. Anecdotally, it is said that people who have small hands have difficulty (for example, Japanese flight attendants, in particular, have had problems). INS has drawn criticism for not providing more support to INSPASS. At many airports, kiosks are not always operating and the times when someone can be first enrolled in the system are limited.

Application Registration Card for United Kingdom Asylum Seekers

The United Kingdom's Home Office has adopted a biometric solution to help identify asylum seekers, or foreign nationals who, upon arriving in the U.K., are unable or unwilling to return to their countries of nationality because of persecution or the fear of persecution. Asylum seekers are issued a smart card known as an Application Registration Card (ARC) that carries templates of the bearer's fingerprints, as well as their photograph, name, date of birth, and nationality. (For more information, go to http://www.biometrics-today.com/jan02news.html#item1.) The ARC, which contains a secure updateable chip to store additional information, is intended to provide fast and positive identification of asylum seekers subsequent to their initial processing at ports of entry or at the Asylum Seekers Unit in Croydon, England. Croydon was selected as the first location to pilot the biometrically enabled ARC owing to the large number of in-country asylum applications that it receives.

The objective is to prevent asylum seekers from doing unlawful things like applying for benefits multiple times in multiple names. Historically, immigrants had been issued a Standard Acknowledgment Letter, a paper document that is easily counterfeited, forged, or otherwise compromised.

The decision to use a fingerprint biometric for the ARC was made easier by the fact that a huge legacy database already existed because fingerprints of asylum seekers had been collected over a long period. To address privacy concerns, the data held in the chip is protected by a software key escrow, and cardholders are informed of the information placed on the microchip. The cost of each card is about £5 (U.K.).

San Francisco Police Department Automatic Palmprint Identification System (APIS)

Just as fingerprints are left behind at crime scenes, so too are palmprints, which can be important clues for solving crimes. Capitalizing on this fact, the San Francisco Police Department (SFPD) uses latent palmprints from crime scenes to identify possible criminal suspects. Palmprint identification is becoming more popular with law enforcement because criminals leave palmprints at approximately 30 percent of all crime scenes. The SFPD uses an Automatic Palmprint Identification System (APIS) to speed up the identification process. The APIS captures the palm's three core areas and converts them to a template for database storage.

The police take the palmprints of a suspected criminal at the time of his arrest, just as they take ten-rolled fingerprints during the booking process. These palm- prints are then digitized and stored in a database. Police also take latent palmprints left at crime scenes; the forensic investigator "lifts" the palmprints, which are then scanned and entered into the palmprint database. Police then try to match the palmprints collected at crime scenes against the stored palmprints of suspects. The APIS performs this identification (one-to-many) search and provides a ranked list of possible matches. A forensic investigator then can hone in on the possible matches for a true match or hit.

The APIS correctly identified a hit-and-run suspect just one month after its implementation. So far the department has over 400,000 palmprints in the APIS database, the largest in the United States. Police officers expect the new system to solve crimes where fingerprints are not always present. If successful, the SFPD's use of palmprints could be replicated by many other law enforcement agencies at the federal, state, and local levels, and taking arrestees' palmprints could become standard operating procedure for the authorities. Just as the FBI has its IAFIS for fingerprints, a national repository for palmprints could also be created, and in the process, more crimes could be solved. Currently, a major operational downside of palmprints is the relatively large image that must be captured and the costs associated with transmitting that data in light of limited bandwidth.

Electronic Arrest Warrant: Gwinnett County, Georgia

Police in Gwinnett County, Georgia, have begun using biometric signatures to reduce the processing time needed to issue arrest warrants. Using video conferencing connected via the Internet, a police officer can contact a judge to present evidence supporting a warrant. If the judge is satisfied, he can authorize the warrant by signing it online. This whole process takes about 15 minutes: a major improvement from the previous system that required the police officer to travel to the courthouse, which could take up to four hours with heavy traffic—a situation that kept officers spending most of the day driving back and forth to the courthouse. (For more information, go to http://www.integratedsolutionsmag.com/articles/1998_07-08/980701.htm.)

All six police precincts, the police headquarters, and the county jail in Gwinnett County can now process electronic arrest warrants. The process works as follows: The officer logs on to the password-protected system and enters data on electronic forms about the accused, victims, witnesses, and nature of the alleged crime. Once the data is entered, the officer clicks an icon on his computer screen to place a videoconference call to the courthouse. Once the videoconference is established, the judge swears in the officer and they proceed to discuss the warrant application.

If the judge determines that the legal requirements have been satisfied, each party signs the arrest warrant using a digitizer pad. Software electronically captures each signature and binds them to the document. Both the judge and the officer print paper copies of the arrest warrant. The judge's copy is physically stored at the courthouse and the officer's copy is presented to the arrestee.

The security of the electronic warrant system was a major implementation concern for Gwinnett County officials. Both officers and judges have passwords that must be entered to begin the arrest warrant process. (A fingerprint recognition system is planned for future use. Judges and officers will log on to the system by placing their finger on a small scanner.) The signature software ensures the signatures on the arrest warrant are secure. Users of the system must first enroll their signatures with the system; users sign their names ten times using the digitizer. The biometric signature software records the time it takes to sign a name, the type of pen strokes used to sign a name, and other distinctive characteristics of each signature. When a user signs their name, it is compared to the record of the signature enrolled in the system in a one-to-one match (verification).

To enhance security, the signature software also binds the signatures cryptographically to the electronic documents. Signatures cannot be altered once they are so bound. If the document is altered, the signature automatically voids itself. All of the electronic documents are stored on the server as read-only memory, so the documents cannot be altered. To access data on the server, a judge's password is needed.

The system has been well received by both police officers and judges as it has significantly reduced processing time for arrest warrants. (Arguably, criminals prefer the old inefficient system.) The electronic arrest warrant system could be particularly useful in rural counties where officers routinely have to travel long distances to get to the courthouse. The system would also be welcome in large cities plagued with rush-hour traffic.

Traffic Court, Miami-Dade County, Florida

Miami-Dade County in Florida, with a population of more than 2 million people, has the fourth-largest traffic court system in the United States. The number of traffic citations has been growing; in 1999 it stood at over 700,000, requiring over 2 million documents to be filed with the Miami-Dade County Traffic Court Division—a huge volume of paperwork to file, store, process, access, and provide to a judge whenever necessary. To ease the problems created by this huge paper trail and to improve service, the county implemented an electronic imaging document system. This system includes a module that enables judges, clerks, prosecutors, defense attorneys, and defendants, using special electronic styluses, to provide "handwritten" electronic signatures on court documents. Signatures are captured electronically and affixed to appropriate forms. More than 8,900 defendant signatures are captured per week.

As a result, documents can be processed and routed electronically, streamlining the workflow. Information technology has thus transformed the Traffic Court Division into a "paperless court," significantly improving its efficiency and effectiveness and making it the first paperless traffic court in the world. The system has improved productivity, saved significant dollars, and provided the public with high-quality documents with appropriate signatures in place. The ability to capture signatures in a legally binding way was a key component of the entire process.

Sarasota County Detention Center, Sarasota, Florida

Since 1998, the Sarasota County Detention Center has used an iris recognition system to authenticate the identities of its approximately 750 inmates. As inmates are brought into the detention center, a device scans their irises, and they are enrolled in the system. Currently, the detention center uses the system only to authenticate the inmates when they enter and leave.

Within the detention center, inmates use photograph identification cards for internal verification. In the past, inmates would switch cards with those inmates about to be released in an attempt to assume their identity and escape. Since its implementation, the iris recognition system has caught eight inmates trying to escape using switched identities. Another individual who had been arrested by the police was released when the iris scan revealed that he was not the person the police wanted—the wanted suspect was a recently released inmate with his iris template still on file.

The Sarasota County Detention Center is pleased with the system, which, including implementation, cost less than $10,000 and has already proved its value through the foiled escapes. The iris recognition system takes seconds to verify an individual and provides positive identification at any time. The database has a text section where, for example, information concerning arrest warrants can be maintained. This feature helped the detention center identify an individual in its charge who had three additional outstanding arrest warrants.

Florida Department of Corrections

The Florida Department of Corrections (FDC) uses its Automated Visitor Registration System II (AVR II) to process prison staff and visitors. The AVR II uses two methods for authentication: hand geometry as the primary and a facial photograph as the back-up. The hand geometry unit employs a miniaturized camera to capture a digital template of the back of the individual's hand. These photographs analyze the size, shape, width, thickness, and surface of the hand. Over 95 measurements of the individual's hand are taken and converted to a template, which is stored in the system's database for future verification (one-to-one matching). The computer also stores each individual's photograph.

On any given weekend, the Florida Department of Corrections processes approximately 10,000 visitors into and out of its prison facilities—a tremendous number of people to verify, track, and monitor. The FDC particularly wanted to improve customer service by reducing the waiting time for visitors, thus making the visit less time consuming and more convenient. Before the installation of AVR II, visitor identification and clearance could take as long as four minutes per person. With 150 people in line at the gate (a not uncommon occurrence), this meant long waits. With AVR II, the new process takes about 10 seconds per person. The FDC also sees the use of biometrics, like hand geometry, important in eliminating the possibility of inmates leaving the prison disguised as staff or other authorized visitors.

Since children visit their parents in jail, the FDC management had to make decisions about how minor visitors would be processed in AVR II. All children are photographed, but they are not entered into the hand geometry system until they reach age 12 because experience showed that their enrollment hand had to be large enough to register on the scanner.

The AVR II is part of the integrated control system and is governed by control room staff. During initial registration (which takes 3–4 minutes), a visitor answers questions, and a high-resolution digital camera mounted on the workstation takes a photograph. Each visitor then receives a personal identification number (PIN), which is a nine-digit number automatically generated by the system and assigned to visitors during this initial process.

A visitor inputs the assigned PIN by typing the digits on a keypad and then places their right hand into the hand geometry reader. The system verifies the visitor by comparing the hand geometry of the hand presented to the reader with the template stored for that person in the system. The system also immediately provides information, including the visitor's photograph, on the control room officer's computer. Upon verifying the identity of the visitor, the control room officer admits the individual at the touch of a button. This entire process takes less than 10 seconds. Visitors use a similar process to exit the institution. The information and related tracking data is automatically available through a central office LAN server.

Intensive Supervision Surveillance Programme, United Kingdom

The United Kingdom's Home Office is experimenting with an Intensive Supervision Surveillance Programme (ISSP) that uses biometric technology to keep track of juvenile repeat offenders who would otherwise be in jail. Juveniles are eligible for ISSP if they have committed four or more offenses in the past 12 months and had at least one previous sentence. Many in the criminal justice community see the ISSP approach as better than custodial sentences, which are widely viewed as ineffective and costly.

The ISSP system continuously tracks the offender 24/7. ISSP does this monitoring by fitting an electronic tag on the offender. This tag is linked to a computerized voice recognition system that telephones the juvenile at various times of the day to check that he is where he supposed to be. The system prompts the juvenile to utter certain phrases and then matches the actual phrase spoken with the biometric voice template on file for the juvenile. Surveillance cameras in town centers can also be configured to recognize the faces of the offenders.

Should the system prove effective, ISSP could easily be extended to the mainstream prison population, particularly in home detention or parole situations.

Trusted Traveler Credential

There has been much discussion about the use of some form of a trusted or registered traveler program for passengers in civil aviation. For example, the Aviation and Transportation Security Act of 2002 provides that the Under Secretary of Transportation for Security may establish requirements to implement trusted traveler programs. This law explains that a major goal of such a program is to expedite the security screening of the trusted travelers, thereby allowing security staff to focus greater resources on those passengers who should be subject to more extensive screening. In the U.S., the Transportation Security Administration, along with other government agencies, is considering various proposals. Using the INSPASS system as a model for a national trusted traveler credential has also been advanced. However, no course of action has been firmly set in the U.S. In the Netherlands, a program has been started and it is discussed next.

Amsterdam, Schiphol Airport, The Netherlands

Amsterdam Schiphol Airport became the world's first airport to employ an automatic border control system using iris recognition for travelers. The Privium system authenticates the identity of registered travelers by cross-referencing a traveler's real-time iris scan with the traveler's pre-registered iris template, which is stored on an encrypted smart card issued to the registered traveler. This program is open to holders of European Economic Area passports (European Union countries plus Norway, Iceland, and Liechtenstein). Some 2,500 people are currently using the Privium system.

The security procedure involves two basic phases: enrollment and verification. In the enrollment phase, the authorities qualify and register the traveler. This process, which includes a passport examination, background check, and iris scan, takes less than 30 minutes. Successful enrollment (registration) results in the traveler being issued a smart card, on which his encrypted iris template is stored.

The second phase verifies the registered traveler at the border control checkpoint. This verification is done when the traveler approaches a gated kiosk and inserts his smart card into the kiosk card reader. The system reads the smart card and allows valid registered travelers to enter a secure, isolated area. The traveler looks into an iris scan camera so that the iris can be matched with the data on the smart card. If a successful match is obtained, the passenger can continue to the gate. If the biometric match fails, or the traveler's passage is not authorized by any external system link, the automatic gate directs the traveler to the front of the queue for the standard manual passport check. The entire automatic border passage procedure is typically completed in seconds.

The system does not use a database but receives data from a smart card chip. This system architecture means that there is no sharing of the iris template information because only the traveler holds this information. The use of individual smart cards to hold the biometric data rather than a centralized biometrics database, coupled with the fact that program enrollment is voluntary, has eased concerns about individual privacy. Due to a strict separation of data on the chip, the card reader is also able to read Dutch Border Police data independently from the biometric information, further easing privacy concerns. As a security and privacy measure, the data is encrypted on the card protecting it from fraudulent use. Additionally, since the system involves no physical contact such as fingerprint or hand geometry biometrics, there are no concerns regarding hygiene.

National Identity

Biometrics can be a critical enabling technology for a national identity system. Chapter 19 provides an in-depth assessment of the feasibility of a national identity system in the U.S. The next section discusses how Malaysia is using biometrics as part of its national identity system.

Malaysia's Government Multi-Purpose Card

Malaysia is the first country to use a biometrically enabled smart card as part of a national identification scheme. The Government Multi-Purpose Card (GMPC), also called "Mykad," electronically incorporates identity, digital thumbprints, and biographical information into a mandatory piece of plastic the size of a credit card. Mykad incorporates encryption technology and other security features including holograms. Apart from the name and address of the cardholder, all other data is protected and can only be accessed through a card reader available only to the authorities.

As the name implies, the Government Multi-Purpose Card is not just an ID but holds a number of applications. (Go to http://www.jpn.gov.my/gmpc.html for more information.) The GMPC applications include:

- **National Identity**   The GMPC will eventually replace the current plastic card-based National Identity Card issued to over 17 million Malaysians. National identity is the anchor application of the GMPC; the unique ID number assigned to every GMPC holder is expected to serve as the secure access key to other applications and systems.

- **National Driving License**   The GMPC will replace the paper-based laminated cards currently held by about 6 million drivers. The GMPC will enhance traffic law enforcement by increasing the accuracy of summons information in government databases and by providing law enforcement with up-to-date driving records.

- **Immigration**   The GMPC will supplement the Malaysian passport to facilitate entry and exit from Malaysian immigration check points. It will not replace the actual passport, since it is required for entry into and exit from other countries.

- **Medical Information (PKI)**   The PKI will enable users to conduct various secured e-commerce transactions using a digital certificate that will ensure authentication, data integrity, and nonrepudiation.

In 1999, the Government of Malaysia and a consortium of local and international companies entered into a contract for development of the card. The program is in two phases. A pilot program to cover the 2 million residents of the Kuala Lumpur area. The second phase is nationwide. The card was launched in September 2001 and the pilot phase should be completed by the end of 2002. The national roll-out is expected to be completed in 2003. As of April 2002, 1.5 million cards had been produced.

Government Services Centers (GSC), equipped with digital cameras, biometric scanners, mobile and desktop card-accepting devices, and key readers, will perform various GMPC-related functions to include:

- Application and enrollment

- Renewal and replacement

- Update of bearer's GMPC and passport information

- Payment of summons and collection of payment

- Renewal of driving license

Law enforcement, immigration authorities, and emergency medical personnel will be issued with mobile card-reading units to read the data on the smart cards. This mobile capability will facilitate, among other things, identity verification using biometrics and access to relevant databases, for example, medical information for an unconscious patient.

Current uses include expedited entry/exit at immigration checkpoints using unmanned automated gates, currently available at Kuala Lumpur International Airport and other international entry/exit points. (Go to http://www .unisys.com/industry-analyst/IndustryAnalyst-03.asp for more information.) Future applications currently being tested include incorporating bank ATM functionality and transit card functionality to pay highway tolls, parking, and an integrated ticketing system for train and bus travel. These future applications are being developed under the Payment Multi-Purpose Card (PMPC) project. Some banks have already tested the PMPC card. The visionary plan is for the GMPC and PMPC functionalities to be merged eventually. Thus, the ultimate objective of the GMPC is to provide a one-stop service center to provide a secure, single common platform for present and future public and private sector applications.

Criticism of the GMPC and public acceptance issues has not really surfaced, in part, because every Malaysian citizen over the age of 12 has long been required to carry a paper identity card containing his thumbprints. By law, each Malaysian must carry his or her government-issued identity card. Moreover, the Constitution of Malaysia does not specifically recognize a right to privacy.

Access Control

The following section discusses controlling logical (computer) access in the school system in Stockholm, Sweden.

Scanning Students: A Stockholm School Goes Biometric[4]

In Stockholm, Sweden, the school system uses fingerprint authentication to log in 80,000 students to its computer network of 19,000 workstations in information technology labs in the city's 174 public schools.

The problems confronting the Stockholm schools are by no means unique to Swedish schoolchildren. Students frequently forgot their passwords, particularly in the lower grades. Teachers spent up to 20 minutes of a 40-minute computer class resetting passwords, wasting time reserved for educational instruction. To avoid wasting time, some teachers and students wrote the passwords down, creating a security risk and setting a bad precedent for proper procedures. Also, students shared passwords, which meant that it was difficult to monitor a student's Internet surfing activities, which might stray into unauthorized areas.

Initially, the school system did a one-year pilot study with 450 students and teachers. Administrators were concerned over how scanners would perform with small fingers in a challenging environment. The pilot results impressed the school administration. The school administration selected fingerprint as the biometric of choice because it was seen as more reliable, easy to use, and relatively inexpensive when compared to other biometric solutions.

During the initial phase of the pilot study, four different fingerprint scanners were used with 60 students enrolled on all four types for preliminary testing. Engineers discovered that devices from two of the vendors, well-suited for adult fingerprints, had difficulty scanning the smaller fingers of children. Consequently, after two months of testing, one scanner and 450 students and teachers at the test site were selected.

To log in, a student enters her username, then places either the left or right index finger on the scanner (both are enrolled so students do not have to remember

---

[4] This example draws heavily on Samir Hamouni, Project Leader for the City of Stockholm, "Swedish School Learns the Value of Biometrics," a presentation delivered at the Biometrics 2002 Conference, November 7, 2002, London, England. Mr. Hamouni also kindly answered the author's many questions.

which one it is). The software captures the image and creates a template that is then compared to the stored template. A one-to-one verification is done, and the user is logged in via a process that takes seconds.

The feedback has been very positive. Teachers feel more like teachers and not password supervisors. Students caught on very quickly and think the technology is "cool." To facilitate future deployments, administrators have created an approved products list from which schools select their hardware and equipment. Also, learning tools to show the students where to place their fingers have helped familiarize them with the system. Several other departments are considering shifting to a biometric logon.

Military Applications/Military Programs

The military has long been interested in biometrics and the technology has enjoyed extensive support from the national security community. The following sections discuss how the U.S. military is using biometrics.

Biometrically Protected Smart Card Pilot Program, Fort Sill, Oklahoma

This case study, adapted from a RAND Report, explains how the U.S. Army experimented with using a biometric on a smart card for its personnel in basic training. From the kernels of this modest pilot test, the Department of Defense decided to adopt a biometrically enabled Common Access Card. This study offers valuable lessons for anyone considering such a combination of the two technologies.

Problem

The U.S. Army sends recruits to basic training at one of five bases in the United States: Fort Sill, Oklahoma; Fort Jackson, South Carolina; Fort Leonard Wood, Missouri; Fort Knox, Kentucky; and Fort Benning, Georgia. Shortly after arrival at the base, the new recruits must buy toiletries, haircuts, and other personal items. To enable them to make these purchases, the Army issues recruits an advance on their pay. Giving these recruits several hundred dollars in cash causes concern because the money is easily lost or stolen. Thus, Fort Sill used a voucher system, while at Fort Knox, the Army issued checks to the recruits and then marched them to the local post exchange (PX) store to buy money orders. These activities took hours to complete and complicated the training schedule. The Army's Training and Doctrine Command (TRADOC) and Finance Command began to look for alternative approaches. Because the Treasury Department's Financial Management Service and DoD's Defense Finance and Accounting Service (DFAS) manage government payments, they became involved in the search for solutions. The Army and Air Force Exchange Service (AAFES) also participated because it wanted to test speeding of throughputs and reduce cash handling at basic training points of sale. Given the objective of a quick, safe, and efficient system of paying recruits, the Army decided to test three different systems of stored value cards containing digital cash:

- Smart cards that were PIN protected
- Smart cards that were biometrically protected
- Smart cards that were open purses, like cash

The Army tested the biometrically protected smart card, shown in Figure 16-1, at Fort Sill, Oklahoma. The biometric used was a fingerprint. Mellon Bank did the system integration. Identicator Technologies provided the biometric technology, with additional integration to the electronic purse done by Product Technologies, Inc.

Program

The biometric smart card pilot program began at Fort Sill in March 1998 and ran for 15 months. Determining the population to be included in the Fort Sill pilot was straightforward, it would include all recruits arriving for basic training. Because Army basic training is a highly controlled environment, recruits have a very limited number of places at which they are allowed to spend money. The Army placed a smart card reader and fingerprint sensor at each location (points of sale) where recruits were allowed to spend money. The Army also gave a keychain-sized card reader to each drill sergeant to allow him to monitor how much money a recruit had on his card.

The first thing done with recruits arriving at Fort Sill was to verify their identities and SSNs and issue them the smart cards with advances on their pay. Army personnel enrolled each recruit into the system using a laptop computer and sensor to scan the recruit's right index finger to obtain a digital representation of the fingerprint. The clerk also scanned the recruit's left index finger as a backup. The clerk then added cash value to the card based on an Army formula: $200 for men; $260 for women. Cards were set to expire in 60 days, at which time

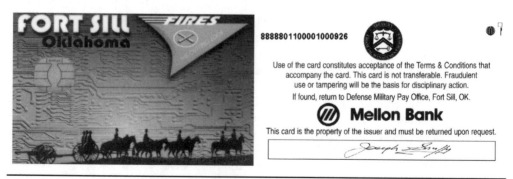

Figure 16-1   The Fort Sill biometrically protected (front and back of card) smart card

all remaining cash transferred to the recruit's bank account, which had been established in the meantime. The Army did not keep a separate record of the fingerprint; only the serial number of the card was linked to the cardholder's name.

The recruit was responsible for keeping track of his smart card, which contained his fingerprint template. At points of sale, the recruit entered his card into the card reader and placed his right or left index finger on the sensor. This template was compared to the template on the card. If they matched, the sale went through with the amount deducted from the card.

Performance

The program team had no reports of fraud and no complaints about failure to use the system. Only 10 people out of the 25,000 enrolled during the pilot program were unable to enroll; thus the failure to enroll rate was extremely low—0.04 percent. This failure to enroll rate is much lower than the advertised 2+ percent for fingerprint technologies. However, these young recruits are prime candidates for fingerprint biometrics. Of those enrolled in the system, only 3 percent failed to gain access to their card with a first fingerprint, but when a second fingerprint was used, there was 100 percent access. The only performance issue for the system was that after several months the sensors for enrollment would wear out and "go bad." The clerks managing the system learned to recognize the signs in advance and replace the sensors as necessary.

Protections

Drill sergeants are very protective of their recruits. During informational sessions with the project team, one drill sergeant expressed concerns that recruits with fundamentalist religious beliefs might object to using the biometric on religious grounds. They were also concerned that fingerprints would be kept after recruits left and were relieved to find out that no fingerprints from this activity would be retained by the Army. Even though sales were linked by serial number to a bank, and account information and names could be drawn from this, no information was gathered about recruit purchases. The drill sergeants were also assured that the template on the card could not be reverse-engineered into a fingerprint image. Because this pilot program did not involve personal information contained in a system of records, it had no Privacy Act implications. At the time of enrollment, each recruit received a brochure explaining how the fingerprint technology worked.

No formal feedback was obtained from the recruits, but reportedly the drill sergeants found the program a great improvement over previous practices. The drill sergeants preferred the smart cards because of reduced risk of theft, which can be time-consuming because they must assist with investigations, file reports, and help the recruit who has lost his money. However, the Army decided that while digital cash was a good solution, biometrics would not be used to protect the card. Experiments with open purse smart cards in the basic training environment worked as well as those protected by a PIN or biometric but at less cost.

Lessons Learned

The program, directed from the top, was accepted without much difficulty. Several reasons explain this success. First, the program provided more time for training by reducing the time spent on administrative tasks. The program reduced from hours to minutes the process of paying recruits and conducting subsequent transactions for sundries, haircuts, and more. In addition, a well- thought- out educational campaign was targeted at the drill sergeants, the Army personnel who have the recruits' interests most at heart and the recruits' lives most in sight. Program managers showed some 300 drill sergeants how the technology worked, explained the limits to the information provided, and answered the sergeants' questions. Finally, the Army conducted the biometrically protected smart card program for a clearly defined purpose in a highly controlled environment with an ideal population.

All DoD training bases are now using open purse smart cards, except for the Marines at Parris Island, South Carolina, who use PINs to secure their cards.

Defense Manpower Data Center (DMDC)

The DMDC operates what is arguably the Department of Defense's largest biometric database. By way of background, the Federal Managers' Financial Integrity Act of 1982 requires federal managers to establish internal controls to provide reasonable assurance that funds, property, and other assets are protected against fraud or other unlawful use. As a result of this legislation, the Department of Defense launched Operation Mongoose, a fraud prevention and detection initiative. Operation Mongoose exposed a number of fraud schemes and indicated that Department of Defense needed to improve servicemember identity assurance procedures. Responding to the need for better fraud prevention measures, the acting Under Secretary of Defense (Personnel and Readiness) gave authority to the DMDC to initiate an electronic fingerprint capture policy in 1997.

In an initial pilot program, DMDC saved an estimated $8 million with 25,000 military retirees living in overseas locations. The program confirmed DMDC's suspicion that military benefits were still being collected on deceased retirees when many failed to appear to enroll their fingerprint in the new identification system. Since 1998, the DMDC has been capturing the right index fingerprint of all active-duty, reserve, and retired military personnel, as well as survivors receiving a military annuity. This potential enrollment pool is 4 million people. The fingerprint is captured during the routine issuance (or reissuance) of military identification cards at DMDC sites. DMDC stores electronic copies of these fingerprints in a comprehensive database known as the Defense Enrollment Eligibility Reporting System (DEERS). DMDC does not store any copies of fingerprints on the actual military identification card. DEERS can be accessed if a person's identity needs to be authenticated.

Pentagon Athletic Club, The Pentagon

The Department of Defense (DoD) Biometrics Management Office (BMO) is spearheading a pilot project that features iris recognition technology for members of the Pentagon Athletic Club to access their facility, which is located near the Pentagon in Arlington, Virginia, and is popular with all ranks for sports and exercise. Participation in the project is voluntary and involves enrolling the iris pattern of the member, which takes less than 3 minutes. To gain access to the club, the system detects the individual's approach. Once the person's eye is several inches from the mirror in the unit, a camera captures an iris image, which is digitally processed and searched against the database of stored templates for a match. When a match occurs, access is granted almost instantaneously. The objective is to do away with the old system, which required members to swipe their card. This meant that members always have to carry their identification cards, particularly inconvenient when members would go out on runs. The iris recognition system will enable not only secure access to the facility for members but also promote convenience for members since they will not have to carry anything on their person. The pilot project also contributes to the Biometrics Management Office's efforts to enhance the military community's awareness of biometrics.

DoD Biometrics Management Office; DoD Biometrics Fusion Center, DoD Common Access Card

The United States military must conduct global operations in difficult conditions, while at the same time, the DoD must manage massive support network to provide for soldiers, their family members, and all those who contribute to national security. Mission success requires increased reliance on information technology because it enables DoD to work smarter and maintain our warfighter's edge. But reliance on IT means that information systems and the data they contain must be fully protected. The DoD has embraced biometrics as a tool to achieve this protection.

DoD has long been experimenting with biometrics. For example, since the 1960s, the National Security Agency has been working on speaker/voice recognition. Recent military operations have made it clear that DoD needs to do a better job of securing its computer systems and networks. In 1999, a DoD Network Vulnerability Assessment of Kosovo highlighted concerns about information assurance. Responding to this Assessment in 1999, Senator Robert Byrd of West Virginia stated in the *Congressional Record* that, "Experience with 'hackers' and DoD exercises indicate that defense systems, often globally linked and readily accessed, are vulnerable to unauthorized penetration of their information networks... I am told that the Department [of Defense] has learned from its experience in Kosovo that this kind of a threat is not limited to major world powers."[5] Congress, with Senator Byrd's support, directed that the Army study biometrics and assess the Biometrics Fusion Center concept—a central DoD facility to test and evaluate biometrics; to serve as a knowledge base for biometrics; and to be involved in storage of biometric data. Upon receiving favorable Army input, Congress established the Army as the DoD Executive Agent for biometrics. Section 112 of Public Law 106-246 states in part: "To ensure the availability of biometrics technologies in the Department of Defense, the Secretary of the Army shall be the Executive Agent to lead, consolidate, and coordinate all biometrics information assurance programs in the DoD."[6]

The DoD has begun implementing a smart card technology across the Department of Defense that will enable it to deploy troops faster and safeguard its people and facilities better. The DoD's Common Access Card (CAC) is a tamper-resistant identification card with an embedded 32-kilobyte memory chip. The CAC has already been issued at many stateside and overseas locations and will eventually be issued to 4 million people, including active-duty military, reservists, DoD civilians, and eligible contractor employees. If a CAC is lost or stolen, the identification and security accesses on the card can be invalidated immediately. Currently, the DoD Biometrics Fusion Center is conducting tests on various biometrics that can be used in conjunction with the CAC. In the near term, future versions of the CAC will be biometrically enabled, meaning the biometric reposed on the card will be used for access control, business processes, etc. To learn more about DoD biometrics, visit http://www.c3i.osd.mil/biometrics/.

DoD DNA Specimen Repository for Remains Identification

While not a "true" biometric application (in the sense that it is not a real-time process), DNA always generates great interest. Therefore, a discussion of one of the world's largest DNA repositories is appropriate. The DNA Repository for Remains Identification along with the Armed Forces DNA Identification Laboratory make up the DoD DNA Registry. The DNA Registry, a Division of the Office of the Armed Forces Medical Examiner, helps the military identify remains of soldiers killed in combat or missing in action. High-velocity weapons and the lethality of the modern battlefield often destroy any chances of using fingerprints or dental records. DNA, however, can almost always be used to identify remains. Although most times the armed forces can identify the dead based on various records, DNA identification provides closure for the family and the biological proof of death required by life insurance companies.

---

[5] *Congressional Record*, 1999. Vol. 145, p. S6650.

[6] U.S. Public Law 106-246, section 112. *Emergency Supplemental Act*, July 13, 2000.

This issue came to a head as the military prepared for Operation Desert Storm with the potential for large numbers of casualties. At the Dover Air Force Base in Delaware, mortuary facilities were expanded, but medical officials were concerned about the ability to identify the dead. DNA techniques had been pursued by the military in its efforts to identify servicemembers missing in action from Vietnam, Korea, and even World War II, but this was a slow process that required the military to find close relatives and obtain samples from them in an attempt to match them to DNA samples from the deceased.

Army pathologists were convinced that the need to identify large numbers of dead service personnel had to be addressed and that a military DNA registry could provide a suitable solution. The Army leadership also became convinced of the utility of such a registry and lobbied for it. In December 1991, authorization and appropriations for the DNA program were received. Since June 1992, DoD has required all military inductees and all active-duty and reserve personnel to provide DNA samples for its DNA Repository at the time of enlistment, reenlistment, annual physical, or preparation for operational deployment. The DNA Repository also contains samples from civilians and foreign nationals who work with the U.S. military in arenas of conflict. DoD stores the samples in freezers at the DNA Specimen Repository in Gaithersburg, Maryland.

Implementation of the program in the Army, which is the Executive Agent of the DNA program for DoD, was not without controversy. Everyone was concerned about privacy, from DoD officials to policymakers to the media. The program office began to hold meetings to educate military personnel about the purpose of the program and the privacy protections that would be used to ensure that DNA data would not be otherwise employed. The education campaign worked, and at all levels military personnel have participated in the program. To date, those who have refused to participate in the DNA registry have been forced to leave the service. (On March 17, 1997, a DoD Directive permitted the armed service branches to exempt certain members from the mandatory DNA collection requirement to accommodate religious practices.) As of 1998, only three servicemembers have refused to submit samples, as opposed to 1.3 million service members who have complied.[7]

Undoubtedly, a number of servicemembers are unwilling participants but have chosen to trust the Army rather than leave the service. In addition to the education campaign, other announcements had to be made about the program. In particular, on June 14, 1995, DoD placed "system of records" notice in the *Federal Register* announcing the establishment of this new system containing personal information. This announcement, required by the Privacy Act, needed to be approved by DoD's Privacy Board, and it was, after 18 months of deliberations.

---

[7] See *Mayfield v. Dalton*, 901 F.Supp. (D. Hawaii 1995) (dismissing all claims of two Marines who refused to participate in DNA program on grounds that it infringed on their constitutionally protected privacy rights).

Another major issue for the program was how long to keep the DNA records. One might assume that they would just be pulled when a servicemember leaves the military, but apparently similarity of service members' names or SSNs as well as clerical error raised the risk of pulling the wrong record. It is also time-consuming to search the repository continually for individual records, particularly when there are more than 3 million records.

Originally, DoD's policy called for destruction of DNA records after 75 years. However, in 1996, DoD changed the destruction schedule to 50 years, to be compatible with standards for military health records. This 50-year period ensures that no servicemember remains in the armed forces when his DNA record is pulled from the database. Also, in 1996, DoD amended its policy to permit servicemembers to request that their DNA samples be destroyed when they leave the service. In other words, servicemembers can opt out of the database. Once a servicemember makes such a request, DoD has six months to destroy the DNA records.

DoD's strict policy on sharing of the specimens ensures that DNA specimens can only be used for:

- Remains identification
- Internal quality-control purposes
- Consensual uses
- Other limited uses as compelled by law

This last category includes a court order authorizing sharing investigation or the approval of the DoD General Counsel or Assistant Secretary of Defense for Health Affairs for prosecution of a felony. The specimens cannot be used without consent for any other purpose, such as paternity suits or genetic testing. In addition, the specimens are considered confidential medical information and are covered by federal laws and military regulations on privacy. This policy has been tested by numerous federal agencies who have asked for access to the data, primarily for law enforcement purposes.

Chapter 17

Searching the FBI's Civil Files: Public Safety v. Civil Liberty

By John D. Woodward, Jr.

In the aftermath of the terrorist attacks of September 11, 2001, Congress and the Executive Branch have increased interest in information systems that can collect, compile, store, and share data about individuals. This data can be used to help identify and profile individuals or anticipate events or trends.[1] Long before September 11, paper records and metal filing cabinets in government offices were rapidly giving way to electronic documents and computer databases. These changes bring greater efficiencies and capabilities. As a Department of Justice working paper explains, "Today's technologies, when applied in a strategic fashion, hold the promise of reduced paperwork, quick information capturing, broad transmittal and access capabilities, improved information quality, and reduced long-term costs."[2]

---

[1] The creation of the U.S. government's Foreign Terrorist Tracking Task Force and the Department of Defense's Total Information Awareness initiative in response to the terrorist attacks are one example of this interest in information systems and how the government may use individual data.

[2] U.S. Department of Justice, Office of Justice Programs, Privacy Impact Assessment for Justice Information Systems Working Paper, August 2000, available at http://www.ojp.usdoj.gov/ archive/topics/integratedjustice/piajis.htm.

Some databases are not controversial. For example, in Chapter 3, Peter T. Higgins explained how the Federal Bureau of Investigation (FBI) developed its biometric showcase, the Integrated Automated Fingerprint Identification System (IAFIS), containing electronic fingerprint submissions for approximately 42.8 million individuals fingerprinted as a result of their arrest or incarceration. IAFIS can compare fingerprint images it receives from a suspect in custody with its huge database of fingerprints and determine whether there is a match within hours, or even minutes—the average search time is 68 minutes.

However, massive government-controlled databases also give rise to civil liberty concerns. Following up on the groundwork laid in Chapter 3, this chapter focuses on one such U.S. government database that has largely escaped public scrutiny. Recently, the FBI has begun taking steps to upgrade its "civil files," which currently store the fingerprints of about 40 million Americans. These people are not terrorists, criminals, arrestees, or suspects. Rather, they are current and former federal government employees, U.S. military members, and naturalized immigrants, along with others. Traditionally, the FBI's civil files system consisted of tens of millions of tenprint cards, or completed paper forms that contained the fingerprints, captured (or "rolled") in ink, of a person's eight fingers and two thumbs. The FBI physically filed these tenprint cards in warehouses. However, the Bureau has established a new, automated civil files system that stores in a comprehensive computerized database the electronic images of those fingerprints received since May 2000. For example, the tenprint card of a Vietnam War era soldier sits in a warehouse, whereas a new Army recruit's fingerprints are electronically stored.

This new civil files system provides the FBI with a solid foundation for an impressive technical capability to search the civil files as part of its national security work, for criminal investigation efforts, or for other reasons. A latent fingerprint found at any crime scene could be searched against the civil files database for a possible match. In this way, searching the civil files might help solve crimes. However, the FBI's new system also raises civil liberty and privacy concerns. To civil libertarians, the system is an example of the "Big Brother" that George Orwell warned us about in his classic book *1984*. To others, the system represents the powerful beginnings of a national identification system that means we inevitably lose our individual privacy. This chapter discusses this new FBI capability in an historical context and highlights the beneficial uses it brings to public safety as well as the concerns it potentially poses to civil liberty and related interests. It concludes by offering several policy recommendations and calling for further public discussion of this issue.[3]

---

[3] An earlier version of this chapter appeared in John D. Woodward, Jr., "Searching the FBI's Civil Files: Public Safety v. Civil Liberty," *U.S. Law Week* (September 17, 2002): 2183; also published in John D. Woodward, Jr., "Searching the FBI's Civil Files: Public Safety v. Civil Liberty," *Privacy & Security Law* (September 2, 2002): 1042. This chapter is based, in part, on the author's previous RAND research published in John D. Woodward, Jr., Katherine W. Webb, Elaine M. Newton, et al., *Army Biometric Applications: Identifying and Addressing Sociocultural Concerns*, 133–145 (2001).

Historical Need for Better Identification

By the late nineteenth century, law enforcement desperately needed better ways to identify criminals, particularly as the criminal justice systems of the western world increasingly based punishment on whether a convicted person had a prior criminal record (Cole 2001 and Beavan 2001). For example, in 1869, England enacted the Habitual Criminals Act, which provided for longer sentences for criminals with previous convictions. Recidivists received lengthier prison sentences and thus had a powerful incentive to assume a false identity to attempt to hide their previous criminal record. Hiding previous misdeeds also was made easy in societies, such as the United States, that encouraged mobility and relocation.

A Frenchman came to the rescue in 1883. Alphonse Bertillon, a Paris police official, devised a system of anthropometrics whereby the authorities, using special tools, recorded a set of precise measurements of an individual's physical features. For example, so-called Bertillon operators measured the distance from a person's elbow to the tip of his index finger, the distance from the top to the bottom of each ear lobe, along with many other measurements. They also made detailed notations of the person's physical characteristics and made a record of the person's peculiar marks, such as scars and tattoos. The following year, Bertillon made 241 positive identifications of recidivists that the police had otherwise missed. Bertillon's successes and fame grew. One French newspaper proclaimed "Bertillonage" as "the greatest and most brilliant invention the nineteenth century has produced in the field of criminology" (Cole 2001).

Bertillonage, however, required a complicated enrollment system involving highly skilled technicians and special equipment that made its deployment difficult, especially in remote areas. Technically, the Bertillon system had significant error rates because of mismeasurements due to operator error, as well as the lack of uniqueness of measurements of physical features that are not independent variables. Moreover, the system had no latent capability, as anthropometrics are not left behind at crime scenes, as are fingerprints.

Based in part on work done by three Britons—Dr. Henry Faulds; Sir Francis Galton, a cousin of Charles Darwin; and Sir Edward R. Henry, a police official who first learned about fingerprints while in British India and who went on to become Commissioner of the Metropolitan Police—fingerprints soon came to be recognized as distinctive and permanent physical features that could be used to identify individuals. Fingerprints had the added advantages of being easy to collect from a criminal in custody and fairly easy to find at many crime scenes.

In 1892, Mark Twain, in *The Tragedy of Pudd'nhead Wilson*, helped popularize this new means of identification when he had Lawyer Wilson declaim in his address to the jury that there are "certain physical marks," like fingerprints, "which do not change their character, and by which [a person] can always be identified—and that without shade of doubt or question." Lawyer Wilson continued that such a mark "cannot be counterfeited, nor can [a person] disguise it or hide it away, nor can it become illegible by the wear and mutations of time."

The FBI's stewardship of the nation's fingerprint data originated with the government's need to have a dependable criminal identification system. In 1905, the Department of Justice (DOJ) established a Bureau of Criminal Identification and two years later, Leavenworth Federal Penitentiary became the headquarters for DOJ's fingerprint card collection. In 1924, two important events occurred that significantly influenced the FBI's fingerprint collection policies. First, Congress authorized the DOJ to begin collecting fingerprint and arrest record information voluntarily submitted by federal and state authorities for federal and state arrests. This new mission fell to the FBI. In that same year, Attorney General Harlan Fiske Stone appointed J. Edgar Hoover as the FBI Director.

Hoover was well qualified to undertake this new information collection mission. His earlier professional experiences had helped him appreciate the necessity for having well-organized information systems. While attending night law school at George Washington University, Hoover had worked as a clerk at the Library of Congress, where he learned about cataloguing and indexing. Hoover began working at the Department of Justice in July 1917, and he quickly rose in government service. As a special assistant to Attorney General Alexander M. Palmer during the "Red Scare" and "Red Raids" of 1919–1920, Hoover helped create a card index of 450,000 people who, in the government's eyes, held radically suspect political views.

Hoover applied the lessons learned from these experiences to improve the FBI's fingerprint system. By June 1925, he had recatalogued all the fingerprint files and he eventually made the FBI the nation's central repository for criminal information, including fingerprint records. In Hoover's obituary in 1972, *The New York Times* described the FBI's centralized fingerprint file as an example of Hoover's "innovation and modernization in law enforcement" and a "landmark in the gradual application of science to police work."[4]

In 1930, Congress officially created the FBI's Identification Division, giving it responsibility for "acquiring, collecting, classifying and preserving criminal identification and other crime records" and authorizing the exchange of these criminal identification records with authorized state and local officials.[5] Thus, as first established, the purpose of the Identification Division was to serve as a central repository of criminal identification data for law enforcement throughout the nation. The FBI's turf expanded in 1933 when the United States Civil Service Commission, the predecessor of the Office of Personnel Management, gave the fingerprint cards of

---

[4] Christopher Lydon, "J. Edgar Hoover Made the F.B.I. Formidable With Politics, Publicity and Results," *New York Times*, May 3, 1972.

[5] *United States Department of Justice v. Reporters Committee for Freedom of Press*, 489 U.S. 749 (1989).

more than 140,000 federal government employees to the FBI, which established a Civil Identification Section. From this humble beginning, the civil files soon grew in size to equal the criminal files—each holds the fingerprints for approximately 40 million people.

Criminal Justice Information Services

The FBI's Identification Division was re-established in February 1992 as the Criminal Justice Information Services (CJIS) Division. CJIS serves as the focal point and central repository for criminal justice information services in the FBI. As the FBI's largest division, its purview includes the National Crime Information Center (NCIC), Uniform Crime Reporting (UCR), the National Instant Criminal Background Check system, and Fingerprint Identification. In addition, CJIS also has responsibility for several technological initiatives, including the aforementioned IAFIS, the NCIC 2000, the National Instant Check System (NICS), and the National Incident-Based Reporting System (NIBRS). The UCR program is a national crime data collection effort encompassing 17,000 federal, state, and local law enforcement agencies that contribute crime statistics. NCIC 2000 is a nationwide information system that supports federal, state, and local criminal justice agencies. NICS is a database that federal firearms licensees may contact for information as to whether the receipt of a firearm by a prospective transferee or purchaser would violate federal or state law. NIBRS is an enhancement to UCR that supports increased data collection and has the capability to break down and combine crime offense data into specific information.

Today, the CJIS Division, through its IAFIS program, houses the world's largest fingerprint repository. Located at a highly secure, campus-like setting in Clarksburg, West Virginia, the CJIS collection is more than four times the size of all fingerprint repositories in Europe combined. CJIS's current file holdings of criminal and civil fingerprint records total more than 219 million. While some fingerprinting is still done using the traditional ink and paper tenprint cards, much of it is being done as a high tech, all-electronic process, leveraging computer capabilities and using biometric technology.

Figure 17-1 illustrates an example of how the process works. A person places his finger on a platen of a live-scan device, and the device then finds the fingerprint and captures it electronically as an image file. This process is repeated for each finger until all ten fingerprints are captured. These image files, along with other relevant personal information, are electronically transmitted to the FBI. Minutiae, or key features of the fingerprint as depicted in the image file, can then be located, plotted, and extracted to produce a much smaller binary record, known as a template. For evidentiary purposes, CJIS retains the compressed images in a subsystem for image comparison. CJIS also maintains the fingerprint minutiae in a subsystem. An image of the card, or the transmission itself, being the best evidence, is maintained in the tenprint certification file for

Current Process

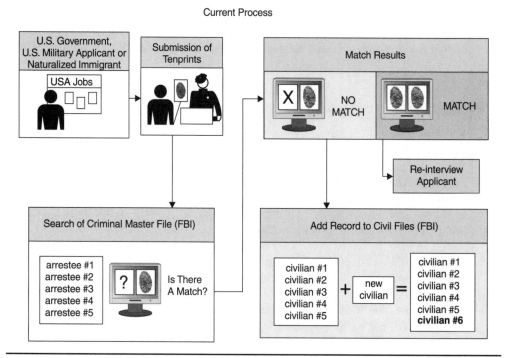

Figure 17-1 The current process

potential production in court should that ever prove necessary. Eventually, all law enforcement fingerprinting will likely be done through this type of biometric process; the cost of the equipment is still a hurdle for many smaller law enforcement offices, however.

Criminal Master File

On August 10, 1999, the FBI inaugurated the full operation of IAFIS. This system enables federal, state, and local criminal justice agencies to transmit fingerprint information electronically to the FBI for processing. Previously, criminal justice agencies mailed ink and paper fingerprint cards to the FBI. After the cards were received, a semiautomated system classified the fingerprints and employees compared them against the fingerprint cards in the FBI's CJIS criminal fingerprint database. This identification process sometimes took weeks or months to complete, particularly when the FBI had to perform growing numbers of background checks. For example, by late 1996, the delays reached 89 days for civil checks and 143 days for criminal checks. Movement delays resulted in an additional 43 days elapsed time from the tenprint card's being taken at the date of arrest to the card's arrival at CJIS for identification. The backlog grew to a peak of nearly 3 million cards. In essence, the criminal master file had grown far too large and the demand for civil and criminal searches had increased such that the criminal master file could not be easily searched.

As Chapter 3 explains, technology, incorporating computer and biometric advances, came to the rescue. For many years, processing fingerprint cards was largely a manual, labor-intensive process. In 1963, the FBI began a partnership with the then National Bureau of Standards to begin automation of the fingerprint search process. Studies to establish the feasibility of minutiae matching were begun and development contracts awarded for prototype fingerprint reading hardware. Throughout the 1960s and 1970s, analyses, studies, prototyping, and engineering development continued with initial automated processing introduced by the FBI in October 1979. In August 1995, the Boston Police Department and the FBI began to experiment with electronic submission of fingerprints and return of criminal history records. Other states, including California, South Carolina, and West Virginia, soon established similar pilot programs, thus laying the foundation for a comprehensive IAFIS approach.

IAFIS represents a significant technological breakthrough for public safety because it can compare the submitted fingerprint images against its huge database of fingerprints and respond with an average search time of 68 minutes. The IAFIS program mission statement summarizes this capability by explaining that its mission is to "provide complete and accurate responses within two hours to criminal fingerprint search requests and twenty-four [hours] for civil fingerprint search requests when such requests are submitted electronically to the FBI." The response produces a criminal history of the person, if one exists, which includes a record of the person's serious offenses on file at the federal level. Even if the person fingerprinted provides a false name or alias identification documents, IAFIS will make a positive identification about 99 percent of the time by matching fingerprints, which a person cannot so easily change or alter.

In practical terms, IAFIS's accurate fingerprint-based identification, combined with its quick response time, means that law enforcement holding a suspect is more likely to know the suspect's true identity and criminal status while he or she is still in custody. Prior to IAFIS, paper-based fingerprint searches took too long to complete, meaning that law enforcement all too often received a suspect's identity and criminal history information too late. For example, pre-IAFIS, police in Richmond, Virginia, arrest John Doe for burglary. Doe is booked and his fingerprints are taken, but because of the 143-day backlog, he appears before a magistrate and posts bail before the fingerprint search is completed. Only after Doe absconds do police learn that Doe's fingerprints matched the FBI's holdings for career criminal Richard Roe, wanted on murder charges in Idaho. With IAFIS, police learn this vital information within two hours of Doe/Roe's arrest for burglary.

This process is sometimes referred to as a National Agency Check (NAC). CJIS runs the fingerprint record it receives against IAFIS, its integrated, automated

How IAFIS Searches a 400 Million Fingerprint Database in 68 Minutes

While an in-depth discussion of the technical operation of IAFIS is beyond the scope of this book, a basic explanation of how IAFIS searches a 400 million fingerprint database with an average search time of 68 minutes might be of interest. It is no easy task to search within minutes the fingerprints of one person against a database representing the fingerprints of 40 million individuals to determine whether there is a match. This type of search is known as identification or a "one-to-many" (1:N) search. IAFIS tries to resolve this dilemma by subdividing the database (the criminal master file) to be searched so that only the relevant portion of it must be searched. This subdivision is done by using a multi-stage classification process of *binning*. Binning is the selection of potential matches based on information intrinsic to the fingerprint that can be readily detected. Specifically, each fingerprint comprises various types of ridge patterns, traditionally classified according to the Henry system, named for Sir Edward R. Henry. IAFIS uses the classifications of left loop, right loop, arch (to include tented arch), and whorl. The ten fingerprints of a person can then be classified accordingly. Ensemble matching is then performed. With ensemble matching, a set of independent samples (fingerprints taken from a person's 10 fingers) is collected from each person being identified and this set of 10 is binned as a group, and then matched against corresponding sets in the database. The net effect in many cases is to further reduce the number of potential matches to be considered. This also reduces the probability of a false match (also known as a false positive), and reduces the processing time required to search the data set, thereby improving system responsiveness. For example, with IAFIS, binning produces a filter rate that can reduce 40 million records to less than 1 million records for most searches.[6]

criminal master file database in Clarksburg, to determine whether the individual has any past criminal involvement.

The criminal master file database contains a comprehensive fingerprint record of individuals fingerprinted as a result of arrest or incarceration, along with other special cases. CJIS has converted all of these fingerprint records into electronic format. In a major undertaking, the FBI paid $32 million to have 32 million cards scanned into the system. Moreover, many state, federal, and

---

[6] See for example, James L. Wayman, "Error Rate Equations for the General Biometric System," *IEEE Robotics and Automation*, 6.1 (March 1999): 35–48.

territorial criminal justice agencies have the capability to transmit electronically their fingerprint records to CJIS. Currently, electronic submissions account for about 60 percent of the CJIS workload. Thus, the criminal master file database is readily and easily searchable. This database includes more than 132 million criminal records, representing 42.8 million individuals who have been arrested or convicted of a criminal offense in the United States. While subject to great daily variability, CJIS receives an average of about 55,000 fingerprint searches and submissions a day for such processing. On February 27, 2002, IAFIS processed a record 72,311 fingerprint submissions. These submissions comprise 45 percent criminal records (about 20,000 to 25,000 criminal records per day) and 55 percent civil records (about 35,000 to 40,000 civil records per day). IAFIS identifies roughly 65 percent of the criminal records as recidivists, so CJIS is adding approximately 7,000 new criminal subjects per day in IAFIS. Many of these are submitted as a result of traditional criminal investigation functions such as:

- The arrestee's booking process: Determining the identity of a person in police custody, and determining whether a person has a prior criminal record. (Arrestees often provide false personal information.)

- Fingerprint evidence from a crime scene: Determining whether a latent fingerprint left at a crime scene can be matched to anyone in the criminal files. (The FBI can do approximately 1,000 latent fingerprint searches per day.)

However, this number also includes growing numbers of criminal history background searches requested by federal and state governments and others for various permit, license, and employment clearances, in addition to federal employment applications and military service.

Congress permits the FBI to charge a user fee for some of these search services. For example, the INS is one of the FBI's largest customers for fingerprint checks for non-law enforcement purposes. INS pays $25 to the FBI for each fingerprint check. For fiscal year 1996, INS paid the FBI $32.5 million to conduct fingerprint checks for benefit applications, with approximately $19.5 million spent for naturalization applications. If the criminal history background search reveals that the individual has past criminal involvement, the fingerprint record becomes part of the criminal master file database. In the case of federal employees and military members, along with others, if the search reveals no criminal history, the fingerprint record is kept in the CJIS civil files database.

Civil Files

The CJIS civil files database maintains approximately 87 million civil fingerprint cards representing approximately 40 million people. Some people have more than one fingerprint record in the database. For example, many military veterans take employment with the federal government. These individuals have been fingerprinted as a result of federal employment applications or military service, for alien registration and naturalization purposes, as well as for voluntary submission for personal identification purposes. For example, Executive Order 10450, *Security Requirements for Government Employees*, dated April 27, 1953, requires federal employees in positions affecting the national security to submit fingerprints. The fingerprints of other individuals who have to undergo background checks for other government mandated employment or licensure requirements do not currently repose in the FBI's civil files. These individuals range from child care workers, lawyers, school bus drivers, state government employees, taxi drivers, and others. For example, all applicants to the Virginia State Bar must submit a tenprint card as part of their bar application. After the card is searched and returned with negative results, it is reposed in the applicant's file with the Virginia Board of Bar Examiners, an agency of the Supreme Court of Virginia.

The civil files database is not yet automated. The vast bulk of its fingerprint records are still the paper and ink variety. As noted, however, since May 2000, the FBI has taken steps to automate the database from "Day One forward" as it receives electronic versions—that is, new fingerprint cards in electronic format. Thus, over time, as CJIS receives more and more electronic images, the civil files will become an increasingly attractive database in which to search for national security, criminal investigation, or other purposes. The FBI also has the option of scanning into the database the pre-May 2000 paper and ink fingerprint records—tenprint cards—to convert them into electronic format just as it did with the criminal master file. However, as the FBI's experience with criminal tenprint cards demonstrates, scanning the existing civil files could be an expensive option—ballparked at $100 million. On the other hand, warehousing costs for the millions of paper tenprint cards are also high.

In the case of the U.S. military, the FBI, with the DoD's blessing and funding, is scanning in the 2.1 million fingerprint records of enlisted personnel dating back to May 1990. This conversion costs about $1.25 per card, including the 10 fingerprint images and accompanying text. To enhance searching capabilities, the FBI is electronically organizing a subfile, known as a Special Latent Cognizant (SLC) file, within the civil files database for these military members. Over time, the FBI could organize an expanded SLC file of fingerprints of DoD employees, military members, and contractors with security clearances, or Department of Energy employees and contractors, and so on. By recording civil fingerprint records electronically into the civil files database and by organizing extensive SLC files, or subsets, within it, the civil files database, like the criminal master file database, would become more easily and readily searchable.

Benefits of Searching Civil Files

Having an electronic civil files database of fingerprint records would make for better public safety because it would enable the government to update its process of ensuring that military members, U.S. government employees, and those with national security clearances have not run afoul of the law. Specifically, it would provide a dependable and regularly updated mechanism to report whether such personnel have been arrested for serious offenses.

Suppose police arrest a person who holds a national security clearance on felony charges. During booking, his fingerprints are taken and transmitted to the FBI for searching against the criminal master file. As this is the person's first and only arrest, no match is made. Currently, no search is made against the largely paper-based civil files. Presumably, it is the arrestee's responsibility to report his arrest to the security officer responsible for his security clearance. The arrestee might not want to honor this obligation for understandable reasons—fear of termination of employment. If the civil files were in an electronic database, the following opportunities present themselves:

- Fingerprint records of an arrestee would be searched against the civil files, a match would indicate the arrestee is a military member, a U.S. government employee, or a person with a national security clearance, and the appropriate security officer could be notified.

- Fingerprint records from the civil files could be easily searched against the criminal master file to vet individuals on a continual basis, instead of the current system of waiting years for these fingerprint searches to be done as part of a person's security reinvestigation.

From a criminal investigative point of view, having the ability to access and search latent fingerprints against all the fingerprint records in the civil files database would seem beneficial for law enforcement purposes. For example, sometimes the only clue the authorities have in a criminal investigation is a latent fingerprint found at a crime scene. Suppose a latent print is found at the scene of a crime committed on a U.S. military base. A search of the criminal master file reveals no matches. The authorities could then search this latent print against the civil files database, which contains fingerprints of armed forces members, DoD civilian employees, and DoD contractors, including those who might have had access to the military base at the time the crime was committed. Figure 17-2 illustrates an example of how this process would work.

The example is not limited to crimes committed at military bases, of course. Anytime there is a latent fingerprint left at a crime scene and no match found in the criminal master file, the FBI could routinely searched the civil files. In this way, more crimes could potentially be more speedily solved through employing these so-called cold searches, or searches in which no information about a suspect is required prior to conducting the search. However, latent searching works

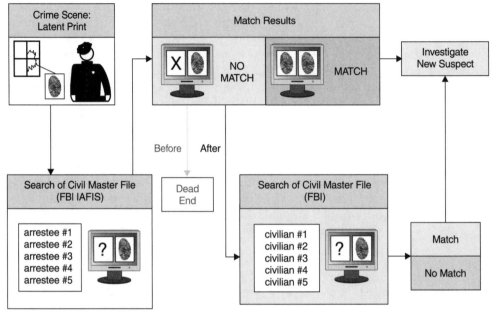

Figure 17-2   Using the FBI's Civil Files

well against the criminal master file because a large percentage of its population is highly recidivist. Conversely, latent searching against the civil files, which represents a law-abiding population, would presumably result in fewer matches.

Searching the civil files also could be an aid in counterintelligence and counter terrorist investigations. For example, if the U.S. authorities learn that an intelligence officer of a foreign government used a particular hotel room to meet with an unknown person, that room could be checked for latent prints. Ideally, the authorities would want to learn the identity of the person with whom the foreign intelligence officer met, because that person might be committing acts of espionage by providing unauthorized information to the intelligence officer or planning terrorist attacks. Any prints recovered from the hotel room could be searched against the civil files for a possible match. A match, while not conclusive evidence that the person is a spy, would help the authorities' investigative efforts. Similarly, if the authorities found prohibited terrorist literature in the possession of a military member, they could examine the literature for fingerprints. Any recovered could be searched against the civil files to help determine who else accessed the literature.

A recent real-life espionage example shows how such searching could aid investigations. Former FBI agent Robert Hanssen will spend the rest of his life in prison without parole for spying for the Soviet Union and Russia over a 20-year period. How did U.S. counterintelligence experts break the case? A fingerprint provided part of the evidence. Thanks to a Russian intelligence official working for the U.S. government, the FBI managed to get possession of materials that Hanssen sent to his Russian contacts. (The Russian spy did not know Hanssen's identity, he only knew that these materials came from a well-placed American working for the Russians.) These materials contained a plastic bag that Hanssen had used in one of his "dead drops" with his Russian handlers. A latent fingerprint remained on the plastic bag. The FBI searched the latent print against its IAFIS criminal master file and matched it to Hanssen. It made the match because the criminal master file contains fingerprint records of arrestees along with a small number of special cases—the FBI routinely enters the fingerprint records of its agents. Just as the FBI searched a latent fingerprint against its criminal master files to find a spy, so, too, could such searches be run against a civil files database.

Moreover, searching civil files also could help in other ways. For example, the military regularly ejects service members for reasons other than criminal conduct. After their discharge from the service, some of these ejectees try to re-enlist in the military under another name. Searching the civil files would soon put a stop to this behavior because when the person tried to re-enlist in alias, his fingerprints would be searched against the civil files database and be matched to the fingerprints he submitted when he first joined the military under a different name. Searchable civil files also would be a helpful way to identify deceased or unconscious persons, particularly in the event of a disaster. For example, fingerprints could be taken from the people the authorities are trying to identify and searched against the civil files for positive identification.[7]

Intuitively, searching the civil files would appear to offer benefits. Empirically, the benefits are not as certain, in part, because many questions have not been fully answered. For example, how many criminals, terrorists, and spies would be identified and how many crimes would be solved by searching the civil files? How much would it cost in dollars and other resources to establish such a searchable civil files system? Is it worthwhile operationally and economically to scan in the paper and ink tenprint cards compiled before May 2000? What are the other costs of such a system, and what trade-offs does the establishment of

---

[7] For example, Lawrence K. Altman, "Now, Doctors Must Identify the Dead Among the Trade Center Rubble," *New York Times*, September 25, 2001; Peter Perl, "Hallowed Ground," *Washington Post Magazine*, May 12, 2002 (explaining that at the Somerset County, Pennsylvania, crash site of United Air Lines Flight 93, "some fragment of each of the dead had been positively identified, either by DNA or, in a few cases, fingerprints").

such a system require, particularly in light of limited resources? A thorough cost benefit analysis could help provide answers.[8]

The FBI's View

The FBI has long considered this kind of searching of the civil files. As early as 1995, the FBI asked its Office of General Counsel (OGC) for its opinion as to whether the FBI could legally conduct such searches of its civil files. Much of the OGC's analysis focused on the Privacy Act of 1974, which regulates the collection, maintenance, use, and dissemination of personal information by federal government agencies.[9] In broad terms, the Privacy Act gives certain rights to the "data subject," or the individual who provides personal information to the federal government, and places certain responsibilities on the "data collector," or the U.S. government agency collecting the personal information. The Privacy Act balances a federal agency's need to collect, use, and disseminate information about individuals with the privacy rights of those individuals. In particular, the Act tries to protect the individual from unwarranted invasions of privacy stemming from a federal agency's collection, maintenance, use, and dissemination of personal information about the individual.

After review, OGC concluded that "using civil fingerprint records for criminal justice purposes is legally unobjectionable."[10] OGC determined that the use of CJIS civil files for criminal justice purposes is consistent with the Privacy Act because it is a "routine use." Under the Privacy Act, the two requirements for routine use are compatibility and Federal Register publication. OGC determined that the compatibility requirement is met because "using fingerprints collected for criminal history check purposes for criminal justice identification purposes is completely compatible with the purposes for which they were first collected." OGC also determined that because the FBI has published properly the routine use in the Federal Register, "after reading the notice, no reasonable person could claim to be surprised to find that [his] fingerprints, once submitted

---

[8] On a related note, Professor David Kaye emphasizes the need for cost benefit analysis in the context of DNA databases used for law enforcement purposes. David H. Kaye, "Commentary: Two Fallacies About DNA Data Banks for Law Enforcement," *Brooklyn Law Review*, 67.1 (2001) 189.

[9] The Privacy Act of 1974, codified at 5 U.S.C. § 552a, as amended, became effective on September 27, 1975; see Office of Information and Privacy, Department of Justice & Office of Information and Regulatory Affairs, Office of Management and Budget, Overview of the Privacy Act of 1974, September 1998, available at http://www.usdoj.gov/04foia/1974intro.htm; see also Office of Legal Education, Executive Office for United States Attorneys, U.S. Department of Justice, Privacy Act, November 1999.

[10] John D. Woodward, Jr., "Searching the FBI's Civil Files: Public Safety v. Civil Liberty," *U.S. Law Week* (September 17, 2002): 2188.

to the FBI, will be used by the Bureau for identification purposes in either a criminal justice or civil setting."

The FBI changed the routine uses set forth in the "Fingerprint Identification Record System" notice in February 1996. The notice reads, in pertinent part:

> Identification and criminal history record information within this system of records may be disclosed as follows: To a Federal, State, or local law enforcement agency, or agency/organization directly engaged in criminal justice activity (including the police, prosecution, penal, probation/parole, and the judiciary), and/or to a foreign or international agency/organization, consistent with international treaties, conventions, and/or executive agreements, where such disclosure may assist the recipient in the performance of a law enforcement function, and/or for the purpose of eliciting information that may assist the FBI in performing a law enforcement function; to a Federal, State, or local agency/organization for a compatible civil law enforcement function; or where such disclosure may promote, assist, or otherwise serve the mutual criminal law enforcement efforts of the law enforcement community.[11]

Similarly, based on its examination of relevant case law, OGC determined that there is no constitutional right to privacy in an individual's identity and criminal history background. In sum, OGC has concluded that there is no legal hurdle preventing the FBI from searching its civil files database. This OGC conclusion suggests that it would be legally unobjectionable for a federal government agency, were it so inclined on policy grounds, to coordinate with the FBI to establish a searchable fingerprint database. Specifically, the agency could have the FBI organize a file consisting of the fingerprint records of the agency's personnel, or various files containing further subsets of the agency's personnel, such as those in a particular geographic area or employment classification, which the FBI could then cold search.

Constitutional Protections

Several Supreme Court decisions have established that an individual has minimal constitutional privileges concerning his fingerprints.[12] Moreover, the courts have upheld numerous federal, state, and municipal requirements mandating fingerprinting for employment and licensing purposes, provided that

---

[11] 61 Federal Register 6386 (Vol. 61, No. 34, February 20, 1996).

[12] For example, *Davis v. Mississippi,* 394 U.S. 721, 727 (1969); and *Schmerber v. California,* 384 U.S. 757, 764 (1966).

the government has a rational basis for requiring fingerprinting. In the federal context, the so-called "rational basis" test means that Congress must show that the fingerprinting requirement bears a rational relationship to a legitimate government objective or interest.[13] The rational basis test is a significantly lesser standard of judicial scrutiny than the compelling state interest test. Courts apply the compelling state interest test when state action affects the exercise of a fundamental right, such as political speech. The courts have upheld government-mandated fingerprinting for employment and licensing purposes in connection with the taking of fingerprints for spouses of liquor licensees, male employees of alcoholic beverage wholesalers, taxi drivers, cabaret employees, bartenders, dealers in secondhand articles, all employees of member firms of national security exchanges registered with the Securities and Exchange Commission, and all individuals permitted unescorted access to nuclear power facilities.

Federal statutes requiring fingerprinting have been challenged in the courts. In *Utility Workers Union of America v. Nuclear Regulatory Commission*, a union representing some 5,170 utility workers in nuclear power plants challenged as unconstitutional that part of a newly enacted federal statute requiring that those workers be fingerprinted. The union claimed the fingerprinting requirement violated the workers' Fourth Amendment and privacy rights. The federal district court disagreed and upheld the fingerprinting requirement. Citing a long line of cases, the court noted that in non-criminal contexts, the judiciary has "regularly upheld fingerprinting of employees."

As for the constitutional right to privacy claim, the court quoted from a leading federal appellate court case:

> Whatever the outer limits of the right to privacy, clearly it cannot be extended to apply to a procedure the Supreme Court regards as only minimally intrusive. Enhanced protection has been held to apply only to such fundamental decisions as contraception...and family living arrangements. Fingerprints have not been held to merit the same level of constitutional concern.[14]

Moreover, in applying the rational basis test, the court noted Congressional concern over an incident of sabotage at a nuclear power plant in Virginia and concluded that "using fingerprints to verify the identity and any existing crimi-

---

[13] For example, *Utility Workers Union of America, AFL-CIO, v. Nuclear Regulatory Commission*, 664 F. Supp. 136, 139 (S.D.N.Y. 1987); *Iacobucci v. City of Newport*, 785 F.2d 1354, 1355-56 (6th Cir. 1986), rev'd on other grounds, 479 U.S. 921 (1986); and *Thom v. New York Stock Exchange*, 306 F. Supp 1002, 1010 (S.D.N.Y. 1969).

[14] *Utility Workers Union of America, AFL-CIO, v. Nuclear Regulatory Commission*, 664 F. Supp. 136, 139 (S.D.N.Y. 1987) (quoting *Iacobucci v. City of Newport*, 785 F.2d at 1357–58).

nal history of workers with access to vital areas or safeguards information is a rational method of clearing these workers."

Similarly, in a case involving a challenge to a New York state regulation requiring fingerprinting of all employees of national stock exchanges, a federal district court found that "possession of an individual's fingerprints does not create an atmosphere of general surveillance or indicate that they will be used for inadmissible purposes. Fingerprints provide a simple means of identification no more."[15] The court observed that as long as the government had a "valid justification...for the taking of the prints under reasonable circumstances, their use for future identification purposes even in criminal investigations, is not impermissible." Thus, it seems unlikely that the federal judiciary would invalidate government searching of the civil files provided there was a rational basis to conduct such searches.

Privacy Concerns

The U.S. government's most powerful law enforcement agency, having a massive, easily searchable fingerprint database potentially corresponding to roughly 15 percent of the nation's law-abiding population, is not without concerns. Searchable civil files combined with the already searchable criminal master file would give the U.S. government the ability to conduct fingerprint searches on about 30 percent of the U.S. population. Many Americans do not trust the government to protect an individual's privacy. As two scholars have noted: "[The] history of government programs indicates that privacy rights are violated routinely whenever expediency dictates."[16] One such case includes the U.S. government's use of Census Bureau information to identify Japanese-Americans to be relocated to internment camps during World War II. Following the attack on Pearl Harbor in 1941, President Franklin Roosevelt issued Executive Order 9066, which authorized military personnel to detain and relocate persons of Japanese ancestry. An estimated 120,000 people, many of whom were U.S. citizens, were held without judicial review. Within one week (in a precomputer age), the government, using census records, had compiled the names and addresses of all ethnic Japanese living in the United States.

There exists a "Big Brother" or Enemy of the State fear that such a database could be used by the state as a tool of oppression. This fear is based on the belief that an oppressive state needs strong identification means at its disposal to surveil the lives of its citizens. Searchable fingerprint databases are one such

---

[15]   *Thom v. New York Stock Exchange*, 306 F. Supp. at 1010.

[16]   John J. Miller and Stephen Moore, "A National ID System: Big Brother's Solution to Illegal Immigration," *Cato Policy Analysis*, September 7, 1995, available at http://www.cato.org/pubs/pas/pa237es.html.

means the state can use to monitor an individual's actions over a period of time. When a person leaves a fingerprint at a certain location, he leaves evidence of his presence there, whether it was a crime scene or the site of a political rally or house of worship. Similarly, large fingerprint databases can make anonymity hard to achieve by making it difficult for a person to change or alter his identity, by, for example, assuming a false name. Using an alias can be an effective way to engage in criminal or terrorist acts, or to engage in political dissent. The Founding Fathers were no strangers to the use of well-chosen noms de plume; James Madison used the alias Publius, in writing his contributions to the Federalist Papers.

At a broader sociocultural level, many Americans, drawing on the nation's frontier experience, believe that a person should have the ability to start his life anew. David H. Kaye has said: "There is a largely unspoken assumption, deeply rooted in American history and culture, that if we are moved to do so, it is possible for us to leave the past behind and to reinvent ourselves in another place." Kaye goes on to explain, "This is a romantic, unrealistic prospect today. The lives we lead leave a trail in medical records, in credit card records, in school records, in employment files—in any records that link to our social security numbers, driver's license numbers and the like."[17] Moreover, feelings and assumptions do not always translate into concrete legal rights. For example, Harvard Law Professor Alan M. Dershowitz has made this point rather starkly: "Finally, there is the question of the right to anonymity. I don't believe we can afford to recognize such a right in this age of terrorism. No such right is hinted at in the Constitution."[18]

Misuse or abusive use of fingerprint information is also a concern. As Simson Garfinkel observed, "The more trust we place in an identification technology, the more rewarding fraud becomes. And the possibility of intentional fraud can never be eliminated" (Garfinkel 2000) Garfinkel and others worry that law enforcement can make identification mistakes as well as commit more nefarious acts such as deliberately modifying or swapping fingerprint files.

Others worry that fingerprint data may be unreliable and its use may lead to errors—for example, the fingerprint of an innocent person falsely matched to a fingerprint left at a crime scene. Simon Cole observes that forensic fingerprint analysis has "an aura of infallibility" surrounding it. He explains: "The claim that no fingerprint has ever appeared twice was first popularized more than a hundred years ago, and by dint of analogy (with other natural objects like snowflakes), lack of contradiction and relentless repetition, this bit of folk wisdom became deeply enshrined." But to Cole, "the relevant question isn't whether fingerprints could ever be exactly alike—it's whether they are ever similar enough

---

[17]   David H. Kaye, "Commentary: Two Fallacies About DNA Data Banks for Law Enforcement," *Brooklyn Law Review*, 67.1 (2001) at 193

[18]   Alan M. Dershowitz, "Why Fear National ID Cards?" *New York Times*, October 13, 2001.

to fool a fingerprint examiner. And the answer, it's increasingly, unnervingly clear, is a resounding yes."[19]

Cole holds a distinct minority view. At least one judge has refused to permit him to testify as an expert witness on fingerprint evidence, explaining: "The record is devoid of any evidence that Dr. Cole possesses any more than an elementary knowledge of latent fingerprint collection and comparison. His approach...can hardly be viewed as generally accepted as reliable in the relevant scientific community...."[20] Judge Brennan found that "Dr. Cole's proposed attack on the scientific underpinning of fingerprint identification is more in the role of an advocate or historian and not as an expert."

Controversy has surfaced in the federal courts over fingerprint evidence.[21] In January 2002, Judge Louis Pollak of the U.S. District Court for the Eastern District of Pennsylvania issued what became a potentially explosive if very short-lived opinion on the use of fingerprint evidence in a court of law. While taking judicial notice of the uniqueness and permanence of fingerprints and while permitting courtroom testimony by fingerprint experts, Judge Pollak refused to allow fingerprint experts to express an opinion that a particular latent print matched or did not match the rolled print of a particular person.[22] However, Judge Pollak reversed himself on March 13, 2002, granting the government's motion for reconsideration.[23] Impressed by the fact that England had recently established a new legal framework similar to U.S. courts with respect to a court's use of expert fingerprint identification testimony, Judge Pollak concluded that "arrangements which, subject to careful trial court oversight, are felt to be sufficiently reliable in England, ought likewise to be found sufficiently reliable in the federal courts of the United States, subject to similar measures of trial court oversight."[24]

---

[19]   Simon Cole, "The Myth of Fingerprints," *New York Times,* May 13, 2001. For a technical discussion of the distinctiveness of fingerprints, see Sharath Pankanti, Salil Prabhakar, and Anil K. Jain, "On the Individuality of Fingerprints," Proceedings of the IEEE Computer Society Conference on Computer Vision and Pattern Recognition (CVPR), Hawaii, December 11–13, 2001.

[20]   *People v. James Hyatt*, Indictment #8852/2000, Supreme Court of the State of New York, County of Kings, Part 23 (precluding Dr. Cole from testifying as an expert before the court and noting that "what Dr. Cole has offered here is 'junk science.' ").

[21]   For example, *United States v. James M. Broten, et al.*, Case No. 01-CR-411 (DNH), (N.D.N.Y. March 25, 2002) (denying the defendant's motion to preclude the government's latent fingerprint identification evidence); *United States v. Byron C. Mitchell*, Cr. No. 96-00407 (E.D. Pa. September 27, 1999) (upholding the admissibility of fingerprint evidence and rejected a challenge by the defense attorney to exclude that evidence).

[22]   *United States v. Plaza*, Cr. No. 98-362-10, (E.D. Pa. January 7, 2002).

[23]   Order, *United States v. Plaza*, Cr. No. 98-362-10, (E.D. Pa. March 13, 2002).

[24]   Order, *United States v. Plaza*, Cr. No. 98-362-10, (E.D. Pa. March 13, 2002).

Unlike credit histories and other data that contain mistakes, fingerprint identification systems, like IAFIS, while not perfect, are based on a physical characteristic that is distinctive and permanent. Moreover, the technology and processes behind such systems, while not infallible, are mature and reliable. Are these convincing reasons to embrace searchable electronic civil files?

Policy Recommendations

Searching the civil files for national security, criminal investigative, or other related purposes presents the classic "public safety versus civil liberty" tradeoff. Balancing public safety and civil liberty concerns suggests three possible approaches to searching the civil files:

- Tilt strongly toward public safety and encourage such searching
- Tilt strongly toward civil liberty and prohibit such searching
- Take some kind of middle ground and permit some form(s) of limited searching, subject to certain conditions

How one decides depends on how one tilts.

The basic issue appears to be whether the state's interest in public safety justifies subjecting presumably law-abiding citizens to a search of their fingerprints for a possible connection to an unlawful act. While a person can easily change his name, he cannot so easily change his fingerprints. Thus, fingerprints are a somewhat immutable marker of a person's identity and as such they are extremely useful for identification. Moreover, fingerprints essentially disclose only identification information.[25] Thus, they thus escape the controversy that surrounds the use of DNA databases for criminal investigative purposes, since many people perceive DNA as containing medical and health-related information.

Concern over such a use also is mitigated by the voluntary nature of the fingerprint submissions, as a condition of employment or licensure, and the established legal basis requiring it. It may be argued that fingerprint submission is more of a Hobson's choice because people, in reality, are forced to submit their fingerprints to the U.S. government if they want a particular position or privilege. The Hobson's choice argument seems most compelling in the case of an

---

[25] Dr. Harold Chen, in his work on dermatoglyphics (the study of the patterns of the ridges of the skin on parts of the hands and feet), notes that "certain chromosomal disorders are known to be associated with characteristic dermatoglyphic abnormalities." He specifically cites Down syndrome, Turner syndrome, and Klinefelter syndrome as chromosomal disorders that cause unusual fingerprint patterns in a person. See Harold Chen, Medical Genetics Handbook 221-226 (1988) quoted in John D. Woodward, "Biometric Scanning, Law and Policy: Identifying the Concerns—Drafting the Biometric Blueprint," *University of Pittsburgh Law Review,* 59.97 (1997) 117.

18-year old conscripted for military service who does his duty, leaves the Service and, as a result, has his fingerprints entered into the federal law enforcement system permanently. With conscription, of course, the state is taking the person's whole body and subjecting it to dangers, hardships, and discomfort; the incremental intrusion of taking a person's fingerprints in this context does not seem like much. Moreover, the effectiveness of the notice given to data subjects can be criticized. While citations to publication in the *Federal Register* might satisfy legal requirements, policymakers, public interest advocates, and John Q. Public might question whether the purpose behind notification is being met. Nonetheless, the fact remains that the law is very comfortable with fingerprinting as a condition of employment or licensure.

Stewardship of the data contained in the civil files as well as who decides when a "match" is made also deserve policy discussion. The FBI's fingerprint identification system is designed so that the same organization that is responsible for finding and arresting the guilty also holds the records that identify them and employs the experts to make their identification. This design is balanced by the fact that the accused, as part of the legal process, can challenge a fingerprint identification and have his own expert explain why it is not a match. An alternative, if controversial, approach could include a system where the fingerprint records are maintained by a neutral organization that could serve as an informational clearinghouse or as an independent identification center. Rather than designating fingerprint identification involving the civil files a law enforcement function and an organizational part of the FBI, fingerprint identification could be treated as more of a scientific and technical process—Does X match Y?—and placed in an appropriate agency overseen by a Department of Homeland Security.

Regardless of whether fingerprint records are entrusted to the FBI or another organization, the steward needs to do a better job of record keeping, particularly in the area of dispositions, or the status of the individual represented in the criminal master file. While the FBI knows from its criminal master file that a person was arrested on a certain date in a certain place, it does not know what happened after the person's arrest in more than 50 percent of the cases. In some cases, it might not even know why a person was arrested. This raises concern since not all who are arrested are proven guilty in a court of law. Similarly, individual fingerprint records would be inputted into the civil files and would stay there forever, long after the individual left military or government service. Therefore, these records would in many ways become outdated and inaccurate, although the fingerprints would still be useful. (For example, a search might match a latent fingerprint to Joseph Snuffy in the civil files but all the database reveals, aside from the search, is that Snuffy left the Army in 1997. Nonetheless, such a lead could be extremely valuable, as the authorities could focus their efforts and develop other information about Snuffy based on it.)

We should not conveniently assume that searching the civil files would produce concrete benefits. Rather, the premise that searchable civil files would contribute to public safety should be subjected to a rigorous cost-benefit analysis. This analysis should include a small pilot program to be established to search against a small portion of the civil files database that can be made electronic to determine the match or "hit" rate. For example, those with high-level national security clearances should be put into the electronic civil files and their status should be periodically updated by searching against the criminal master file. In this way, we will have a better basis for judgment.

Searching the civil files has not yet become a reality. But it is neither the state of the technology nor the state of the law that prevents it from becoming so. The question is one of public policy. Before such searching of the civil files is undertaken, full public discussion of this issue would be wise, especially at a time when the nation's legislative and executive branches are focused on public safety and homeland security concerns prompted by the September 11 terrorist attacks. At a minimum, such a discussion should include the perceived benefits and costs associated with such use of information in a government-controlled database. Before searching the civil files, we should search for more complete answers.

Chapter 18

Private-Sector Programs

By John D. Woodward, Jr.

This chapter reports on various examples of private sector use of biometrics.[1]

The examples are by no means all-inclusive. Some of the programs analyzed did not enjoy success; InnoVentry's biometrically enabled cash checking system went belly-up in 2001. However, the programs discussed hopefully make it clear that the private sector is using biometrics in many diverse ways. Many industries like the security, convenience, and efficiency that biometrics offer. Casinos have aggressively incorporated biometrics into their security systems. Others include financial institutions, ranging from a small credit union serving health care workers in the Virginia Tidewater to a financial giant like Charles Schwab. University students, hospital workers, employees of a popular haberdashery, customers, and many others are participating in various biometric-based programs.

---

[1] Julius Gatune provided extremely helpful research assistance in the preparation of this chapter. This chapter's sections discussing the use of biometrics by the Riverside Health System Employees Credit Union, the Columbia Presbyterian Hospital, the University of Georgia, and Kroger Supermarkets are based on work published in *Army Biometric Applications*, by John D. Woodward, Jr., Katharine W. Webb, et al., RAND 2001 in Appendix B, Program Reports, reprinted by permission.

Casinos

Casinos, highly incentivized to provide foolproof, yet noninvasive, security, have been leading-edge adopters of facial recognition. The gaming industry also uses biometrics for access control and customer service applications. For these reasons, the casino industry merits in-depth consideration as a case study.

Facial Recognition in Casinos: Gambling on Success?

"There's a lot of money in Vegas and that attracts people who want it. Somebody is always going to be trying to beat the house."

—Earl Carroll, director of surveillance at the San Remo, quoted in "Technology Has Spawned a Dramatic Improvement In Casino Surveillance," *Gaming Magazine*, December 12, 2000.

"A card-counting team can take a casino for $200,000 in an hour."

—Robert Schmitt, CEO of Biometrica, Inc., quoted in *Security Watch*, May 2000.

When asked why he robbed banks, career criminal Willie Sutton answered, "Because that's where the money is." The criminal class that hits the nation's casinos would no doubt give a similar answer—except unlike banks, casinos offer free drinks, no-cost frills, more convenient hours, and other attractions. Moreover, while Willie usually "packed heat," in the form of a Thompson submachine gun—"You can't rob a bank on charm and personality"—casino thieves are usually the white collar variety who try to beat the casinos with creativity and technical gadgetry.

In a given year, an estimated $40 million in illegal gains walk out the doors of Las Vegas' grand casinos. Casinos want to stop this outflow. The industry has been looking to the emerging technology of facial recognition as a way to stop the hemorrhaging. Because casinos have been an early adopter of facial recognition, this chapter begins with a detailed analysis of why casinos have embraced this biometric technology.

Facial recognition, though a relatively new biometric technology, has received enthusiastic acceptance by the gaming industry. In fact, many casinos were early adopters; Trump Marina, for example, installed a system in 1997 (well before facial recognition gained public notoriety in the aftermath of the Super Bowl surveillance episode in January 2001, discussed in Chapter 14). While casinos are highly secretive about their security measures, many deploy facial recognition systems. According to the International Biometric Group, a U.S.–based biometric consulting firm, facial recognition is used in "probably 75 percent of Las Vegas casinos to catch card counters or people who have been barred from casinos." Beverly Griffin, co-owner of Las Vegas-based Griffin Investigations, which provides security systems for casinos, estimates the penetration rate at 50 percent and growing. (For more information, refer to Chris Jones' "Biometrics enhance security at casinos; airport use possible," at http://www.biometricgroup.com/a_press/InBusinessLasVegas_Oct2001.htm.) Biometrica Systems Inc., recently reacquired by Viisage, claims to have sold its facial recognition systems to more than 100 casinos in the U.S., according to Jim Pepin, the company's vice president of sales and marketing in a *Los Angeles Times* article on February 2, 2001.

Indeed, a partial listing of the casinos that have installed facial recognition systems includes Park Place Entertainment, Trump Casinos, MGM Mirage, Harrah's Entertainment, Isle of Capri Casinos, Venetian, and Bellagio. Foxwoods Casino in Connecticut, the world's largest, also uses facial recognition.

At Trump Casinos, in Atlantic City, New Jersey, surveillance cameras linked to a facial recognition system record everything that happens in the casino—every casino game, everyone who walks in and out the doors, and every hand that is dealt. The cameras periodically move to different locations, which makes it difficult to locate and somehow disable them. If Trump Marina's surveillance cameras zoom in on a suspicious character, the facial recognition program can capture his face, and convert it into template. Casino security personnel may also add extra personal identification information, like sex and race, to bin (or further narrow) the search. The facial recognition software then compares it to images of casino undesirables. If the face provides a probable match, the database gives a wealth of investigative data on the suspected undesirable, including height, weight, aliases, and known associates. Trump Casinos can also dial into the Casino Information Network, a system that allows it to exchange investigative data and photos with 50 other casinos around the world. The network enables casinos to track teams of cheaters, who move from state to state and casino to casino. Once an undesirable person or group is identified, casino security can then either decide to expel them or watch them more closely.

The casino industry's extensive deployment of facial recognition may seem surprising given criticisms of how ineffective the technology is. For example, in May 2002, Barry Steinhardt, the director of the American Civil Liberties Union's Technology and Liberty Program, stated, "Even with recent, high-quality photographs and subjects who were not trying to fool the system, the face-recognition technology was less accurate than a coin toss. Under real world conditions, Osama Bin Laden himself could easily evade a face recognition system."[2] In light of these concerns, why would a profit-oriented industry be among its biggest deployers? Several reasons may help explain why the gaming industry "gambled" on facial recognition.

---

[2]   ACLU, "Data on Face-Recognition Test at Palm Beach Airport Further Demonstrates Systems' Fatal Flaws ACLU Says," May 14, 2002, http://www.aclu.org/news/2002/n051402b.html.

Business Strategy for the Casino Market

Early on, facial recognition vendors teamed up with established private investigative and consulting firms that already had a solid gaming industry client base. This synergy helped to crack the casino market. For example, Viisage/Biometrica, a provider of facial recognition systems, worked with CVI LLC, a company that publishes the Casino Information Database, used by many casinos. Visionics, another provider, works with the Griffin G.O.L.D. casino security database system, which is an established source of intelligence within the gaming community.

These strategic alliances helped make facial recognition acceptable among casino security officials, and gave the casinos the confidence to try facial recognition. The investigative firms already had the databases from which the facial recognition systems could be populated—after all, you have to be able to match a face to faces of "bad guys." "Bad guys" for casinos include any number of (male and female) undesirables, such as blatant cheaters, card counters, pick pockets, and many others. In exchange, the facial recognition system provided the investigative firms with a means to further automate their databases.

Casino Attitude Toward Facial Recognition

For the casino industry's security strategy, facial recognition is part of its defense-in-depth. Casinos do not see the technology as a solution to their problems but rather as an additional weapon in their surveillance arsenal. This approach means that the casinos are more tolerant of facial recognition's shortcomings. If the facial recognition systems can reduce, narrow, or otherwise screen the number of people that their expert "human hawks" have to scrutinize, it is all for the better. In this sense, facial recognition systems nicely complement the work of casino security officers but do not replace them, in a business where any help is welcome.

In an *Associated Press* interview in 1999, Derk Boss, the director of surveillance for the Stratosphere Hotel Casino and Tower in Las Vegas explained how facial recognition is an improvement, "The old mug shot books, you had to look through there and hope you could find it. It makes it a lot easier and brings it up to high technology—where we all want to be." The *Associated Press* concluded, "In the past, casinos counted on pit bosses with good memories to spot the undesirables. The high-tech methods are bound to give them an edge." (For more information, see Angie Wagner's "High-Tech Raises the Odds Against Casino Cheats," at http://www.canoe.com/CNEWSFeatures9912/21_casino.html.)

Interestingly, a leading biometric authority shares some of this "pit boss" attitude toward the technology as well. Speaking at a conference in August 2002 (as reported in *Security Focus*), Dr. James Wayman of San Jose State University explained that at best, facial recognition systems limit the range of possible matches to a third of all possible positive match candidates. In other words, the technology performs a screening function. The systems have a "failure to acquire" rate, which means a certain percentage of the time the system does not recognize a face against a background. The failure to acquire rate is affected by such factors as environmental conditions (lighting, shading), the subject's cooperation or lack thereof, and quality control issues. In an August 7, 2002, article by Ann Harrison, entitled "Researcher: Biometrics Unproven, Hard To Test," Wayman noted, "The idea that this operates automatically is entirely incorrect.... They are nothing more than investigative tools, they are not automatic systems." (For more information, go to http://online.securityfocus.com/news/566.)

J.C. Herz, in an article for *Wired*, entitled "Seen City: From surveillance cams to facial scans, in Las Vegas the whole world is watching," has summarized how casinos use this technology:

> If a person's template closely matches one in the database, a record pops up, with the image of a card-counter or criminal along with a list of his aliases and associates. The software never makes a positive identification—it just alerts the staff. Then it's up to human operators to decide how good the match is—and whether to escort the person off-site and send out a bulletin over an intra-casino network.... In one sense, the technology just automates what casinos have been doing for years, with pan-and-scan cameras, mug books, and sharp memories. But speed and networking do make a difference, especially since the databases are shared.

(For more information, go to http://www.wired.com/wired/archive/9.12/vegas.html.)

Keeping the Technological Edge

Given the high stakes involved and the creativity and determination of the criminal element, the gaming industry emphasizes security and tries new ideas. Casino "undesirables" tend to be very technology savvy, highly motivated, and adaptive. They routinely use hidden transmitters, miniature cameras, and computers in their attempts to beat the house.

Casinos do not like to feel that they are always one step behind. They try to be proactive with respect to technology and thus are more willing to try a new technology, like facial recognition, and even help it develop by using it. In an article for *Wired*, "Casinos Fight Back with Tech," written by Vince Beiser, Andy Andersen—a private investigator who specializes in casino security—explained, "We've got to get into high technology, because the cheaters have." (For more information, go to http://www.wired.com/news/technology/0,1282,19463,00.html.) The casinos see the technology as a means by which they can keep up with the cheaters; they know they have to stay ahead in technology, because, just as a casino never closes, its enemies never sleep.

Success with Facial Recognition

Anecdotal evidence suggests that facial recognition systems have been successful in catching at least some undesirables in the casino world. Success stories include:

> "[T]he system was installed at Trump Marina in 1997. Three days later, it helped the casino nab eight baccarat cheats."
>
> —Reported in "Casinos Using Facial Surveillance," *Gaming Magazine*, February 26, 2001.

> "The first day [the] system was installed, a major casino discovered a long-sought-after cheating ring, potentially saving themselves several thousands of dollars."
>
> —Reported in "To Catch a Thief," *CasinoGuru.com*, August 3, 1999.

> "After having this advanced technology for only a couple of weeks, we used the Visionics system to identify a known suspect who had registered under a false name," said Dan Eitner director of surveillance at the Venetian.
>
> —Reported in "Facial Recognition Ready for Prime Time?" *Security Watch*, May 2000.

as well as this detailed account by Andy Newman, entitled "Face-Recognition Systems Offer New Tools, but Mixed Results," in the *New York Times* on May 3, 2001:

> Detective Sean Boero and his partner were walking the casino floor at the Atlantic City Hilton...when, behind a pile of red chips at a craps table, they spotted a familiar face. It was a petty thief and card cheat named Sammy with a long criminal record.... They called headquarters to see if there were any warrants for his arrest. No dice.

> That might have been the end of it. But Detective Boero...went back to his office, called up Sammy's digital mug shot on a computer and hit Search. Up popped a bunch of mug shots of men who looked, to varying degrees, like Sammy [ ]. Several were of Sammy himself under different names, Detective Boero said. He checked for warrants on those names. Two of Sammy's alter egos were wanted for theft.

> Detective Boero raced back to the casino... The detective approached and gave Sammy the news. "He just smiled and said, 'You got me,' " Detective Boero later remarked.

Each of these reported events could perhaps be explained by the casino's good fortune, the undesirable's bad luck, or as part of the casino's slick public relations effort to hype deterrence (to make the undesirables think that the casino has impenetrable security so they go elsewhere). Or maybe the technology actually worked.

Casino Surveillance: 360°, Pan, Tilt, and Zoom

As Jim Wayman has made clear, a well-known problem with facial recognition systems is "failure to acquire" a good shot of the target. Criminals are noncooperative subjects; they do not want to be identified and will take extreme steps to alter their appearance. To improve the chances of getting a good shot of the target and to reduce the failure to acquire rate, surveillance cameras should offer maximum versatility and speed: they should be able to rotate 360 degrees so that targets can be followed throughout the casino and have a capability to zoom in quickly on the target's face to capture it when opportunity presents itself. Casino surveillance cameras generally satisfy these requirements and also feature widely deployed, but concealed, equipment. For example, cameras are hidden behind smoked glass fixtures in the casino's ceiling. The zooming power is such that the serial number on a dollar bill or the year on a coin can be viewed. At major casinos like the Bellagio, Mandalay Bay, and the Venetian, there are more than 1,000 concealed surveillance cameras recording patrons' movements.

Facial recognition technology works best when it gets help. Casinos are highly incentivized to give it all the help it needs by using many state-of-the-art cameras to monitor well-lighted casino floors, where well-trained casino security officers and other staff are on the look-out for anything suspicious. If these human hawks see something strange, they can communicate that information to the camera operators to pan, tilt, and zoom to get a good shot of the target. And casino security only needs one good shot of the target. Operators can input information like race, gender, sex, and age to further narrow the search. Thus, a key to success is the synergy between the facial recognition system and the human hawks and camera operators who make it work.

Low Cost of Facial Recognition Systems

While costs of any new technology have to be carefully considered, casinos, because of the high emphasis they place on security, do not regard the money spent on facial recognition as much of a hindrance. Compared to the overall security budget for a casino, the cost of adding facial recognition is almost insignificant. In a May 2000 *Security Watch* article entitled, "Facial Recognition Ready for Prime Time?" Charles Gaunther of Trump Marina estimated that, "We probably saved the price of the system in the first six months." (For more information, go to http://www.bbpnews.com/pdf/PT.pdf.)

Casinos also already have the necessary surveillance camera infrastructure, and facial recognition taps into this legacy network. Therefore, the marginal cost of adding facial recognition systems to this infrastructure is low because the major investments have already been made.

To encourage casinos to try the technology, the leasing arrangements that many facial recognition vendors offer do not require casinos to make an outright commitment to the technology. For example, a casino can add a facial recognition capability for as little as $675 a month. The casino can always discontinue the lease if it decides that using the technology is not worthwhile. Having no long-term commitment makes the systems easier to adopt.

Multiple Uses

Facial recognition can go beyond surveillance of undesirables. It can have multiple uses, such as enhancing customer service by alerting casino staff to the arrival of a preferred customer or "high roller" who can then be given V.I.P. service, at which the casinos excel. In some ways, quickly identifying the highly desirable customers is as important as identifying the undesirable ones.

Customer Relations Management (CRM) systems utilizing facial recognition systems have been devised. Boyd Gaming Corp. has obtained patent rights for a preferred player tracking and identification system, which adds iris and facial scanning technology to slot machines, and will incorporate other features.

Facial recognition, along with other biometrics, may also provide new business opportunities, especially for online/Internet gambling where there is a strong need to verify the identity of an online gambler. Facial recognition systems have also been helpful for the gaming industry's public relations in that casinos have used the systems to track problem gamblers who have voluntarily chosen to be excluded from casinos. Thus, facial recognition can be a good public relations tool showing that casinos care.

Enhanced Value of Existing Databases

Casino databases not only have personal data (for example, race, gender, height, weight, aliases used) on undesirables, but also information on techniques, accomplices, venues frequented, and so on. Thus, once the system identifies a potential cheater, various helpful details can be called up from the database to help human hawks with further investigation. Using facial recognition, casinos can develop new profiles for all undesirables—card counters, cheaters, slip-and-fall artists, lifters, pickpockets, and other casino pests. (For more information, go to http://www.bbpnews.com/pdf/PT.pdf.)

The fact that facial recognition not only identifies an undesirable but also identifies his associates and their methods means that even a low match rate is good enough. The human hawks only need a lead. If the software is not very good at catching all the suspects, the fact that undesirables tend to operate in groups means that one match easily leads to others, once the security officials investigate further. Thus, the marginal return on a match is much higher in a casino setting.

Use of Other Biometrics

Casinos are using other biometrics for a variety of purposes. For example, Oneida Bingo and Casino in Green Bay, Wisconsin, uses biometrics to secure money. Money is concentrated in four areas, which include the vault, "hard" and "soft" count rooms, and the "cage." Coins are counted in the hard count area. Dollar bills are counted in the soft count area. Visitors go to the cage to exchange chips for money or to receive bills for coins, and vice versa.

Employees who work in the vault, cage, and count rooms are the only ones permitted in those areas. Initially, ID cards and magnetic stripe readers restricted access to those areas. However, some employees lost their cards and other employees were giving their cards to people who weren't authorized to enter those areas. As a result, anyone in possession of a card could easily enter the vault.

The casino installed hand geometry readers to control access to restricted areas. More than 200 employees use the readers. The employees are first enrolled into the system and their hand geometry template is stored. To use the devices, employees enter an ID number on the reader's keypad, which allows the system to know who is attempting to gain access. The employees place their hand flat on the reader, which generates a three-dimensional image of the hand, including its length, width, and thickness. That image is then compared to a stored image. When the individual's identity has been verified, a door automatically unlocks.

The casino is also using hand geometry readers for time and attendance, which solves the problem of employees clocking for their friends. Employees use separate hand readers for time and attendance and access control.

Though facial recognition systems are still in their infancy, the casino experience demonstrates that when expectations are realistic and the technology is applied properly, they can serve as a useful tool in casino security and even in business applications, such as customer relations management and access control. A major key in successful use of facial recognition systems is having the right attitude and making the necessary adjustments to help the technology work. Knowing the technology's limitations is crucial for success. The casinos' experiences serve as good testimony for how facial recognition systems can be applied in a specific security-conscious environment.

Customer Service Applications for Financial Institutions

Although conservative in nature, financial institutions have increasingly been willing to use new technologies due, in part, to the intense competition in this sector. Fraud is also a major concern. Because of its potential advantage of lowering costs, providing better service, and enhancing security, biometrics is a very attractive technology to financial institutions. At the same time, financial institutions demand high-performance rates, favorable cost-benefit analyses, and controversy free applications.

Riverside Health System Employees Credit Union, Newport News, VA

According to Bill Rogers, the publisher of *Biometric Digest*, over a dozen credit unions in the U.S. have adopted biometrics for customer service applications. Table 18-1, based on Rogers' industry research, shows some of the leading examples. In this section, we discuss how one credit union, serving 3,300 members in Virginia's Tidewater region, is using biometrics for customer service.

Credit Union Location Web Address	Data Proc. Vendor Biometric Integrator Bio Software & Type	Number	Members Assets
Purdue Empl. CU W. Lafayette, IN www.purdueefcu.com	Summit Info Systems Real Time Data SAFLINK—Fingerprint	9 Kiosks	60,000 $330 Mil
Riverside Health Systems FCU Newport News, VA www.rhsecu.org	Real Time Data Real Time Data SAFLINK—Fingerprint	3 Kiosks	3,300 $5 Mil
Birmingham Post Office FCU Birmingham, AL	EPL Real Time Data SAFLINK—Fingerprint	1 Kiosk	3,000 $18 Mil
Fiberglass Fed. CU Newark, OH www.fiberglass.org	EPL Real Time Data SAFLINK—Fingerprint	1 Kiosk	11,900 $63 Mil
First Financial CU West Covina, CA www.fffcu.org	Summit Info Systems Real Time Data SAFLINK—Fingerprint	10 Kiosks	61,500 $472 Mil
Georgia Power Fed. CU Atlanta, GA www.georgiapowerfcu.com	Summit Info Systems Real Time Data SAFLINK—Fingerprint	2 Kiosks	7,700 $46 Mil
Kern Schools Fed. CU Bakersfield, CA ww.ksfcu.org	EPL Real Time Data SAFLINK—Fingerprint	7 Kiosks	95,800 $665 Mil
Publix Empl. Fed. CU Lakeland, FL www.pefcu.com	EPL Real Time Data SAFLINK—Fingerprint	1 Kiosk	81,000 $266 Mil
Y-12 Fed. CU Oak Ridge, TN www.y12fcu.org	EPL Real Time Data SAFLINK—Fingerprint	1 Kiosk	47,300 $212 Mil
NWS Credit Union Yorktown, VA www.nwsfcu.org	Real Time Data Mgmt. Real Time Data SAFLINK—Fingerprint	Teller Stations	7,000 $25 Mil
Houston Municipal CU Houston, TX	Fiserv Galaxy Plus Fiserv Galaxy Plus SAFLINK—Fingerprint	Teller Stations	12,800 $17.1 Mil
Chief Pontiac CU Pontiac, MI www.chiefpontiac.com	Fiserv Galaxy Plus Fiserv Galaxy Plus SAFLINK—Fingerprint	Teller Stations	14,500 $64.5 Mil
Georgia Telco CU Atlanta, GA www.gatelco.org	EPL Real Time Data SAFLINK—Fingerprint	4 Kiosks	78,200 $712 Mil
Kraft Foods Fed. CU White Plains, NY www.kffcu.org	Summit Info Systems Real Time Data SAFLINK—Fingerprint	3 Kiosks	40,800 $310 Mil
Synthetics Fed. CU Hopewell, VA	Real Time Data Real Time Data SAFLINK—Fingerprint	1 Kiosk	3,700 $14 Mil

Table 18-1   Biometric Credit Unions (from Bill Rogers', *Biometric Digest*)

Credit Union Location Web Address	Data Proc. Vendor Biometric Integrator Bio Software & Type	Number	Members Assets
Aberdeen Proving Ground FCU Aberdeen, MD www.apgfcu.com	Summit Info Systems Real Time Data SAFLINK—Fingerprint	3 Kiosks	70,000 $355 Mil
City & County Empl. CU St. Paul, MN www.ccfcu.org	Summit Info Systems Real Time Data SAFLINK—Fingerprint	2 Kiosks	33,200 $211 Mil
Michigan First CU Southfield, MI www.dtcu.cc	CPU Processing Real Time Data SAFLINK—Fingerprint	1 Kiosk	52,800 $305 Mil
Health Associates Fed. CU Orange, CA www.hafcu.org	Symitar Systems, Inc. Real Time Data SAFLINK—Fingerprint	1 Kiosk	6,000 $25 Mil
Front Royal Fed. CU Front Royal, VA www.rmaonline.netfrfcu	Real Time Data Real Time Data SAFLINK—Fingerprint	1 Kiosk	7,660
Wright Patt CU Fairborn, OH www.wright-patcu.org	Summit Info Systems Real Time Data SAFLINK—Fingerprint	3 Kiosks	150,200 $600 Mil
C-Mar CU Marietta, GA	EPL Real Time Data SAFLINK—Fingerprint	1 Kiosk	10,600 $35 Mil
Delta Employees CU Atlanta, CA	Symitar Systems, Inc. Real Time Data SAFLINK—Fingerprint	2 Kiosks	140,000 $1.8 Bil
Metro One CU Concord, CA	Summit Info Systems Real Time Data SAFLINK—Fingerprint	2 Kiosks	21,000 $145 Mil
Mission Fed. CU San Diego, CA	Symitar Systems, Inc. Real Time Data SAFLINK—Fingerprint	2 Kiosks	130,000 $1 Bil
Redwood CU Santa Rosa, CA	Symitar Systems, Inc. Real Time Data SAFLINK—Fingerprint	2 Kiosks	98,000 $700 Mil
South Metro Fed. CU Arlington, VA	FiTECH Real Time Data SAFLINK—Fingerprint	1 Kiosk	2,000 $22 Mil
State Department Fed. CU Arlington, VA	Summit Info Systems Real Time Data SAFLINK—Fingerprint	1 Kiosk	57,000 $432 Mil

Table 18-1   Biometric Credit Unions (from Bill Rogers', *Biometric Digest*) *(continued)*

The Riverside Health System in Newport News, Virginia, includes three hospitals, 10 nursing homes, several wellness and fitness centers, three retirement communities, and over 200 medical offices. The credit union serving this system is fairly small, employing a handful of staff. In 1997, as part of its move into the information age, credit union management decided to add an automated kiosk known as "Money Buddy"—the virtual teller that enables 24/7 electronic customer service. Money Buddy, installed in July 1998, serves two locations where it offers features such as allowing customers to print account statements, transfer funds between accounts, apply for loans, make loan payments, and process withdrawals. Money Buddy requires account numbers and a fingerprint for customer access; customers do not need a card or PIN.

Credit union customers include many military and government families— given the large number of military installations in the area. Perhaps because of the clientele's experience with on-base security measures, most have come to see the Money Buddy's fingerprint system as more protective than invasive. The credit union educated its customers about how the biometric process works. For example, the credit union's promotional materials made it clear that, "Unlike the F.B.I., Money Buddy's finger image scanning system does not keep a picture of your finger print. In addition, the stored information cannot be used to recreate your print in any fashion," since the Money Buddy scanner converts the finger image into a 1024 character numeric code. "That number and only that number is stored in a local database along with your account number. Each time you access Money Buddy and your account, the new scan is converted into a number and compared to the stored number." The credit union deletes an account holder's fingerprint template when they close the account.

The system has encountered few operational problems. Of over 500 customers currently enrolled, only about 10 are so-called "failures-to-enroll," meaning they are unable to use the system because the scanner cannot capture their fingerprint data well enough. These ten customers use the "work-around"—a PIN with no card required. Smaller problems include climatic and occupational factors that alter individuals' fingerprints. Specifically, skin dryness that accompanies health care workers' frequent hand washings can lead to fingerprint distortions. These dryness problems can be resolved by adding a bit of oil to the finger by rubbing it behind the ear. A carpenter who is a credit union member has worn his fingerprints almost completely smooth by virtue of his work; he uses a PIN as a work-around.

Experts explain that credit union clients benefit from biometrics because the credit unions can automate more banking services at member locations, such as at employee work sites. Also, the use of biometrics, because it provides greater security, can provide additional benefits to members. For example, a credit union can offer higher withdrawal limits for special transactions, such as members needing down payment funds toward the purchase of a new car.

InnoVentry Facial Recognition Cash Checking Machines

InnoVentry set out to use facial recognition to help improve the check cashing process for the "non-banked," or the estimated 37 million Americans who do not have an account with a financial institution. The non-banked must rely on commercial check-cashing services, which can be expensive and inconvenient. In

1998, InnoVentry embarked on a strategy featuring unsupervised ATM kiosks, known as Rapid Payment Machines (RPM) that used facial recognition technology to identify customers. InnoVentry sought to reduce fraud, which has long plagued the check-cashing industry. Dr. Joseph Atick, whose company, then known as Visionics, provided the "FaceIt" facial recognition technology, claimed in an interview with *Bank Technology News* that "The fraud rates with our check-cashing clients are down to half a percent because of the facial recognition biometrics." InnoVentry's major participants included Wells Fargo & Co., Cash America International Inc., and Diebold, a leading ATM maker. Investors pumped over $250 million into the venture.

As an operational decision, InnoVentry located its RPM kiosks in high-traffic retail stores that offered a safe, well-lit environment with extended hours. InnoVentry's RPMs could be found throughout the United States, including Ohio, Pennsylvania, Arizona, Arkansas, California, Colorado, Florida, Georgia, Illinois, Louisiana, Massachusetts, Michigan, Nevada, North Carolina, Texas, and Wisconsin. It had agreements with major retail chains including Circle K, Kroger, Wal-Mart, and Albertson's Race-Trac to install the ATMs in their premises. (For more information, go to http://www.business-journal.com/LateNov00/Dieboldcontract.html.)

To enroll, a customer phoned a central call center using a telephone attached to the RPM. The customer service representative then got personal information, along with the enrollee's social security number. A camera in the RPM kiosk captured a digital photograph of the customer's face. Facial recognition software then generated a biometric template from the photograph. (For more information, go to http://www.dss.state.ct.us/digital/news24/bhsug24.htm.) To cash their checks and receive cash, customers inserted their checks into the RPM and followed the instructions on an interactive touch screen. For authentication, a customer entered his or her social security number, and InnoVentry then verified the claimed identity by doing a one-to-one match—comparing the facial image presented to the template on file for the customer. On average, the transaction could be completed in less than three minutes. At the height of its operation, InnoVentry had enrolled 2.5 million people, cashed 8.0 million checks, and installed 1,400 RPMs (for more, go to http://www.biometrics-today.com/novdec01news.html). Over $4 billion worth of checks had been cashed (for more, go to http://www.banktechnews.com/btn/articles/btnsep01-1.shtml).

Despite these impressive numbers, the business model failed. InnoVentory shut down in the Fall of 2001. Simply put, the cost of running the machines could not be covered by the charges generated, set at a small percentage of the value of each cashed check. More specifically, according to Ken Rees, the former InnoVentry chief operating officer, the cause of failure was the higher than expected failure rate of the technology in authenticating customers, which translated to lost revenue. As reported by *ATM & Debit News* in February 2002, Rees said that at some locations, up to 30 percent of attempts to authenticate users of InnoVentry's RPMs failed; most locations had failure rates of about 5 percent.

Many of those failures involved "false non-match" or "false rejection" errors, otherwise known as the "upset customer" scenario. This scenario occurred when the InnoVentry system failed to recognize authorized customers already enrolled. As a result, two things happened: the customer did not get her money leading to her becoming upset, and she promptly called the InnoVentry help desk from the RPM telephone because she needed her money. These calls to the help desk cost InnoVentry money because they require human intervention and additional resources. This problem, combined with the relatively high capital cost of installation of an RPM and the small percentage charge per check-cashing transaction, meant that Innoventry had to be a high volume, automated operation to be successful. Too many false non-matches exacerbated the problem. Another problem has been attributed to poor choice of some sites, which proved problematic and failed to generate enough profits. Being first into this non-banked market with its innovative approach meant that InnoVentory was working on a new paradigm and consequently it took many months to discover whether a site worked. By then it was too late. As one financial industry insider explained, "Being a pioneer sometimes means you end up with an arrow in your back."

The key lessons learned include:

- Site selection must be done with care.
- Performance in real-world situations can be very different from test situations.
- Accuracy of biometrics is crucial to success.
- Lower the fixed cost so that impact of error management costs is lessened.

AGLA Improving Customer Service Through Streamlined Processes

American General Life and Accident Insurance Company (AGLA), based in Nashville, Tennessee, has more than 7,000 field agents who work directly with clients. This work generated lots of paper documents for matters such as amending insurance policies, paying insurance premiums, and completing policy applications. Under the paper-based regime, forms with manually executed signatures were sent to AGLA headquarters where staff sorted them and manually entered data into the computer system. This process was inefficient and prone to data entry errors, thus costly and damaging to customer perceptions of the company. As a result, AGLA decided to use biometric signature software to capture client signatures at remote sites via electronic networks. This implementation of an electronic document management system cuts processing time and cost, which in turn improves the agents' efficiency. Such a system required capturing each client's legally binding signature on electronic documents so that it appears on a computer screen exactly as it does when printed.

Starting in 1997, AGLA embarked on a solution whereby it added electronic signature software to the portable, pen-based computers used by the company's 7,000 agents. The software allowed agents to make beneficiary changes to policies and capture the customer's signature on an electronic form that looks, on screen, exactly like the paper version. Agents can send electronic versions of documents, such as beneficiary changes, to Nashville via modem. The system checks the forms for completeness and errors, and if they pass, the electronic document gets automatically posted to a database. AGLA does not keep a paper copy, just the signed electronic original; however, one printed copy is mailed to the customer.

The system has allowed AGLA to reduce the time, and consequently the cost, it takes to issue or amend a policy. The error rate in electronically captured applications and forms is reportedly low, and processing time and cost have been cut. In addition, the streamlined process boosts customer satisfaction. Some lessons learned from the electronic signature example: People are used to providing a signature for documents and the use of an electronic signature is a very natural extension of that process. Companies are also used to requiring signatures so, again, the use of an electronic signature is a very natural extension of that policy. Both parties thus find it easy and nonthreatening to accept electronic signatures on electronic documents. Chapter 15 explains how the U.S. legal system accommodates the use of this kind of biometric-based electronic signature. Other insurance and financial companies have also fielded the technology.

ING DIRECT Online Banking

Headquartered in Wilmington, Delaware, ING DIRECT is the operating name of ING Bank, a federally chartered savings bank, and part of ING, the eleventh largest financial institution in the world. ING DIRECT, as an online bank, has implemented fingerprint biometrics to allow its customers to be verified over the Internet. Customers log on by entering their account number and PINs and then put their finger on a biometric reader located on the mouse or keypad. The fingerprint image captured verifies their identity. ING DIRECT's management believed that the use of a fingerprint was convenient and gave the appearance of strong security, thus acting as a strong deterrent. In launching the program in 2000, Arkadi Kuhlmann, President and CEO of ING DIRECT, said, "The biometric mouse is an easy and convenient way for consumers to access their bank accounts online in a secure way." The pilot study involved 500 customers in seven countries, each of whom was given a plug-and-play computer mouse equipped with a fingerprint reader. (To avoid charges of specie-ism, please note that some IT aficionados refer to it as a biometric "hamster," defined as a computer "mouse" that also includes a thumbprint scanner.) Enrollment is strictly voluntary and designed to decrease fraud and provide customers with a fast, convenient, and easy option. Wary customers are still able to do business the "old-fashioned" way. The good news, according to Brenda Rideout (overseer of the biometric pilot project) as reported by *eWeek* in 2000, "We had thought there would be much more concern about 'Big Brother' and somebody taking your fingerprint. People seem to be quite open to this technology and not quite as concerned as we had thought they'd be." The bad news: the hardware costs over $100 per mouse, plus the accompanying software, making it "much too high to be a universal product."

Bank Hapoalim, Signature Recognition

Bank Hapoalim, Israel's dominant financial institution with offices in Europe and America, has 2.5 million active accounts. Hapoalim uses electronic signatures, or "dynamic signature verification," to help authenticate its customers. When a customer opens an account, the lower section of the papers to be signed rests on a special electronic pad that follows the pen's movements during the customer's signature. The signature of each customer then gets converted to a template that facilitates reliable authentication by electronic scanners in bank branches in Israel and around the world. The signing pad's level of sensitivity can be adjusted depending on the level of security required. When a customer wants to do a transaction with the bank, the software authenticates the signature, using the stored signature template. Hapoalim's customers can now transact business with almost any branch as the database can authenticate the signature from any location. The signatures of old account-holders were scanned into the system. The system uses "PenFlow" technology produced by WonderNet, Ltd., an Israeli company.

Standard Bank of South Africa

As early as 1996, Standard Bank of South Africa, the country's second-largest banking group and the first bank in South Africa to use ATMs, experimented with fingerprint readers in the bank's automated kiosks at several branches. During enrollment, a customer had their fingerprint and facial photograph taken and digitized. Both the fingerprint template and the photo were stored with other relevant customer information. The bank then issued the enrolled customer a smart card with the stored details. When the customer entered an automated terminal to transact business, he or she placed the smart card into the reader. The system read the customer information from the smart card, and the ATM screen would instruct the person, by name, to place a finger on the fingerprint-reading device. A small photo of the enrolled cardholder was also retrieved from the database and displayed on the ATM screen at this time. If the customer's live fingerprint sample matched the fingerprint template stored on the smart card, access to the system was granted.

As part of the lessons learned, any organization implementing biometrics needs to know its customer base. At Standard Bank's sites, a large number of mineworkers used the ATM kiosks. As *Banking Technology Online* has reported, due to the "hands on" nature of their work, the mineworkers' fingerprints had weathered and degraded to such an extent that the error rates were not considered satisfactory, so the project has been shelved.

Bank of Hawaii, Waianae Branch

The Bank of Hawaii, one of the Aloha State's leading financial institutions, uses hand geometry at its Waianae branch to meet the demand for faster, more convenient banking services. Hand geometry provides automated customer access to safe-deposit boxes, thus eliminating the need for a vault attendant. During enrollment, the hand geometry system measures finger length, width, thickness, and the surface area of the customer's hand. During use, the customer enters a PIN, which points the system to the customer hand geometry template, then places their hand in a wall-mounted, biometric hand geometry reader. If the identity is verified (through a one-to-one match), the hand geometry system admits the customer to the vault and automatically logs the entry. To add another layer of security, the bank videotapes all unattended transactions with a digital video system as the customer is entering the door to the vault area.

About 500 customers with safe-deposit boxes have enrolled. The hand geometry system eliminates the need for a bank attendant, thus lowering the bank's operating expenses. The system also has improved customer service because enrolled customers can access their safe-deposit boxes any time during banking hours. "We chose [this approach] because it enables us to provide self-service delivery, and we're satisfied with the safety aspects of it," said Harvey Chang, vice president and project manager, Hawaii Branch Division. The Bank of Hawaii's system is known by the trade name, PassVault by Diebold; Recognition Systems, Inc. provides the hand geometry readers.

Charles Schwab—Voice Services

Charles Schwab & Co., the well-known discount brokerage house with over $500 billion in funds under management, uses voice recognition technology to authenticate customers accessing their account information by telephone. Schwab compares the phrase stated by the customer over the telephone with a stored digital voice print from a customer-dictated phrase. Using biometrics allows Schwab to identify customers by their distinctive voice prints, thus reducing the opportunity for password theft and other types of fraud. Once authenticated, customers can then use the automated system to obtain stock quotes. The Schwab system recognizes the names of more than 13,000 securities said in more than two million different ways, since most companies have dozens of variant pronunciations and names such as "IBM" or "IBM Incorporated" or "International Business Machines." (For more information, go to http://www.sri.com/news/releases/9-17-96.html.) Operating over the telephone, which can be a noisy and difficult environment for speech recognition, the system gives customers real-time stock quotes for virtually all companies traded on U.S. stock exchanges. According to Cicily Baptist, Schwab's vice president in charge of development and deployment of the speech system, "We'll use this new technology to make it easier for our customers to get into their accounts. For those customers who join this program, the technology will be able to identify their voices so they'll no longer need to remember their PIN."

As reported in *Knowledge Management Magazine* (January 2000), Schwab "retired" the original name for the service, "Voice Broker," in September 1999 and replaced it with the more generic phrase, voice services, as part of its business strategy. Baptist explained that, "The purpose [behind Voice Broker] was not to name the product and sell the product but to integrate the service and have it used to obtain information. It should be seamless to the customer; we don't want to call attention to it."

Schwab voice services receive an average of 100,000 callers each day, adding up to more than 1.5 million calls a year. This service gives Schwab clients the freedom and flexibility to handle their finances on their own time without the hassle of having to wait for a customer service representative. (For more information, go to http://www.tmcnet.com/tmcnet/columns/mia052200.htm.) The program has the potential to grow in that Schwab has some 6.3 million customer accounts.

On a related note, company founder Charles Schwab, who long struggled with dyslexia, began the Schwab Foundation for Learning, a nonprofit dedicated to helping youngsters with "differences." The foundation uses word processors with speech-recognition software to help dyslexic older students.

Amec Capital Projects U.K.— Biometric Payment Authentication

Amec Capital Projects Limited is conducting pilot studies on the use of biometric signature software to process and authenticate subcontractor payment certificates. Before adoption of the software, these certificates were prepared as an Excel document that was printed and then signed by the surveyor and the contract manager on site. These were then photocopied and forwarded by mail to the appropriate company director for further signature. After review, the director signed them and sent them by internal mail to the accounts department for processing. (For more information, go to http://www.itcbp.org.uk/itcbp/AllPubs/biometric.pdf.)

With the electronic signature software, the documents are generated on site, electronically signed by authorized signatories, and e-mailed to the appropriate director for review and further signature. The director then e-mails them to the accounts department where the treasurer authenticates the signatures to ensure that the documents have not been altered. The biometric signature software produces a biometric token that has the signature dynamics, the token is then embedded on the document along with other details about the document binary composition. This signature can then be validated to confirm that the originator signed the document and that the contents have not been altered.

Installation and training were done in one day. The benefits realized included faster payment process, less paperwork, and saving time. An improvement that has been suggested is to use a fingerprint stamp where a pre-enrolled signature is released from a database by means of a fingerprint keyboard.

Amec plans to continue with the trials after tackling some of the business processes that need to be changed.

Time and Attendance/Employee Verification

Biometric applications for human resource management are growing as organizations look for better ways to account for employees and resources. Managers must be able to track attendance. Biometrics can help without requiring close supervision. To consider a well-known example, a problem in monitoring attendance using conventional time and attendance systems is that employees clock for their friends (also known as "buddy punching"). With biometrics, every employee clocks for themselves and the problem of buddy punching is eliminated, with money saved in the process.

Men's Wearhouse

Men's Wearhouse uses biometrics to verify its employees. The specialty retailer began adding fingerprint readers to the keyboards of its point-of-sale terminals in 1999. Every store in the 600-unit chain will eventually use a fingerprint reader to capture employee time and attendance and provide associates with access to online information and learning tools. The fingerprint reader also ensures that the person at the cash register is the right person. As *Newsweek* reported, "The most unusual time-saving feature of the new registers is a fingerprint scanner that lets managers make returns and exchanges more swiftly because the computer instantly recognizes them. With the old system, employees had to go through several screens and passwords to handle returns." Jeff Marshall, the company's chief information officer and architect of the system, explains, "I know who is in the register, when they were in it, and what transactions took place when they were in it." The device offers "much more security than a key on a chain," notes Marshall.

Men's Wearhouse has long been considered something of a technological innovator in the retail industry. For example, the company spent $10 million on customized software for touch-screen registers to provide instant inventory and related information.

Columbia Presbyterian Hospital, New York, NY

This New York hospital has used a hand geometry scanner system for its 8,000 staff for two primary purposes: to monitor time and attendance and to control physical access. The hospital wanted better time and attendance practices because of perceived inaccuracies in bookkeeping. In 1997, the first year of the system's operation, fraud reduction led to an estimated savings of more than $1 million. The use of hand geometry has also contributed to better access control, leading to better building security.

A few minor problems have been associated with the hand geometry system. Employees expressed some initial privacy concerns (for example, "Is this taking my fingerprints?"), but the use of the system has become routine, users have become habituated, and concerns appear to have subsided. Scanning problems can occur due to environmental conditions, such as when the lens or scanning surfaces become dirty. Wearing of bandages, long sleeves, and other add-ons can also distort the hand image, whether during the initial scan for enrollment or during subsequent verifications. Employees' data are deleted from the system upon their separation from the hospital.

Physical Access

A major concern for many organizations is controlling access so that only authorized people are allowed in various locations. Traditional access control methods depend on human guards, who cost money and can be compromised, or PINs, passwords, cards, keys or tokens, which can be stolen or forgotten. Using a biometric ensures that only the person who has the biometric gets access, thus improving security.

University of Georgia, Athens, GA

The University of Georgia has one of the longest-running biometric applications in the United States, going back 30 years. The university uses hand recognition systems for physical access purposes.

Early on, the University of Georgia realized that it needed to restrict access to its student dining facilities. Prior to 1972, the university used a punch card system that was ineffective and easily circumvented. In 1972, it implemented a hand geometry system. In 1995, the university implemented a much improved three-dimensional biometric hand geometry system. At that time, 5,400 students—those on the university's meal program—enrolled in the new system. Because of the success of the program, both in terms of student reaction and of curtailing unauthorized access to the dining facilities, the university decided to expand the system to address other physical access needs on campus. The same hand geometry system is now used to grant access to the 17 residence halls housing 5,600 students. Since 1998, the University of Georgia has required all 31,000 "Bulldogs" to enroll in the hand geometry program, which prevents unauthorized access to the university's sport and recreation facilities, and other places.

The university administration received relatively few complaints from the student body. But, some operational problems have surfaced. For a successful reading to take place, the individual must be comfortable with the system. At the University of Georgia, many students quickly get habituated because they use the system multiple times every day, so they become accustomed to the procedure. If individuals have suffered trauma (for example, broken hands are not uncommon on a university campus), they have trouble using the system.

Marshall Field Garden Apartment Homes, Chicago, IL

Marshall Field Garden Apartment Homes (MFGAH), an inner-city housing project consisting of a 10 building, 628 unit gated community in Chicago, Illinois, uses hand geometry readers to improve residential security. (For more information, go to http://www.axiomsecurity.com/perspectives/presentations.html.) The key objective was to provide decent, safe, and sanitary affordable housing at MFGAH. Specifically, MFGAH management sought to address the following concerns:

- Gang and illegal drug activity, vandalism, violence, and related factors that had a negative impact on the quality of tenant life
- Unauthorized occupants, who add to maintenance costs

A specialized access control system integrates biometric hand geometry devices with single-person passage portals. Users are enrolled in the access control system, assigned PINs, and have their hand geometry captured when they arrive at the community. The PINs associate individuals with apartments and indicate whether the users are residents, guests, or staff members. The system records more than 10,000 transactions per day for 6,000 users.

Users, including children and the elderly, guests, and staff use their hand as a key to pass through the single-person portals. The single-person-passage uses two interlocking doors and an occupancy sensor to prevent "tailgating." The occupancy sensor determines whether the single-person passage portal is vacant, occupied by one person, or occupied by more than one person by the location of the weight distributed on its floor. When it senses single-person occupancy, the door the user entered through locks, and the person proceeds to the hand geometry device, enters a PIN on the keypad, and presents the hand to the device for verification. Using infrared, the unique hand geometry is compared to the user's stored template created during enrollment. Software also checks whether the user has current authorization. If the user is a tenant, she is given unlimited access for the term of her lease. Guest access is set electronically. If the user does not have current access authorization, she must exit the portal via the door through which she entered. A user who has a correct match and authorization proceeds through the second door, thus gaining access to the community.

Templates are automatically updated with each verification—adjusting to gradual changes in users' hands that occur as they grow, age, or experience weight changes. If a user's hand geometry changes dramatically, for instance if he breaks a finger, a new template can be created.

Guest are enrolled on their first visit and assigned a PIN, the duration of authorization depends on his status—a visiting friend, a pizza delivery person, a baby sitter, and others. A previously enrolled guest whose access rights have expired can be reactivated on his return for subsequent visits. To eliminate the need for many re-enrollments for guests, enrollment information remains on file even after access authorization has expired.

For exception handling (or work-around) purposes, a bypass mechanism enables a guard to override the system, for example, for a caregiver pushing a person in a wheelchair, or a parent with a stroller, or emergency responders. Video cameras monitor and record the bypass portal lanes to prevent unauthorized entry. The whole system can release all doors in case of power failure, fire alarm, or emergency.

Crime is prevented through deterrence, limiting access to the unauthorized public, and denying access to specific "undesirable" individuals even if the tenant has approved the visit. Potential criminals worry that the system can provide information about them or block escape routes.

Audit trails provided by the system have been used as an effective alibi to show that a person accused of having committed a crime at a certain location actually was present elsewhere. The audit trails have also been used to aid police to surprise tenants who have arrest warrants outstanding. The audit reports can also show usage patterns to help with resource allocation decisions.

Some tenants have complained vigorously about the intrusiveness of the technology. But some of the complainers have been dismissed as those who were engaged in criminal activities and felt threatened by the system. The complaints reduced as these individuals moved out or got evicted. Some tenants also complained about the lack of privacy, in particular single people who might have overnight visitors, as well as security being too extreme for a housing project.

The result of improved security has been higher occupancy rates. Many tenants have expressed their overall satisfaction; they feel a tremendous increase in a sense of personal safety. Children can play in the inner courtyard without being exposed to drug dealing, and prostitution has been stopped. The crime rate has reportedly dropped significantly in the Marshall Field Garden Apartment Homes.

Customer Service, Retail Applications

Keeping customers happy and satisfied wins their loyalty—a main business objective. As the saying goes, "The customer is the king," but you have to know the king first and that is where biometric technology comes in. By allowing organizations to automatically identify customers, biometrics improves convenience.

Kroger Supermarkets, Various Locations, TX

Kroger, the country's largest grocery company, with about 3,600 stores nationwide, has recently completed a trial of fingerprint biometrics recognition in conjunction with check cashing in its stores. Because of the trial program's success, Kroger fielded the system in 250 stores nationwide by the first quarter of 2000.

Kroger uses a fingerprint scanning system. In each store, approximately 45 percent of all Kroger customers write checks to pay for their purchases. These customers are given the opportunity to participate in the fingerprint-scanning program. A Kroger executive said that about 8,000 to 10,000 customers per store participated in the test phase of the program. Kroger reportedly has been pleased with the program's performance as well as the overall reduction of check fraud in its stores. In the six trial stores, approximately 1,000 incidents of check fraud took place each month before Kroger implemented the system. The pilot stores have had zero incidents of check fraud since implementation. This dramatic drop in the incidence of fraud has created a large enough savings that the system should pay for itself within a year.

In 2002, Kroger has been experimenting with a new retail point-of-sale system in several of its stores in College Station, Texas. Shoppers who enroll free of charge to use "SecureTouch-n-Pay," the finger image machine, simply walk up to the cashier station and pay with their fingerprint. A Kroger executive explained that Kroger experienced very little negative reaction from customers to the use of fingerprint scanning. Customers have been pleased at the hassle-free process. No longer do they need to show an ID card but simply put their finger on the scanner and within a second the process is over. After a customer places his finger on the scanner, the data collected are matched to a local database on the store workstation containing the records of that store's customers. If the fingerprint is not in the store's local database, the computer searches the main Kroger database off-site. If the customer is found in the main database, the individual is identified and the local database then receives the customer's record for future transactions.

Kroger was initially concerned that their senior citizen customer base might express concerns over the program but found that this group was the most enthusiastic about the biometrics system. The seniors are highly motivated with regard to fraud and security and welcomed the fingerprint scanners. Kroger did discover that seniors tend to have drier hands than younger people, which at first hampered getting a good read on the scanner. Kroger made adjustments and now the system operates well for this customer group.

United Retail's Jet Stores, Various Locations, South Africa

United Retail's Jet Stores in South Africa are using facial recognition for a preferred customer service application. Specifically, United Retail is using the technology to register customers' faces along with their credit card and related data on a voluntary basis. When a customer approaches the counter, a small camera next to the cash register scans her face. The attendant can refer to the stored customer details and the attendant can give more personalized service, thus making the customers feel preferred. United intends to create a loyalty program to reward registrants and to eliminate the need for them to carry credit cards. All that the customer needs is his or her face to complete a transaction. United Retail chose facial recognition because it is passive; the customer does not need to do anything.

Computer and Network Access

Information is the lifeblood of any organization. However, the value of this information is fully realized only if authorized employees can properly access and share it—thus the need for computer networks and access controls. Access to computer networks is traditionally provided through passwords supplied to the user. But, as explained in detail in Chapter 1, employees, in the age of "password overload," have trouble remembering passwords and thus pick ones that are easy to remember (and easily compromised), or write them somewhere convenient (where they can be easily obtained by unauthorized people). When they do not pick easy ones to remember (like a favorite sports team) or write them down in secret places (like on a sticky note under the keyboard or mouse pad), employees tend to forget their passwords. Thus, many hours are lost and resources squandered as system administrators provide them with new passwords. Biometrics provide a solution by not requiring a person to remember his or her password, saving headaches for users and systems administrators, and most of all by keeping information secure.

Blue Cross & Blue Shield of Rhode Island

Blue Cross & Blue Shield of Rhode Island (BCBSRI) is in the process of implementing an enterprise-level computer security system based on biometrics. The new system replaces existing password protection with fingerprint authentication to control access to the health insurance provider's main computer network. Eventually, the system is expected to include over 1,000 BCBSRI employees. By creating stronger authentication, BCBSRI will better safeguard patient medical records and sensitive company data and meet the patient protection requirements of the federally mandated Health Insurance Portability and Accountability Act (HIPAA), which goes into effect in 2003.

Implementation of the new biometric security solution will occur in several phases. A pilot test was done over a period of one year and the results were favorable. Full rollout began in July 2002. "The results of the pilot project confirmed that we can provide increased convenience for our employees, while securing our networks and gaining a number of other organizational benefits, such as reducing the burden of password management for our help desk administrators," said Victor Pigoga, Director, Data/Voice Communications for BCBSRI. "It also assures our customers that we are committed to investing in cutting-edge technology to protect the privacy of their health information." (For more information about the BCBSRI security, go to http://www.saflink.com/80102.html.)

California Commerce Bank (CCB)

"Almost all major financial institutions are now at least piloting some type of biometric technology for internal use; many of the implementations, however, have remained confidential." (For more information, refer to "Bridging the Gap," at http://securitysolutions.com/ar/security_bridging_gap/.)

The California Commerce Bank (CCB) is one of the few banks to go public about its use of biometrics to control computer and network access. CCB has implemented a system to allow employees to use fingerprint authentication to access sensitive customer data. Most banks require a series of passwords and PINs to give employees access to different levels of information and different databases. CCB uses biometric fingerprint scanners attached to employee workstations to authenticate users. The need for greater security, better productivity, and lower cost led to a biometric solution. Security needs required that only authorized personnel could access certain information. "We have an open-space office," explained Salvador Villar, CCB's President, in the article, "Fingerprint Verification for Data Access," from Bankers' Hotline. "When employees step away from their desks, we need to be sure that no one can get to their information." (For more information, go to http://www.bankersonline.com/articles/bhv11n02/bhv11n02a21.html.) Passwords cost an estimated $200 per user per year due to fixing problems related with forgotten passwords.

Chapter 19

Biometrics and the Feasibility of a National ID Card

By Martin C. Libicki and John D. Woodward, Jr.

The terrorist attacks of September 11, 2001, have caused Americans to reevaluate the balance between domestic security and civil liberties. This chapter concentrates on one proposal raised post-09/11 that strikes at this balance: U.S. government adoption of a national identification card (or national ID) as part of a comprehensive nationwide identity system. National ID cards received heightened media attention from the *Wall Street Journal*, October 8, 2001, when Larry Ellison, the CEO of Oracle Corp.—the world's largest database systems vendor—in an article named, "Smart Cards: Digital IDs Can Help Prevent Terrorism," called for "the government to phase in digital ID cards" and to interlink existing government databases in such a way as to have a more comprehensive national database about individuals.

A national ID card proposal is bound to be controversial, complicated, and "not that easy" as a recent report of the National Research Council has made plain (Kent and Millett, eds. 2002). In the context of a national identification card system, biometrics is viewed as an enabling technology that will help make such a system effective by binding a person to his identity.

The national identification card debate is not new in the United States and has long enjoyed lively discussion. For example, in 1975, Frances G. Knight, the Director of the Passport Office at the U.S. Department of State, advocated the issuance of a national ID card, with fingerprints, to every citizen. By the time she retired two years later, she had few overt supporters for her idea largely because policymakers—and lawmakers—feared negative public reaction. In 1980, the Select Commission on Immigration and Refugee Policy, chaired by Rev. Theodore M. Hesburgh, avoided recommending a national ID card or a mandatory work card scheme for the U.S. In 1994, the congressionally established Commission on Immigration Reform, chaired by former Representative Barbara Jordan, also considered the national ID card issue. Jordan, however, stopped short of proposing a national ID card scheme in her congressional testimony, endorsing the idea of a more secure ID document for workers and a better database for employers to verify the identity and citizenship of any employment applicant. Similarly, then Senator Alan Simpson argued at the time that such a card would only be presented for employment at the time of hire or when applying for federally funded benefits.

As the above examples help demonstrate, the nation's lawmakers considered national ID card schemes based primarily on concerns about illegal immigrants coming to the United States and working illegally or receiving unauthorized federal benefits.

Prior to September 11, 2001, the conventional wisdom about national ID cards seemed to be that most Americans didn't want and would not abide them—period. Since 9/11, the conventional wisdom is arguably changing although the White House claims it is not interested. Three specific characteristics of the terrorist attacks have made a national identity system of some sort a plausible, if not necessarily probable, approach to serve domestic security purposes:

- All nineteen hijackers being dead, no after-the-fact risk of arrest, prosecution, and punishment could have deterred their actions, or can forestall similar terrorist actions—this is the grave problem posed by "one-time-use" terrorists. However, those who might aid and abet them may be deterred by such risk.

- Of the nineteen, apparently only a few of them appeared on any U.S. government watch list: Al Hamsi and Al Midhar; a third, Mohammed Atta, had a bench warrant outstanding in Broward County, Florida, for failing to appear in court on a traffic violation. There was no evidence readily available to the U.S. government that would have merited surveillance of the other seventeen.

- None of the nineteen were U.S. citizens. (Among the thousand plus foreign nationals in custody two months after the attack, few were U.S. citizens.)

The first two characteristics suggest that two traditional tools of law enforcement—arrest and preemption based on intensive surveillance of specific individuals—were and would have been of limited relevance in this case, or in future similar cases. This observation suggests one (but not necessarily only one) alternative: law enforcement must use extensive surveillance based on a larger population set of people, most of whom, by definition, are unlikely to do anything at all illegal, but a small number of whom might do something very bad.

But who does law enforcement surveil? Surveilling one class of Americans but not another would, for the most part, be invidious and legally objectionable (with long recognized exceptions: parolees have, by their own criminal actions, set themselves apart for special treatment by the state). This is where the third characteristic—no hijacker was a U.S. citizen—achieves relevance. Law and custom permit distinctions to be made between the country's three hundred million citizens and its several million non-citizens. These include non-citizens present in the United States for tourism, transit, business, study, certain work, and in the case of resident aliens, because they live here. Being fewer in number, the noncitizens are easier to track and, arguably, should be tracked to some extent by the government.

Hence the thinking behind this chapter. If the U.S. government could track the major movements and critical activities of non-citizens present in the United States, it might be able to pick up warnings or clues of future terrorist attacks or other comparable crimes. In this way, the authorities, in a forward-looking way, might be able to preempt such attacks. Even if potential attackers lived so as to minimize or anonymize ostensible movements and critical activities, forcing them to do so would likely complicate their planning and throw off their operations. Some would-be terrorists may be deterred by the cost of avoidance or the fear of making telltale mistakes prior to committing their terrorist acts. Others may make mistakes in any case. By correlating major movements and critical activities, it may be possible to deter accomplices who are willing to help suicide bombers, but who are not willing to die or suffer incarceration. Finally, a regime of surveillance and detection of certain sensitive activities (such as renting crop-dusting airplanes and purchasing certain controlled substances) could make it more difficult for certain classes of people to use them for illegal purposes.

In fairness, even an extensive surveillance system can merely reduce, at best, the risk of future terrorist acts. The best set of well-collected warnings or clues is next to worthless if it is unclear what they are warnings of or clues to. For example, on August 17, 2001, federal authorities had in their custody (as a visa violator), Habib Zacarias Moussaoui, a foreigner who had apparently asked Minnesota flight school instructors to train him in flying jet aircraft but not in landing them. Had there been a template that included the modalities of what actually happened on September 11, Moussaoui's case would have rung loud alarm bells; however, no such template was taken seriously by officialdom. (Even though French authorities reported that Moussaoui had associated with terrorist groups and a local FBI field office, arguably seeing parts of an inchoate template and hearing some mild alarm bells, thought the circumstances called for a search warrant to be issued under the Foreign Intelligence Surveillance Act, a request demurred by FBI headquarters.)

The next terrorist attack may also catch the nation unaware particularly if it uses another novel or unanticipated approach. However, three factors make extensive surveillance potentially worthwhile:

- The possibility that *ancillary modalities* (for example, how operations are financed and supported, how operatives are recruited and kept on track) may be repeated from one attack to the next

- The likelihood that the authorities, having been surprised once, will be entertaining a much more varied set of templates against which to evaluate any warnings or clues

- The likelihood that the authorities' tracking of non-citizens' major movements and critical activities could be helpful for any post-event (or after-the-fact) analysis

However, if U.S. citizens perpetrate the next such terrorist attack or are the ones called upon to help foreigners with such an attack, the benefits of surveilling only non-citizens would be largely ineffective. Although U.S. citizens have been involved in terrorism, foreign terrorists remain the primary concern.

Aside from the above, one immense operational problem of conducting extensive surveillance of non-citizens has to be addressed. The kind of national identification system needed to track non-citizens can be easily evaded if non-citizens can credibly claim to be citizens. Non-citizens bent on terrorism would be incentivized to do just that (credibly claim to be citizens) and could do so fairly easily because there are relatively few circumstances in which Americans have to show a government issued identification. Although people are asked to show some form of government-issued identification before they board a plane or after they are pulled over in a vehicle by the authorities, the quality of such identification varies widely (for example, exploiting a now closed legal loophole, many hijackers procured Virginia driver's licenses with a minimum of valid information).

So any foreign terrorist wishing to escape scrutiny once inside the U.S. need only acquire one, or better yet, multiple driver's licenses, which can be easily obtained from a corrupt DMV official or mass produced by a forgery artist. Armed with these fake ID documents, the foreign terrorist escapes scrutiny because he is using his forged driver's license for identification purposes. Because of this reality, it would be pointless to ask for hard identification only from foreigners, without asking for equally hard identification from everyone else (meaning, Americans).

Thus, establishing an extensive surveillance and identification system for non-citizens present in the U.S. would not be that helpful since foreign terrorists will evade the surveillance and identification system by masquerading as Americans with (fraudulent) driver's licenses. To be effective, a similar system of surveillance and identification is required for citizens (and non-citizens) that is a national ID system.

Thesis and Constitutionality Issues

The remainder of this chapter examines whether a national ID system is feasible. That is, can one envision a national identification system that contributes to the fight against terrorism and crime; proves technologically feasible and hard to defraud; remains consistent with our legal and political values; and yet has built-in protection against potential abuses?

This chapter does not argue that there must be a national ID system. Such an argument would have to establish that the data collected through surveillance and identification would be worthwhile, and would establish—by appealing to some set of values—that the gains in domestic security, factoring in both good and bad side-effects, are worth the loss in civil liberties. At best, this chapter only examines the feasibility of such a national identification card system and its ability to maximize its utility for certain domestic security and minimize some of its less desirable effects or loss of civil liberties. A system may meet all such tests and be judged, on balance, undesirable or unaffordable.

We will not attempt to assess the legality of a national identification card system in all of its particulars. Those wanting a rich analysis of the constitutionality of national identification card schemes will have to look elsewhere. There *are* reasons to believe a national ID system would not be illegal, although it may not necessarily be constitutional to compel individuals to provide some of the information that *could* be considered pursuant to a national identification system (for example, requiring citizens to produce their national ID cards on a police officer's random demand; requiring citizens to provide DNA samples from their bodily fluids).

That said, a few words on the subject of privacy, discussed elsewhere in this book, are in order because many objections to national identification systems are based on privacy grounds. The concept of privacy fuses two separate, if related, ideas.

The first idea, long recognized by law and society, is the general right of individuals to keep certain of their words and acts private. No one should know about the individual's private words and private acts except other people to whom the individual has deliberately revealed them. Such people are likely to be known to the individuals beforehand; in any case, the individual makes the decision to entrust a person with his private words or acts. Thus, human nature being what it is, some people can keep a secret and some cannot. Alice tells Bob in confidence about her innermost thoughts, Bob promptly blabs to Carol. And as the previous chapter makes clear, privacy gets legally complicated because the word "privacy," like the phrase "national identification card," is nowhere to be found in the text of the U.S. Constitution, leading the U.S. Supreme Court and others to construe its meaning.

The second idea, which is clearly *not* so protected by law, covers the conversion of local information into global information. Local information reveals what takes place in public and, potentially, in front of strangers. Global information is that information which is made available to all. With specific exceptions (for example, an act that takes place before a live broadcast) information becomes globalized through the process of recording, storing, and making such records available to those not there at the time and the place who may, in fact, be somewhere across the globe. In other words, if one has revealed something about oneself to *one* completely random stranger in public, he cannot then complain if *other* strangers can therefore access such information about him. Examples of local information might be what someone purchases at a grocery store, when someone walked into a shopping mall, or what someone has festooned on their lawn.

Granted, many of us might be troubled to learn that complete strangers are systematically collecting and archiving such information in gigantic databases that are accessible by other complete strangers. Indeed, most of the current concern about Internet privacy is of precisely this nature and there may yet be legislation to curb corporations and others from converting information captured for one purpose (such as to complete a transaction) from being applied to another (such as to facilitate cross-marketing) without the data subject's consent.

The second notion of privacy also comes into play when government officials collect biometric data (like a photograph of someone's face) from people in public; for that matter, there are no prohibitions against the government collecting fingerprints that one "leaves behind" in any public location either.

The last issue, briefly noted, concerns the constitutionality of the government's demand that individuals present identification as a condition of entry to private or public spaces. For example, ticketed passengers must show photo identification prior to boarding a commercial flight. This requirement is presumably based on a Federal Aviation Administration regulation grounded in the government's responsibility to ensure public safety. After September 11, other activities may be deemed to fall under the public safety penumbra. Similarly, requirements to show identification to cross national borders or enter government sites (such as military installations) raise no serious challenge either.

It is less clear and more problematic, however, whether or not the government can demand identification of those who walk on public streets, enter public buildings, or transact public business, exercising their rights as citizens or performing their duties as taxpayers. As the Supreme Court has explained in *Florida v. Royer,* 460 U.S. 491, 497-498 (1983), a law enforcement officer does not violate the Fourth Amendment when he approaches an individual in a public setting and asks him questions. However, the Court has made it clear that "[t]he person approached [ ] need not answer any question put to him; indeed he may decline to listen to the question at all and may go on his way."

Noting that there is no right to anonymity "hinted at in the Constitution," law scholar Alan Dershowitz opined in the *New York Times,* October 24, 2001, that we cannot "afford to recognize such a right in this age of terrorism."

Basic Parameters of an Identification System

The fundamental purpose of an identification system is to determine and report the identity of a person who would cross or encounter a specified checkpoint, for example, an entrance to a sensitive place, passage from one place to another, or the right to perform certain acts (for example, drive a truck transporting hazardous materials). Such a system should be governed by several objectives:

- Maximum reliability (people are who they claim to be)

- Sufficient effectiveness (people present identification often enough to serve the purposes of domestic security and accountability)

- Minimum intrusiveness (people are not asked to present identification too often and data collectors must be specifically authorized to require people to present identification)

- Minimum hassle (the act of presenting identification should not be too onerous)

- Minimum essential retention (necessary data is correctly reported and recorded; non-necessary data is discarded, especially data concerning U.S. citizens not under criminal investigation)

It becomes clear that these objectives must be traded off: information should be collected often enough, but not too often. Such a system must be carefully designed and justified to optimize among them.

Two other objectives, although not essential, are highly desirable:

- **Simplicity**   Identity cards should be simple, both to minimize the cost of their issuance, but also to minimize the amount of information that can be illicitly extracted from the physical card, itself.

- **Convenience**   ID card holders ought to be able to use them, if *they* so choose, for other identification purposes; this could be a great convenience for the cardholder.

An ID card as such should be seen as a *logical bridge between a person and a set of data about this person*. Indeed, the primary role of a national ID system is to give everyone enrolled a unique alphanumeric (think of it as a person's name plus enough extra digits to distinguish the country's various John Smiths). The alphanumeric is the link across the bridge.

Were it no easier to read the card directly than to swipe the card into a networked reader, send the alphanumeric to the database, and get information back electronically, there absolutely would be no reason to include *any* more information in the card. The database would contain the rest (for example, biometrics, certain transactional events, and relevant interactions with the government—plus whatever other information the user deems convenient—such as credit card memberships).

From the standpoint of security and privacy, there are valid reasons for making it difficult for anyone to read the contents of the identity card itself. More importantly, there are valid reasons for limiting access to the database of a person's datasets containing biometric data as well as information on the various comings and goings that having an identity card makes it possible to collect and track. Minimizing what is on the card helps establish a system that can be guarded with tight access controls.

The remainder of this section discusses the various components of a national ID system: the card itself, the databases it feeds, optional authentication features of an ID card, and how to validate the ID process.

National Identification Card

One essential requirement for the national identification card is for it to contain a unique identification alphanumeric for its holder, for example, the holder's name plus enough extra bytes to distinguish people with identical names. But there is no requirement that the alphanumeric be easily readable. One can imagine identity cards that are completely blank—as are many proximity cards and similar products, such as ExxonMobil's SpeedPass, a proximity device used as a credit card substitute. Blank cards have the great advantage in that they cannot be asked for casually. The mythologized street cop hassling random passers-by for their national identification cards would be nearly impossible to envision under this scenario—unless the street cop were willing to carry a device that could read such cards electronically. Authorized people, conversely, could read the card and, with a small time lag, a photograph, and other personal identifying information could be presented to them. So, there is no concrete need to store such information on the card itself.

In practice, it makes sense to include the person's photograph on the ID card. If nothing else, it enables people to pick out which one is theirs when mixed (for example, a husband and wife toss them on the dresser prior to bedtime, wake up and cannot remember whose is whose).

A photograph on the national ID card also permits authorities running checkpoints to verify, more or less, that the person presenting himself is holding the identity card that he is supposed to hold. Although a networked checkpoint could also do this verification, such a facility would require sufficient bandwidth to return a good photograph quickly. People who access the Web over dial-up phone lines know that even a 56K connection can take a second or two to return sufficiently detailed images (and in many parts of the United States, 56K is a luxury). Many checkpoints do not need to be connected to a network in real-time—only those that do a hard check on holders or which use personal information in the database to permit or deny access. The rest, those that collect information for later analysis, can dial the network when the phone lines are not in use or store the information and transmit it later. As such, the fundamental notion is that the card is read by a device which verifies that the information has been validated by the U.S. government, which passes the contact information forward into a central database, and may return biometric information (to permit a fraud check on the card) as well as access permission. Such a fraud check could be as basic as comparing the presenter's face with the face returned by the network, or as stringent as doing a one-to-one comparison of a biometric presented, such as a fingerprint or an iris, with its stored template.

Conversely, the national ID card should be designed so that it can only be read by checkpoint authorities, and not any official (for example, street policemen) for whatever reason. This design feature can be achieved by legal and technical means. Legal means would include making it a criminal offense for overzealous police officers to demand such ID cards unless certain criteria were met and providing for stiff penalties for violators. Police officers could be required to give an equivalent *Miranda*-like warning when stopping individuals on the street: "You have the right to refuse to produce your national identification card."

Exploiting technical means includes encrypting the alphanumeric; this step requires the card-reading device (CRD) to have decryption keys. If there is only one such key, and a card-reading device falls into the wrong hands, the degree of tamper resistance required to hide the key indefinitely is likely to be very high, and perhaps not feasible. Devious and clever cryptographers and electrical engineers do exist. Alternatively, card-reading devices could forward encrypted traffic to one central point (plus backups) for decryption prior to entering in the database. If few such points are guarded they should be safe; but it also means that checkpoints cannot control access in real-time if the network is down or otherwise very slow. Access control is a network problem with or without encryption.

There are various ways to encode information onto an ID card, each with its own features and risks:

- A magnetic strip is easy to read and copy.

- A bar code could also be swept by a wand and read, but if information is encrypted and authenticated, there will be too many bits to be read by a swipe. Something that can read a two-dimensional barcode will be needed instead.

- A proximity card is easy to read, and does not have to be removed from a wallet or purse to work. The next generation of embedded chips can hold enough bits to carry encryption and authentication data. Proximity cards can also be read without their holders knowing it—a way of clandestinely tracking holders who may otherwise avoid checkpoints. But this requires that people move past the checkpoint through a narrow opening such as a turnstile, and card-reading devices be powerful and sensitive enough to detect ID cards from a distance.

- If the card is engineered as a powered electronic device, as opposed to a passive conveyor of information, it can, itself, query the card-reading device and respond only to those specifically authorized to read a card (for example, the card may be used as a credit card and thus accessible to some merchants but not others and not to state policemen who ask for driver's licenses). In addition, a powered device with a keypad can permit messages to be digitally signed, and power requires an energy source, like batteries, which adds logistical complications (for example, batteries die).

National Identification Databases

If an identity card is a bridge into a database, then the contents of the database are what matter. Such a national identification database system would be organized by the alphanumeric of the national ID card holders. The database system would hold personal identification information about each national ID card holder, such as citizenship status and proof of citizenship (for example, birth certificate and naturalization papers) for holders.

The system would consist of four types of national identification databases that would hold: biometric data, checkpoint events, ancillary government data, and optional authentication features, such as a private digital signature key. Each database would be keyed to a person's unique alphanumeric.

Biometric Data

This database stores a combination of physical characteristics (for example, iris, face, fingerprints) or personal traits (for example, voice, signature) that can identify an individual, either within a restricted set or globally.

- As discussed in Chapter 4, a face is an example of a biometric, and photography can capture faces unobtrusively, or at least without great inconvenience. Photographs of people's faces are, however, somewhat limited as biometric identifiers because faces are not robust and not highly distinctive. In other words, they change over time (and sometimes unexpectedly) and are not unique. Many people look like each other (at least at the level of detail that characterize drivers licenses). How pictures are taken can influence what people look like because environmental factors come into play—lighting, shading, pose, movement, and more. The science of categorizing faces according to objective criteria (such as are entailed in facial recognition) is still developing. But, a face is still robust and distinctive enough to make a facial image a useful must because, at a minimum, it permits checkpoint authorities to visually verify that the person is holding the identity card he is supposed to hold).

■ As discussed in Chapter 6, a manually executed signature, like a photograph, is not globally unique but it has long been recognized by law and custom as a way to confirm one's identity. We are regularly asked to put our signature on a variety of documents. Putting a person's dynamic signature in a database would make it harder for people to masquerade as someone else with a similar enough face. It would also allow for cross comparisons when other checkpoint-related documents are signed (for example, the rental forms for the crop duster).

■ As discussed in Chapter 5, the human iris is a highly distinctive identifier. Collecting it deliberately involves looking at a camera from a short distance away, which requires cooperation from the subject. While somewhat of a "new" biometric, the iris, because of its inherent distinctiveness and robustness, has tremendous potential as a way individuals can easily establish or confirm their identity.

■ Fingerprints have long been recognized to be globally distinctive; they have long been used by law enforcement for identification. As explained in Chapters 3 and 17, the FBI has fingerprints (of the ten, rolled variety) on file for over 80 million people already (for example, 40 million in the IAFIS's Criminal Master File—as a result of individuals being arrested for felony offenses—and 40 million in the largely "paper" civil files, submission of finger prints being required as a condition of federal government employment, military service, or naturalized citizenship). As explained in detail in the upcoming section, "Biometric Data: Freezing Identity," the use of fingerprints is the only established, proven way to identify a person when searching against a large-scale database.

■ As discussed in Chapter 7, DNA, like fingerprints, is both globally distinctive and apt to be left behind. But the deliberate extraction of DNA is intrusive, controversial, and expensive. Moreover, at this juncture, no commercially viable DNA-based systems can find a match in near real-time. Given the other medical or health-related information that might be inferred from a DNA sample, compelling people to produce DNA will assuredly raise vehement policy and legal objections.

Biometrics will be used to verify the presented ID card, and there are limits to what biometric data can be collected easily. Capturing irises and collecting fingerprints require specialized devices, are modestly intrusive, and take little time. Fingerprint matching can be done fairly quickly, in part because rather than processing the entire latent print, the biometric fingerprint system extracts key features of the fingerprint to form a template, or computer readable series of zeroes and ones, that are unique to the fingerprint captured.

It is theoretically possible to take photographs at checkpoints, compare them to a database of possibilities, and identify people that way. Doing so reliably requires that environmental factors be strictly controlled: same pose for everyone under the same lighting and background conditions as the database photographs, and still needs to be checked by someone. At this stage of facial recognition's development, it is much more useful to compare a photograph against a small data set (hundreds) of possibilities than it is to compare it against a large set (hundreds of millions) required for automatic identification. Searching a face against millions of faces results in too many false matches (false positives, possibles), which would require extensive human intervention to resolve.

Biometric Data: Freezing Identity

A primary purpose of requiring biometrics is to make certain that national identification card holders have their identities frozen or fixed; they are not and cannot masquerade as another identity in the pool of ID card holders in the U.S. In other words, "One ID card holder, one identity." This use of biometrics is also referred to as negative identification, and is similar to the social services applications of biometrics as discussed in Chapter 13.

The following example illustrates freezing or fixing identity in the national ID context. John Doe, with supporting documentation, applies for his national ID card in Virginia where he has one issued. He then appears as Richard Roe with supporting documentation and applies for a national ID card in Kentucky. If only a check of the name is run to determine if the same person has previously applied for a card, no hit is made because John Doe does not match Richard Roe. John Doe/Richard Roe thus receives two national ID cards. By using a biometric capable of identification in a large-scale database, John Doe/Richard Roe would not be able to hide from the fact that he had applied for an ID card, because while John Doe/Richard Roe can fraudulently change his name and get fraudulent supporting documentation, he cannot so easily alter his biometric. When Richard Roe applies, his biometric would be taken and would match John Doe and his previous application in Virginia.

The use of the biometric is crystal clear in theory but the conceptual waters soon get muddied as reality intrudes. This use of a biometric to freeze a person's identity is not a silver bullet. It only freezes identity—terrorists and other ne'er-do-wells can still apply for and receive national ID cards. Also terrorists or other ne'er-do-wells can still apply for and receive national ID cards using an alias identity; however, they are effectively locked into only one identity whether it is their true name or their alias.

Moreover, to freeze identity effectively means that the U.S. government must collect biometrics from all citizens and other residents. The national identity card and biometric enrollment must be mandatory. Thus the U.S. government must confront difficult political and policy considerations because exempting certain people from this biometric enrollment requirement jeopardizes the security of the system. If Terry the Terrorist does not have to have a national ID card and provide a biometric to the USG, he won't. In effect, the identity freeze melts away.

A secondary purpose of requiring a biometric is to enable the U.S. government to search the biometric against a "watchlist" database consisting of undesirables, such as suspect terrorists and wanted criminals. A major drawback to this process is that the search only works if the database contains the biometric of the undesirables. However, watchlist data may be available. The FBI has a start with its IAFIS Criminal Master File, and a complete set of fingerprints for many wanted criminals is on record (from recidivism).

Given that every U.S. citizen and resident would have to apply for a card, the biometric database of cardholder applicants will become very large, very quickly: there are roughly 300 million citizens. This biometric database would become the world's largest biometric database. A major technical challenge presents itself: As the size of the database increases, the number of matching errors also increases. In a verification system, where the sample is compared only to the template corresponding to the claimed identity, false matches are rare, except in cases of forgery. However, in an identification system as proposed here, each cardholding applicant will have to be biometrically enrolled and searched for a match against a portion of the database (containing hundreds of millions of records). The chance of falsely matching at least one of them will be much higher than the single-match False Match Rate. A rough approximation of the False Match Rate (FMR) for the System is: $FMR(SYS) = N * FMR$, where N is the number of records (templates) in the database and FMR is the false match rate for a single comparison. (A more precise approximation is: $FMR(SYS) = 1-(1-FMR^m)^{P*N}$ where N is the number of records (templates) in the database, m is the number of measures for each individual enrolled, P is the penetration rate and FMR is the false match rate for a single comparison (assumed equal across all measures and users).)

As explained in Chapter 17, fingerprint-based biometric systems try to resolve this dilemma by reducing N, that is by subdividing the database to be searched so that only part of it must be searched. This subdivision is done by using a multistage classification process of "filtering" and/or "binning." Filtering uses external information (data not having to do with the actual fingerprint) to select the search set within the database. An example of a characteristic used for filtering is the gender of the person being identified. Binning is selection of potential matches based on information intrinsic to the fingerprint that can be readily detected (such as pattern types like loops, whorls, and arches). Ensemble matching is then performed. With ensemble matching, a set of independent samples (for example, fingerprints taken from four different fingers) is collected from each person being identified and is binned and filtered as a group, then matched against corresponding sets in the database. The net effect in many cases is to further reduce the number of potential matches to be considered (Wayman 1999, 35–48). This reduces the probability of a false match, and also reduces the processing time required to search the data set and thereby improves system responsiveness. The fraction of the database actually being tested for potential matches is called the *Penetration Rate*.

Error rate considerations are an absolutely critical factor in deciding the type of hard biometric to collect and how many of them to collect. Error rate considerations are a major reason why collection of ten rolled fingerprints is attractive to many experts. Using ten rolled fingerprints for a search against a large database results in fewer false matches (or false positives, "possibles," or "candidates" compared to using one or two fingerprints for the search.

Along these lines, the prestigious National Institute of Standards and Technology (NIST) has been conducting technical studies of error rate analysis over large-scale databases for "flat" prints compared to "rolled" prints, and "flat" prints compared to "flat" prints. Flat prints (or images) reveal the center of the finger and require only a minimum of unique identifying points. "Flats" are more often called "plain" or "simultaneous impressions"—and "slaps" by some experts.

Rolled prints capture unique identifying points on the entire finger surface area in order to collect the maximum number of unique identifying points. Strictly from an identification perspective, rolled prints are preferred because they give the system more data with which to work.

Collecting ten flats has been referred to by some as the "bop-bop-bop" technique (that is, touch one hand's fingers—touch both thumbs—touch the other hand's fingers). The "bop-bop-bop" collection process would be considerably faster than typical live scan (rolled) procedures. Also, flats tend to have less pressure distortion of friction ridge detail (though little fingers are often partially or completely missing in typical four-finger plain impressions). (Some minor technical adjustments could help, for example, finger separators or molded channels could be built into a special platen to reduce the need for software separation of friction ridge detail "running together" from adjacent fingers and the need for strong software logic to decipher which finger is the middle, ring, etc.) However, while many subject matter experts are optimistic about the use of ten flats, there is currently no authoritative U.S. government finding that the use of x number of flat prints would achieve desirable results for searching large-scale databases and searching watchlist database containing partial latent fingerprints. NIST is working on such a study.

In this context, if one is serious about establishing a national identification card system, these questions must be answered:

- What biometric(s) should be used to enable one-to-many searching against a large-scale database (containing upwards of 3 billion fingerprints representing 300 million individuals)?
- Can we successfully use 2, 4, X, 10 (flat or rolled) fingerprints or 1 or 2 irises, or other biometircs, for searching against a large-scale database of this size to freeze identity within acceptable performance parameters?

- Can we successfully use 2, 4, X, 10 (flat or rolled) fingerprints or 1 or 2 irises, or other biometrics, for searching against a watchlist database containing partial latent fingerprints of undesirables? What is the trade-off of using ten flats for this searching as opposed to ten rolled?

- Depending on the answers to the above and faced with the prospect of collecting biometric data from hundreds of millions of individuals, what specific biometrics and technologies should be used?

Checkpoint Events

Records of who was where when are the *raison d'être* of the database. Individual checkpoints may also contain other information. One that controlled access to the transportation of hazardous materials may well indicate which and how much hazardous material and what kind of vehicles (and with their license numbers) were involved.

Although there is shortage of neither imagination nor storage to support a limitless selection of checkpoints, after some point there is a shortage of rationale. Insofar as the purpose is to inhibit terrorism (and other comparable crimes), checkpoints ought to be those that either restrict access to potentially dangerous objects, sensitive sites (for example, the Hoover Dam), or transactions possibly associated with terrorist activities. They should be few enough so that it is plausible for someone who did not wish to present a card to go about everyday business, albeit of a restricted sort, for weeks or months at a time.

Events on or since September 11 suggest that a national ID card could be presented to:

- Travel on airlines, trains, and ships (requiring it for mass transit is probably too intrusive)

- Cross international borders

- Rent or acquire certain machinery, notably planes, ships, and trucks (but would it be too intrusive to require it for auto rental?)

- Purchase certain chemicals and certain other products

- Transfer very large quantities of cash and for other financial transactions

- Enter certain parts of government buildings (but likely not required for accessing government buildings such as tax offices and courts)

- Register for university, college, and other educational programs (many non-citizens are in the U.S. on student visas; not all of them show up at their schools), and perhaps on random days, to enter school

In practical terms, many of these checkpoints already exist in some form and already require some sort of identification (a driver's license, social security number, or passport) to engage in the checkpoint event (air travel, large cash transfers, or crossing international borders). So, the major change would be the transition from any easily obtainable, easily forged ID card to one that is much harder to forge and can be recorded to a database. That is, the physical act of showing identification would not change much; the permanence and reliability of the act would.

Extending the list of checkpoints further may expose sensitivities. If "certain other products" were interpreted to include firearms, for instance, it would be far easier to facilitate their registration (so gun advocates would be horrified) but a background check could be run in real-time (so advocates of a waiting period for firearm purchase would not be able to hide behind the background check requirement).

Finally, if the national ID card is used to restrict access to certain sites or permit authorities to be alerted to the presence of a suspect individual, this information also needs to be kept in a database (even if the primary purpose of the database is to refresh local CRDs periodically).

Ancillary Government Data

A national ID card may also be used to limit fraud in entitlement programs, validate employment eligibility, and license drivers.

Whether or not it is so used ought to make little difference for its use against terrorism and similar crimes. Rarely are these latter uses associated with terrorism; while Mohammed Atta had a bench warrant for driving without a license, so do millions of nonterrorists. More often than not, they are not even associated with everyday violent crime. But, in all three cases, a unique national ID card serves legitimate public policy purposes such as:

- Minimizing duplicate benefits payments
- Restricting illegal immigration
- Preventing people whose license is revoked in one state from getting one in another state

The more uses to which a single identification number is put, the broader a dossier the authorities can compile on any one individual. Are there ways to shield those who object from unwarranted scrutiny while serving the public policy interests of fraud reduction, immigration control, or public safety?

Many public-sector jobs require a background check and submission of fingerprints and are thus legitimate checkpoint events (since it adds very little to what is already an intrusive process that citizens voluntary undergo). Should a person's being hired for a private-sector job also be a checkpoint event for a national ID card check? Mid-1990s concerns over illegal immigration, did, in fact, drive an earlier wave of proposals for a mandatory national ID card system. Mandating a national ID card would make it difficult for employers of illegal aliens to claim that they broke the law inadvertently since their hiring had to be correlated with some identification presentation. On-the-job presentation would require that all employers own CRDs, which would add to business costs. Alternatively, a government office or other designated party could validate a job-seeker's ID card, confirm his legal status, and then send a validated message to the prospective employer. This message could tie the job-seeker's ID to a biometric, like a photograph.

A currently existing checkpoint event such as claiming benefits for any number of entitlement programs could be made a checkpoint event requiring presentation of a national ID card as well. A claimant could present a national ID card or submit to ID enrollment and biometric collection at the time of claimancy. A request-for-benefits code and an alphanumeric would be forwarded to a relevant database. The database would indicate whether or not the card is valid and whether or not the claim ought to be honored (for example, a duplicate application exists). The benefits office registers the claimant with an ID number that is either the alphanumeric itself, or if the claimant objects, a separate identification alphanumeric (such as JohnDoe0017886MDUC) unique to the benefits office. For these latter applicants, the benefits office never sees the true alphanumeric; however, some central database does record the local ID number (as well as the issuing office code to remove inadvertent duplication between offices). Also, a central database would record other transactional events such as changes in claimancy (for example, a person went off welfare).

Similar procedures could govern driver's licenses. People present their national ID card to the state department of motor vehicles, a cross-check is run against a national database that would contain public safety information from all the U.S. states and territories (for example, to determine license status, outstanding warrants). To protect citizen sensitivities, those who object to having their alphanumeric on the license are issued a license number with a separate driver's license ID; only a national database can correlate the two. A policeman who pulls over an errant driver would see either a national ID card with an alphanumeric embossed on it (and which can be taken to a card-reading device if fraud is suspected) or a regular driver's license. The national ID card, of course, would not include the information normally found on driver's licenses, but such information can be readily retrieved from digital cell phones or laptop computers (if kept up to date). Here, the national ID facilitates the issuing of drivers licenses but isn't a driver's license.

General Tenets

There is no requirement that biometric identification and checkpoint events need be kept in the same database or by the same institution; it suffices only that they be indexed by a person's unique alphanumeric. The same holds true for other information. A global database of educational credentials and licenses could, if needs arise, be kept by a third institution. It is the indexing that matters. And indexing is a major operational concern because many government agencies have been known to garble or otherwise incorrectly report and record data in their charge. Consistent indexing and correlation is an anti-error record integrity mechanism.

Finally, common sense dictates that the biometrics database and the access control database are:

- Housed on nonstop servers with enough processing and networking power to communicate to checkpoints and legitimate queries without undue delay (they may have to be cached locally to serve overseas users)

- Backed up and, if necessary, distributed so they can function in the event of physical damage, network outages, or computer attacks (including denial-of-service attacks)

In other words, they should be comparable to the information systems that validate credit cards on a now-routine basis. Nevertheless, the enormity of these technical challenges should not be underestimated.

Optional Authentication Features

A national ID card would be even more useful (and it would mollify those who would carry such a card) if it could be used for general authentication substituting credit cards, driver's licenses, concealed carry permits for firearms, health information, membership cards, electronic purses, and more. Since the alphanumeric on the ID card would be encrypted, those who would use the alphanumeric for collateral purposes have to make it generally readable—as long as the choice of whether to hand it over remains private (similar strictures apply to social security cards; alas, such strictures are not universally understood and people give out such information freely).

The national ID card does not need to indicate which credit cards or membership groups the user belongs to. But if these groups use unique alphanumerics to indicate membership then tendering a reliable alphanumeric should permit it to be read and compared to the database (issuers, of course, will need either network connections or a physical store of numbers to verify this fact, but this is no different than what is already routinely done for credit card purchases).

The card could even hold a user's digital signature, which would work much as the government's digital signature would. Applying the card electronically to a message (or providing a keypad on the card that would permit a message to be generated) would validate the message (for example, "I agree to pay $50 for this shirt.") better than a manually executed signature does.

Cards get stolen, and some protection must be in place that prevents the thief from making off with goods and services and saddling cardholders with the bill. For this reason, the last few bytes of the private key should be supplied by the user (as a PIN is) rather than on the card itself. A stolen card whose photograph does not match the face of the thief is normally of limited use—assuming merchants are honest. But since the whole purpose of a digital signature is to permit users to commit to payment via a signed bit-string and some merchants are not honest or conduct e-commerce, some PIN is required. This requirement will not end fraud; PINs can be copied during use or users can be coerced into yielding them—but it should help, especially if there is a robust way to communicate to the database that the private key has been compromised.

A lost or stolen card would generally require that the user get a new private key, an act that requires personal validation, but the alphanumeric would stay the same. Such a card must be revoked if the user is to no longer assume responsibility for the debts (and other actions) incurred by its use. Perhaps a phone call that supplied an alphanumeric and a PIN should suffice to get the card suspended for a while followed by a more authenticated revocation process. Fraudulent revocation can be reversed in a similar fashion. Revocation can be instantly applicable and communicated in subsequent calls to the database by a vendor.

Finally a national database would hold a record of all public keys (in some cases several keys for users who opted for multiple keys to serve multiple purposes). It is critical that access to these latter records is separate from access to the mandatory records. Many people are likely to ask for the public key to check whether transactions are legitimate. Mandatory records are of legitimate interest only to a specified few.

Verifying the ID Process

It is highly desirable that the information in the national ID card be complemented by a set of bytes that authenticates what it contains and is encrypted so that it can be read only by those authorized to do so.

The standard technique for authenticating the card is a digital signature. In this case, the government's private key, a digitized photograph on the card, and the alphanumeric are inserted into an algorithm that generates a signature byte-string. Anyone who knows the government's public key can insert the key with the byte-string into a second algorithm, which then generates the original personal ID and the photograph. Attempts to change the alphanumeric, the photograph or both would reveal a mismatch with the byte-string. This process works because private keys and their associated public keys are unique to each other. Knowing the private key permits one to derive the public key, but it is computationally infeasible to derive the private key from the public key. Success at using the decoding algorithm establishes that only someone with the government's private key could have linked the picture and the alphanumeric. Authentication can permit local card-reading devices without network access to limit fraud. This method, however, requires some way of reading the card that can transfer more bits than is currently possible with proximity card readers.

It does no good to authenticate the card, itself, if the process by which the photograph (as well as other biometrics) and alphanumeric are associated can be spoofed—that is, the branch office that sent the data to the federal government is negligent or complicit with a phony enrollment process. To date, the enrollment process to get U.S. passports appears to be a rarely defrauded way of associating a photograph with a unique identity. In electronic terms, various passport offices would have to capture the information, sign it with their own private key, send it to a central source that would verify the original source of the information, take the information itself, and then sign it with its own private key. That signature machine would have to be tightly guarded. Overseas users (with certain exceptions discussed later), would undergo a similar process to get U.S. visas, which would be, in effect, their identification cards. There is an unavoidable tradeoff between the number of such collection points and their reliability. The more locations, the easier it is for citizens and travelers to get their cards. However, with more locations comes a greater chance that one of them is sloppy or corrupt—the terrorists may well seek out such offices for precisely that reason. Security can be raised by double-signing all collections and carefully guarding signature machines, but not without cost and hassle. The bottom line is that as the number of enrollment points increases, the reliability of the entire system becomes more problematic.

People who get duplicate alphanumerics may break the correlation among suspicious events or among suspect relationships (since, with duplicate alphanumerics, events would appear to refer to different people). Attempts to deny people access or privileges on the basis of past events could be defeated by someone who carries a card—and thus an identity—which is much cleaner. Here biometrics capable of identification help. When an applicant tries to enroll into the identity card system, his biometric would be captured and that biometric record would be checked against the entire set of ID card holders for any possible match in a "one to many" search (1:N). The larger the global database, the more difficult it is to do this large-scale search cleanly.

So while the danger still exists that John Doe can use a forged birth certificate to fraudulently enroll in the national identification card system as Richard Roe, Doe cannot create any more false aliases or go back to being John Doe because his biometric records are indelibly associated with Richard Roe. Further, if John Doe had ever been arrested as John Doe and had his fingerprints entered into the system, then his attempt at creating an alias identity (Richard Roe) would be stopped in its tracks because the fingerprint match done at enrollment would find him out.

Preventing non-citizens from claiming to be U.S. citizens will also prove problematic. Even with over eighty million fingerprints on file (a little over half are currently IAFIS-like searchable), which leaves six times as many Americans without them. In theory, a claim of citizenship can be backed up with a copy of a stolen or fraudulent birth certificate. This, in practice, does not seem to be much of a problem with the passport process (although with so many things associated with a national ID card, the incentive to commit fraud would increase). Collecting biometric information for non-citizens (all of whom, by definition, are born else-where) before they come into the United States makes it possible for subsequent biometric matching to defeat the birth certificate ruse. This does not solve the problem of those who are already in the United States at the time of initial en-rollment or who sneaked past borders controls by entering the U.S. surrepti-tiously through its relatively porous border. The U.S. government might collect and photograph birth certificates from state and local authorities in order to pick out invented documents (by their absence from the official records), sub-tract records of death certificates to prevent another avenue of fraud, and ask for information on schooling (most schools these days have some sort of student pictures) for those who generate suspicion. But this effort is Herculean.

Enrolling a non-citizen (for example, through the visa process) and giving them an alphanumeric still does not capture a person's true history back home—absent overseas tracking based, perhaps, on reliable biometric data. This was a problem with the nineteen hijackers. Who they said they were is known; who they actually were before coming to the United States is, in many cases, a matter of dispute. For non-citizens the quality of the existing history is related to how well-documented their lives were in the past, and such informa-tion may only be relevant to the small percentage of non-citizens that merit in-vestigation. For citizens a lot depends on the age at which people would get national identity cards. Until people can legally drive or sign a contract there are limits to how much large-scale mischief they can assist in; those that do cross the law are photographed and fingerprinted in any case.

Critical Issues

Now for the potential show-stopping issues. This section addresses:

- Transition and enrollment
- Protection of information
- Consequences of inevitable faults
- Costs
- Reciprocity with other countries
- Mission creep

Transition and Enrollment Issues

This national identity system has three primary components: ID cards, an ID registry, and a system of checkpoints. None now exist, except for bits and pieces of the registry. Normally, trying to bring three components up simultaneously—one of which requires public compliance and the other corporate compliance (for example, those who rent crop dusters)—well in advance of effective results is daunting to say the least. But it is not impossible.

The target population (largely non-citizens), for instance, already gets some sort of U.S. government–issued identification cards (for example, visas—but see below). Upgrading the quality of these documents is a modest step; improving the quality and collecting biometric information along with the issuing U.S. passports (which have a ten-year update cycle) could be done. Holders of government identification cards (government employees and contractors) could follow shortly behind. Such cards could then be read at points of entry with little further ado. Starting small is also important to gain an understanding of how well the system works as well as its likely costs, error rates, and reliability.

Granted, for a time, there will be people passing existing checkpoints (for example, boarding airlines) without national ID cards. Thus, non-citizens may be tempted to count themselves among them. Until such time as having such cards is mandatory (at least for passing the specified checkpoints), terrorists or criminals may be inhibited by biometric collection that can be matched against a database of the holder population. This, however, will not catch people who sneak into the United States from over the border (or in the bellies of freighters) and do not have visas, passports, or employee ID cards.

As the number of checkpoints and the population of national ID holders grow, each will drive the other; both, in turn will increase the number of institutions who choose to use the one common ID card (and keep their own membership data based on alphanumerics). This will further encourage people to get ID cards who otherwise have little expectation of traversing checkpoints.

Protection of Information

Inherent in an ID system meant to monitor non-citizens and those under legal constraint (such as warrant, arrest, parole, declaration of mental incompetence) is the promise that the movements of ordinary citizens should not routinely become matters of additional governmental scrutiny. Such distinctions leave behind the issue of whether it is fair and/or constitutional for judges to assume that any criminal sentence brings with it the categorization as someone whose movements are to be recorded forever after. However, laws requiring convicted child molesters to register their location with the police and laws that publicize this type of information achieve a measure of categorization that society by and large seems to embrace.

Protecting everyone else from unnecessary scrutiny—both governmental and private sector—requires some way of preventing checkpoint records from growing willy-nilly. One way is to acquire data on everyone, pick out those who are not to be monitored and either withhold such contact information from the database or send it into that part of the database that can only be looked at through a legal procedure (such as under a court order).

Withholding the information has problems. The card-reading device may have no way of telling who is in which category; the database (or a device fed by the database) has to. Embedding such information in the alphanumeric (for example, non-citizens and others get a different code) means that people who can be monitored at some points in their life and ought not be monitored at other points would need two different alphanumerics. Generating that second alphanumeric would inform recipients that they are under suspicion (and would thus be self-defeating). More importantly, there will be reason to go back into the file and collect information on people (for example, those under suspicion or are applying for a sensitive job) who previously were not of interest. Keeping such data can also reveal whether someone is trying to use the national ID card of someone in the restricted database—when they were spotted at two distant places at roughly the same time.

Ascertaining that restricted information is not put into the less-restricted database may be a challenge, but it could be met by several means, such as:

- Entrusting both databases to a bureaucracy that has no vested interest in unwarranted disclosure

- Permitting auditing by ombudsmen trusted by people who do not trust the government, but who are trusted by the government to keep data confidential

- Penalizing deliberate violations of privileged databases

Such protection only goes so far; some trust in the probity of government combined with the law of large numbers (any widespread subversion is bound to leak out) will, realistically, be required to ensure that safeguards are followed.

Faults

Systems are rarely fault-free, and faults, invariably, have consequences. Four types of faults—bad records, improperly revealed information, inoperative networks, and CRDs—are worth noting.

Bad records are a problem when people make bad decisions based on them. One argument against mandating IDs for employment (so as to discourage illegal immigration) is that a one percent error rate would keep a million legal Americans out of work while problems were fixed (compared to an estimated population of two to three million employable illegal aliens). The system discussed here will also inevitably contain errors, both in registering people and in tracking their whereabouts. The best that can be said is that the consequences of those errors will be mitigated by the fact that at least tracking will be largely automated (proper systems design convert some ambiguous errors into obvious ones). The consequences of error are also softened insofar as the purpose of collecting checkpoint information is more to suggest (for example, that a person may be engaged in suspicious activity) than decide (for example, to give someone access or not).

By one estimate, one percent of all data guardians are tempted to leak information. With a comprehensive database built atop a national ID system, there is more information to reveal and hackers will be incentivized to break in and cyberterrorists to destroy. But since most of it is a record of events that are public anyway, few of which are *per se* embarrassing, the potential for greater harm is limited. Also, getting information on U.S. citizens (not under court jurisdiction) from checkpoint files can and should be strictly guarded, in much the same way that other sensitive systems are (for example, by access controls, presentation of valid warrants, and logs).

As a general principle, except for a handful of people permitted to scan the database to ensure the integrity of the software, every request for information should be based on the following:

- Through a specific logged query that requests a yes/no answer (for example, to test for fraud)

- For permission to transfer a record from sensitive to general files upon presentation of a warrant (for example, for arrest or pursuant to a judge's ordered change-of-status)

- To execute software to check for a specific pattern of activities that may predict a major crime and based on specific warrants

- To scan a person's record to look for errors on checkpoint events, a power granted to a very select group of people (computers can do much of the work) and, which, in turn, may perhaps not be returned in electronic (and thus easily collated) form

Networks and equipment fail. In most cases, network failures mean only that real-time information has to be replaced by storing information on-site and releasing it once the network returns. In other cases, network failures may make it difficult to validate cardholders against network-stored biometrics, which may lead to some people being denied access to services or places. The same holds for card-reading device failures, which may result in no one being checked and, in some cases, denied access for everyone—so throughput issues must be carefully considered.

Costs

The costs of a national ID system can only be guessed at this time. Advocates of national identity cards usually low-ball their estimates at the five-to-twenty dollars a head level, but consider:

- The national ID card itself has more embedded technology than its paper counterparts

- This national ID card is likely to have a great deal more biometric information behind it and would be required to perform phenomenal and unprecedented identification searching of 100's of millions of records

- The costs of card-reading devices and stations, networking costs, and database creation, operation, and maintenance must be factored in

- Large systems rarely come in under budget

Offsetting such costs is the potential of a national ID system to consolidate and rationalize not only federal, state, and local databases but also private ones. Yet, as long as there are many cases where presentation of an ID (for example, to policemen, benefit workers, and hospital clerks) is voluntary, government agencies will not be able to abandon alternative indexing schemes altogether. Cost savings will depend, in large part, on what percentage of citizens choose to make their alphanumeric broadly available, and what percentage insist on other (prior) arrangements for drivers' licenses, benefits claimancy, credit cards, and memberships. Similarly, the savings to the private sector will also depend on this percentage, which in turn will influence how many such entities are willing to piggyback on the optional features of the ID card as opposed to retaining their own separate system for all members.

Reciprocity

Not surprisingly, a national identification system designed to track citizens of other countries has international ramifications. Canadians do not need passports to come to the United States and most Europeans do not need visas. What do they use for ID cards? How standardized must ID systems be across countries? What data should be shared with foreign countries (and with which ones)? Might the standards, technologies, and databases established for a U.S. national ID system facilitate authoritarianism overseas? Would an ID card from a country whose citizens can enter the United States without a visa suffice as an alternative to a U.S.–issued ID? Many difficult questions remain to be answered.

Reliability

Foreign identity documents would have to meet U.S. standards for authentication and for the capture of biometric information. Unfortunately, it takes only one corrupt civil servent to issue such an identity document to create a loophole for terrorists. Plugging such holes may require the United States to make controversial distinctions among foreign nations.

Globally Unique Identification

No foreigner should have more than one alphanumeric. This rule not only requires foreign countries to have the biometric systems that can catch duplications, but also they need to be willing and able to check applicants against the files of other countries based on such biometrics. This means that every country has to collect at least one globally unique biometric.

Confidentiality

If the United States is going to insist that other nations make compatible identity cards, these nations will likely insist on being able to read U.S. national ID cards as well, and not only physically but also cryptographically (since the cards are encoded to inhibit casual perusal). If these countries are given the U.S. decryption key (or keys, if multiplied as above) then they must protect the key (or keys) as well as they are protected here. Alternatively, those who go abroad can have an additional alphanumeric encoded into their card, the key to which is provided to foreign countries. If that key is compromised and it wafts back to the United States (as is likely) then those people with an alternative alphanumeric may be subject to ID checks by unauthorized persons. For those who go overseas, a second ID card (or a third) that contains a second alphanumeric would solve the problem.

Data sharing is another issue. Terrorism is an international problem; the plot against the World Trade Center and Pentagon was apparently hatched in Germany (and supported by travel through Spain, Malaysia, and other countries). The United States would be helped if non-citizens were monitored in friendly states and the data shared—but then the United States must be prepared to share data as well. Can the United States trust that other nations would adhere to similar standards of data confidentiality and appropriateness? Perhaps, again, with traditional allies, this is a minor issue; Europeans complain about lax U.S. data privacy regimes. But even close allies have different mores; certain speech acts are crimes in France and Germany but are considered protected speech here.

The real problem comes if a U.S. national ID system were to enable malevolent regimes to control their population better. Merely the fact that people who travel to the United States (or, perhaps, also Europe, etc.) have electronically readable cards may make it easier for foreigners to demand to read these so that cardholders (many of whom may be mere dissidents) can be tracked more efficiently. If the United States demands intelligence from unsavory countries to fight terrorism, can it resist demands that it provide checkpoint data collected here on what the oh-so-helpful regime considers their enemies (for example, dissidents)?

Mission Creep

The possibility remains that even a national ID system based on certain privacy-protecting rules and designs would make it that much easier to evolve into an ID system with less protection.

Such an argument invites three responses:

■ One can reject outright any attempt to judge policy not by what it is but by what it can become, and the latter is pure speculation

■ One can maintain that the country's dense fabric and long history of civil liberties and civil rights provide considerable protection against abuse

■ One can meet the argument head on and assess those features of a national ID system that dispose it toward or away from mission creep.

Clearly, a national database and a reliable alphanumeric identifier *do* permit a national identity system program to grow. Biometrics change slowly if at all; therefore, once a national database is amassed, it has considerable persistence from one year to the next, and it can be turned to many ancillary ends. Similarly, once the work has been done to build a unique authenticated alphanumeric, the uses to which it can be put (for example, to order education, benefits, employment, and health records) represent a considerable temptation. Neither of these expansions requires the national ID card itself; the database suffices.

When it comes to the ID card, however, some persistence against mission creep can be engineered into the national ID card itself, notably the lack of a visible alphanumeric and the requirement that the alphanumeric be difficult to read (because it requires decryption electronics). One saving grace would be the cost and hassle of recalling and reissuing easy-to-read cards once a population of hard-to-read cards was universal. Ultimately, politics and psychology will determine mission creep. Making changes in the national ID card's use a matter of federal legislation (rather than administration regulation) can publicize any attempt at mission creep. If people buy into a national ID because their promised scope is limited, and then this trust is violated, negative public reaction may squelch mission creep. Conversely, if people get used to being in a database, as well as owning and carrying ID cards (even if only required for checkpoint access), perhaps missions will creep unimpeded and that may not be good policy either.

Part VI

Appendixes

place index finger in window

Appendix A

Resources

Chapter 1

Adams, and Sasse. "Users Are Not the Enemy." *Communications of the ACM.* 42, no. 12 (December 1999).

Anderson, and Kuhn. "Tamper Resistance—A Cautionary Note." Proceedings of the Second USENIX Workshop on Electronic Commerce. 1996. Berkeley: USENIX Association.

Brittain, and Paquet. "The Cost of a Nonautomated Help Desk." Research Note DF-14-7228. Gartner, Inc. January 14, 2002.

Computer Emergency Response Team. "Advisory CA-1994-01: Ongoing Network Monitoring Attacks." February 3, 1994.

Denning, Dorothy. 1994. *Information Warfare and Security.* Boston: Addison-Wesley.

Junkel, Richard. 1999. "Hand Geometry Based Verification." *Biometrics: Personal Identification in Networked Society.* Jain, Bolle, and Pankanti, eds. Boston: Kluwer Academic Publishers.

Smith, Richard E. "The Strong Password Dilemma." *CSI Computer Security Journal.* Summer 2002. http://www.smat.us/sanity/.

Smith, Richard E. 2002. *Authentication: From Passwords to Public Keys.* Boston: Addison-Wesley.

Thalheim, Krissler, and Ziegler. "Body Check." *c't* magazine. 11 (2002): 114. http://www.heise.de/ct/english/02/11/114/.

U.S. General Accounting Office. "Identity Fraud: Information on Prevalence, Cost, and Internet Impact Is Limited." Report GAO/GGD-98-100BR. May 1998.

U.S. General Accounting Office. "Identity Fraud: Prevalence and Cost Appear to Be Growing." Report GAO-02-363. March 2002.

Wilkes, Maurice. 1968. *Time-sharing Computer Systems.* London: Macdonald.

Chapter 3

ANSI Standard For Forensic Identification. Automated Fingerprint Identification Systems. Glossary of Terms and Acronyms. October 6, 1988.

Beavin, Colin. 2001. *Fingerprints: The Origin of Crime Detection and the Murder Case That Launched Forensic Science."* New York: Hyperion.

Cole, Simon. 2001. *Suspect Identities: A History of Fingerprinting and Criminal Investigation.* Harvard University Press.

Faulds, Henry. "Skin Furrows of the Hand." *Nature.* xxii, 1880.

Galton, Francis. 1892/1965. *Finger Prints.* London: Macmillan and Co./New York: De Capo Press.

Jain, Anil, L. Hong, S. Pankanti, and R. Bolle, eds. "An Identity-Authentication System Using Fingerprints." Proceedings of the IEEE. vol. 85, no. 9 (September 1997): 1365.

Lee, Henry C., and R. E. Gaensslen, eds. 1991. *Advances in Fingerprint Technology.* Elsevier.

Newcombe, Tod. "Finger Imaging Points to Welfare Savings." *Government Technology.* 1996. http://www.govtech.net/magazine/gt/1996/apr/welfare/welfare .phtml.

Sodhi, G. S., and Jasjeet Kaur. "On Henry's Fingerprint Classification System." *Fingerprint Whorld.* 28, no. 110 (October 2002): 200.

Trauring, Mitchell. "On the Automatic Comparison of Finger Ridge Patterns for Personal-Identity Verification." *Nature.* 197, no. 4871 (1963): 938.

Chapter 4

Alivin, Martin, and Mark Przybocki. "The NIST Speaker Recognition Evaluations: 1996–2001." National Institute of Standards and Technology. Gaithersburg, MD. 2001.

ANSI/NIST-CSL. "Data Format for the Exchange of Fingerprint, Facial, and Scars Marks and Tattoo (SMT) Information." ANSI/NIST-CSL 1a-2000 (Amendment). 2000.

Burrows, Tina-Louise. 1996. *Speech Processing with Linear and Neural Network Models.* Cambridge, U.K.: Cambridge University Engineering Department.

Choudhury, T. "Current State of the Art." January 2000. http://www-white .media.mit.edu/tech-reports/TR-516/node8.html.

Cole, Ron, et al. "Survey of the State of the Art in Human Language Technology." Web Edition. Cambridge University Press and Giardini. 1997.

DoD CounterDrug FERET. http://www.dodcounterdrug.com/facialrecognition/FERET/feret.htm.

Dottington, G., W. Liggett, A. Martin, M. Przybocki, and D. Reynolds. "Sheep, Goats, Lambs and Wolves: An Analysis of Individual Differences in Speaker Recognition." NIST Speech Group. http://www.nist.gov/speech/tests/spk/1998/icslp_98/sld001.htm.

Fant, Gunnar. "Acoustic Theory of Speech Production." 1960. The Hague, Netherlands: Mouton and Co.

Fejfar, A., and W. Haberman. "Automatic Identification of Personnel Through Speaker and Signature Verification—System Description and Testing." Proceedings of Carnahan Conference on Crime Countermeasures." July 1977. Oxford, U.K.

History of the [MIT] Speech Communications Group. http://web.mit.edu/speech/www/history.html.

IBM ViaVoice. http://www-3.ibm.com/software/speech/.

Jebara, T. "3D Pose Estimation and Normalization for Face Recognition." Center for Intelligent Machines. McGill University. 1995. http://web.media.mit.edu/~jebara/uthesis/thesis.html.

Matthew, T., and A. Pentland. "Eigenfaces for Recognition." *Journal of Cognitive Neuroscience*. 3, no. 1 (1991): 71–86.

Minsky, M., and S. Papert. 1969. *Perceptrons*. Cambridge, MA: MIT Press.

NIST FERET database. http://www.itl.nist.gov/iad/humanid/feret/.

Microsoft. "Office XP Speaks Out: Voice Recognition Assists Users." http://www.microsoft.com/PressPass/features/2001/apr01/04-18xpspeech.asp.

Ostermann, J. "Animation of Synthetic Faces in MPEG-4." *Computer Animation*. Philadelphia, Pennsylvania. (June 8–10, 1998): 49–51.

Penev, P., and J. Atick. "Local Feature Analysis: A General Statistical Theory for Object Representation." *Network: Computation in Neural Systems*. 7 (1996): 477–500.

Phillips, P. J., P. Rauss, and S. Der. "FacE REcognition Technology (FERET). Recognition Algorithm Development and Test Report, ARL-TR-995." 1996. United States Army Research Laboratory.

Phillips, P., H. Wechsler, J. Huang, and P. Rauss. "The FERET Database and Evaluation Procedure for Face Recognition Algorithms." *Image and Vision Computing*. 16, no. 5 (1998): 295–306.

Scansoft, Inc. http://scansoft.com/.

Smithsonian Speech Synthesis History Project. http://www.mindspring.com/~ssshp/ssshp_cd/ss_ibm.htm#TASS2.

SpeakerKeyFAQ (ITT Industries), http://www.biometrics.org/REPORTS/SpeakerKeyFAQ.html.

Suzuki, M., and S. Kitamoto. United States Patent No. 4,054,749 (issued 18 October 1977). Method for Verifying Identity or Difference by Voice. Washington D.C.: U.S. Government Printing Office.

The NIST Speech Group. http://www.nist.gov/speech/index.htm.

The VoiceXML Forum. http://www.voicexml.org/.

Wechsler H., P.J. Phillips, V. Bruce, S.F. Fogelman, and T.S. Huang, eds. "Face Recognition: From Theory to Applications." NATO ASI Series. Springer-Verlag. 1998.

Chapter 5

Daugman, J. "How Iris Recognition Works." 1998. University of Cambridge. http://www.cl.cam.ac.uk/users/jgd1000/irisrecog.pdf.

Daugman, J. "John Daugman's Webpage, Cambridge University, Computer Laboratory." 1998–2002. http://www.cl.cam.ac.uk/~jgd1000/.

Daugman, J. United States Patent No. 5,291,560 (issued 1 March 1994). Biometric Personal Identification System Based on Iris Analysis. Washington D.C.: U.S. Government Printing Office.

Defense Advance Research Projects Agency. "Iris Recognition at a Distance (IPTO Project with Sarnoff Corporation)." 2001. http://www.darpa.mil/ipto/psum2001/M237-0.html.

EyeDentify Corporation. Wommelgem, Belgium. 2002. http://www.eye-dentify.com/.

EyeTicket Corpration. McLean, Virginia. "EyeTicket Corporation Webpage." 1997–2002. http://www.eyeticket.com.

Flom, L., and A. Safir. United States Patent No. 4,641,349 (issued 3 February 1987). Iris Recognition System. Washington D.C.: U.S. Government Printing Office.

Iridian Technologies, Inc. "KnowWho Authentication Server, Product Specifications." 2001. http://www.iridiantech.com/.

Mansfield, T. "Biometric Authentication in the Real World." The National Physical Laboratory (NPL) Center for Mathematics and Scientific Computing. 2001. Middlesex, United Kingdom.

Mansfield, T., G. Kelly, D. Chandler, and J. Kane. "Biometric Product Testing Final Report." 2001. The National Physical Laboratory (NPL), Center for Mathematics and Scientific Computing. Middlesex, United Kingdom.

Orkand Corporation. "Personal Identifier Project: Final Report." April 1990. State of California Department of Motor Vehicles Report DMV88-89. Reprinted by the U.S. National Biometric Test Center.

Retinal Technologies, Incorporated. http://www.retinaltech.com/.

University of Albany Library. "Finding Aid for the Carleton P. Simon Papers, 1881–1952, 1956 (APAP-073)." December 16, 1988. http://library.albany.edu/speccoll/findaids/apap073.htm.

Medical References

Diabetic Retinopathy. http://www.stlukeseye.com/Conditions/DiabeticRetinopathy.asp.

FA Hall of Fame. http://www.pasadenaeye.com/faq/faq10/faq10_rose_ text .html.

Fluorescein angiogram (FA). http://www.stlukeseye.com/eyeq/FluoresceinAngiogram.asp.

Fluorescein Angiography movie. http://www.opsweb.org/Op-Photo/Angio/FAMovie/FAMovie.htm.

Fluorescein Angiography. http://www.pasadenaeye.com/faq/faq10/faq10_text.html.

Ophthalmic Fluorescein and Indocyanine Green Angiography. http://www.vrmny.com/angiography.htm.

Chapter 6

Ali, F., and R. Pavlidis. "Syntactic Recognition of Hand-written Numerals." IEEE Transactions on Systems, Man, and Cybernetics. 7, no. 7 (1977).

Boldridge, A.G., and R.W. Freund. United States Patent No. 4,035,768 (issued 12 July 1977). Personal Identification Apparatus. Assigned to Veripen Incorporated, New York, New York. CynerSign Inc. http://www.cadix.com.my/products/csign/cybersign.html.

Fejfar, A., and W. Haberman. "Automatic Identification of Personnel Through Speaker and Signature Verification—System Description and Testing," Proceedings of Carnahan Conference on Crime Countermeasures." July 1977. Oxford, U.K.

Gaines, R., W. Lisowski, S. Press, and N. Shapiro. "Authentication by Keystroke Timing, RAND Report R-256-NSF." 1980. RAND Corporation.

Gupta, G., and A. McCabe. "A Review of Dynamic Handwritten Signature Verification." 1997. James Cook University. Townsville, Australia.

Interlink Electronics, Inc. http://www.interlinkelec.com.

Joyce, R., and G. Gupta. "Identity Authentication Based on Keystroke Latencies." Communications of the ACM 33. (February 1990): 168–176.

Leclerc, F., and R. Plamondon. "Automatic Signature Verification: The State of the Art—1989–1993." International Journal on Pattern Recognition and Artificial Intelligence. 8, no. 3 (1994): 643–660.

Leggett, J., and G. Williams. "Verifying Identity via Keystroke Characteristics." International Journal Man-Machine Studies. 1 (1988): 67–76.

Mayer, A., F. Monroe, M. Reiter, and A. Rubin. "The Design and Analysis of Graphical Passwords." New York University. Bell Labs, Lucent Technologies, AT&T Labs-Research.

Monrose, F., and A. Rubin. "Keystroke Dynamics as a Biometric for Authentication." Future Generation Computer Systems. 16 (2000): 351–359.

Monrose, F., M. Reiter, and S. Wetzel. "Password Hardening Based on Keystroke Dynamics." 2001. Bell Labs, Lucent Technology. Murray Hill, NJ. Published online. Springer-Verlag.

Ord, T., and S.M. Furnell. "User Authentication for Keypad-based Devices Using Keystroke Analysis." 1999. Spinnaker International Ltd., Plymouth, United Kingdom.

Peacock, A. "Learning User Keystroke Latency Patterns." Computer Based Learning Unit. University of Leeds. http://pel.cs.byu.edu/~alen/personal/CourseWork/cs572/KeystrokePaper/.

Salem, R. United States Patent No. 4,197,524 (issued 8 April 1980). Tap-acuated Lock and Method of Actuating the Lock. Washington D.C.: U.S. Government Printing Office.

Song, D. X., D. Wagner, and X. Tian. "Timing Analysis of Keystrokes and Timing Attacks on SSH." 1999. University of California, Berkeley. For DARPA contract N6601-99-28913.

Wacom Technology Corp. http://www.wacom.com/.

Wong, C., M. Gouda, and S. Lam. *IEEE/ACM Transactions on Networking*. 8, no. 1 (February 2000).

Young, J., and R. Hammon. United States Patent No. 4,805,222 (issued 14 February 1989). Method and Apparatus for Verifying an Individual's Identity. Washington D.C.: U.S. Government Printing Office.

Chapter 7

Angelfire.com. http://www.angelfire.com/hi5/bluetooth/biometrics.html.

Barron, Janet J. "Knock, Knock. Who's There? Will the Science of Biometrics Replace Passwords and PINs?" *High Technology Careers*. http://www.hightechcareers.com/doc100/biometrics100.html.

BBC News. "Police Play It by Ear." January 2, 1999. http://news.bbc.co.uk/1/hi/sci/tech/246713.stm.

BBC News. "U.K. Ear Print Catches Murderer." December 15, 1998. http://news.bbc.co.uk/1/hi/uk/235721.stm.

Biel, Lena, O. Pettersson, and L. Philipson. "ECG Analysis: A New Approach to Human Identification." *IEEE Transactions on Instrumentation and Measurement*. 50, no. 3 (2001): 808–812.

Boucher Ferguson, Renee. " Advanced Biometrics Gives Security a Hand." *eWEEK*. November 29, 2000. http://www.zdnetindia.com/techzone/resources/security/stories/8530.html.

Burger, M., and W. Burger. 1998. "Ear Biometrics." *Biometrics: Personal Identification in Networked Society*. Jain, A., et al., eds. Kluwer Academic Publishers.

Cameron, David. "Skin Chips." *MIT Technology Review*. August 8, 2002. http://www.technologyreview.com/articles/print_version/wo_cameron080802.asp.

Cameron, David. "Walk This Way." *MIT Technology Review*. April 23, 2002. http://www.technologyreview.com/articles/print_version/wo_cameron042302.asp.

Carreira-Perpinan, Miguel A. "Compression Neural Networks for Feature Extraction: Application to Human Recognition from Ear Images" (in Spanish). 1995. Master's Thesis, Faculty of Informatics. Technical University of Madrid, Spain. http://www.dcs.shef.ac.uk/~miguel/papers/msc-thesis.html.

Carreira-Perpinan, Miguel A., and A. Sanchez-Calle. "A Connectionist Approach to Using Outer Ear Images for Human Recognition and Identification." http://www.dcs.shef.ac.uk/~miguel/papers/ps/ear-abstract.pdf.

Clarke, Roger. "Human Identification in Information Systems: Management Challenges and Public Policy Issues." http://www.anu.edu.au/people/Roger.Clarke/DV/HumanID.html.

Collins, Robert T., R. Gross, and J. Shi. "Silhouette-Based Human Identification from Body Shape and Gait." 2002. Robotics Institute, Carnegie Mellon University. http://citeseer.nj.nec.com/502776.html.

Cutler, Ross. "Face Recognition Using Infrared Images and Eigenfaces." http://www.cs.umd.edu/~rgc/pub/ir_eigenface.pdf.

Davis, Ann. "The Body as Password." *Wired*. July 1997. http://www.wired.com/wired/archive/5.07/biometrics_pr.html.

Forensic Fact Files: Information on Forensic Science. http://www.nifs.com.au/FactFiles/Fingerprints/what.asp?page=what.

Forensic-Evidence.com. "Ear Identification in the News Again; This Time It's Ear Photographs." 2001. *Identification Evidence*. The Netherlands. http://www.forensic-evidence.com/site/ID/IDearNews.html.

Forster, J. P., M. S. Nixon, and A. Prugel-Bennet. "New Area Based Metrics for Gait Recognition." University of Southampton. http://eprints.ecs.soton.ac.uk/archive/00005983/02/avbpa09.pdf.

Garfinkel, Simson. 2001. *Database Nation: The Death of Privacy in the 21st Century*. Sebastopol, CA: O'Reilly. http://www.oreilly.com/catalog/dbnationtp/chapter/ch03.html.

Gross, Ralph, and Shi Jianbo. "The Motion of Body (Mobo) Database." 2001. Robotics Institute, Carnegie Mellon University. http://citeseer.nj.nec.com/506226.html.

Guevin, Laura. "Picking Your Brain in The Name of Security." August 19, 2002. http://www.tmcnet.com/tmcnet/columns/laura081602.htm.

Hartel, Pieter, C. Slump, and R. Veldhius. "Multidisciplinary Postdoc Project Proposal: Smart Hand-held Objects." November 8, 2001. Distributed and Embedded Research Group, University of Twente. http://wwwhome.cs.utwente.nl/~pieter/projects/smartobjects.pdf.

Hoogstrate, A. J., H. van den Heuvel, and E. Huyben. Referenced September 2, 2002. "Ear Identification Based on Surveillance Camera Images." Netherlands Forensic Institute. May 31, 2000. http://www.forensic-evidence.com/site/ID/IDearCamera .html.

Howard, Toby. "Biometrics Come of Age." *Personal Computer World*. January 2001. http://www.cs.man.ac.uk/aig/staff/toby/writing/PCW/biom.htm.

Human Identification at a Distance (HID). http://www.equinoxsensors.com/products/HID.html.

Hurley, David J., M. S. Nixon, and J. N. Carter. "Force Field Energy Functionals for Image Feature Extraction." *Image and Vision Computing*. 20 (2002): 311–317.

IRID, Inc. (Infrared Identification Incorporated). http://www.iridinc.com; "Sarcon Technology Could Assist Firefighters, Automobile Makers." 2001. http://www.sarcon.com/news_&_info/oakridger080201.htm.

IRID, Inc. "Basic of Infrared Imaging." 2002. http://www.iridinc.com/IR%20Imaging.htm.

Izarek, Stephanie. "Smart Gun, Smart Solution?" FoxNews. January 25, 2001. http://www.foxnews.com/printer_friendly_story/0,3566,664,00.html.

Jain, A., and S. Pankathi. "Automated Fingerprint Identification and Imaging Systems." TJW Research Center, IBM. http://researchweb.watson.ibm.com/ecvg/pubs/sharat-forensic.pdf.

Jarvis, Angela. "Biometric Identification." Forensic-Evidence.com. http://www.forensic-evidence.com/site/ID/ID_Biometric_jarvis.html.

Krochmal, Mo. "Biometrics Makes Scents for Computer Users." *TechWeb News*. September 1, 1999. http://www.techweb.com/wire/story/TWB19990901S0009.

Little, James J., and Jeffrey E. Boyd. "Recognizing People by Their Gait: The Shape of Motion." *Journal of Computer Vision Research*. MIT Press. 1, no. 2 (Winter 1998). http://citeseer.nj.nec.com/little96recognizing.html.

McBride, Jonah. "Human Gait Recognition Curve Matching." May 15, 2002. http://www.lems.brown.edu/vision/courses/computer-vision/projects/McBride/pres_files/CV-final.html.

McCormick, John. "Keep Networks Safe with Body Language." *Government Computer News*. April 27, 1998. http://www.gcn.com/archives/gcn/1998/april27/rev2.htm.

McFarling, Usha Lee. "Researchers Smell Success in Developing 'Robo-Noses.' " *Seattle Times*. March 9, 1999. http://archives.seattletimes.nwsource.com/cgi-bin/texis.cgi/web/vortex/display?slug=nose&date=19990309.

Moenssens, Andre A. 1971. "Alphonse Bertillon and Ear Prints." *Fingertip Techniques*. Chilton Book Co.

Moenssens, Andre A. "Lip Print Identification Anyone?" Forensic-Evidence.com. http://www.forensic-evidence.com/site/ID/ID00004_10.html.

Morgan, J. "Court Holds Earprint Identification Not Generally Accepted In Scientific Community." Forensic-Evidence.com. http://www.forensic-evidence.com/site/ID/ID_Kunze.html.

Nakajima, K., et al. "Footprint-Based Personal Recognition." *IEEE Trans on Biomedical Engineering*. 47, no. 11 (2000): 1,534–1,537.

National Law Enforcement and Corrections Technology Center. "Technology in Law Enforcement." *TechBeat*. Fall 2000. http://www.nlectc.org/virlib/InfoDetail .asp?intInfoID=246.

New Jersey Institute of Technology. "Section 4: Technology Assessment." *Personalized Weapons Technology Project Progress Report With Findings and Recommendations*. April 15, 2001. http://www.njit.edu/pwt/reports/VolumeI/ 11Sect4-Technologies.htm#Biometric.

Niyogi, Sourabh A., and Edward H. Adelson. "Analyzing and Recognizing Walking Figures in XYT." *Proceedings of Computer Vision and Pattern Recognition*. June 1994. Seattle, WA. (TR #223). http://citeseer.nj.nec.com/ niyogi94analyzing.html.

Pacchioli, David. "The Nose That Glows." *Research / Penn State*. 20, no. 3 (September 1999). http://www.rps.psu.edu/sep99/nose.html.

Pearce, T. C., et al. "Handbook of Machine Olfaction: Electronic Nose Technology." Unpublished Book. http://www.le.ac.uk/eg/tcp1/book/Chapter1/ch1_1.pdf.

Polemi, D. 1997. "Biometric Techniques: Review and Evaluation of Biometric Techniques for Identification and Authentication." Institute of Communication and Computer Systems National Technical University of Athens. ftp://ftp.cordis .lu/pub/infosec/docs/biomet.doc.

Polich, John. "P300 Clinical Utility and Control of Variability." *Journal of Clinical Neurophysiology*. 15, no. 1 (January 15, 1998): 14–33.

Registratiekamer. "At Face Value—On Biometrical Identification and Privacy." September 1999. http://www.cbpweb.nl/documenten/av_15_At_face_value.htm.

Sang-Kyun, Im, et al. "A Biometric System by Extracting Hand Vein Patterns." *Journal of Korean Physical Society*. 38, no. 3 (March 2001): 268–272. http:// ini.cs.tu-berlin.de/~schoener/sem-biometry/im01_hand_vein_patterns.pdf.

Sebastian, Donald. "'Smart Guns'? Not So Fast Say NJIT Researchers." News@NJIT. http://www.njit.edu/Publications/twanext/2001.06a/index1.html.

Selinger, A, and A. Diego Sokolinsky. "Appearance-Based Facial Recognition Using Visible and Thermal Imagery." Equinox Corporation. http://www .equinoxsensors.com/publications/andreas_face.pdf.

Sense Holdings. "Biometric Information—How Does This Stuff Work?" http://www.senseme.com/scripts/biometrics/biometrics.htm.

Shakhnarovich, Gregory, L. Lee, and T. Darrell. "Integrated Face and Gait Recognition from Multiple Views." Proceedings of IEEE Conference on Computer Vision and Pattern Recognition. 2001. http://www.ai.mit.edu/people/ gregory/papers/cvpr2001.pdf.

Srivastava, A., and Liu XiuWen. "Statistical Hypothesis Pruning for Identifying Faces from Infrared Images." Florida State University, Tallahassee. http://calais.stat.fsu.edu/anuj/postscripts/IRFacePaper.pdf.

Woodward, Jr., John D. "Biometric Scanning, Law & Policy: Identifying the Concerns." *The University of Pittsburgh Law Review*. Fall 1997.

Woodward, Jr., John D. "Biometric Scanning, Law & Policy: Identifying the Concerns—Drafting the Biometric Blueprint." *The University of Pittsburgh Law Review*. 59, no. 97 (Fall 1997).

Chapter 8

Cambier, James L. Personal e-mail to Valorie S. Valencia. March 7, 2002.

Derakhshani R., and S. A. C. Schuckers. "Determination of Vitality From a Non-Invasive Biomedical Measurement for Use in Fingerprint Scanners." *Pattern Recognition* (forthcoming).

Eastern Province Herald. "Stupid Crimes: True Stories About Dumb Criminals." *Eastern Province Herald*. April 2000.

Hill, E., and Stoneham. "Practical Applications of Pulse Oximetry." http://www.nda.ox.ac.uk/wfsa/html/u11/u1104_01.htm.

Kallo, et al. United States Patent No. 6,175,641 (issued 16 January 2001). Detector for Recognizing the Living Character of a Finger in a Fingerprint Recognizing Apparatus. Washington D.C.: U.S. Government Printing Office.

Lapsley, et al. United States Patent No. 5,737,439 (issued 7 April 1998). Anti-Fraud Biometric Scanner that Accurately Detects Blood Flow. Washington D.C.: U.S. Government Printing Office.

Matsumoto, T., H. Matsumoto, K. Yamada, and S. Hoshino. "Impact of Artificial Gummy Fingers on Fingerprint Systems." Proceedings of SPIE. Vol. #4677. Optical Security and Counterfeit Deterrence Techniques IV. 2002.

Osten, et al. United States Patent No. 5,719,950 (issued 17 February 1998). Biometric, Personal Authentication System. Washington D.C.: U.S. Government Printing Office.

Phelps, Robert W. "Pulse Oximetry and Its Advances." November 1999. http://www.anesthesiologynews.com/specreps/an/sr0001/02report.htm.

Thalheim, Lisa, J. Krissler, and P. M. Ziegler. "Body Check: Biometrics Defeated." *c't* magazine. November 2002: 114. http://www.heise.de/ct/english/02/11/114.

Valencia, Valorie S. "Biometric Liveness Testing." Paper presented at the CardTech SecurTech Conference. New Orleans, LA. April 25, 2002.

Willis, David, and Mike Lee. "Biometrics Under Our Thumb." *Network Computing*. June 1, 1998. http://www.networkcomputing.com/910/910r1side1.html#bio.

Young, Kevin. "Biometric Security." *PC Magazine*. February 8, 1999.

Chapter 11

BioLab University of Bologna. "Fingerprint Verification Competition (FVC2000) Home." September 14, 2000. http://bias.csr.unibo.it/fvc2000.

Biometrics Working Group, CESG/NPL. "Best Practices for Biometric Testing." Ver. 1.0. January 2000. http://www.cesg.gov.uk/technology/biometrics/index.htm.

Computer Science Department, University of Bologna. "Synthetic Fingerprint Generator (SfinGe) Home." Version 2.5. September 4, 2002. http://bias.csr.unibo.it/research/biolab/sfinge.html.

Daugman, J. United States Patent No. 5,291,560 (issued 1 March 1994). Biometric Personal Identification System Based on Iris Analysis. Washington D.C.: U.S. Government Printing Office.

Fejfar, A., and W. Haberman. "Automatic Identification of Personnel Through Speaker and Signature Verification—System Description and Testing." Proceedings of Carnahan Conference on Crime Countermeasures. July 1977. Oxford, U.K.

Jain, Anil, Sharath Pankanti, and Salil Prabhakar. "On the Individuality of Fingerprints." 2001. Michigan State University. IBM Research Center. Digital Persona, Inc.

Mansfield, T., G. Kelly, D. Chandler, and J. Kane. "Biometric Product Testing Final Report." The National Physical Laboratory (NPL), Centre for Mathematics and Scientific Computing. 2001. Middlesex, United Kingdom.

Phillips, P. J., et al. "Face Recognition Vendor Test 2002." http://www.frvt.org/FRVT2002/default.htm.

Phillips, P. J., et al. "FRVT 2000 Evaluation Report." Department of Defense Counterdrug Technology Development Program Office. http://www.frvt.org/FRVT2000/documents.htm.

Phillips, P. J., P. Rauss, and S. Der. "FacE REcognition Technology (FERET). Recognition Algorithm Development and Test Report, ARL-TR-995." 1996. United States Army Research Laboratory.

Underwriters Laboratories, Inc. http://www.ul.com.

Chapter 12

American Banker. "FutureBanking." *American Banker.* October 21, 1996.

Associated Press. "Fingerprints Suggest Gay Link: Researchers Say Higher Percentage Have More Ridges on Left Hand." December 26, 1994.

Bevier, Lillian R. "Information About Individuals in the Hands of the Government: Some Reflections on Mechanism for Privacy Protection." *William & Mary Bill of Rights Journal.* 4, no. 455 (1995): 458.

Clarke, R. "Human Identification in Information Systems: Management Challenges and Public Policy Issues." *Information Technology & People.* December 1994.

EPIC. *Privacy & Human Rights.* (2002): 1–8.

Gavison, Ruth. "Privacy and the Limits of the Law." *Yale Law Journal.* 89, no. 421 (1980): 428.

Haapaniemi, Peter. "A Passkey Without A Peer." *Exec.* December 1998. http://www.unisys.com/execmag/1998-12/journal/feature.htm.

Hancock, Elise, and Melissa Hendricks. "In Short—Health & Medicine." *John Hopkins Magazine.* June 1996. http://www.jhu.edu/~jhumag/696web/hlthmedc.html.

Johns Hopkins Bayview Medical Center. "Clues at Our Fingertips." http://www.jhbmc.jhu.edu/Motil/finger.html.

Mell, P. "Seeking Shade in a Land of Perpetual Sunlight: Privacy as Property in the Electronic Wilderness." *Berkeley Technology Law Journal.* 1997.

Miller, John J., and Stephen Moore. "A National ID System, Big Brother's Solution to Illegal Immigration." Cato Policy Analysis No. 237. September 7, 1995.

Smith, Robert Ellis. "The True Terror Is in the Card," *New York Times Magazine.* September 8, 1996.

Smith, Robert Ellis. *Ben Franklin's Web Site.* 2000. http://www.gigalaw.com/bookshelf/benfranklin.html.

Tomko, George. "Biometrics as a Privacy-Enhancing Technology: Friend or Foe of Privacy?" Privacy Laws & Business 9th Privacy Commissioners'/Data Protection Authorities Workshop. Santiago de Compostela, Spain. September 15, 1998. http://www.dss.state.ct.us/digital/tomko.htm.

U.S. Department of Health. Education and Welfare, Records, Computers and the Rights of Citizens: Report of the Secretary's Advisory Committee on Automated Personal Data System. Cambridge: MIT Press. 1973.

Legal References

Daubert v. Merrell Dow Pharmaceuticals (1993).

Olmstead v. United States, 277 U.S. 439 (1927).

The T. J. Hooper, 60 F.2d 737 (2d Cir.) cert. denied, 287 U.S. 662 (1932) (Hand J.).

Chapter 13

Aaron, David L. "The EU Data Protection Directive: Implications for the U.S. Privacy Debate." Testimony Before the Subcommittee on Commerce, Trade, and Consumer Protection. U.S. House of Representatives. March 8, 2001. http://energycommerce.house.gov/107/hearings/03082001Hearing49/Aaron102.htm.

Alderman, Ellen, and Caroline Kennedy. 1995. *The Right to Privacy.* New York: Vintage.

Allen, Anita L. 1991. "Legal Issues in Nonvoluntary Prenatal Screening in AIDS." In *Women and the Next Generation: Towards a Mutually Acceptable Public Policy for HIV Testing of Pregnant Women and Newborns.* Faden, Ruth R., et al., eds. Oxford University Press.

Bevier, Lillian. "Information About Individuals in the Hands of Government: Some Reflections on Mechanisms for Privacy Protection." *William & Mary Bill of Rights J.* 4, no. 455 (1995): 457.

Bork, Robert H. 1990. *The Tempting of America: The Political Seduction of the Law.* New York: Free Press.

Cate, Fred H. 1997. *Privacy in the Information Age.* Washington D.C.: Brookings Press. 57, 63.

Electronic Privacy Information Center and Privacy International. 2002. "Privacy & Human Rights." http://www.privacyinternational.org/survey/phr2002/.

Flaherty, David H. "Privacy in Colonial New England." (1972): 87–88.

Goldberg, Steve. 1996. *Culture Clash: Law and Science in America.* New York University Press: 114, 115.

Hixson, Richard F. 1987. *Privacy in a Public Society: Human Rights in Conflict.* Oxford University Press.

Katsh, M. Ethan. 1995. *Law in a Digital World.* Oxford University Press.

Lessig, Lawrence. 1999. *Code and Other Laws of Cyberspace.* New York: Basic Books.

OMB (1987) (quotations omitted).

Roch, Michael P. "Filling the Void of Data Protection in the United States Following the European Example." *Santa Clara Computer & High Technology Law Journal.* 12, no. 71 (1996): 89.

Schwartz, Paul M. "Privacy and Participation: Personal Information and Public Sector Regulation in the United States." *Iowa Law Review.* 80, no. 553 (1995): 574–575.

Scott, W., and M. Jarnagin. 1868. *Treatise Upon the Law of Telegraphs, Appendix.* 457–507. New York: Little, Brown & Co.

Strauss, Peter L., et al. *Gellhorn & Byse's Administrative Law: Cases & Comments.* 874 (1995).

Tribe, Laurence. "The Constitution in Cyberspace: Law and Liberty Beyond the Electronic Frontier." 1991. http://www.epic.org/free_speech/tribe.html.

Warren, Samuel D., and Louis D. Brandeis. "The Right to Privacy." *Harvard Law Review.* 193 (1890).

Westin, Alan F. 1967. *Privacy and Freedom.* New York: Atheneum.

Legal References

10 U.S.C. § 774 (1999).

5 U.S.C. § 552a(a)(4).

5 U.S.C. § 552a(a)(5).

5 U.S.C. § 552a(e)(3).

5 U.S.C. § 552a(e)(4).

5 U.S.C. § 552a(e)(10).

5 U.S.C. § 552a(g)(4);

5 U.S.C. § 552a(i)(2).

5 U.S.C. § 552a(j).

Article 1, E.U. Data Protection Directive, or Directive 96/46/EC

Article 1, E.U. Privacy Directive, or Directive 96/46/EC.

Britt v. Naval Investigative Serv., 886 F.2d 544, 555 (3d Cir. 1989).

Buchanan v. Wing, NYSC, Appellate Division, Third Judicial Department, December 4, 1997, 79341.

Clavir v. United States, 84 F.R.D. 612, 614 (S.D.N.Y. 1979).

Daniels v. Williams, 474 U.S. 327 (1986).

Davis v. Mississippi, 394 U.S. 726–727.

Department of Justice (1998) at "Definitions: D. Record."

Doe v. Attorney General, 941 F.2d 780, 795 (9th Cir. 1991).

Doe v. City of New York, 15 F.3d 264, 267 (2d Cir. 1994).

Employment Division, Department of Human Resources of Oregon v. Smith, 494 U.S. 889 (1990).

Fadjo v. Coon, 633 F.2d 1172, 1175–1176 (5th Cir. 1981).

Goldman v. Weinberger, 475 U.S. 503 (1986). AFR 35-10, 1-6.h(2)(f) (1980).

Griswold v. Connecticut, 381 U.S. 479, 483, 484 (1965).

Griswold v. Connecticut, 381 U.S. at 500 (Harlan, J., concurring), (quoting *Palko v. Connecticut*, 302 U.S. 319, 325 (1937)).

Henke v. United States Dep't of Commerce, 83 F.3d 1453, 1460 n.12 (D.C.Cir.1996).

In re Crawford, 1999 U.S. App. LEXIS 24941, *7 (9th Cir. 1999), (citing *Whalen v. Roe*, 429 U.S. 589, 599–600 (1977)).

J.P. v. DeSanti, 653 F.2d 1080, 1090 (6th Cir. 1981).

Kostyu v. United States, 742 F.Supp. 413, 416–417 (E.D. Mich. 1990).

Moore v. City of East Cleveland, 431 U.S. 494 (1977).

Olmstead v. United States, 277 U.S. 438 (1928).

Pilon v. United States Department of Justice, 796 F.Supp. 7, 12 (D.D.C. 1992).

Planned Parenthood of Southeastern Pennsylvania v. Casey, 505 U.S. 833 (1992).

The Privacy Act of 1974, codified at 5 U.S.C. § 552a, September 27, 1975.

Quinn v. Stone, 978 F.2d 126, 133 (3d Cir. 1992).

Roe v. Sherry, 91 F.3d 1270, 1274 (9th Cir. 1996).

Skinner v. Railway Labor Executives' Ass'n, 489 U.S. 602, 617 (1989).

State of Connecticut Department of Social Services. Office of Administrative Hearings and Appeals, *Notice of Decision.* November 10, 1998.

Thom v. New York Stock Exchange, 306 F.Supp. at 1010.

Tobey v. N.L.R.B., 40 F.3d 469, 471–473 (D.C. Cir. 1994).

U.S. Constitution, Amendment XIV.

U.S.C. § 552a(b).

United States Postal Serv. v. National Ass'n of Letter Carriers, 9 F.3d 138, 144 (D.C. Cir. 1993).

United States v. Dionisio, 410 U.S. 1, 93 (1973).

United States v. Westinghouse, 638 F.2d 570, 577 (3d Cir. 1980).

Utility Workers Union of America, at 136, 138–139. Section 606 of the Omnibus Diplomatic Security and Anti-Terrorism Act of 1986, codified as section 149 of the Atomic Energy Act of 1954, 42 U.S.C. § 2169 (1986). 10 C.F.R. § 73.57 implements the statute.

Vernonia Sch. Dist. 47J v. Acton, 515 U.S. 646, 652 (1995).

Whalen v. Roe, 429 U.S. at 592 n.6.

Whalen v. Roe, 429 U.S. at 592 n.6. (Brennan, J., concurring).

Whalen v. Roe, 429 U.S. at 592 n.6. (Stewart, J., concurring).

Whalen v. Roe, 429 U.S. at 602 (footnote omitted).

Whalen v. Roe, 429 U.S. at 603–04.

Whalen v. Roe, 429 U.S. at 605.

Wilson v. Pennsylvania State Police, CA 94-6547, 1999 U.S. Dist. LEXIS 3165 *5 (E.D. Pa. March 11, 1999), (U.S. Mag. Judge Hart), (citing *Whalen v. Roe*, 429 U.S. at 599–600).

Chapter 14

Agre, Phil E. "Your Face Is Not a Bar Code: Arguments Against Automatic Face Recognition in Public Places." June 2, 2002. http://dlis.gseis.ucla.edu/people/pagre/bar-code.html.

Armey, Dick, and the ACLU. "Proliferation of Surveillance Devices Threatens Privacy." July 11, 2001. http://freedom.house.gov/library/technology/aclu.asp.

Commonwealth of Virginia General Assembly. House Bill No. 454. "Orders for Facial Recognition Technology." 2002.

Stanley, Jay, and Barry Steinhardt. "Drawing a Blank: The Failure of Facial Recognition Technology in Tampa, Florida." July 3, 2002. ACLU. http://archive.aclu.org/issues/privacy/drawing_blank.pdf.

United Kingdom. Parliamentary Office of Science and Technology. "Biometrics & Security." *Postnote*. No. 165 (November 2001).

Wayman, James L. "Biometrics: The State of the Technology." Proceedings of CardTech/SecurTech 2001. May 15, 2001.

Legal References

Planned Parenthood of Southeastern Pennsylvania v. Casey, 505 U.S. 833, 851 (1992).

United States v. Dionisio, 410 U.S. 1, 14 (1973).

Whalen v. Roe, 429 U.S. 589, 605 (1977).

Chapter 15

Dessent, Michael H. "Digital Handshakes in Cyberspace Under E-SIGN: 'There's a New Sheriff in Town!'" *University of Richmond Law Review*. 35, 943 (January 2002).

Forrester Research. Programme and Presentations for the Seminar on Revenue Implications of E-Commerce. WTO Committee on Trade and Development. April 22, 2002.

IBIA Privacy Principles. http://www.ibia.org/privacy.htm.

Implementation of Paperwork Elimination Act. Office of Management and Budget. January 26, 2001. http://www.whitehouse.gov/omb/fedreg/gpea2.html#iis1.

In re National Institute of Standards and Technology—Use of Electronic Data Interchange to Create Valid Obligations, file B-245714 (Comptroller Gen'l, 1991).

Mesenbourg, Thomas L. "Measuring Electronic Business: Definitions, Underlying Concepts, and Measurement Plans." U.S. Census Bureau. http://www.census.gov/epcd/www/ebusines.htm.

Mitchell, Mary. General Services Administration. "The State of Federal eGovernment and eBusiness." January 23, 2001. http://www.egov.gov/presentations/DigGovMI12001/sld001.htm.

Office of Management and Budget Guidance on Implementing the Electronic Signatures in Global and National Commerce Act (E-SIGN Act). http://www.whitehouse.gov/omb/memoranda/esign-guidance.pdf.

Smedinghoff, Thomas J., and Ruth Hill Bro. "Electronic Signature Legislation." http://profs.lp.findlaw.com/signatures/signature_4.html.

U.S. Department of Commerce. Economic and Statistics Administration. National Telecommunications and Information Administration. *A Nation Online: How Americans Are Expanding Their Use of the Internet.* February 2002. http://www.ntia.doc.gov/ntiahome/dn/.

U.S. Department of Commerce. *E-stats.* March 18, 2002. http://www.census.gov/eos/www/papers/estatstext.pdf.

Legal References
21 CFR 11.3(7) (Definitions).

21 CRF 11.70 (Signature/record linkage).

31 U.S.C. § 1501(a)(1).

The Electronic Signatures in Global and National Commerce Act (E-SIGN), P.L. 106-229, 15 U.S.C.A. § 7001 et seq. (2000).

The Government Paperwork Elimination Act of 1998 (GPEA), P.L. 105–277, Title XVII, codified at 44 U.S.C.A. § 3501 et seq.

Smith v. Maryland, 442 U.S. 735 (1979).

U.S. Department of Commerce. *The Emerging Digital Economy II.* June 1999.

UCC §1–201(39).

UCC §1–201(46).

United States v. Miller, 425 U.S. 435 (1976).

Chapter 16

"Government Multi-Purpose Card." Malaysia. http://www.jpn.gov.my/gmpc.html.

"Government of Malaysia and the Card." Malaysia. http://www.msc.com.my/mdc/flagships/mc.asp.

"Kuala Lumpur International Airport and Other International Entry/Exit Points." http://www.unisys.com/industry-analyst/IndustryAnalyst-03.asp.

"One Claim Only for Afghans." *Biometric Technology Today.* October 2002.

Electronic Arrest Warrant: Gwinnett County, Georgia. http://www.integratedsolutionsmag.com/articles/1998_07-08/980701.htm.

Elsevier Advanced Technology. "Biometric Smart Identity Card for United Kingdom Asylum Seekers." http://www.biometrics-today.com/jan02news.html#item1.

Hamouni, Samir. "Swedish School Learns the Value of Biometrics." Presentation delivered at the Biometrics 2002 Conference. November 7, 2002. London, England.

Mintie, David. Connecticut's Department of Social Services. Interview.

van der Harst, Machiel. "Keeping an Eye on Afghan Refugee Aid Claims." Presentation delivered at the Biometrics 2002 Conference. November 8, 2002. London, England.

Legal Reference
Mayfield v. Dalton, 901 F.Supp. (D. Hawaii 1995).

Chapter 17

Altman, Lawrence K. "Now, Doctors Must Identify the Dead Among the Trade Center Rubble." *New York Times*. September 25, 2001.

Beavan, Colin. 2001. *Fingerprints: The Origins of Crime Detection and the Murder Case that Launched Forensic Science*. New York: Hyperion.

Chen, Harold. *Medical Genetics Handbook*. (1988): 221–226.

Cole, Simon A. 2001. *Suspect Identities: A History of Fingerprinting and Criminal Identification*. New Haven, Conn.: Harvard.

Cole, Simon. "The Myth of Fingerprints." *New York Times*. May 13, 2001.

Foreign Terrorist Tracking Task Force. Department of Justice. "Attorney General Orders New Steps to Share Information Relating to Terrorism with Federal Agencies as well as State and Local Government." April 11, 2002. http://www.usdoj.gov/opa/pr/2002/April/02_ag_211.htm.

Garfinkel, Simson. "Database Nation: The Death of Privacy in the 21st Century. (2000): 43.

Kaye, David H. "Commentary: Two Fallacies About DNA Data Banks for Law Enforcement." *Brooklyn Law Review*. 67.1 (2001): 189.

Lydon, Christopher. "J. Edgar Hoover Made the F.B.I. Formidable With Politics, Publicity and Results." *New York Times*. May 3, 1972.

Miller, John J., and Stephen Moore. "A National ID System: Big Brother's Solution to Illegal Immigration." *Cato Policy Analysis*. September 7, 1995. http://www.cato.org/pubs/pas/pa237es.html.

Perl, Peter. "Hallowed Ground." *Washington Post Magazine*. May 12, 2002.

Sharath Pankanti, Salil Prabhakar, and Anil K. Jain. "On the Individuality of Fingerprints." Proceedings of the IEEE Computer Society Conference on Computer Vision and Pattern Recognition (CVPR). Hawaii. December 11–13, 2001.

Twain, Mark. 1900. *The Tragedy of Pudd'nhead Wilson*. Hartford, Conn.: American Publishing Company.

U.S. Department of Justice, Office of Justice Programs. "Privacy Impact Assessment for Justice Information Systems Working Paper." August 2000. http://www.ojp.usdoj.gov/archive/topics/integratedjustice/piajis.htm.

Wayman, James L. "Error Rate Equations for the General Biometric System." *IEEE Robotics and Automation*. 6.1 (March 1999): 35–48.

Woodward, Jr., John D. "Biometric Scanning, Law and Policy: Identifying the Concerns—Drafting the Biometric Blueprint." *University of Pittsburgh Law Review*. 59.97 (1997): 117.

Woodward, Jr., John D. "Searching the FBI's Civil Files: Public Safety v. Civil Liberty." *U.S. Law Week*. (September 17, 2002): 2183.

Woodward, Jr., John D. *Privacy & Security Law*. (September 2, 2002): 1042.

Woodward, Jr., John D., et al. *Army Biometric Applications: Identifying and Addressing Sociocultural Concerns*. (RAND 2001): 133–145.

Legal References

"Fingerprint Identification Record System" notice in February 1996. 61 Fed. Reg. 6386 (Vol. 61, no. 34, February 20, 1996).

Davis v. Mississippi, 394 U.S. 721 (1969).

Iacobucci v. City of Newport, 785 F.2d 1354, 1355–1356 (6th Cir. 1986), rev'd on other grounds, 479 U.S. 921 (1986).

Order, United States v. Plaza, Cr. No. 98-362-10 (E.D. Pa. March 13, 2002).

People v. James Hyatt, Indictment #8852/2000, NYSC, Kings County, Part 23.

The Privacy Act of 1974, codified at 5 U.S.C. § 552a. September 27, 1975.

Schmerber v. California, 384 U.S. 757 (1966).

Thom v. New York Stock Exchange, 306 F. Supp 1002, 1010 (S.D.N.Y. 1969).

United States Department of Justice v. Reporters Committee for Freedom of Press, 489 U.S. 749 (1989).

United States v. Byron C. Mitchell, Cr. No. 96-00407 (E.D. Pa. Sept. 27, 1999).

United States v. James M. Broten, et al. Case No. 01-CR-411 (DNH), (N.D.N.Y. March 25, 2002).

United States v. Plaza, Cr. No. 98-362-10 (E.D. Pa. Jan. 7, 2002).

Utility Workers Union of America, AFL-CIO, v. Nuclear Regulatory Commission, 664 F. Supp. 136, 139 (S.D.N.Y. 1987).

Chapter 18

"Casinos Using Facial Surveillance." *Gaming Magazine*. February 26, 2001. http://www.gamingmagazine.com/managearticle.asp?c=610&a=.

"Facial Recognition Ready for Prime Time?" *Security Watch*. May 2000. http://www.bbpnews.com/pdf/PT.pdf.

"Fingerprint Verification for Data Access." *Bankers' Hotline*. 11, no. 2 (February 2001). http://www.bankersonline.com/articles/bhv11n02/bhv11n02a21.html.

"SAFLINK Biometric Security Software Chosen by Blue Cross & Blue Shield of Rhode Island For Network Security Solution." August 1, 2002. http://www.saflink.com/80102.html.

ACLU. "Data on Face-Recognition Test at Palm Beach Airport Further Demonstrates Systems' Fatal Flaws ACLU Says." May 14, 2002. http://www.aclu.org/news/2002/n051402b.html.

Amec Capital Projects U.K.—Biometric Payment Authentication. http://www.itcbp.org.uk/itcbp/AllPubs/biometric.pdf.

Beiser, Vince. "Casinos Fight Back with Tech." *Wired*. 1999. http://www.wired.com/news/technology/0,1282,19463,00.html.

Emigh, Jacqueline. "Bridging the Gap." *Access Control & Security Systems*. 2002. http://securitysolutions.com/ar/security_bridging_gap/.

Green, Jennie. "To Catch a Thief." *CasinoGuru.com*. 2002. http://www.casinoguru.com/features/0899/f_080399_tocatch.htm.

Harrison, Ann. "Researcher: Biometrics Unproven, Hard To Test." August 7, 2002. http://online.securityfocus.com/news/566.

Herz, J. C. "Seen City: From Surveillance Cams to Facial Scans, in Las Vegas the Whole World Is Watching." *Wired*. 2001. http://www.wired.com/wired/archive/9.12/vegas.html.

InnoVentry's RPMs. 2000. http://www.business-journal.com/LateNov00/Dieboldcontract.html.

Jones, Chris. "Biometrics Enhance Security At Casinos; Airport Use Possible." *INBUSINESS*. October 19, 2001. http://www.biometricgroup.com/a_press/InBusinessLasVegas_Oct2001.htm.

Marshall Field Garden Apartment Homes. http://www.axiomsecurity.com/perspectives/presentations.html.

Newman, Andy. "Face-Recognition Systems Offer New Tools, but Mixed Results." *New York Times*. May 3, 2001.

Wagner, Angie. "High-Tech Raises the Odds Against Casino Cheats." December 21, 1999. http://www.canoe.com/CNEWSFeatures9912/21_casino.html.

Woodward, Jr., John D., et al. *Army Biometric Applications*. Appendix B: Program Reports. RAND 2001.

Chapter 19

Ellison, Larry. "Smart Cards: Digital IDs Can Help Prevent Terrorism." *Wall Street Journal*. October 8, 2001.

Kent, Stephen T., and Lynette Millett, eds. *IDs—Not That Easy: Questions about Nationwide Identity Systems*. Computer Science and Telecommunications Board. National Research Council. 2002.

Wayman, James L. "Error Rate Equations for the General Biometric System." *IEEE Robotics and Automation*. 6, no. 1 (March 1999): 35–48.

Legal References
Florida v. Royer, 460 U.S. 491 (1983).

Appendix B

Publicly Held Companies Offering Biometric Services

Source: *Biometric Information Directory* published by Bill Rogers of *Biometric Digest*

Company Name	Country	Internet URL
AcSys Biometric Corp.	Canada	http://www.acsysbiometrics.com
AcSys Biometrics USA, Inc.	USA	http://www.acsysbiometricsusa.com
ActivCard, Inc.	USA	http://www.ankari.com
affinitex	Canada	http://www.affinitex.com
AiT	Canada	http://www.ait.ca
Aware, Inc.	USA	http://www.aware.com
BIO-key International	USA	http://www.bio-key.com
Biometric Technology Today	UK	http://www.compseconline.com
Biometrica Systems, Inc.	USA	http:///www.biometrica.com
BioPassword by Net Nanny Software, Inc.	USA	http://www.biopassword.com
Bioscrypt, Inc.	Canada	http://www.bioscrypt.com
CMC Limited	India	http://www.cmcltd.com
Communication Intelligence Corp. (CIC)	USA	http://www.cic.com
ComnetiX Computer Systems, Inc.	Canada	http://www.comnetix.com

Company Name	Country	Internet URL
Datastrip, Inc.	USA	http://www.datastrip.com
delSecur	Canada	http://www.delsecur.com
Diebold, Inc.	USA	http://www.diebold.com
Digital Descriptor Systems, Incorporated	USA	http://www.ddsi-cpc.com
Dreammirh Co., Ltd.	Korea	http://www.dreammirh.com
Elsevier Advanced Technology	UK	http://www.compseconline.com
Exact Identification Corp.	USA	http://www.aprint.com
Fingerprint Cards AB	Sweden	http://www.fingerprint.se http://www.fingerprints.com
Finx Group, The	USA	http://www.finxgroup.com
Gartner Group, Inc.	USA	http://www.gartner.com
Global Capital Securities Corporation	USA	http://www.gcapsecurities.com
Hypercom Corp.	USA	http://www.hypercom.com
ID Technologies	USA	http://www.idtek.com
Identix, Inc.	USA	http://www.identix.com
IMAGIS Technologies	Canada	http://www.imagistechnologies.com
Infineon Technologies	Germany	http://www.infineon.com
Infineon Technologies Corp.	USA	http://www.infineon.com/fingertip
Information Technologies, Ltd.	India	http://www.amexit.com
ITT Industries	USA	http://www.speakerkey.com
Keyware Technologies	USA	http://www.keyware.com
Kronos, Inc.	USA	http://www.kronos.com
LCI SmartPen N.V.	Belgium	http://www.smartpen.net
Leapfrog	USA	http://www.leapfrog-smart.com
Locus dialogue— Division of Info Space	Canada	http://www.locusdialogue.com
NEC Corporation	Japan	http://www.nec.co.jp http://www.nec.com
Net Nanny Software, Inc.	USA	http://www.biopassword.com
Nuance	USA	http://www.nuance.com
Omron	USA	http://www.society.omron.com/itc/index.htm
Precise Biometrics AB	Sweden	http://www.precisebiometrics.com
Printrak, A Motorola Company	USA	http://www.motorola.com/printrak
Purchasing Research Service	UK	http://www.purchasingresearchservice.com
Recognition Systems	USA	http://www.handreader.com
Ringdale, Inc.	USA	http://www.ringdale.com

Company Name	Country	Internet URL
Safetek International, Inc.	USA	http://www.safetekinc.com
SAFLINK Corporation	USA	http://www.saflink.com
Secure Enterprise Solutuions, Inc.	Canada	http://www.weprovidesecurity.com
Sense Holdings, Inc.	USA	http://www.senseme.com
Sense Technologies, Inc.	USA	http://www.senseme.com
Sensormatic	USA	http://www.sensormatic.com
SNP SPrint Pte. Ltd.	Singapore	http://www.snp.com.sg
Sony CPCE	UK	http://www.world.sony.com/puppy
Sony Electronics, Inc.	USA	http://www.sony.com/puppy
SpeakEZ, Inc. (A division of T-NETIX, Inc.)	USA	http://www.speakezinc.com
SpeechWorks International	USA	http://www.speechworks.com
SSP Solutions, Inc.	USA	http://www.sspsolutions.com
STMicroelectronics	USA	http://www.st.com
SyntheSys Secure Technologies, Inc.	USA	http://www.synthesysusa.com
T-Netix	USA	http://www.t-netix.com
Triton Secure Limited	Australia	http://www.tritonsecure.com/
TSSI LTD.	UK	http://www.tssi.co.uk
Viisage Technology	USA	http://www.viisage.com
Visionics Corporation	USA	http://www.visionics.com

NOTE

When looking at these publicly held companies, it's important to remember that not all of them are purely biometric vendors. Many sell non-biometric products and services and derive a large majority of their revenue from non-biometric sources. This list is non-inclusive. It is for information purposes only.

Index

INTERNATIONAL CONTACT INFORMATION

AUSTRALIA
McGraw-Hill Book Company Australia Pty. Ltd.
TEL +61-2-9900-1800
FAX +61-2-9878-8881
http://www.mcgraw-hill.com.au
books-it_sydney@mcgraw-hill.com

CANADA
McGraw-Hill Ryerson Ltd.
TEL +905-430-5000
FAX +905-430-5020
http://www.mcgraw-hill.ca

**GREECE, MIDDLE EAST, & AFRICA
(Excluding South Africa)**
McGraw-Hill Hellas
TEL +30-210-6560-990
TEL +30-210-6560-993
TEL +30-210-6560-994
FAX +30-210-6545-525

MEXICO (Also serving Latin America)
McGraw-Hill Interamericana Editores S.A. de C.V.
TEL +525-117-1583
FAX +525-117-1589
http://www.mcgraw-hill.com.mx
fernando_castellanos@mcgraw-hill.com

SINGAPORE (Serving Asia)
McGraw-Hill Book Company
TEL +65-863-1580
FAX +65-862-3354
http://www.mcgraw-hill.com.sg
mghasia@mcgraw-hill.com

SOUTH AFRICA
McGraw-Hill South Africa
TEL +27-11-622-7512
FAX +27-11-622-9045
robyn_swanepoel@mcgraw-hill.com

SPAIN
McGraw-Hill/Interamericana de España, S.A.U.
TEL +34-91-180-3000
FAX +34-91-372-8513
http://www.mcgraw-hill.es
professional@mcgraw-hill.es

**UNITED KINGDOM, NORTHERN,
EASTERN, & CENTRAL EUROPE**
McGraw-Hill Education Europe
TEL +44-1-628-502500
FAX +44-1-628-770224
http://www.mcgraw-hill.co.uk
computing_neurope@mcgraw-hill.com

ALL OTHER INQUIRIES Contact:
Osborne/McGraw-Hill
TEL +1-510-549-6600
FAX +1-510-883-7600
http://www.osborne.com
omg_international@mcgraw-hill.com